Lecture Notes in Computer Science   11513

Commenced Publication in 1973
Founding and Former Series Editors:
Gerhard Goos, Juris Hartmanis, and Jan van Leeuwen

More information about this series at http://www.springer.com/series/7409

Dilma Da Silva · Qingyang Wang ·
Liang-Jie Zhang (Eds.)

Cloud Computing – CLOUD 2019

12th International Conference
Held as Part of the Services Conference Federation, SCF 2019
San Diego, CA, USA, June 25–30, 2019
Proceedings

Springer

Editors
Dilma Da Silva
Texas A&M University
College Station, TX, USA

Qingyang Wang (ID)
Louisana State University
Baton Rouge, LA, USA

Liang-Jie Zhang (ID)
Kingdee International Software
Group Co., Ltd.
Shenzhen, China

ISSN 0302-9743   ISSN 1611-3349 (electronic)
Lecture Notes in Computer Science
ISBN 978-3-030-23501-7   ISBN 978-3-030-23502-4 (eBook)
https://doi.org/10.1007/978-3-030-23502-4

LNCS Sublibrary: SL3 – Information Systems and Applications, incl. Internet/Web, and HCI

This Springer imprint is published by the registered company Springer Nature Switzerland AG
The registered company address is: Gewerbestrasse 11, 6330 Cham, Switzerland

Preface

The International Conference on Cloud Computing (CLOUD) has been a prime international forum for researchers and industry practitioners alike to exchange the latest fundamental advances in the state of the art and practice of cloud computing, to identify emerging research topics, and to define the future of cloud computing. All topics regarding cloud computing align with the theme of CLOUD.

CLOUD 2019 was part of the Services Conference Federation (SCF). SCF 2019 had the following ten collocated service-oriented sister conferences: 2019 International Conference on Web Services (ICWS 2019), 2019 International Conference on Cloud Computing (CLOUD 2019), 2019 International Conference on Services Computing (SCC 2019), 2019 International Congress on Big Data (BigData 2019), 2019 International Conference on AI & Mobile Services (AIMS 2019), 2019 World Congress on Services (SERVICES 2019), 2019 International Congress on Internet of Things (ICIOT 2019), 2019 International Conference on Cognitive Computing (ICCC 2019), 2019 International Conference on Edge Computing (EDGE 2019), and 2019 International Conference on Blockchain (ICBC 2019). As the founding member of SCF, the First International Conference on Web Services (ICWS) was held in June 2003 in Las Vegas, USA. The First International Conference on Web Services—Europe 2003 (ICWS-Europe 2003) was held in Germany in October 2003. ICWS-Europe 2003 is an extended event of the 2003 International Conference on Web Services (ICWS 2003) in Europe. In 2004, ICWS-Europe was changed to the European Conference on Web Services (ECOWS), which was held in Erfurt, Germany. To celebrate its 16th birthday, SCF 2018 was held successfully in Seattle, USA.

This volume presents the accepted papers for the 2019 International Conference on Cloud Computing (CLOUD 2019), held in San Diego, USA, during June 25–30, 2019. For this conference, each paper was reviewed by three independent members of the international Program Committee. After carefully evaluating their originality and quality, 24 papers were accepted.

We are pleased to thank the authors, whose submissions and participation made this conference possible. We also want to express our thanks to the Program Committee members, for their dedication in helping to organize the conference and in reviewing the submissions. We would like to thank Prof. Hai Jin, who provided continuous support for this conference.

Finally, we would like to thank Dr. Jing Zeng for his excellent work in organizing this conference. We look forward to your great contributions as a volunteer, author, and conference participant for the fast-growing worldwide services innovations community.

May 2019

Dilma Da Silva
Qingyang Wang
Liang-Jie Zhang

The original version of the book was revised: For detailed information see correction chapter. The correction to the book is available at https://doi.org/10.1007/978-3-030-23502-4_25

Organization

General Chair

Hai Jin — Huazhong University of Science and Technology, China

Program Chairs

Dilma Da Silva — Texas A&M University, USA
Qingyang Wang — Louisiana State University–Baton Rouge, USA

Services Conference Federation (SCF 2019)

SCF 2019 General Chairs

Calton Pu — Georgia Tech, USA
Wu Chou — Essenlix Corporation, USA
Ali Arsanjani — 8x8 Cloud Communications, USA

SCF 2019 Program Chair

Liang-Jie Zhang — Kingdee International Software Group Co., Ltd., China

SCF 2019 Finance Chair

Min Luo — Services Society, USA

SCF 2019 Industry Exhibit and International Affairs Chair

Zhixiong Chen — Mercy College, USA

SCF 2019 Operations Committee

Huan Chen — Kingdee International Software Group Co., Ltd., China
Jing Zeng — Kingdee International Software Group Co., Ltd., China
Liping Deng — Kingdee International Software Group Co., Ltd., China
Yishuang Ning — Tsinghua University, China
Sheng He — Tsinghua University, China

SCF 2019 Steering Committee

Calton Pu (Co-chair) — Georgia Tech, USA
Liang-Jie Zhang (Co-chair) — Kingdee International Software Group Co., Ltd., China

CLOUD 2019 Program Committee

Gerald Baumgartner	Louisiana State University, USA
Feng Chen	Louisiana State University, USA
Haopeng Chen	Shanghai Jiao Tong University, China
Jingshu Chen	Oakland University, USA
Dazhao Cheng	University of North Carolina at Charlotte, USA
Jai Dayal	Intel, USA
Roberto Di Pietro	Hamad Bin Khalifa University, USA
Shahram Ghandeharizadeh	Qatar
Liting Hu	Florida International University, USA
Marty Humphrey	University of Virginia, USA
Danesh Irani	Google, USA
Yasuhiko Kanemasa	Fujitsu Laboratories Ltd., Japan
Krishna Kant	Temple University, USA
Mukil Kesavan	VMware, USA
Wubin Li	Ericsson Research, Canada
Yao Liu	SUNY Binghamton, USA
Salvo Marcuccio	University of Pisa, Italy
Aziz Mohaisen	University of Central Florida, USA
Supratik Mukhopadhyay	Louisiana State University, USA
Nagendra Kumar Nainar	CISCO, USA
Mara Nikolaidou	Harokopio University of Athens, Greece
Li Pan	Shandong University, China
Chen Qian	University of California at Santa Cruz, USA
Shaolei Ren	University of California, Riverside, USA
Ruediger Schulze	IBM Germany Research & Development GmbH, DE, Germany
Huasong Shan	JD Silicon Valley R&D Center, USA
Jun Shen	UOW, Australia
Byung Chul Tak	Kyungpook National University, South Korea
Yuzhe Tang	Syracuse University, USA
Anand Tripathi	University of Minnesota, USA
An Wang	Case Western Reserve University, USA
Chen Wang	IBM Thomas J. Watson, USA
Wei Wang	The University of Texas at San Antonio, USA
Yan Wang	SUNY at Binghamton, USA
Yuehua Wang	Texas A & M University – Commerce, USA
Pengcheng Xiong	Amazon, USA
Dianxiang Xu	Boise State University, USA
Feng Yan	University of Nevada, Reno, USA
Iling Yen	University of Texas at Dallas, USA
Yifan Zhang	SUNY Binghamton, USA
Ming Zhao	Arizona State University, USA

Contents

Ultra-Low Power Localization System Using Mobile Cloud Computing

Junjian Huang[1], Yubin Zhao[1(✉)], XiaoFan Li[2], and Cheng-Zhong Xu[3]

[1] Shenzhen Institutes of Advanced Technology,
Chinese Academy of Science, Shenzhen, China
{huangjj,zhaoyb}@siat.ac.cn
[2] State Radio Monitoring Center Testing Center, Beijing, China
lixiaofan@srtc.org.cn
[3] State Key Lab of IoTSC, Department of Computer and Information Science,
University of Macau, Macau, Macao, Special Administrative Region of China
czxu@um.edu.mo

Abstract. In the existing positioning system based on bluetooth (BT), the interference of the positioning device signal, the slow processing speed of the positioning data and the large energy consumption of the positioning device affect the system positioning accuracy and service quality. In this paper, we propose an Ultra-Low power indoor localization system using mobile cloud computing. The mobile cloud server reduces the signal interference of the positioning device, improves the positioning accuracy and reduces the system energy consumption by controlling the working mode of the positioning device. A simultaneous localization and power adaptation scheme is developed. In the real experiment evaluation, our proposed system can localize the area of a terminal located within 3 m distance with 98% accuracy and average positioning error less then 1.55 m. Compare with other BLE system, 97% average energy consumption of our system is reduced.

Keywords: Energy consumption · Mobile cloud computing ·
Bluetooth · Indoor localization

1 Introduction

As people's indoor activities increase, the demand for indoor positioning increases, and indoor positioning systems are rapidly developed. Indoor positioning system combined with mobile cloud computing can provide users with real-time fast location service [1,2]. Users can obtain real-time positioning information or search for lost children [3,4] by accessing the mobile cloud server

Y. Zhao—This work was partially supported by National Nature Science Foundation of China (No. 61801306), Shenzhen Fundamental Research (No. JCYJ20180302145755311), Shenzhen Discipline Construction Project for Urban Computing and Data Intelligence, Open Fund of IPOC (No. IPOC2018B002).

D. Da Silva et al. (Eds.): CLOUD 2019, LNCS 11513, pp. 1–10, 2019.
https://doi.org/10.1007/978-3-030-23502-4_1

through the Internet. However, the current positioning servers are not ideal because of the large signal interference, long response time and large energy consumption [5,6].

In the current indoor location research, RSSI-based localization technique is widely used in the Bluetooth low power (BLE) system [7,8]. Distance measurement can be extracted through RSSI [9,10]. The more accurate the distance calculated by RSSI, the more accurate the positioning. A stronger signal is less susceptible to interference [11], and the RSSI value obtained is more accuracy. In the realistic environment, a large number of beacons are deployed, generating a large amount of positioning information. Increased positioning information will increase the burden on the mobile cloud server, and the service response time will increase. At the same time, severe signal interference affects the quality of RSSI value. A large number of positioning devices lack reasonable management and monitoring, which increases system energy consumption and damage. Therefore, the control of beacon's working modes are also as important as the position estimation method [12,13].

In this paper, we propose an mobile cloud computing based Bluetooth low energy (BLE) localization system. A simultaneous localization and power adaptation scheme is proposed to reduce the total power consumption and guarantee position estimation accuracy. The first contribution is that a min-max based positioning algorithm is developed to obtain the information of targets. By turning off a large number of beacons that are far away from the user, the acquisition of invalid positioning data and interference of signals can be reduced. We verify that the system obtain higher positioning accuracy due to the reduction of interference and operate simply. The second contribution is the energy conservation method that monitors the working modes of beacons using the mobile cloud computing architecture. Electricity consumption is greatly reduced in the entire service compared to the process without control. In the real experiment, we find that the system can keep strong robustness for long-time services is possible by monitoring working status of beacons and finding early fault.

The rest of the paper is organized as follows: Sect. 2 describes the architecture of the system proposed followed by details of the composition of the proposed system, the function of the proposed system, which including localization function and energy conservation control. This is then followed by experiments and the discussion of the experimental results in Sect. 3. Conclusions are presented in Sect. 4.

2   Proposed Positioning System

2.1   System Architecture

The proposed system consist of five parts: user, data collection unit (DCU), data transmission unit (DTU), the mobile cloud server. The user requests the location service by accessing the mobile cloud server, and uploads the BT information of the device including the name and physical address, and then keep the BT on until the end of the service request. DCU consists of a certain number of beacons. DCU will periodically search for mobile terminal data, which contains

Bluetooth information and RSSI values, and then upload the data to the mobile cloud server through the DTU. The DTU connects the DCU to the mobile cloud server. The mobile cloud server can not only obtain the position data from DCU through the DTU, but also transmit the control instruction management DCU through the DTU. The filtering of all positioning data and the calculation of user location are done in the mobile cloud server. The mobile cloud server manages the DCU according to the location of the user, reducing the energy consumption of DCU. After the location information is calculated, it is uploaded to the mobile cloud server, and the user can obtain his location by accessing the mobile cloud server. The system architecture is show in Fig. 1.

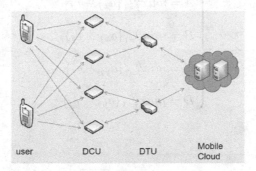

Fig. 1. System architecture

The mobile cloud server mainly implements two functions, one is positioning and the other is energy conservation control. During the positioning process, RSSI measurements to the target is collected through beacons of the DCU and forwarded to the mobile cloud server through a nearby DTU. The target terminal is equipped with BLE chips and broadcast mobile terminal data periodically to the beacons. Mobile cloud server calculate the location with enough data through min-max algorithm and confirm a area which represent position. During the energy saving control process, the cloud server generates energy adaptation scheme according to the location of mobile terminal to control and deduce the power consumption for DCU.

2.2 Localization Function

In the localization function, mobile terminal such as SmartPhone request service from the mobile cloud server and open BLE to broadcast the information (e.g., ID). Beacons upload the ID and RSSI extracted from the information broadcasted by the user. The server filters out the data including the mobile device according to the ID, and selects the RSSI value for the positioning calculation according to the set threshold.

In this paper, the positioning calculated by Min-Max algorithm. The Min-Max also known as Bounding Box algorithm, is a simple and straightforward method. We can calculate r_j based on RSSI of each beacon j of which location $a_j = (a_{xj}, a_{yj})$. Building bounding box given by $[a_{xj}-r_j, a_{yj}-r_j] \times [a_{xj}+r_j, a_{yj}+r_j]$, its side length is twice that of r_j. Overlap region (OR) of all bounding box conclude the position, its vertices $V = \{(A, D), (B, D)(A, C), (B, C)\}$ as Fig. 1 obtain from 1. The center of OR can be estimated to be the position $(x, y) = (\frac{A+B}{2}, \frac{C+D}{2})$. In Fig. 2, the midpoints $M = \{a(\frac{A+B}{2}, D), b(\frac{A+B}{2}, C), c(A, \frac{C+D}{2}), d(B, \frac{C+D}{2})\}$ of each side of the bounding box can represent the boundary of OR, serves as a basis of the energy conservation control method.

$$\begin{cases} A = max_{j=1}^{N}\{a_{xj} - r_j\} \\ B = min_{j=1}^{N}\{a_{xj} + r_j\} \\ C = min_{j=1}^{N}\{a_{yj} + r_j\} \\ D = max_{j=1}^{N}\{a_{yj} - r_j\} \end{cases} \quad (1)$$

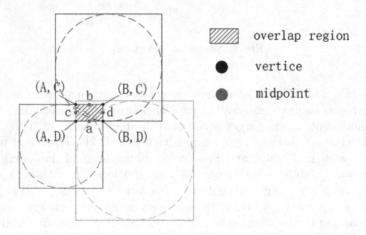

Fig. 2. Bounding box and midpoints which represent the boundary of OR

The users can access the mobile cloud server to get the current localization. In this system, only the mobile terminal broadcast signal. In an ideal state, signal interference is reduced. Therefore, enhancing the terminal's transmit power can improve robustness of RSSI and make positioning more accurate. In the search phase, user can search the people who only wear a devices that can broadcast such as Smartband through server.

2.3   Energy Conservation Control

We divide the plane region into multiple rectangular units, which are composed of subregions with equal areas. Each rectangular unit contains a DCU. The server judges the rectangular unit where the terminal is located based on the OR and operate open the DCU. Beacon has three working modes: working mode, standby mode and sleep mode. Operate the working mode of beacon according to the feature point of OR in subregion.

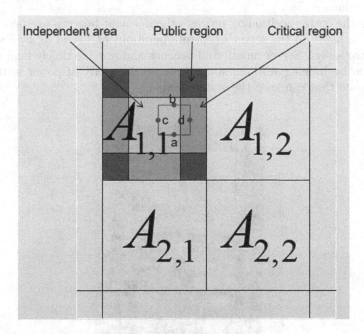

Fig. 3. The rule of trigger regional division (Color figure online)

The subregion consists of three special areas, which trigger different control actions. There are three operating conditions:

Independent region control: The yellow part in Fig. 3 is called the independent area. When OR overlaps with independent region, such as a, c, and b points, only the beacons in subregion $A_{1,1}$ are set to work mode, and the beacons of other subregions are set to wait mode. The beacon in the rectangular area not overlaps with OR is set to sleep mode.

Critical region control: The green part in Fig. 3 is called the critical region. Terminal will cross over to the next subregion, if OR overlaps with critical region, such as d point. To avoid losing positioning, the beacons in another subarea adjacent to critical region such as $A_{1,2}$ participates in positioning work with working mode.

Public region control: The green part in Fig. 3 is called the public region. If OR overlaps with public region, beacons in four adjacent areas will be set to work mode. Server operate more beacons to participate in positioning work.

The server judge a cross-regional behavior by the distance between the terminal and the next rectangular area that can prevent loss of positioning due to the user's sudden return to the original rectangular area. Beacons in the second rectangular will be open and wait if distance is within the threshold. Only the beacons in the current rectangular area will be open if the distance exceed the threshold value.

During the entire positioning process, the dormant beacons are periodically woken up to listen to the server's control operations and send its own working status to the server. Server monitor all beacons and provide timely maintenance information by judging working status include electricity of power source and working mode that can keep the system stable.

Fig. 4. The development board

3   Experiment and Analysis

3.1   Experiment Condition

In order to calculate the distance between the beacons and the target, an RSSI that can be obtained by BT of the beacon is used. The beacon contains a Node32s development board with ESP-WROOM-32 that has built-in BLE and WiFi modules. Figure 4 is a physical map of the development board. The development board also has a variety of energy-saving modes, among which the deep sleep mode consumes the lowest energy. The development board's consumption data comes from its technical manual as shown in Table 1.

Table 1. Work energy consumption

Working parameters	Power consumption (3.3 V)
Wi-Fi Tx packet 19.5 dBm	225 mA
Wi-Fi/BT Rx and Sniffer	90 mA
BT Broadcast 10 dBm	90 mA
Deep Sleep	0.9 mA

3.2 Positioning Experiment and Analysis

The positioning experiment was set up in a $8.86 * 5.86\,\mathrm{m}^2$ laboratory, as shown in Fig. 5, with the blue circle representing the beacon. The beacons are mounted on a wall 1.2 m high, beacon in the center is arranged on a shelf. Terminal are mounted on a shelf 1.2 m high. The scanning frequency of beacon was 0.5 Hz. The terminal contains an Node32s development board whose transmitting power is 10 dBm to broadcast BT signal. The server obtains data transmitted by all beacons and calculate positioning with three optimal RSSI within the threshold range that is $-10\,\mathrm{dBm}$ to $-75\,\mathrm{dBm}$.

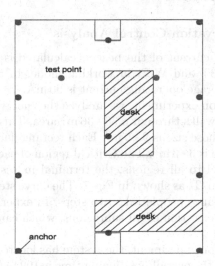

Fig. 5. The actual experiments environment.

The two fixed positions show in Fig. 5 have been considered to test the estimation accuracy. The RSSI acquisition time is $T = 2.2\,\mathrm{s}$, in which the BT search time is 2 s and the WiFi transmission time is 0.2 s. Position estimation has been performed 1000 times. The position error is the Euclidian distance between the estimated position and the real position.

Figure 6 show the CDF of localization errors at two fixed position. These result combine with the datum of two test points demonstrate that the proposed

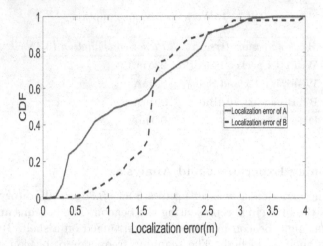

Fig. 6. CDFs of localization errors of the trajectories with two fixed positions.

position method achieves around 3 m 98% localization error and the average error for positioning is around 1.55 m.

3.3   Energy Conservation Control Analysis

The average operating current of the beacon calculated is 102.3 mA according to operating time of BT and WiFi in working mode. In waiting mode, WiFi operate sniffer that average operating current is 90 mA.

Through a simulation experiment, we analyze the energy consumption of the system when a person walks through a $36 * 36\,\text{m}^2$ area. This area is divided into 16 rectangular areas whose size is $9 * 9\,\text{m}^2$. Each rectangular area is divided into 9 subregions whose size is $3 * 3\,\text{m}^2$. The Critical region of each subregion is 0.5 m wide. In order to travel to all regions, the terminal moves in a 5-step Hilbert curve at a step of 1.12 m/T, as shown in Fig. 7. The curve step length of 1.12 m is approximately the distance people take two steps. In experiments, 169 beacons are arranged at the intersection of all subregions, which can reduce the number of points in the system.

During the simulation experiment, the system has located 1024 times according to Hilbert curve, so the overall positioning time is $1024 * T$. At the positioning i, the energy consumption of positioning can be expressed as W_i, there are P_i beacons in working mode, Q_i beacons in waiting mode and S_i beacons in sleeping mode. All of beacons with working mode which current is 102.3 mA work in the experiment without control. The W_i of each positioning is the same. By (2), we can calculate the total energy consumption W.

$$\begin{cases} W_i = 3.3 * (102.3 P_i + 90 Q_i + 0.9 S_i) * \frac{T}{3600} \\ \\ W = \sum_{i=1}^{n} W_i \end{cases} \qquad (2)$$

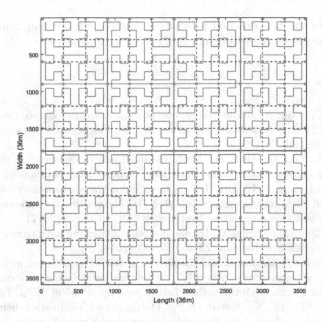

Fig. 7. Trajectories and the anchor deployment.

Table 2. Positioning energy consumption

Positioning operation	W	Mean
With control	1055.33 mWh	6.244 mWh
Without control	25702.318 mWh	211.256 mWh

The Table 2 show that energy consumption contrast without control has been reduced significantly, and average energy consumption reduced 30 times. The energy conservation control method has its own research and application value in practice and it is worth further study and optimization.

4   Conclusion

In this paper, we propose and implement the positioning system which use mobile cloud computing with high accuracy and low energy consumption. Most signal interference and energy consumption can reduce with control of the mobile cloud server. Each terminal simply broadcasts its BT signal while signal collection and positioning computations are done at the server side by beacons and the mobile cloud server. By controlling the working mode of the beacon according to the area where the terminal is located, it can reduce the acquisition of invalid data that increases the mobile cloud server load, at the same time the energy consumption of the system can be reduce. Furthermore, the mobile cloud server monitors the performance of the beacons and provides guarantee for the maintenance of the nodes that the system can work normally for a long time.

References

1. Liu, J.W.S., et al.: A building/environment data based indoor positioning service. In: 2015 IEEE International Conference on Data Science and Data Intensive Systems (DSDIS). IEEE (2015)
2. Jung, S.-H., Lee, G., Han, D.: Methods and tools to construct a global indoor positioning system. IEEE Trans. Syst. Man Cybern. Syst. **48**, 906–919 (2017)
3. Wang, J.J., Hwang, J.G., Park, J.G.: A novel indoor ranging method using weighted altofrequent RSSI measurements. In: 2017 11th International Conference on Signal Processing and Communication Systems (ICSPCS). IEEE (2017)
4. Chen, Q., Ding, D., Zheng, Y.: Indoor pedestrian tracking with sparse RSS fingerprints. Tsinghua Sci. Technol. **23**(1), 95–103 (2018)
5. Jondhale, S.R., et al.: Issues and challenges in RSSI based target localization and tracking in wireless sensor networks. In: International Conference on Automatic Control and Dynamic Optimization Techniques, pp. 594-598. IEEE (2017)
6. Elnahraway, E., Li, X., Martin, R.P.: The limits of localization using RSS. In: International Conference on Embedded Networked Sensor Systems, pp. 283–284. ACM (2004)
7. Alippi, C., Vanini, G.: A RSSI-based and calibrated centralized localization technique for Wireless Sensor Networks. In: IEEE International Conference on Pervasive Computing and Communications Workshops, p. 301. IEEE Computer Society (2006)
8. Zhai, S., et al.: Coverage hole detection and recovery in wireless sensor networks based on RSSI-based localization. In: IEEE International Conference on Computational Science and Engineering, pp. 250–257. IEEE (2017)
9. Piccinni, G., Avitabile, G., Coviello, G.: A novel distance measurement technique for indoor positioning systems based on Zadoff-Chu Sequences. In: New Circuits and Systems Conference. IEEE (2017)
10. Soewito, B., Faahakhododo, I., Gunawan, F.E.: Increasing the accuracy of distance measurement between access point and smartphone. In: International Conference on Knowledge, Information and Creativity Support Systems, pp. 1–6. IEEE (2017)
11. Singh, A.D., Vishwakarma, S., Ram, S.S.: Co-channel interference between WiFi and through-wall micro-Doppler radar. In: 2017 IEEE Radar Conference (RadarConf). IEEE (2017)
12. Kajikawa, N., et al.: On availability and energy consumption of the fast connection establishment method by using Bluetooth classic and Bluetooth low energy. In: Fourth International Symposium on Computing and NETWORKING, pp. 286–290. IEEE (2017)
13. Ksentini, D., Elhadi, A.R., Lasla, N.: Inertial measurement unit: evaluation for indoor positioning. In: International Conference on Advanced NETWORKING Distributed Systems and Applications, pp. 25–30. IEEE (2002)

A Method and Tool for Automated Induction of Relations from Quantitative Performance Logs

Joshua Kimball[✉] and Calton Pu

Georgia Institute of Technology, Atlanta, GA 30332, USA
{jmkimball,calton.pu}@gatech.edu

Abstract. Operators use performance logs to manage large-scale web service infrastructures. Detecting, isolating and diagnosing fine-grained performance anomalies require integrating system performance measures across space and time. The diversity of these logs layouts impedes their efficient processing and hinders such analyses. Performance logs possess some unique features, which challenge current log parsing techniques. In addition, most current techniques stop at extraction leaving relational definition as a post-processing activity, which can be a substantial effort at web scale. To achieve scale, we introduce our *perftables* approach, which automatically interprets performance log data and transforms the text into structured relations. We interpret the signals provided by the layout using our template catalog to induce an appropriate relation. We evaluate our method on a large sample obtained from our experimental computer science infrastructure in addition to a sample drawn from the wild. We were able to successfully extract on average over 97% and 85% of the data respectively.

Keywords: Information integration · Data cleaning · Data extraction

1 Introduction

Our experimental computer science infrastructure, *elba*, generates huge volumes of data from large numbers of diverse experiments and systems topologies, which support our empirical-based method for understanding computer systems' more fundamental behavior. As we show later, we have run over 20,000 experiments on *elba* over the last three years generating over 100 TB of data spread across 400K various log files. To isolate and diagnose nuanced, fine-grained performance anomalies, we need to support a broad array of experimental configurations, since these bugs can materialize under a range of conditions. For example, experimental artifacts like logs can vary in number and layout *per experiment* making data extraction and subsequent analysis challenging to perform at scale. Recent approaches like DeepLog operate over arbitrary text and attempt to isolate "macro-level" system events like crashes [1]. Our automated relation induction approach, *perftables*, operates over the diverse performance monitoring outputs with the objective of isolating much more precise (shorter and transient) events.

© Springer Nature Switzerland AG 2019
D. Da Silva et al. (Eds.): CLOUD 2019, LNCS 11513, pp. 11–25, 2019.
https://doi.org/10.1007/978-3-030-23502-4_2

The layout diversity observed across these performance logs stems from our infrastructure's enormous experimental parameter space and its diversity of instrumentation. Resource monitoring is one particularly good illustration. Elba infrastructure currently features five resource monitors: iostat, systat (sar), collectl, oprofile and lockmon. Each execution (of a given monitor) can have very different output even though each of these programs accepts a fixed number of parameters. For example, toggling a runtime parameter to change the resources being monitored alters the layout of the monitor's log file. Assuming each resource monitoring decision is binary, there can be as many as 2^n possible layouts for a performance monitor capable of measuring up to n resources. (From this point forward, layout and format are used interchangeably.) Given this, the number of possible layouts is exponential in the number of resources being monitored. This makes a naïve approach of writing a parser for each unique format simply intractable. In our data set, we have found the number of distinct layouts to number in the hundreds (under the most conservative accounting). Data variety and volume at our scale impedes automated data extraction and subsequent data analysis, creating an enterprise data-lake-scale data management challenge for our infrastructure [2]. The longer data remains unprocessed, the more unwieldly its management becomes [3].

Previous Work. Approaches from previous work in automated information extraction has generally fallen into one of two categories: wrapper induction and supervised learning techniques [4, 5]. Wrapper induction techniques have been applied to documents with explicit record boundaries like HTML [4, 6, 7]. Supervised techniques have been applied to similar domains. Work on extracting relations from web lists also shares some parallels with work on information extraction [8].

Previous work from the systems and programming language communities on log dataset extraction also feature similar work [9]. Work from the systems community has generally relied on source code interposition techniques to decorate logging statements corresponding to specific string literals which are found in the output [10]. Work from the programming language community has primarily used examples to either synthesize transformations or automatically generate a transformation program from user provided transformation actions. RecordBreaker is one such example of this latter approach [9], and it along with Datamaran are the most similar approaches to ours [11].

Example 1.1. Most previous work assumes record boundaries have been established beforehand or can be easily established using repeated patterns found in explicit structures such as the HTML DOM tree. As Gao et al. explain, log files have no natural record boundaries or explicit mechanisms like HTML tags for determining them [11]. In addition, log files can have nested structures and variable length records, i.e. records which span a variable number of rows. Log files also include noise such as formatting concerns and various metadata as shown in Fig. 1.

Performance logs present some specific and unique challenges. First, performance logs output formats are impacted by two implicit factors: the computer architecture of the system components being monitored and the actual behavior of the system under study. This latter characteristic suggests layout is at least partially runtime dependent, thus the layout of a given performance log for a given execution is not known a priori.

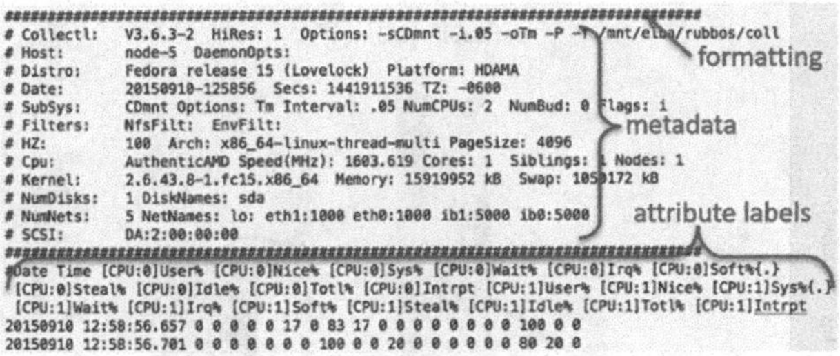

Fig. 1. collectl multi-core

Example 1.2. Figures 1 and 2 shows the performance output from the same performance monitor bootstrapped with the same monitoring parameters but running on different systems. Figure 1 displays the output for the multicore system while Fig. 2 depicts the single core system. Clearly, the output is significantly different holding all else constant. The impact of these implicit factors on the layout of the output underscores the need for an unsupervised approach.

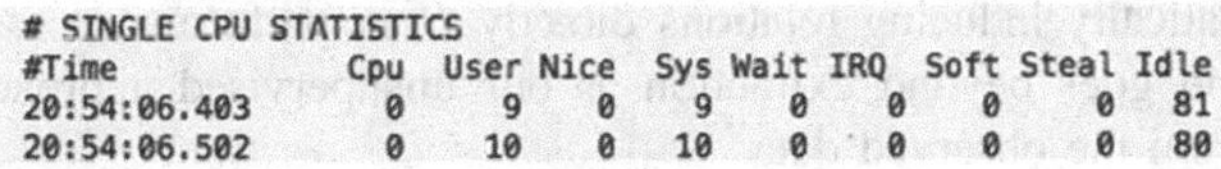

```
# SINGLE CPU STATISTICS
#Time           Cpu  User Nice  Sys Wait  IRQ  Soft Steal Idle
20:54:06.403      0     9    0    9    0    0    0    0   81
20:54:06.502      0    10    0   10    0    0    0    0   80
```

Fig. 2. collectl single core

Secondly, performance logs often contain multiple, related record types. In addition, record types can have degenerative sub-structures such as variable length attributes. This characteristic only adds to the complexity of comparing records once they are found. Prior work has assumed records are independent, so this work contains no mechanism for evaluating the relationships among records. This step is critical to realizing an end-to-end unsupervised approach. Information must be able to be extracted and directly represented in relations.

Example 2. Figure 4 shows a snippet of a log file containing process and context switch data from two sampling periods. First, notice that each active process appears on a separate line. Since each sampling period has a different number of active processes, each sampling period spans a variable number of lines. Also, the sampling period is the record in this case. Under a record type independence assumption, each region of data, i.e. the regions containing data about context switches and processes respectively, would be treated as their own record types. In this case, the two sampling periods not the data regions constitute the two record structures, which also happen to span a variable number of rows, i.e. variable length records.

While assuming independent record types is suitable for simple extraction, it is impractical at our scale. In our case, once the data has been extracted, it would still require significant transformation to get it into the correct relational form. This last example also demonstrates the need for an approach to identify record boundaries over

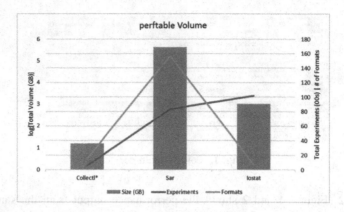

Fig. 3. perftables usage

a (potentially large) variable number of rows due to the impact of runtime factors can have on the layout.

Approach Overview. In this paper, we present *perftables*—our unsupervised algorithm for automatically inducing relations directly from performance monitoring log files. Our method goes beyond extraction as our unsupervised approach constructs tables directly from the observed data.

To accomplish this objective, we have defined a small set of pattern-based templates. We use a set of delimiters to first convert text into tokens. Then we transform each token sequence into a sequence of data type labels by applying a series of data type functions to each token. Next, we lazily match these sequences of data labels to one of our templates based on similarity. Once data has been matched to a template, the template can be used to extract the data and separate semantically meaningful metadata from "noise." To detect record boundaries, we induce a graph over the matching template instances. Finally, we construct relations from the template-matched data according to the record structure detected in the graph.

Generally, our method differs from previous work in its ability to handle logs with runtime dependent layouts. Due to the impact of runtime behavior on log output, multiple record types and variable length records are particularly prevalent in performance logs. For example, we have observed over 100 distinct layouts generated from several distinct runtime configurations across 3 monitoring programs. Specifically, *perftables* does not depend on pre-defining record boundaries. Moreover, it does not assume record boundaries appear over some constant, fixed number of lines. Its lazy approach obviates the need for such a hyperparameter.

Secondly, our method goes beyond extraction and induces relations directly from the log text data. Previous work has relegated schema definition and data transformation to manual post-extraction tasks—a significant burden at our infrastructure's scale. To analyze experimental data at our scale, we require an approach that can extract and transform unstructured log data into structured (relational) data with as little human supervision as possible. As Fig. 3 shows, we have used *perftables* to successfully extract with more than 98% accuracy over 250 GB of data from over 1 TB of log data.

In this paper, we demonstrate how our approach efficiently, accurately and automatically identifies and extracts relations from performance log files. Specifically, we have developed a small set of layout pattern-based templates, which support data extraction and attribute identification. Secondly, we have developed a set of algorithms to automatically identify record boundaries even in the presence of irregular and variable length records. We also show how our templates support automatically defining relations from matching data. Finally, we demonstrate the effectiveness (accuracy and efficiency) of our templates inside our environment and provide coverage for performance log data beyond our domain.

```
Linux 2.6.32-279.22.1.el6.x86_64 (Mysql2)    04/14/2014

09:42:47 PM   cswch/s
09:42:48 PM   2080.00

09:42:47 PM        PID  minflt/s  majflt/s    %user   %system  nswap/s  CPU
09:42:48 PM          1      0.00      0.00     0.00      0.00     0.00    0
....{95}....
09:42:48 PM      14615    294.00      0.00     0.00      0.00     0.00    0
....
09:45:18 PM   cswch/s
09:45:19 PM   1819.00

09:45:18 PM        PID  minflt/s  majflt/s    %user   %system  nswap/s  CPU
09:45:19 PM          1      0.00      0.00     0.00      0.00     0.00    0
....{90}....
09:45:19 PM      14631      0.00      0.00     0.00      0.00     0.00    0
```

Fig. 4. Long variable length records. Intermediate rows, indicated by braces, were removed for space considerations.

2 Terminology and Problem Statement

In this section, we will formally define our problem of unsupervised table extraction from performance log files.

Definition 2.1 (Data Type Sequence). By applying one or more delimiters to a string, it can be transformed into a sequence of tokens. This process is typically referred to as tokenization.

A best-fitting data type description can be estimated for each token by applying a data type function to each one. For example, if a token consists of the characters "123" then a data type description function might return "INT" to indicate integer as the best-fitting data type for this character sequence. By applying a data type function to every token in a sequence, a sequence of data type labels can be constructed. We refer to this sequence of labels as a data type sequence for short.

Definition 2.2 (Layout Template). A Layout Template is a regular expression for data type sequences. We say the data type sequence matches a layout template *iff* the regular expression of a layout template matches the string form of a data type sequence.

Definition 2.3 (Layout). A layout is a specific arrangement of data. Formats or layouts like those depicted in the previous Figures use formatting characters like whitespace and other special character delimiters like "#" or ":" and the order of metadata and data and their orientation to accomplish two objectives: partition data from metadata and metadata from "noise" and express relationships among the data. For example, metadata which immediately precedes data can be assumed to describe the data that follows it. In short, a layout is a sequence such that order can be used to partition the sequence into data and metadata constituent parts.

Formally, a layout, L, consists of text that can be divided into rows separated by newline characters, i.e. "\n." A layout consisting of n rows is $<r_1, r_2, ..., r_n>$. Applying some tokenization function, f, to the ith row r_i results in m tokens $<t_{i1}, t_{i2}, ..., t_{im}>$, and applying some function g to one or more successive t_{ij} determines its membership in M or D, the sets of metadata and data respectively.

Example 3. In the performance monitoring domain, layout explicitly encodes or aligns the measurements to corresponding resources. It expresses relationships among data visually. In Fig. 2, each line expresses the relationship between time and a magnitude for each of the resources being measured. Specifically, at 20:54:06.403, the CPU utilization is 19%, i.e. 100% - Idle%. It also shows the components of this utilization: User and (Sys)tem. Since the values appear on the same line, the layout is expressing a co-occurrence between these components of utilization at time, 20:54:06.403. In the multi-core case in Fig. 1, we see each CPU core (and corresponding components of utilization) are represented as separate columns. Once again, the layout expresses a co-occurrence among these cores' measurements at time 12:58:56.657. In both Figures, the preceding labels describe the data, and more specifically, that a label at a specific position corresponds to data at the same position in a subsequent row. The presence of labels provides an additional important signal. Specifically, knowing labels exist and their location in a file provides information about the location of the data they describe. Moreover, labels immediately preceding values in a tabular-like orientation suggests order can be used to match values to labels—an important signal that could be used during processing. In this respect, these files exhibit some self-describing characteristics.

Definition 2.4 (Log Data). Consider a file F with m layouts $<l_1, l_2, ..., l_m>$. Given our layout definition, interpreting each of the file's layouts can help us separate data from metadata and segregate useful labels from other metadata. Our goal is to find a layout that most closely matches the observed data, so it can be used to extract a Table T from this data. This is a subjective goal as solutions will have a different number of tables, columns and records. We obviously want to maximize the amount of information that can be reliably extracted. Instead, we need to formulate the problem as an optimization task.

Problem. The task is to find the best fitting Layout Template or Templates given the text. Once we have matched a template to an observed layout, we can use the template to construct a table T containing some number of columns and a maximal number of rows from the matching data. So, our refined problem is to extract a table T from the given log data using the best fitting layout L so that the number of extracted tuples is maximized.

3 Model

In this section, we identify the layout patterns our model covers and its assumptions. Our model reduces layout patterns into sequences of coarse-grained data type labels. By casting each token to a best-fitting data type, we can begin to "see" the format patterns more explicitly. Our model also includes a collection of Layout Templates that are expressed as regular expressions over the same alphabet as the one for data type labels. Layout templates not only express data composition but also a specific ordering. These model components combined with a few other reasonable assumptions enable us to automatically extract relations from performance log data.

3.1 Visual Structural Cues and Layouts

Performance log files are often formatted to support human readability and comprehension. As such, humans can use visual cues provided by a file layout to easily separate data from metadata. Unfortunately, performance log text does not explicitly and consistently identify the regular structures that are visually obvious.

We can view the problem of automatically extracting data from performance log files as one of interpreting the file layout. Our task is to find a mechanism to convert the visual cues provided by the layout into something more explicit to support automated detection and extraction. As we will show, the arrangement or sequence of data types seems to sufficiently approximate the layout's visual cues.

We previously defined layout as a sequence of metadata and data in which order can be used to differentiate data from metadata. Figure 5 depicts some of the most common layout structures appearing in performance logs. Each "row" in the figure represents a line, and each "cell's" shading indicates whether it represents a data (grey) or metadata (lavender) element. Gaps among the cells indicate breaks or irregularities, i.e. NULLs. Each example in the figure can be described by their orientations of data to metadata: tabular, horizontal, vertical, or series of independent tabular structures. We use these graphical models as a basis for defining our collection of Layout Templates, which relate sequences of data types to data and metadata distinctions.

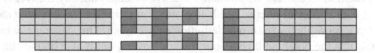

Fig. 5. Common layouts (Color figure online)

3.2 Layout Templates

To support our broader identification and segmentation tasks, we have defined a set of *data layout templates*, or *layout templates* for short, to codify each of the layouts pictured in Table 1. Specifically, our templates are defined using regular expressions over the same alphabet used for representing data type sequences (S, D, N). We name these patterns after the basic data type sequences they describe.

Table 1. Template definitions

Type	Pattern
Uniform (U)	$U = \{S+ \mid (D \mid N)+\}$
Alternating (A)	$A = \{D?(SN)+ \mid D?(NS)+\}$
Tag (G)	$G = \{S(D \mid N)+\}$
Tabular (T)	U_{Si}, U_{N+j} where $0 <= i < j < n$
Horizontal (H)	$A+_i, A+_{i+1}$ where $0 <= i < n$
Vertical (V)	$G+_i, G+_{i+1}$ where $0 <= i < n$
Series	$(T_i \mid H_i \mid V_i)+$ where $0 <= i < n$

Note: Series template describes sequences of other layout templates.

For example, Fig. 2 could be expressed as a sequence of four matching patterns: U_S, U_S, U_N, U_N. (A note on notation: an alphabetic subscript on a basic pattern refers to the specific branch taken in the pattern definition.)

Our templates express varying degrees of restrictiveness. This follows the intuition that the more structure or regularity the data exhibits, the more specific the matching rules can be. Accordingly, our templates can be applied using the best fit principle.

3.3   Assumptions

Our method makes several assumptions about files and their layouts, which enable the application of our templates. While these assumptions might appear to be restrictive, we demonstrate in our evaluation that all log files in our sample, including those collected from the wild, respect these assumptions.

Layout Templates Coverage Assumption. This assumption makes explicit the set of files our approach covers. Our approach begins by assuming files observe a left-to-right, top-to-bottom orientation. Specifically, our method covers files that match our Series layout template. Stated differently, our method can process log files that can be expressed as an ordering of our Layout Templates.

For our method to achieve its ultimate objective to automatically recover relations, the order of data in files of interest needs to matter; order must have semantic meaning. This assumption originates from our definition of a Layout. Our coverage assumption not only restricts the potential layouts our method covers, but it also bounds the search space and limits the set of files from which we can automatically materialize relations.

Token Creation Assumption. This assumption concerns the process of applying some regularly occurring delimiter to split a text of interest into tokens. Specifically, we assume each character in a text is either used for formatting or as part of a data value. Under this assumption, a character used as a delimiter cannot also be part of a data value.

Said differently, characters used as delimiters should not split semantically meaningful data. For example, using a colon ":" as a delimiter on text containing datetime would split semantically meaningful tokens, since the corresponding date entity is now represented as a series of independent tokens. Under this assumption, a colon character needs to either be a delimiter or part of a value for a given text.

While this assumption seems to be restrictive, we add flexibility by limiting the context under which the assumption must be true. Previous work has assumed delimiter characters need to be pre-identified or apply uniformly to a file. This has typically been referred to as tokenization or chunking. In our case, we assume the context for evaluation is the text between two consecutive newline characters, i.e. a line of a file.

In our domain, whitespace is frequently used for formatting and layout purposes. From this experience, we have found using whitespace characters as delimiters usually respects this assumption.

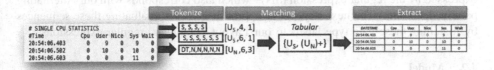

Fig. 6. perftables approach

4 · perfTables Approach

Our approach consists of four steps: tokenizing the file, matching data type sequences to layout templates, identifying candidate relations and records and finally extracting relations. Our layout templates are projected onto a file after a file has been transformed into sequences of data type labels. We create this tokenized representation by applying user-provided (or a default set) of delimiters to the file. Next, we create sequences of data type labels by inferring the best fitting coarse-grained data type for each token. We match our Layout Templates to these data type label sequences using a backtracking approach. Once data type sequences have been matched to templates, we use information from the matched data to identify candidate relations and their constituent records. Finally, we this information and the matchings to form relations.

4.1 Token Creation

First, a file is broken up into tokens using either a set of user-provided or default delimiters. The default set consists of white space characters, pipe (|), comma and quotation marks.

Specifically, each line can be converted into a "row of tokens" by applying one or more of these delimiters to it. After the file has been tokenized, we now consider each line of the file to be a row. Specifically, a row r with m tokens is expressed: $r = <t_0, t_1, t_2, ..., t_{m-1}>$.

The default delimiters are used to bootstrap or initialize our method. Users can supply supplemental delimiters; however, we have found our default set to be reliable for performance log data.

Sequences of Data Type Labels. Each token in the row can be evaluated for fit among three coarse-grained data types: DATETIME, NUMBER and STRING. We represent each token in the row with a label corresponding to the best fitting coarse-grained data type: S for STRING, D for DATETIME and N for NUMBER. At the end of this encoding step, each row is represented by a sequence of S, D and N characters. We call these sequences of data type labels sequences for short.

The next step in our method involves analyzing these patterns for the implicit semantic clues expressed in the layout. For example, a row with the sequence S, N, S, N, S, N describes a sequence of alternating STRING and NUMBER data. This layout suggests data is located at the positions corresponding to the "N" labels, and its metadata is located at the "S" label positions. (Note: the preceding sequence can be expressed by the regular expression (SN)+ which also corresponds with our Alternating pattern definition.) The next step in our approach involves evaluating these sequences by matching these data type labels to our Layout Templates' regular expressions.

4.2   Model

During this step, we interpret the sequences and match them to our templates to identify candidate tables. The objective of this step is to identify those rows that "belong together."

Matching Sequences to Layout Templates. After tokenizing the file, we try to match sequences of data type labels to the best fitting layout template. Not knowing a file's layout *a priori* motivates the need for a lazy, adaptive approach to matching. Accordingly, these sequences are lazily evaluated according to their topological order.

Backtracking. We match sequences to templates using a backtracking algorithm. This approach optimizes the best-fitting template through a process of elimination. We evaluate sequences according to their topological order. Each data type label sequence's string form is matched to each of the regular expressions accompanying each template definition. Only matching templates are preserved until only one remains. The process restarts once a sequence invalidates the remaining template, but not before the remaining template and its span of matching rows is added to an array of template, row span tuples. Once all rows' sequences have been matched to templates, a *table candidate* can be induced from the constituent rows corresponding to each matching template, row span tuple.

4.3   Extracting Relations

Besides helping to isolate common patterns, our Layout Templates provide another important function. They provide some of a matching file's missing semantic information. Specifically, they use the location and position of matching data to impart relational model semantics. For example, based on data type, composition and position, a piece of matching text might be used as attribute labels. These mapping rules also support data alignment, i.e. determining which labels (if they exist) correspond to which data. In this respect, our templates provide a convenient abstraction for aligning matching data to the constructs of the relational model.

Each template specifies how matching data can be separated into attributes and attribute labels. For example, some of our definitions use sequence or a common token index to align labels and corresponding attribute data.

Candidate Attribute Labels. Each template includes rules for identifying the location of *label candidates*. Each label candidate must be a string, but each string is not necessarily a label candidate. The mapping rules accompanying each template make this noise, label or data distinction. For example, in Fig. 6, the rows with similar size, {Us, 6, 1} and {Un, 6, 3}, were paired, and the row matching a uniform string pattern can be conveniently used as semantically appropriate attribute labels in defining a relation for the data matching {Un, 6, 3}.

Given this mapping between our templates and relational model constructs, we can automatically infer a schema (one or more relations) directly from this log data. For now, we assume each instance of a template matching data is independent. We show in our Evaluation how our approach accommodates situations when this is not true.

5   Evaluation

We explore our method's performance primarily along two dimensions: accuracy and processing time. We assess its performance across two different datasets. The first data set originates from our substantial experimental systems infrastructure. We use it to conduct a broad array of systems experiments to assess experimental systems performance. To support this work, we need to collect an enormous amount of performance data.

5.1   Elba Dataset Characteristics

As Fig. 3 shows, we have used *perftables* to process tens of thousands of experimental systems' performance data on the order of hundreds of GBs. Our experimental systems infrastructure primarily relies on three monitoring software programs: collectl, sar (systat) and iostat. As we briefly discussed earlier, these monitors can generate a large variety of layouts. Figure 7 shows the log diversity generated by these three monitors in our environment.

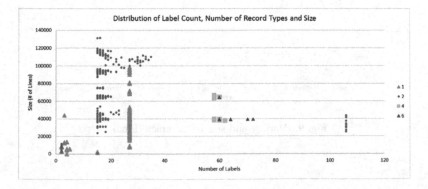

Fig. 7. Data volume and variety for three Elba performance monitors

Gao et al. developed a convenient categorization for describing layout variety. We adapt their categorization as follows: we differentiate interleaved and non-interleaved records precisely. In the following graphs, non-interleaved record structures are represented by "1," and in the interleaved case, we enumerate the number of record structures present in files to illustrate the variety of layouts more explicitly. We don't explicitly separate files with single lines from those with multiple lines in the interleaved case (Fig. 8).

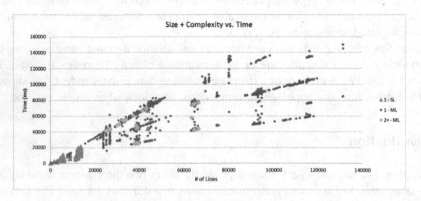

Fig. 8. Variety and size on performance (Elba)

Runtime and Accuracy. Figure 9 shows *perftables* performance by varying size and variety. The sub-linear trend highlights the effectiveness of our lazy approach.

We consider variety in terms of the number of repeated record structures that appear in a file. Even files with multiple record structures, *perftables* performs in sub-linear time.

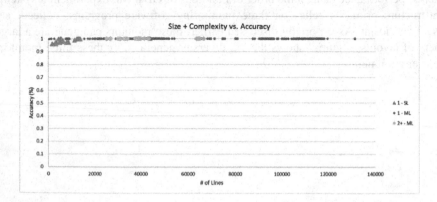

Fig. 9. Variety and size on accuracy (Elba)

5.2   GitHub Dataset Characteristics

The second dataset comes from the wild via a popular public source code repository, GitHub. We eliminated those files from the sample that did not originate from performance monitoring programs. This small, quasi-random sample helps us assess the validity of our assumptions by testing the generalizability of our approach. We retrieved this dataset by querying Github for keywords such as "log," "nagios," and "top." The latter two terms refer to two popular open source resource monitoring tools. Given their wide spread use, we thought they should be included in our sample. Table 2 details our GitHub sample's characteristics. While our quasi-random sample was small, it covers 7 unique monitors not currently deployed in our infrastructure, including: top (profile and process), vmstat (vmware), oprofile, nagios, logstat (kvm) and a bespoke CPU/network monitoring tool.

Table 2. GitHub sample characteristics

Record types	# of samples	Average size (# of lines)
One (single line)	5	3500
One (multi-line)	2	3000
Two or more	1	4000

Github Accuracy. In the following figure, we demonstrate the ability of our method to extend beyond the monitors and their corresponding outputs defined in our environment. On average, we were able to correctly extract over 90% of the data obtained from GitHub into relations. We were only able to extract approximately 75% of the nagios log data due to our approach treating network message labels as attribute labels instead of elements of an enumeration. Despite this result, repairing this error can be accomplished with some simple post-processing (Fig. 10).

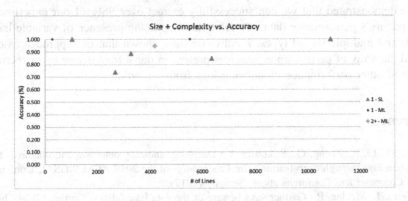

Fig. 10. Variety and size on accuracy (GitHub)

6 Related Work

Previous work has formulated similar log data extraction problems as uncovering some unobserved "template" (structure) from the observed text (data). Some previous work has relied on machine learning techniques to divine such structure from the data [12, 13]. There are two general limitations with such approaches. First, they are dependent on the availability of data, so in this sense, these methods are biased based on the composition of the corpus [8, 14]. Secondly, using supervised machine learning methods usually means manually curating labels for a training data set, and this data set should contain enough variety to account for potential bias. Unfortunately, to the best of our knowledge such a data set is not publicly available, and given the enormous parameter space, it is not likely to be sufficiently varied if one did exist.

Instead of trying to "learn" structure (bottom-up) as others have done, we project structure onto the text (top-down) using a collection of pattern templates. These templates correspond to frequently occurring layouts. Previous work in automated data extraction has used some regularities among HTML tags to separate data from its presentation [15]. For example, groups of specific HTML tags signal more regular substructures like tables and lists. In this respect, our types function like these groups of HTML tags [5].

7 Conclusion

In this paper, we introduced our approach, *perftables*, for automatically inducing relations from the log data generated by commonly used performance monitoring tools. The reasons for extracting this data into a relational form are many: facilitates integrating event and resource data across space (which node/ component) and time (when did the event happen or when was the measurement made), supports automated analysis techniques like machine learning and ultimately enables researchers to glean patterns across a vast volume of experiments occurring over many years.

We demonstrated that we can successfully extract over 98% of our experimental infrastructure's performance data into relations despite the presence of variable length records and multiple record types. Finally, we have shown that our approach extends beyond the array of performance monitors present in our infrastructure by collecting a sample of other performance monitoring logs from the wild.

References

1. Du, M., Li, F., Zheng, G., Srikumar, V.: DeepLog: anomaly detection and diagnosis from system logs through deep learning. In: Proceedings of the 2017 ACM SIGSAC Conference on Computer and Communications Security (2017)
2. Rivera, J., Meulen, R.: Gartner says beware of the data lake fallacy. Gartner (2014). http://www.gartner.com/newsroom/id/2809117
3. Stein, B., Morrison, A.: The enterprise data lake: better integration and deeper analytics. PwC Technol. Forecast. Rethink. Integr. **1**, 18 (2014)

4. Agichtein, E., Gravano, L.: Snowball: extracting relations from large plain-text collections. In: Proceedings of the Fifth ACM Conference on Digital Libraries (2000)
5. Arasu, A., Garcia-Molina, H.: Extracting structured data from web pages. In: SIGMOD Conference (2003)
6. Liu, L., Pu, C., Han, W.: XWRAP: an XML-enabled wrapper construction system for web information sources. In: Proceedings of 16th International Conference on Data Engineering (Cat. No. 00CB37073) (2000)
7. Han, W., Buttler, D., Pu, C.: Wrapping web data into XML. ACM SIGMOD Rec. **30**, 33–38 (2001)
8. Cafarella, M.J., Halevy, A., Wang, D.Z., Wu, E., Zhang, Y.: WebTables: exploring the power of tables on the web. Proc. VLDB Endow. **1**, 538–549 (2008)
9. Fisher, K., Walker, D., Zhu, K.Q., White, P.: From dirt to shovels - fully automatic tool generation from ad hoc data. In: POPL (2008)
10. He, P., Zhu, J., Zheng, Z., Lyu, M.R.: Drain: an online log parsing approach with fixed depth tree. In: 2017 IEEE International Conference on Web Services (ICWS) (2017)
11. Gao, Y., Huang S., Parameswaran, A.G.: Navigating the data lake with DATAMARAN - automatically extracting structure from log datasets. In: SIGMOD Conference (2018)
12. Chu, X., He, Y., Chakrabarti, K., Ganjam, K.: TEGRA. In: Proceedings of the 2015 ACM SIGMOD International Conference on Management of Data, New York, NY, USA (2015)
13. Cortez, E., Oliveira, D., Silva, A.S., Moura, E.S., Laender, A.H.F: Joint unsupervised structure discovery and information extraction. In: SIGMOD Conference (2011)
14. Elmeleegy, H., Madhavan, J., Halevy, A.Y.: Harvesting relational tables from lists on the web. In: PVLDB (2009)
15. Senellart, P., Mittal, A., Muschick, D., Gilleron, R., Tommasi, M.: Automatic wrapper induction from hidden-web sources with domain knowledge. In: Proceedings of the 10th ACM Workshop on Web Information and Data Management (2008)

Systematic Construction, Execution, and Reproduction of Complex Performance Benchmarks

Rodrigo Alves Lima[1]([⊠]), Joshua Kimball[1], João E. Ferreira[2], and Calton Pu[1]

[1] Georgia Institute of Technology, Atlanta, USA
{ral3,jmkimball,calton.pu}@cc.gatech.edu
[2] University of São Paulo, São Paulo, Brazil
jef@ime.usp.br

Abstract. In this work, we present the next generation of the Elba toolkit available under a Beta release, showing how we have used it for experimental research in computer systems using RUBBoS, a well-known n-tier system benchmark, as example. In particular, we show how we have leveraged milliScope – Elba toolkit's monitoring and instrumentation framework – to collect log data from benchmark executions at unprecedented fine-granularity, as well as how we have specified benchmark workflows with WED-Make – a declarative workflow language whose main characteristic is to facilitate the declaration of dependencies. We also show how to execute WED-Makefiles (i.e., workflow specifications written with WED-Make), and how we have successfully reproduced the experimental verification of the millibottleneck theory of performance bugs in multiple cloud environments and systems.

1 Introduction

A performance benchmark (hereinafter referred to simply as a benchmark) typically involves running an artificial workload (e.g., simulating user interactions) on an instrumented application (i.e., specialized with code to record detailed execution logs) deployed on a single or multiple computing nodes whose resources of interest (e.g., CPU, memory, disk I/O) are monitored while the workload is running. Benchmarks are commonly used to evaluate and compare the performance of applications under different configurations and systems through the execution of equivalent, if not equal, workloads. For example, TPC [22] is a well-known family of benchmarks to evaluate and compare, among other relevant metrics, the number of transactions a database system can process per second.

Also, in experimental research in computer systems, hypotheses have to be confirmed by compelling evidence found in both resource monitoring logs (e.g., CPU utilization) and execution logs (e.g., response times) generated by the execution of carefully constructed benchmarks. As an illustrative case, we – project Elba researchers – and our collaborators have executed thousands of large-scale benchmarks over the years to study interesting phenomena in cloud computing

© Springer Nature Switzerland AG 2019
D. Da Silva et al. (Eds.): CLOUD 2019, LNCS 11513, pp. 26–37, 2019.
https://doi.org/10.1007/978-3-030-23502-4_3

environments, leading to the discovery of previously unknown transient resource bottlenecks (e.g., in CPU utilization, disk I/O) with the duration of only a few tens or hundreds of milliseconds that start to happen at quite low average utilization levels (e.g., less than 40% in the case of CPU). Later, we would also confirm the hypothesis that these so-called millibottlenecks can propagate through the components of a distributed system and have their effects amplified, causing significant performance bugs (e.g., response time long tail problem) [15].

Currently, one of our major research goals is to discover and study new types and sources of millibottlenecks. So far we have been able to discover millibottlenecks in CPU utilization due to many causes: garbage collector of the Java Virtual Machine 1.5 [23,25], DVFS (dynamic voltage and frequency scaling) for energy savings [24], and interference from noisy neighbors in consolidated cloud environments [12]. We have also found disk I/O millibottlenecks due to dirty page flushing [26].

Although executing complex benchmarks (e.g., of n-tier systems) is essential to collect the data needed to achieve our goal of discovering and studying new types and sources of millibottlenecks, their construction is challenging. For example, performance debugging of distributed systems requires the analysis of detailed event logs to reconstruct the complete execution path of anomalous requests (e.g., the ones taking seconds to be processed, while the majority is still being served within a few milliseconds) across different computing nodes; further, when looking for their root causes, aforementioned millibottlenecks pose a resource monitoring challenge due to their short life spans and variety – to support their observation, we need a diverse set of resource monitors with low overhead and very short sampling periods (at 50 ms intervals, we can reliably detect millibottlenecks of 100 ms or longer).

Furthermore, reproducibility is a cornerstone of the scientific method: the research community must be able to independently validate published results by reproducing their experiments. As a result, an increasing number of academic journals (e.g., Science [17]) now require the submission of software, scripts, and data used to obtain claimed results along with the article itself.

Automation of complex benchmark workflows is thus essential to guarantee that the original sequence of tasks or, alternatively, another correct sequence of tasks (i.e., one satisfying orchestration dependencies such as server initialization order) is precisely followed when reproducing them. Common tasks include copying artifacts from remote servers, installing libraries, configuring software, initializing applications, running workloads, and archiving results.

However, ensuring the reproducibility of benchmarks usually demands more than simply releasing their software, scripts, and data – it is also necessary to satisfy their hidden and implicit dependencies (e.g., required libraries, compiler versions). Manually recreating complex benchmark environments used in published research is typically intricate, error-prone, and time-consuming so, in previous versions of our benchmarks, hidden software dependencies such as required libraries were satisfied through the use of pre-built operating system images; in turn, implicit dependencies such as network naming conventions adopted in our benchmarks' scripts limited their execution to a single scientific cloud infrastructure called Emulab [5].

Benchmarks should therefore rely on as few hidden and implicit dependencies as possible to be highly configurable and easily portable. For example, the use of pre-built operating system and container images to satisfy hidden software dependencies makes it difficult to increase the configuration spaces of benchmarks (e.g., adding support to multiple library versions would require building an exponential number of these images, one for each possible combination of library versions), which is also critical to our goal of discovering and studying new types and sources of millibottlenecks. Moreover, restricting the execution of benchmarks to a single public cloud infrastructure due to the network naming conventions adopted in their scripts is a major inconvenience because computing nodes are becoming an increasingly scarce resource in these cloud infrastructures. For a better understanding of benchmark dependencies, we refer the reader to Table 1.

Table 1. Commonly found benchmark dependencies according to their target.

Benchmark dependency target	Example
Filesystem	Existence of configuration files
Hardware	Size of CPU cache to flush
Scientific cloud infrastructure	Network naming convention
Software	Libraries and initialization parameters
Server	Proper initialization
Workload	Duration and size

In summary, three concrete needs arise from these software instrumentation, resource monitoring, workflow automation, and dependency management challenges to construct, execute, and reproduce complex benchmarks:

1. Low-overhead software specialization to record detailed logs of interesting events (e.g., request arrivals, remote procedure calls) across computing nodes while a benchmark workload is running.
2. Fine-grained (order of milliseconds), low-overhead tools to monitor many different resources (e.g., CPU, memory, network, disk I/O) of computing nodes while a benchmark workload is running.
3. An appropriate workflow language for the specification of benchmarks, ideally enabling the declaration of all sorts of dependencies so it becomes easier to meet them at runtime (e.g., by adding workflow tasks to install software dependencies instead of relying on pre-built operating system and container images) and to eventually extend configuration spaces (e.g., by adding alternative workflow execution paths to support multiple public cloud infrastructures).

In this work, we present the next generation of the Elba toolkit available under a Beta release, showing how we have used it for experimental research in computer systems using RUBBoS, a well-known n-tier system benchmark, as example. We first show, in Sect. 2, how we have leveraged milliScope – Elba toolkit's monitoring and instrumentation framework – to collect log data from benchmark executions at unprecedented fine-granularity, as well as how we have specified benchmark workflows with WED-Make – a declarative workflow language whose main characteristic is precisely to facilitate the declaration of dependencies; further, the execution of workflows specified with WED-Make is driven by declared dependencies themselves, guaranteeing their satisfaction. Then, in Sect. 3 we show how to execute WED-Makefiles (i.e., workflow specifications written with WED-Make). Next, in Sect. 4 we show how we have successfully reproduced the experimental verification of the millibottleneck theory of performance bugs, first presented in [15], in multiple cloud environments and systems, relying on as few hidden and implicit dependencies as possible. Finally, we present related work in Sect. 5 and summarize our conclusions in Sect. 6.

2   RUBBoS Monitoring and Workflow Specification with the Elba Toolkit

2.1   RUBBoS Benchmark

Most of our studies on interesting phenomena in cloud computing environments have stemmed from executions of RUBBoS [16] – an n-tier system benchmark that simulates user requests to a bulletin board web application similar to Slashdot [19]. As shown in Fig. 1, the RUBBoS web application is composed of 4 tiers: Apache HTTP servers [21], Tomcat application servers [1], C-JDBC middleware servers [2], and MySQL database servers [10].

When the workload is running, the RUBBoS client application generates HTTP requests simulating 24 types of user interactions (e.g., creating and viewing stories). Specifically, this client application sends HTTP requests to the Apache servers, responsible for serving HTML pages, which often need to forward these requests to the Tomcat servers, responsible for handling the application logic. These Tomcat servers send SQL queries to the C-JDBC servers, which forward them to the MySQL servers.

2.2   RUBBoS Monitoring with milliScope

milliScope [9] is our resource and event monitoring framework for n-tier systems, built precisely to discover and study transient phenomena such as millibottlenecks in cloud computing environments.

The resource monitoring component of milliScope contains open-source tools like *sar* [20], *Collectl* [4], and *iostat* to monitor resources like CPU, memory, network, and disk I/O with low-overhead and fine granularity. These tools have all been reliably used in production systems for quite a few years and are under active development.

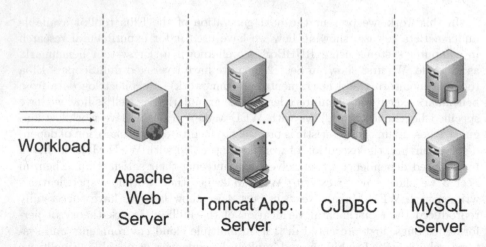

Fig. 1. RUBBoS architecture.

The event monitoring component of milliScope comprises software (e.g., Apache HTTP Server, Tomcat application server) specialized with low overhead event loggers that mainly serve the purpose of identifying execution boundaries of requests (i.e., instants of time that each server was called and returned a response for every request). To impose minimum overhead, these event loggers simply extend native log components. As messages pass from one server to another, unique identifiers generated for each request are logged along with a timestamp and the event type (e.g., sent message to Tomcat server, received message from Tomcat server). In this way, it is possible to reconstruct the complete execution path of requests, as shown in Fig. 2.

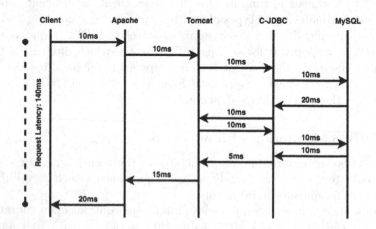

Fig. 2. Reconstruction of the execution path (with latency data) of a request generated by the RUBBoS client application, showing its execution boundaries.

By integrating the fine-grained monitoring of many different resources and highly detailed event logging, both with low-overhead, milliScope has enabled us to analyze the performance of distributed systems across a wide variety of use cases – in particular, finding correlations between millibottlenecks and interesting events like server queue overflows and very long response times.

2.3   RUBBoS Workflow Specification with WED-Make

WED-Make, the major novelty of this new Elba toolkit release, is a workflow language for the specification of complex benchmarks that facilitates the declaration of dependencies. A WED-Makefile (i.e., a workflow specification written with WED-Make) comprises:

- an initial guard;
- a final guard;
- a set of tasks.

In a WED-Makefile, the initial guard explicits dependencies to start the workflow execution. These dependencies are declared as logical predicates defined over variables of interest (like in Bash, a $ has to be placed in front of the variable identifier to retrieve its value). In the following, we present the initial guard specified in the RUBBoS WED-Makefile:

```
initial_guard:
  - $WEB_NET_NODES != ""
  - $APP_NET_NODES != ""
  - $MIDDL_NET_NODES != ""
  - $DB_NET_NODES != ""
```

In the RUBBoS WED-Makefile, variables with suffix _NET_NODES represent the hostnames of computing nodes provisioned for each tier (WEB, APP, MIDDL, and DB). Hence, to start the execution of the RUBBoS workflow, these variables have to be defined (i.e., their values have to be different than the empty string).

On the other hand, the final guard defined in a WED-Makefile explicits dependencies to terminate the workflow execution. For example, after running the RUBBoS workload, a compressed archive containing log data generated by all computing nodes must be created and stored. As we can see in the final guard of the RUBBoS WED-Makefile presented below, the only dependency to terminate the execution of the RUBBoS workflow is exactly to check whether the path to this archive has already been set (variable BENCH_RESULTSTARBALL represents the path to this archive).

```
final_guard:
  - $BENCH_RESULTSTARBALL != ""
```

In a WED-Makefile, each task has a name, a script written in Bash, and a guard expliciting dependencies for the execution of this script. It is worth noting that the variables used in task guards can be interchangeably used as

Bash variables with the same identifiers in task scripts. The RUBBoS work-flow comprises around 90 tasks for copying artifacts from remote servers, installing libraries, configuring software, initializing applications, running work-loads, archiving results, etc. In the following, we present the task specified in the RUBBoS WED-Makefile to collect resulting log data from Apache HTTP servers.

```
- name: WebCollectResultsApacheServer
  guard:
    - $WEB_NET_NODES != ""
    - $WEB_NET_USERNAME != ""
    - $WEB_HTTPD_HOMEDIR != ""
    - $WEB_FS_RESULTSDIR != ""
    - $WEB_HTTPD_STOPPEDAT != ""
    - $WEB_HTTPD_RESULTSDIR = ""
  bash: |
    readonly WEB_HTTPD_RESULTSDIR="$WEB_FS_RESULTSDIR/httpd"
    local web_net_node
    local sessions=()
    local n_sessions=0
    local session
    for web_net_node in $WEB_NET_NODES; do
      ssh -T -o UserKnownHostsFile=/dev/null \
          -o StrictHostKeyChecking=no \
          -o BatchMode=yes \
          $WEB_NET_USERNAME@$web_net_node "
        mkdir -p $WEB_HTTPD_RESULTSDIR
        cp $WEB_HTTPD_HOMEDIR/logs/access_log \
            $WEB_HTTPD_RESULTSDIR/\$(hostname -s)_HTTPD_mscope_access.log
        cp $WEB_HTTPD_HOMEDIR/logs/mod_jk.log \
            $WEB_HTTPD_RESULTSDIR/\$(hostname -s)_HTTPD_modjk.log
      " &
      sessions[$n_sessions]=$!
      let n_sessions=n_sessions+1
    done
    for session in ${sessions[*]}; do
      wait $session
    done
```

In this example, declared dependencies ensure that:

- $WEB_NET_NODES != "" – hostnames of provisioned computing nodes were defined for the web tier.
- $WEB_NET_USERNAME != "" – username to remotely access these computing nodes was defined.
- $WEB_HTTPD_HOMEDIR != "" – Apache directory was already created in these computing nodes.
- $WEB_FS_RESULTSDIR != "" – directory to store resulting log data was already created in these computing nodes.

- $WEB_HTTPD_STOPPEDAT != "" – Apache HTTP server was already stopped.
- $WEB_HTTPD_RESULTSDIR = "" – directory to store resulting log data specifically from the Apache HTTP server was not created in these computing nodes yet.

We also remark that the task script of the previous example sets the value of WEB_HTTPD_RESULTSDIR. Therefore, this script can be successfully executed at most once because the logical predicate $WEB_HTTPD_RESULTSDIR = "" is part of its associate guard.

To our benefit, we already had an implementation of the RUBBoS workflow (in an ad-hoc way, though, with an orchestration script dictating the order in which task scripts had to be executed). Thus, our work mainly consisted in porting it to a WED-Makefile, finding and declaring its hidden and implicit dependencies.

3 RUBBoS Execution

3.1 Execution Model

The execution of WED-Makefiles is inspired by the WED-flow approach for modeling workflows [6]: as previously mentioned, it is driven by declared dependencies. More specifically, dependencies declared in guards have to be satisfied by the data state of workflow instances (i.e., by the valuation of their variables).

Therefore, before executing a workflow specified in a WED-Makefile, the initial data state (i.e., the initial valuation of variables) must be defined in a separate configuration file written as a plain Bash script. Global variables resulting from the execution of this configuration file are the initial data state. In the following, we present an example of RUBBoS workload configuration with 500 concurrent connections:

```
readonly BENCH_TYPE="read-write"
readonly BENCH_WORKLOAD="500"
readonly BENCH_UPRAMPTIMEINMS="180000"
readonly BENCH_SESSIONRUNTIMEINMS="180000"
readonly BENCH_DOWNRAMPTIMEINMS="60000"
```

We remark that some variables are not supposed to be defined in the configuration file (e.g., variables representing the start time of servers). In this case, like in Bash, their values are initialized with empty strings.

If the initial guard specified in the WED-Makefile is satisfied by the initial state, the workflow execution can be started. Then, once the dependencies for executing a task are satisfied, the execution of its script can be triggered. Global variables resulting from the execution of a task script are used to update the current data state. For example, at the end of the execution of the script of task WebCollectResultsApacheServer, presented in Sect. 2, the value of variable WEB_HTTPD_RESULTSDIR is updated. Finally, the workflow execution is terminated when the final guard defined in the WED-Makefile is satisfied by the current data state.

3.2 Implementation

The execution of WED-Makefiles needs concurrency control capabilities because more than one task guard can be satisfied at the same time (e.g., for tasks mounting filesystems in computing nodes of different tiers). Therefore, we have used the PostgreSQL [14] database management system to implement execution engines for WED-Makefiles, leveraging its battle-tested concurrency control mechanisms to maintain the ACID properties of transactions.

In summary, the WED-Makefile is first translated to SQL commands that create a single table and multiple stored procedures that constitute the execution engine itself. This table's columns and rows represent, respectively, variables and workflow instances (i.e., each row represents exactly the data state of the correspondent workflow instance), as shown in Fig. 3. These stored procedures instantiate workflows, check the satisfaction of guards, and even encapsulate task script executions (more specifically, we have used PostgreSQL 9.6 with a plugin called *plsh* [13] that enables stored procedures written in Bash to be run inside transactions).

···	BENCHMARK_ TYPE	BENCHMARK_ WORKLOAD	BENCHMARK_ UPRAMPTIMEINMS	···
...	read-write	500	180000	...
...	read-only	400	180000	...

Fig. 3. WED-Makefile execution engines store the data state of ongoing and past executions of the workflow in database tables.

An inconvenience of using a single table, however, is the fact that most open-source database management systems use a row-level locking mechanism to guarantee serializability, thus preventing two or more concurrent transactions (task scripts, in this case) to operate on the same row (workflow instances, in this case). However, there clearly exists a natural separation of variables in n-tier benchmarks like RUBBoS – one group of variables for each tier. Hence, to achieve maximum parallelism when executing RUBBoS, we have split that single table into multiple tables – one for each group of variables related to the same tier – to be joined by execution identifiers.

4   RUBBoS Reproduction

As aforementioned, the initial data state of instances of a workflow specified in a WED-Makefile has to be defined in a separate configuration file containing parameters (e.g., software versions, workload size and duration). Reproducing a benchmark workflow specified in a WED-Makefile should thus just be a matter of using the same parameters used in the original benchmark execution. However, hidden and implicit dependencies commonly frustrate attempts to reproduce benchmark executions.

In the case of RUBBoS, hidden software dependencies such as required libraries were satisfied through the use of pre-built operating system images, hindering our ability to increase its configuration space. We remark that finding these hidden dependencies is difficult because they can only be found when the benchmark execution fails for not meeting them, but we still managed to implement tasks to install most needed software and libraries at runtime (i.e., building those custom operating system images at runtime), expliciting their dependencies, and eventually abandoning the pre-built operating system images.

On the other hand, finding implicit dependencies such as hard-coded values (e.g., directory paths) and embedded Emulab [5] network naming conventions in RUBBoS scripts was trivial with a tool like *grep*. In this way, we easily declared these dependencies. Later, we would also add alternative workflow execution paths to support a newer public cloud infrastructure called CloudLab [3].

5   Related Work

Other approaches have been proposed for monitoring resources and events in computer systems. We highlight Dapper [18], which uses sampling to reduce event monitoring overhead, and SysViz, a Fujitsu product with limited adoption.

Another workflow language based on WED-flow is WED-SQL [11]. In a similar way, execution engines are generated for workflows specified with WED-SQL through the translation to SQL commands.

To enable the constructions of benchmarks with large configuration spaces, Mulini [8] has leveraged template-based code generation techniques to render custom Bash scripts to implement and orchestrate benchmark executions.

Recently, the Popper convention [7] proposed the use of DevOps configuration tools to manage the execution of reproducible experiments. For example, Popper suggests using containers (e.g., Docker images) to meet software dependencies and configuration tools (e.g., Ansible) to orchestrate experiments.

6   Conclusions

Benchmark executions have led us to the discovery of previously unknown interesting phenomena in cloud computing environments. However, the needs for low-overhead software specialization to record detailed event logs, low-overhead monitoring of many different resources with fine-granularity, and an appropriate workflow language to handle benchmark dependencies have posed significant challenges to the construction, execution, and reproduction of complex benchmarks.

Unlike widely adopted ad-hoc approaches, the new release of our Elba toolkit presented in this paper enables the systematic construction, execution, and reproduction of complex benchmarks needed to achieve our goal of discovering and studying new types and sources of millibottlenecks. In particular, milliScope has enabled us to collect log data from benchmark executions at unprecedented fine-granularity. In turn, WED-Make, the major novelty of this new Elba toolkit release, not only facilitates the declaration of benchmark dependencies but also guarantees their satisfaction.

References

1. Apache Tomcat. http://tomcat.apache.org/. Accessed 17 Mar 2019
2. C-JDBC. https://c-jdbc.ow2.org/. Accessed 17 Mar 2019
3. CloudLab Scientific Cloud Infrastructure. https://cloudlab.us/. Accessed 17 Mar 2019
4. Collectl Performance Monitoring Tool. http://collectl.sourceforge.net/. Accessed 17 Mar 2019
5. Emulab Scientific Cloud Infrastructure. https://emulab.net. Accessed 17 Mar 2019
6. Ferreira, J.E., et al.: Transactional recovery support for robust exception handling in business process services. In: 2012 IEEE 19th International Conference on Web Services, pp. 303–310. IEEE (2012)
7. Jimenez, I., et al.: Popper: making reproducible systems performance evaluation practical. Technical report UCSC-SOE-16-10, UC Santa Cruz School of Engineering (2016)
8. Jung, G., Pu, C., Swint, G.: Mulini: an automated staging framework for QoS of distributed multi-tier applications. In: Proceedings of the 2007 Workshop on Automating Service Quality: Held at the International Conference on Automated Software Engineering (ASE), pp. 10–15. ACM (2007)
9. Lai, C.-A., et al.: milliScope: a fine-grained monitoring framework for performance debugging of n-tier Web services. In: 2017 IEEE 37th International Conference on Distributed Computing Systems (ICDCS), pp. 92–102. IEEE (2017)
10. MySQL. https://www.mysql.com/. Accessed 17 Mar 2019
11. Padilha, B., Roberto, R.L., Schwerz, A.L., Pu, C., Ferreira, J.E.: WED-SQL: an intermediate declarative language for PAIS execution. In: Jin, H., Wang, Q., Zhang, L.-J. (eds.) ICWS 2018. LNCS, vol. 10966, pp. 407–421. Springer, Cham (2018). https://doi.org/10.1007/978-3-319-94289-6_26
12. Park, J., et al.: Performance interference of memory thrashing in virtualized cloud environments: a study of consolidated n-tier applications. In: 2016 IEEE 9th International Conference on Cloud Computing (CLOUD), pp. 276–283. IEEE (2016)
13. PL/sh. https://github.com/petere/plsh. Accessed 17 Mar 2019
14. PostgreSQL. https://www.postgresql.org/. Accessed 17 Mar 2019
15. Pu, C., et al.: The millibottleneck theory of performance bugs, and its experimental verification. In: 2017 IEEE 37th International Conference on Distributed Computing Systems (ICDCS), pp. 1919–1926. IEEE (2017)
16. RUBBoS Benchmark. http://jmob.ow2.org/rubbos.html. Accessed 17 Mar 2019
17. Science Magazine. https://www.sciencemag.org/. Accessed 17 Mar 2019
18. Sigelman, B.H., et al.: Dapper, a large-scale distributed systems tracing infrastructure (2010)
19. Slashdot Bulletin Board. https://slashdot.org/. Accessed 17 Mar 2019
20. sysstat: Performance Monitoring Tools for Linux. https://github.com/sysstat/sysstat. Accessed 17 Mar 2019

21. The Apache HTTP Server Project. https://httpd.apache.org/. Accessed 17 Mar 2019
22. TPC Benchmarks. http://www.tpc.org/information/benchmarks.asp. Accessed 17 Mar 2019
23. Wang, Q., et al.: An experimental study of rapidly alternating bottlenecks in n-tier applications. In: 2013 IEEE Sixth International Conference on Cloud Computing, pp. 171–178. IEEE (2013)
24. Wang, Q., et al.: Impact of DVFS on n-tier application performance. In: Proceedings of the First ACM SIGOPS Conference on Timely Results in Operating Systems, p. 5. ACM (2013)
25. Wang, Q., et al.: When average is not average: large response time fluctuations in n-tier systems. In: Proceedings of the 9th International Conference on Autonomic Computing, pp. 33–42. ACM (2012)
26. Zhu, T., et al.: Limitations of load balancing mechanisms for n-tier systems in the presence of millibottlenecks. In: 2017 IEEE 37th International Conference on Distributed Computing Systems (ICDCS), pp. 1367–1377. IEEE (2017)

Multiple Workflow Scheduling with Offloading Tasks to Edge Cloud

Hidehiro Kanemitsu[1][(✉)], Masaki Hanada[2], and Hidenori Nakazato[3]

[1] School of Computer Science, Tokyo University of Technology
and Waseda Research Institute for Science and Engineering,
Waseda University, Tokyo, Japan
kanemitsuh@stf.teu.ac.jp
[2] Faculty of Informatics, Tokyo University of Information Sciences, Tokyo, Japan
mhanada@rsch.tuis.ac.jp
[3] School of Fundamental Science and Engineering, Waseda University, Tokyo, Japan
nakazato@waseda.jp

Abstract. Edge computing can realize a data locality among a cloud and users, and it can be applied to task offloading, i.e., a part of workload on a mobile terminal is moved to an edge or a cloud system to minimize the response time with reducing energy consumption. Mobile workflow jobs have been widely used due to advance of computational power on a mobile terminal. Thus, how to offload or schedule each task in a mobile workflow is one of the current challenging issues.

In this paper, we propose a task scheduling algorithm with task offloading, called priority-based continuous task selection for offloading (PCTSO), to minimize the schedule length with energy consumption at a mobile client being reduced. PCTSO tries to select dependent tasks such that many tasks are offloaded so as to utilize many vCPUs in the edge cloud; in this manner, the degree of parallelism can be maintained. Experimental results of the simulation demonstration that PCTSO outperforms other algorithms in the schedule length and satisfies the energy constraint.

Keywords: Task scheduling · Workflow scheduling · Offloading ·
Task offloading · Edge cloud

1 Introduction

With multicore household PCs and smartphones being widespread in recent years, the types of applications covered by them became diverse. For instance, applications dealing with image processing, face recognition, and more heavy loaded ones can be handled by parallel processing schemes. Though cloud computing is based on the virtualization of computational resources such as CPU, RAM, and storage to achieve overcommitment, effectively utilizing them for various objectives is still a challenging issue. For instance, there is a problem

© Springer Nature Switzerland AG 2019
D. Da Silva et al. (Eds.): CLOUD 2019, LNCS 11513, pp. 38–52, 2019.
https://doi.org/10.1007/978-3-030-23502-4_4

regarding data communication overhead if the data size between a cloud system and a client can be a bottleneck. In such a case, an edge infrastructure [1], which takes the role of a bridge between them, is deployed. Furthermore, a large amount of data can be stored at the edge for data caching. In particular, storing data from mobile terminals such as smartphones or executing tasks of mobile terminals at the edge can save energy at mobile terminals. In such an offloading scheme [2–8], how to minimize the schedule length along with reducing energy consumption at the mobile terminal is a challenging task.

As for the job to be executed at a mobile terminal, a general representation can be expressed as a directed acyclic graph, or workflow [6–8], where each task has data dependencies with others as the precedence constraint. This job model is called as a mobile workflow job, and how to schedule tasks in a mobile workflow job is called an NP-complete problem.

In this paper, we propose a task scheduling algorithm with task offloading, called priority-based continuous task selection for offloading (PCTSO), for mobile workflow in an edge cloud environment. The PCTSO algorithm tries to check whether each task should be executed at the mobile terminal. If not, the task is offloaded to the edge cloud with generating the new communication between the mobile terminal and the edge cloud. The proposed algorithm is based on a list-scheduling scheme and the objective is to minimize the schedule length along with satisfying the energy consumption constraint. Experimental results of the simulation demonstrate that PCTSO outperforms other algorithms in terms of the schedule length along with satisfying the energy constraint.

The remainder of this paper is organized as follows. Section 3 describes the assumptions and the basics for understanding the proposed algorithm. Section 4 presents and explains the details of the proposed algorithm. Section 5 presents the experimental results. Section 2 shows the related work in terms of task offloading. Finally, Sect. 6 concludes this paper.

2   Related Work

Literature [2] proposes a task offloading algorithm for minimizing the total energy consumption at a mobile client with satisfying the deadline for task execution. Literature [3] proposes a task offloading algorithm by checking each time slot whether a task should be locally executed or offloaded. This approach aims to minimize the total delay for whole task execution with satisfying the energy constraint with linear programming. Literature [5] assumes multi-user environment with weighting both the response time and the energy consumption depending on each user's requirement.

As for task offloading for a workflow, literature [6–8] have been proposed. Task offloading can be applied for fault tolerance purpose in order to resume the task execution in a cloud [6], or load balancing among a cloud and a mobile client [8]. In literature [7], each task is offloaded to a cloudlet to minimize both the execution delay and the energy consumption at a mobile client. If one task is accepted for offloading to a cloudlet, successor tasks of the task are checked

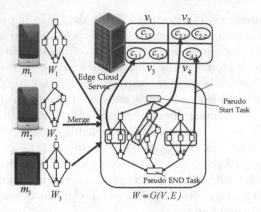

Fig. 1. Assumed situation

if they can be offloaded the same cloudlet or not. If both the execution delay and the energy consumption are reduced by offloading them, they are assigned to the cloudlet.

Above mentioned algorithms check each task for offloading in one-by-one basis. As a result, offloaded tasks and locally executed tasks may exist on a path in a workflow. This characteristics can lead to the fact that many tasks cannot be offloaded and therefore the energy consumption at a mobile client cannot be reduced so much. In PCTSO algorithm, the set of tasks in a path are selected for offloading. Thus, more tasks can be offloaded than conventional algorithms, thereby the reduction of the energy consumption is achieved.

3   System Model

In this section, we describe the assumed system, jobs to be handled in the system, and the objective function. Table 1 shows whole definitions used in this section.

3.1   Assumed System

In an edge cloud system, we assume there is an edge cloud server having multiple VM instances, where the set of available vCPUs (virtual CPUs) is defined as C_{vcpu} and C_{vm} as the set of VM instances (i.e., $|C_{vm}| \leq |C_{vcpu}|$). The i-th VM instance is defined as v_i, and the j-th vCPU in the i-th VM instance is defined as $c_{i,j} \in C_{vcpu}$. We suppose that an edge cloud server has the fixed number of VM instances, i.e., $|C_{vm}|$ is the fixed value and no more VM instances cannot be launched.

Since each VM instance can have one or more vCPUs, let the number of vCPUs in v_i be defined as $N_{vcpu}^i \geq 1$. Let the processing speed for each vCPU be the same as α_{vm}. The set of mobile clients is defined as M, and each mobile clients as $m_i \in M$. The processing speed at i-th mobile client is defined as α_i.

Table 1. Notations for objective function.

Parameter	Explanation	Definition
C_{vm}	Set of VMs	
C_{vcpu}	Set of vCPUs	
$c_{i,j}$	j-th vCPU in i-th VM	
M	Set of mobile clients	
m_k	k-th mobile client	
$W_k = G_k(V_k, E_k)$	k-th workflow	
$W = G(V, E)$	The merged workflow	
t_i	i-th task in W	
$e_{i,j}$	Data comm. from t_i to t_j	
$d_{i,j}$	Data size of $e_{i,j}$	
$pred(t_i)$	Predecessor tasks of t_i	
$suc(t_i)$	Successor tasks of t_i	
$T_p(t_i, m_k)$	Proc. time of t_i on m_k	Defined at (1)
$T_c(d_{i,j}, r_k)$	Comm. time of $d_{I,j}$ on r_k	Defined at (2)
r_k	Comm. bandwidth of m_k	Defined at (3)
ω	Background noise power	
τ	Energy consumption per cycle	
$E_{exec}(t_i, m_k)$	Energy consump. to execute t_i on m_k	Defined at (4)
$E_{in}(e_{i,j}, m_k)$	Energy consump to receive $d_{i,j}$ on m_k	Defined at (5)
$E_{out}(e_{i,j}, m_k)$	Energy consump to send $d_{i,j}$ on m_k	Defined at (5)
$A(t_i)$	Assignment target of t_i	
$T_f(t_i, A(t_i))$	Finish time of t_i on $A(t_i)$	Defined at (6)
$T_{dr}(t_i)$	Data ready time of t_i	Defined at (7)
$T_s(t_j, A(t_j))$	Start time of t_i on $A(t_i)$	Defined at (8)

3.2 Assumed Job Model

As for a workflow job, it is known as an abstraction of a job, in which each task has data dependencies with others. Each task corresponds to a set of instructions, i.e., one executable file or one execution unit. In this paper, we rename a workflow job as "workflow". Each mobile client has one workflow to be executed. Let the number of workflows be M, i.e., the number of mobile clients. Each workflow is expressed as $W_k = G_k(V_k, E_k)$, and the set of workflows is defined as W. However, for simplicity of notation of workflows, each workflow job is supposed to be combined into a larger workflow as W for scheduling, where $W = G(V, E)$ and each task and edge are defined as $t_i \in V$ and $e_{i,j} \in E$, respectively. The pseudo START task t_{pstart} and the pseudo END task t_{pend} are added to generate the "merged workflow" by connecting them to every workflow, where $w_{pstart} = w_{pend} = 0$. By generating such a merged workflow, every task can be simultaneously taken into account for prioritizing of scheduling [15].

In a workflow, let $pred(t_i)$ be the set of predecessor tasks of t_i, and let $suc(t_i)$ be the set of successor tasks of t_i. If $pred(t_i) = \emptyset$, t_i is called the START task, and if $suc(t_i) = \emptyset$, t_i is called the END task.

Figure 1 describes how each workflow is merged into W and how each task is assigned. In this figure, three workflows, i.e., W_1, W_2, and W_3 are merged into W. In W, the pseudo START task and the pseudo END task are added as the new START task and the END task. Without loss of generality, both their workloads, the communication time from the pseudo START task, and the communication time to the pseudo START are set to zero. In this assumption, several tasks in W is assigned to vCPUs on the edge cloud server.

3.3   Cost Model

The workload of t_i is w_i and the resultant data size of t_i, i.e., that must be sent from t_i to t_j is defined as $d_{i,j}$. As for the pseudo START task and the pseudo END task, we assume $w_{pstart} = w_{pend} = 0$ and $d_{pstart,i} = d_{j,pend} = 0$ for $\forall t_i, t_j \in V$. The processing time of t_i on m_k is defined as

$$T_p(t_i, m_k) = \frac{w_i}{\alpha_k}, \tag{1}$$

and the communication time of $d_{i,j}$ over the wireless link between m_k and the edge cloud server is defined as

$$T_c(d_{i,j}, r_k) = \begin{cases} 0, & A(t_i), A(t_j) \in C_{vcpu} \; or \; A(t_i), A(t_j) = m_k \\ \dfrac{d_{i,j}}{r_k}, & otherwise, \end{cases} \tag{2}$$

where $A(t_i)$ is the assignment target of t_i, and $A(t_i) \in C_{vcpu}$ means that t_i is executed on a vCPU in the cloud. r_k is the data rate of wireless communication between the edge cloud server and m_k, which is defined by Shannon's theorem as follows:

$$r_k = \beta_k \log_2 \left(1 + \frac{p_k g_k}{\omega + \sum_{i \neq k, CN_i = CN_k} p_i g_i} \right), \tag{3}$$

where β_k is the communication bandwidth of m_k, p_k is the transmission power and receiving power of m_k, g_k is the channel gain between m_k and a base station, ω is the background noise power, and CN_k is the communication channel used by m_k. It is obvious that r_k becomes smaller if more mobile terminals use the same channel as m_k.

As for the energy consumption for executing t_i on m_k, it is defined as $E_{exec}(t_i, m_k)$, and for transmitting $e_{i,j}$ from the edge cloud server to m_k, or m_k to the edge cloud is defined as $E_{in}(e_{i,j}, m_k)$ or $E_{out}(e_{i,j}, m_k)$, respectively. They are defined as follows:

$$E_{exec}(t_i, m_k) = \tau_k w_i, \tag{4}$$

where τ_k is the coefficient determined for each $m_k \in M$ in terms of the energy consumption per cycle; that is, we assume $w_i \propto E_{exec}(t_i, m_k)$ for $\forall m_k \in M, \forall t_i \in V$. As for the energy consumption related to sending the data to a mobile client and the edge cloud server, we define

$$E_{in}(e_{i,j}, m_k) = p_k T_c(d_{i,j}, r_k), A(t_i) \in C_{vcpu},$$
$$E_{out}(e_{i,j}, m_k) = p_k T_c(d_{i,j}, r_k), A(t_j) \in C_{vcpu}. \tag{5}$$

3.4 Schedule Length

In this section, we present how the start time of each task t_i on $A(t_i)$, i.e., $T_s(t_i, A(t_i))$ is determined when scheduling tasks and how the schedule length is derived. At first, we define several notations for deriving both $T_s(t_i, A(t_i))$ and the schedule length. Suppose the finish time of t_i is defined as $T_f(t_i, A(t_i))$, then we have

$$T_f(t_i, A(t_i)) = T_s(t_i, A(t_i)) + T_p(t_i, A(t_i)), \tag{6}$$

where $A(t_i) \in M \cup C_{vcpu}$. The set of free tasks is defined as $fList$; that is, the set of tasks whose predecessor tasks have been scheduled. For each task in $fList$, the data ready time can be derived. Data ready time (DRT) is the maximum data arrival time from all predecessor tasks. Note that DRT is the earliest start time for each task and the actual start time can be later than DRT. This is because t_j cannot start execution when a task $t_h \notin pred(t_j)$ such that $A(t_h) = A(t_j)$ is scheduled before t_j. DRT of t_j at m_k is derived as follows:

$$T_{dr}(t_j) = \max_{t_i \in pred(t_j)} \{T_f(t_i, A(t_i)) + T_c(d_{i,j}, r_k)\}, \tag{7}$$

where $T_c(d_{i,j}, r_k) = 0$ if $A(t_j) \in C_{vcpu}$ and $A(t_i) \in C_{vcpu}$, or both t_i and t_j are assigned to m_k by the definition given by (2). Then we can derive the start time, i.e., $T_s(t_j, A(t_j))$ with DRT as follows:

$$T_s(t_j, A(t_j)) = \max \left\{ \max_{\substack{t_i \notin pred(t_j), \\ A(t_i)=A(t_j)}} \{T_f(t_i, A(t_i))\}, T_{dr}(t_j) \right\}. \tag{8}$$

The schedule length is the finish time of the END task and is defined as follows:

$$T_f(t_{end}, A(t_{end})) = T_s(t_{end}, A(T_{end})) + T_p(t_{end}, A(t_{end})), \tag{9}$$

3.5   Objective Function

The original energy consumption of W_i at m_l is $\sum_{t_k \in V_i} E_{exec}(t_k, m_l)$. With aforementioned definitions, the objective function is defined as follows:

Objective Function 1. *Minimize* $T_f(t_{end}, A(t_{end}))$
subject to :

$$\sum_{A(t_i)=m_k} E_{exec}(t_i, m_k) + \sum_{\substack{A(t_i) \in C_{vcpu}, \\ A(t_j)=m_k}} E_{in}(e_{i,j}, m_k) + \sum_{\substack{A(t_i)=m_k, \\ A(t_j) \in C_{vcpu}}} E_{out}(e_{i,j}, m_k)$$

$$\leq \sum_{t_j \in V_i} E_{exec}(t_j, m_k) \, for \, \forall m_k \in M, \, and$$

$$T_f(t_{end}^i) \leq \sum_{t_j^i \in V_i} T_p(t_j^i, m_k) \, for \, \forall m_k \in M. \tag{10}$$

4   PCTSO Algorithm

4.1   Overall Procedures

As defined in Sect. 3.2, each workflow job is supposed to be merged into a larger one, i.e., $W = G(V, E)$. From (10), each mobile client's energy consumption for the task scheduling algorithm must be lower or equal to the original execution.

Initially, each mobile client m_k has its own workflow $W_k = G_k(V_k, E_k)$. The initial schedule length $SL_{init}(W_k)$ and the initial energy consumption $E_{init}(m_k)$ are defined as follows:

$$SL_{init}(W_k) = \sum_{t_i \in V_k} \frac{w_i}{\alpha_k}, E_{init}(m_k) = \sum_{t_i \in V_k} E_{exec}(t_i, m_k) = \tau_k \sum_{t_i \in V_k} w_i. \tag{11}$$

From the objective function in Sect. 3.5, the PCTSO algorithm tries to achieve $T_f(t_{end}, A(t_{end})) \leq SL_{init}(W_k)$ and $E_{init}(m_k)$ must be made smaller for each $m_k \in M$.

Algorithm 1 presents the entire procedure of the PCTSO algorithm. From lines 2 to 14, PCTSO iterates procedures to output the schedule during $UEX \neq \emptyset$. At line 3, t_{pivot}, having the maximum *level* value in $fList$ is selected, where $fList$ is the free task list. A task is called "free" if and only if all its predecessor tasks have been scheduled. Then, at line 4, the set of continuous tasks S_{free}, starting from t_{pivot}, is generated by calling $CTSO$ as Algorithm 2. Then, for each task in S_{free}, it is assigned to the idle time slot of a vCPU to start execution as early as possible. Then PCTSO updates both UEX and $fList$ by tracing $suc(t)$, where $t \in S_{free}$ (lines 9–10 or 12 to 14). When all tasks have been traced, i.e., $UEX = \emptyset$, PCTSO finishes.

In the following sections, we present (i) the criterion for selecting a pivot task from $fList$ and (ii) the criterion on how the set of tasks is selected for offloading to the edge cloud server or the mobile client.

Algorithm 1. PCTSO Algorithm

Input: Set of vCPUs C_{vcpu}, Set of mobile clients M, and the merged workflow W.
Output: The mapping from $t_i \in V$ to $C_{vcpu} \cup M$ and the schedule.
   /* UEX is the set of unscheduled tasks and $fList$ is the set of free tasks. The
START tasks at line 1 are not pseudo tasks.   */
1   $UEX \leftarrow V$, $fList \leftarrow$ START tasks
2   **while** $UEX \neq \emptyset$ **do**
3      $t_{pivot} \leftarrow$ the task satisfying (14) from $fList$
     /* Call Algorithm 2.   */
4      $S_{free} \leftarrow CTSO(t_{pivot})$
5   **if** $S_{free} \neq \emptyset$ **then**
6   **while** $S_{free} \neq \emptyset$ **do**
7            $t \leftarrow$ head of S_{free} and remove t from S_{free}
8   Assign t to the idle time slot of a vCPU via the insertion-based technique.
9   Remove t from UEX and $fList$
10   Update $fList$ by tracing $suc(t)$

11   **else**
       /* If no task is assigned to a vCPU, update the state with scheduling t_{pivot}
on m_k.   */
12   Assign t_{pivot} to the idle time slot of m_k
13   remove t_{pivot} from UEX
14   Update $fList$ by tracing $suc(t_{pivot})$

15 **return** V

4.2 Pivot Task Selection Policy

We provide details regarding the task selection policy from the free task list
($fList$). The remaining time duration from t_i to the END task on m_k is
defined as

$$rlevel(t_i) = \max_{t_j \in suc(t_i)} \{T_c(d_{i,j}, r_k) + T_p(t_j, A(t_j)) + rlevel(t_j)\}. \qquad (12)$$

As the start time of t_i can be derived by (8) by assuming that t_i is executed on
m_k. Then, the priority for the task selection i.e., $level(t_i)$ is defined as

$$level(t_i) = T_s(t_i, A(t_i)) + T_p(t_i, m_k) + rlevel(t_i), \qquad (13)$$

where $T_s(t_i, A(t_i))$ is the start time when t_i is executed on m_k. $level(t_i)$ is the
dominant path for the schedule length if every task that can be executed after
t_i is allocated to respective cloud, provided that r_k dominates the bandwidth.
PCTSO algorithm tries to minimize the schedule length by minimizing the start
time of a task in the dominant path. For each task $\in fList$, the task satisfying
the following condition is selected for scheduling.

$$\max_{t_i \in fList} \{level(t_i)\}. \qquad (14)$$

4.3 Continuous Task Selection for Offloading

There is no guarantee that both the schedule length and the energy consumption
at the mobile client m_k are made smaller by assigning a task to a vCPU. Thus,

Algorithm 2. CTSO Algorithm

Input: t_i having the maximum *level* value in $fList$.
Output: S_{free}: the set of continuously selected tasks.

```
1  S_free ← {t_i}
   /* t_min is the best task for ΔSL(S_free).                                      */
2  t_pred ← t_i, t_min ← ∅
3  ΔSL_pre ← ΔSL(S_free)
   /* Fetch successor tasks of t_pred as S that become free after t_fred has been
   scheduled.                                                                      */
4  while S ← chkFreeCandidate(t_pred) ≠ ∅ do
5  |   t_min ← NULL
6  |   while t ∈ S do
7  |   |   S_free ← S_free ∪ {t}
   |   |   /* ΔSL(S_free) is defined at (18).                                       */
8  |   |   if ΔSL(S_free) ≤ ΔSL_pre ∧ ΔSL(S_free) ≤ 0 then
9  |   |   |   if (19) is satisfied with A(t) ∈ C_vcpu, ∀t ∈ S_free then
10 |   |   |   |   ΔSL_pre ← ΔSL(S_free)
11 |   |   |   |   t_min ← t
12 |   |   |   else
13 |   |   |   |   S_free ← S_free − {t}
14 |   |   else
15 |   |   |   S_free ← S_free − {t}
16 |   t_pred ← t_min
   /* If no task is added to S_free, the case of S_free = {t_i} must be checked.    */
17 if S_free = {t_i} then
18 |   if ΔSL(S_free) > 0 ∨ (19) is not satisfied then
19 |   |   S_free ← ∅
20 return S_free
21 Function chkFreeCandidate(t_can):
22 |   S_out ← ∅, FindFlg ← true
23 |   while t_suc ∈ suc(t_can) do
24 |   |   while t ∈ pred(t_suc) do
   |   |   |   /* If the predecessor task is t_can, ignore the check and go to the next
   |   |   |   loop.                                                                */
25 |   |   |   if t = t_can then
26 |   |   |   |   continue
27 |   |   |   else
   |   |   |   |   /* If at least one predecessor task ∈ UEX, break the loop as
   |   |   |   |   "false".                                                         */
28 |   |   |   |   if t ∈ UEX then
29 |   |   |   |   |   FindFlg ← false
30 |   |   |   |   |   break
31 |   |   if FingFlg = true then
32 |   |   |   S_out ← S_out ∪ {t_suc}
33 |   |   FindFlg ← true
34 |   return S_out
```

---

assigning a task to a vCPU is accepted if both the schedule length and the energy consumption are made smaller by inserting an idle time slot of the vCPU. Here, we model how the schedule length is reduced as follows. First, suppose that the selected task is $t_i \in fList$ and t_i is supposed to be offloaded to a vCPU $c_{p,q}$ from m_k. Then, we have the time difference generated by offloading t_i as follows:

$$\Delta T_p(t_i) = T_p(t_i, c_{p,q}) - T_p(t_i, m_k), \tag{15}$$

$$\Delta T_s(t_i) = T_s(t_i, c_{p,q}) - T_s(t_i, m_k), \tag{16}$$

and $T_c(d_{i,j}, r_k)$ is newly generated, where $t_j \in suc(t_i)$ and t_j is placed at m_k. Thus, one condition to reduce the schedule length by offloading t_i is

$$\Delta SL(t_i) = T_c(d_{i,j}, r_k) + \Delta T_p(t_i) + \Delta T_s(t_i, A(t_i)) \le 0, \tag{17}$$

where $\Delta SL(t_i)$ is the increment of the schedule length in case that no data waiting time is generated for all tasks that are scheduled after t_i. Even if $\Delta SL(t_i) > 0$ by offloading t_i, there is one possibility for $\Delta SL(t_i \cup t_j) \le 0$ by offloading t_i and t_j, where $t_j \in suc(t_i)$ when $T_c(d_{i,j}, r_k)$ is much larger than $T_p(t_j, A(t_j))$ because $T_c(d_{i,j}, r_k)$ is localized among VMs in a cloud. Thus, offloading several tasks, having dependencies on each other, can lead to the reduction of both schedule length and energy consumption at a mobile client. Here, suppose that t_i is selected from $fList$ as a candidate for offloading and we assume that $t_{i+1} \in suc(t_i), t_{i+2} \in suc(t_{i+1}), \ldots, t_{i+r} \in suc(t_{i+r-1})$. At $t_{i+j} \in suc(t_{i+j-1})$, suppose that tasks in $pred(t_{i+j})$ have already scheduled, except for t_{i+j-1}. We define such tasks as being put into S_{free}; that is, tasks satisfying the following condition are put into S_{free}.

$$\Delta SL(S_{free}) = T_c(d_{i+r,s}, r_k) + \sum_{t_i \in S_{free}} \Delta T_p(t_i) + \Delta T_s(t_i) \le 0, \tag{18}$$

where t_s is supposed to be placed on m_k. Figure 2 shows an example of how S_{free} is generated, provided that t_i is selected from $fList$. This figure assumes that $\Delta SL(S_{free}) > 0$ for $S_{free} = \{t_i\}$ such as (b), while $\Delta SL(S_{free}) < 0$ if more tasks are added to S_{free} such as (c) and (d). From Fig. 2(b), (c), and (d), we observe that the main factor for $\Delta SL(S_{free}) > 0$ is the communication time between a vCPU in C_{vcpu} and the mobile client m_k, which occurs at the output data communication of the last task in S_{free}. If such a communication time is small with compared to the sum of the task execution times of S_{free}, i.e., $\Delta T_p(S_{free})$, we can have $\Delta SL(S_{free}) < 0$. Thus, even if we have $\Delta SL(t_i) > 0$,

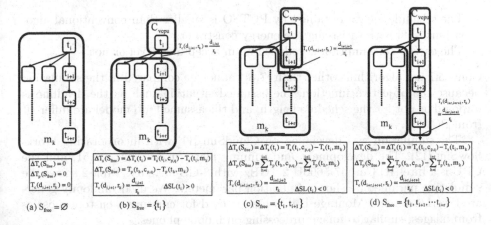

Fig. 2. Example of continuous task selection for offloading

$\Delta SL(S_{free}) < 0$ is possible depending on the relationship between the newly generated communication time and the sum of the processing times in S_{free}.

As for the energy constraint, for all tasks $\in V_k$, the following condition must be satisfied to schedule the selected task.

$$\sum_{A(t_i)=m_p} E_{exec}(t_i, m_p) + \sum_{\substack{A(t_i) \in C_{vcpu}, \\ A(t_j)=m_p}} E_{in}(e_{i,j}, m_p) + \sum_{\substack{A(t_i)=m_p, \\ A(t_j) \in C_{vcpu}}} E_{out}(e_{i,j}, m_p)$$

$$< \sum_{t_j \in V_i} E_{exec}(t_j, m_p). \tag{19}$$

If both (18) and (19) are satisfied, each task in S_{free} is selected for scheduling and is inserted into an idle time slot of a vCPU s.t, $T_f(t_k, c_p)$ is minimized, where $t_k \in S_{free}$.

The detailed algorithm to derive S_{free} is shown in Algorithm 2, called continuous task selection for offloading (CTSO). During lines 4 to 16, CTSO tries to construct S_{free} by tracing successor tasks of t_{pred} in S_{free}. At line 8, if $\Delta SL(S_{free})$ takes the minimum value and $SL(S_{free}) \leq 0$, S_{free} is updated by adding the task t as t_{min}. Otherwise, S_{free} is not varied as line 13 and 15. As procedures in lines 4 to 16 assume that S_{free} has two or more entries, at line 17, CTSO checks the case of $S_{free} = \{t_i\}$. Then, CTSO returns S_{free}. The condition for offloading t_i is accepted is $\Delta SL \leq 0$; that is, during that each task is added to S_{free}, the algorithm finds S_{free} such that $\Delta SL(S_{free})$ is minimized and $\Delta SL(S_{free}) \leq 0$. As $\Delta T_s(t_i, A(t_i))$ is not varied during each task is added to S_{free}, we have only to see the behaviors of $T_c(d_{i+r,s}, r_k)$ and $\sum_{t_i \in S_{free}} \Delta T_p(t_i)$.

5   Experimental Results

5.1   Objective and Method

We conducted preliminary experimental comparisons by a simulation and confirmed advantages of PCTSO algorithm in terms of:

- The schedule length obtained by PCTSO is smaller than conventional algorithms [7,8] with satisfying the energy constraint.
- The energy consumption is reduced in an acceptable level or not.

Conventional algorithms other than [7,8] cannot be compared in the simulation because the objective function, the assumed situation such as the deadline is imposed or not for the schedule length, and the assumed job model are different from PCTSO.

The simulation was developed on CloudSim [11] with incorporating WorkflowSim [12]. The development and running platform are jdk1.7.0.51, and the CPU is a Intel(R) Core i7-5600U 2.6 GHz with 8-GB memory. Table 2 shows the simulation parameters. shows simulation parameters. We used randomly generated workflows and Montage [14], which is used for creating a custom mosaics from images, similar to image processing on mobile phones.

Table 2. Setup parameters for the simulation

Target	Variables	Values
Single job	$|V_i|$ for Random Workflow	$\{30, 50, 100, 1000\}$
	$|V_i|$ for Montage Workflow	$\{25, 50, 100, 1000\}$
	CCR	$\{0.1, 1.0, 5.0, 7.0, 10.0\}$
Multiple jobs	CCR	$\{0.1, 1.0, 3.0\}$ or $\{5.0, 7.0, 10.0\}$
	$|V_i|$ for Random Workflow	$\{30, 50, 100\}$ in normal distribution
	$|V_i|$ for Montage Workflow	$\{25, 50, 100\}$ in normal distribution
	$\sharp$ of workflows $= |M|$	$\{5, 10, 20, 30\}$
System	α_k of M	$\{1\,\text{GHz}, 1.5\,\text{GHz}, 2.0\,\text{GHz}\}$
	$\alpha_{i,j}$ of C_{vcpu}	$3.0\,\text{GHz}$
	$\sharp$ of vCPUs per VM	2
	$\sharp$ of VMs: $|C_{vm}|$	50
	β_k: bandwidth	$\{10\,\text{Mbps}, 20\,\text{Mbps}, 30\,\text{Mbps}, 40\,\text{Mbps}, 50\,\text{Mbps}\}$
	ω: background noise	$-100\,\text{dBm}$ [13]
	p_k: trans. and recv. power	$100\,\text{mW}$
	g_k: gain from the base station	Randomly chosen from $0.1 \leq g_k \leq 1.0$

In other comparison targets described in Sects. 5.2 and 5.3, we compared the schedule length of PCTSO with the algorithm having one-by-one task checking basis; that is, if the schedule length or the energy consumption is made larger if one task is offloaded, the task is assigned to the mobile client, not taking its successor tasks into account. We name this case as "Non-PCTSO". Also we compared PCTSO with algorithms [7,8], named as "Cloudlet" [7] and "LB" [8] in this paper, respectively. The objective of "Cloudlet" is to minimize both the schedule length and the energy consumption, while that of "LB" is the balance the assigned workload among the cloud and a mobile user.

As a comparison metric, we use schedule length ratio (SLR)[9].

$$SLR = \frac{SL}{\sum_{t_k \in CP_w} T_p(t_k, c_{i,j})}, \tag{20}$$

where CP_w is the critical path of W in terms of the total execution time on a path; that is, only the workload of each task on a path is considered and the data size for each edge on the path is not. SL in (20) is the schedule length of W. As we assume every vCPU to have the same frequency, $c_{i,j}$ in (20) takes the same value among vCPUs.

5.2   Comparison by Single Workflow

We conducted comparisons for single random workflow and Montage workflow. Both the schedule length and the energy consumption are averaged by 100 tries with varying CCR [10], the number of tasks. Figure 3 shows the comparison results in terms of the SLR for those workflows. For Fig. 3(a) and (b), we observe that the schedule length by PCTSO has the smallest in the all CCR cases. In particular, the difference of SLR between that of PCTSO and that of Non-PCTSO gets larger in cases of CCR = 7.0 and 10.0. This is because that only tasks having small outgoing data are offloaded in Non-PCTSO and a few number of tasks are offloaded. In PCTSO, more tasks are executed in the edge cloud and energy consumption is reduced with compared to other algorithms. Table 3 shows the comparison results of the energy consumption by single workflow, i.e., random workflow and Montage workflow. Values in the table is the reduction ratio to the original execution, i.e., all tasks are executed at the mobile client. PCTSO only guarantees that the energy consumption with PCTSO is lower than that of original execution, and it does not try to minimize it. However, since the number of offloaded tasks in PCTSO is larger than that of Non-CTSO, the energy consumption by PCTSO is better than Non-CTSO, Cloudlet and LB in all CCR cases. From these results we can conclude that continuously assigning dependent tasks can lead to the effective energy reduction.

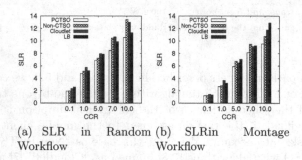

(a) SLR in Random Workflow   (b) SLRin Montage Workflow

Fig. 3. Comparison of SLR by single workflow.

Table 3. Comparison of energy saving in single workflow.

CCR	Random workflow				Montage workflow			
	PCTSO	Non-CTSO	Cloudlet	LB	PCTSO	Non-CTSO	Cloudlet	LB
0.1	16.31%	13.47%	14.23%	13.51%	21.52%	14.39%	17.91%	18.01%
1	15.73%	11.87%	13.77%	12.84%	18.58%	13.83%	15.91%	15.8%
5	12.95%	9.38%	10.23%	11.85%	16.73%	9.11%	11.96%	12.19%
7	10.79%	5.12%	6.03%	7.59%	14.15%	8.21%	9.09%	10.35%
10	9.31%	4.68%	4.46%	6.3%	11.77%	6.67%	7.11%	7.33%

5.3 Comparison by Multiple Workflows

The schedule length in the multiple workflow case is the maximum makespan among multiple workflows, and we averaged the schedule length in 100 tries for each case of multiple workflows, i.e., 5, 10, 20, 30, 50 workflows. Figure 4 shows the results of SLR in multiple workflows. From Fig. 4(a) (b), it can be seen that PCTSO outperforms other algorithms in terms of SLR in every case, which is similar to the single workflow case.

As for the energy consumption, we derived the reduction ratio in mobile clients, and Table 4 shows the averaged reduction ratio for each number of workflows. In every case, the energy consumption by PCTSO is the highest, while the energy consumption ratio by Non-CTSO is lower than that of Cloudlet and LB. From this results, continuous task selection in multiple workflows can lead to the reduction of both the schedule length and the energy consumption.

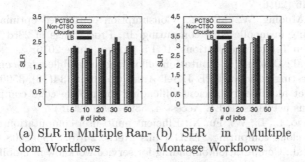

(a) SLR in Multiple Random Workflows   (b) SLR in Multiple Montage Workflows

Fig. 4. Comparison of SLR by multiple workflow.

Table 4. Comparison of energy saving in multiple workflows.

♯ of jobs	Random workflow				Montage workflow			
	PCTSO	Non-CTSO	Cloudlet	LB	PCTSO	Non-CTSO	Cloudlet	LB
5	15.94%	10.58%	11.13%	11.05%	18.18%	10.36%	10.36%	11.04%
10	16.53%	8.99%	11.91%	12.7%	16.48%	8.84%	13.37%	14.02%
20	17.68%	9.78%	11.84%	11.3%	16.71%	9.44%	13.5%	15.84%
30	13.37%	10.7%	10.73%	13.35%	15.27%	11.01%	12.98%	12.22%
50	13.97%	5.06%	9.6%	10.78%	13.97%	6.3%	10.43%	12.45%

6   Conclusion

In this paper, we proposed a task scheduling algorithm with offloading tasks to an edge cloud, called PCTSO. PCTSO is based on offloading tasks and priority based scheduling algorithm. PCTSO tries to continuously select dependent tasks for offloading in order to minimize the schedule length under the energy constraint. From experimental results, we conclude that PCTSO can be applied to the case that multiple workflows must be finished as early as possible, with reducing the energy consumption for each mobile client.

As a future work, we take the mobility of each client into account, and we will implement PCTSO as a realistic software.

Acknowledgment. The research leading to these results has been supported by the EU-JAPAN initiative by the EC Horizon 2020 Work Programme (2018–2020) Grant Agreement No. 814918 and Ministry of Internal Affairs and Communications, "Federating IoT and cloud infrastructures to provide scalable and interoperable Smart Cities applications, by introducing novel IoT virtualization technologies (Fed4IoT)".

References

1. Shi, W., et al.: Edge computing: vision and challenges. IEEE Internet Things J. **3**(5), 637–646 (2016)
2. Tianze, L., Muqing, W., Min, Z.: Consumption considered optimal scheme for task offloading in mobile edge computing. In: Proceedings of 23rd International Conference on Telecommunications (ICT), 6 pages, June 2016
3. Mao, Y., et al.: Dynamic computation offloading for mobile-edge computing with energy harvesting devices. IEEE J. Sel. Areas Commun. **34**(12), 3590–3605 (2016)
4. Zhang, K., et al.: Energy-efficient offloading for mobile edge computing in 5G heterogeneous networks. IEEE Access **4**, 5896–5907 (2016)
5. Chen, X., Jiao, L., Li, W., Fu, X.: Efficient multi-user computation offloading for mobile-edge cloud computing. IEEE Trans. Netw. **24**(5), 2795–2808 (2016)
6. Deng, S., et al.: Computation offloading for service workflow in mobile cloud computing. IEEE Trans. Parallel Distrib. Syst. **26**(12), 3317–3329 (2015)
7. Gao, B., et al.: From mobiles to clouds: developing energy-aware offloading strategies for workflows. In: Proceedings of ACM/IEEE International Conference Grid Computing (CCGrid), pp. 139–146 (2012)
8. Jia, M., et al.: Heuristic offloading of concurrent tasks for computation-intensive applications in mobile cloud computing. In: Proceedings of IEEE INFOCOM Workshop on Mobile Cloud Computing, pp. 352–357 (2014)
9. Topcuoglu, H., Hariri, S., Wu, M.Y.: Performance-effective and low-complexity task scheduling for heterogeneous computing. IEEE Trans. Parallel Distrib. Syst. **13**(3), 260–274 (2002)
10. Sinnen, O.: Task Scheduling for Parallel Systems. Wiley, Chichester (2007)
11. Calheiros, R.N., Ranjan, R., Beloglazov, A., De Rose, C.A.F., Buyya, R.: CloudSim: a toolkit for modeling and simulation of cloud computing environments and evaluation of resource provisioning algorithms. Softw. Pract. Exp. **41**(1), 23–50 (2011)
12. Chen, W., Deelman, E.: WorkflowSim: a toolkit for simulating scientific workflows in distributed environments. In: Proceedings of IEEE International Conference on E-Science, pp. 1–8, October 2012
13. Rappaport, T.S.: Wireless Communications: Principles and Practice. Prentice-Hall, Upper Saddle River (1996)
14. Bharathi, S., et al.: Characterization of scientific workflows. In: Proceedings of Third Workshop on Workflows in Support of Large-Scale Science, pp. 1–10 (2008)
15. Zhao, H., Sakellariou, R.: Scheduling multiple DAGs onto heterogeneous systems. In: Proceedings of International International Parallel and Distributed Processing Symposium (IPDPS 2006) (2006)

Min-Edge P-cycles: An Efficient Approach for Computing P-cycles in Optical Data Center Networks

Amir Mirzaeinia[1]([⊠]), Abdelmounaam Rezgui[2], Zaki Malik[3], and Mehdi Mirzaeinia[4]

[1] Department of Computer Science and Engineering,
New Mexico Institute of Mining and Technology, Socorro, USA
amirzaei@cs.nmt.edu
[2] School of Information Technology, Illinois State University, Normal, USA
arezgui@ilstu.edu
[3] Department of Business Analytics, Texas A&M University-Commerce,
Commerce, USA
zaki.malik@tamuc.edu
[4] Department of Electrical Engineering, AmirKabir University of Technology,
Tehran, Iran
m.mirzaeinia@aut.ac.ir

Abstract. Effective network protection requires that extra resources be used in failure events. Pre-configured protection cycles (P-cycles) are proposed to protect mesh-based networks using few extra resources. A number of heuristic methods have been developed to overcome the complexity of finding optimum P-cycles in dense optical networks. The processing time of existing approaches depends on the number of working wavelengths. As the number of working wavelengths is increasing in modern networks, the processing time of current P-cycle computing approaches will continue to increase. In this paper, we propose an approach, called Min-Edge P-cycle (MEP), that addresses this problem. The core of the proposed approach is an iterative algorithm that uses the minimum-weight edge in each iteration. Our approach provides the same redundancy requirements as the previously known unity cycle method but it does not depend on the number of working wavelengths. The new approach can significantly reduce the processing time of computing P-cycles in large scale optical, server-centric data center networks, e.g., BCube, FiConn, and DCell networks.

1 Introduction

Over the last decade, data center (DC) networks have been growing both in terms of number and size. These DC networks are used for various applications such as web search engines, social networks, gaming, and distributed data processing systems such as MapReduce. Many companies, e.g., Google, Amazon, Facebook,

© Springer Nature Switzerland AG 2019
D. Da Silva et al. (Eds.): CLOUD 2019, LNCS 11513, pp. 53–66, 2019.
https://doi.org/10.1007/978-3-030-23502-4_5

and Microsoft, have various kinds of DC networks to serve their own needs or external tenants (cloud users).

Modern data centers may have thousands of servers connected together through different data communication networks. Addressing failures in DC networks has been the focus of significant research. A Ponemon Institute report shows that there are seven different main reasons for data center outages [16]. These reasons are UPS system failure, cybercrime (distributed denial of service), accidental human error, water/heat failure, weather related, generator failure, and IT equipment failure. According to this report (Fig. 1), the average cost of an outage increased by seven percent from $690,240 in 2013 to $740,357 in 2016 with single incident losses reaching a high of $2.4 million [16].

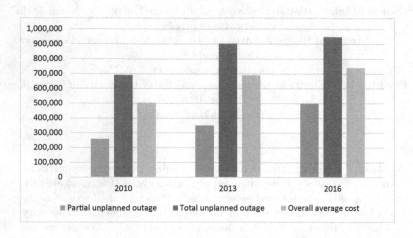

Fig. 1. Cost (in $) for partial and total shutdown [16].

In parallel with this trend in terms of failure costs, optical technologies are increasingly used to interconnect computing and storage resources within and between DCs [19]. This has triggered interest in new approaches to address failures in these optical data center networks [17]. In general, failure recovery is more time efficient when done at the lowest layer such as optics than at higher layers such as the data link or IP layers. The high capacity and greatly reduced switching time are key characteristics of the fiber that make it a good selection for physical transmission in DC networks. However, finding backup paths at failure time is a time consuming process. Therefore, the first solution to minimize the restoration time is pre-configured backup bandwidth. Pre-configured backup bandwidth is a costly process. Redundant bandwidth sharing was developed as an approach to reduce this cost. If the backup redundant bandwidth is not properly designed, then certain network topologies, such as mesh networks, need more redundant bandwidth.

To have a network capable of managing any service outage, different points need to be considered. These points are traffic or service restoration time and link bandwidth or other network equipment provision. In a typical point-to-point communication, an extra link could be deployed to make it fault tolerant against link failure. However, this method is not efficient because the backup link is not shared among the working links, i.e., an additional one hundred percent extra resources are required. This is called one-for-one protection technique. Another method is sharing the backup path among several working paths. This is more efficient in terms of required extra resources. Ring-based networks and Pre-configuration protection cycle (P-cycle) are proposed to achieve fast switching time and low extra resources requirement. P-cycle will be explained in more detail in Sect. 3.

To the best of our knowledge, there is no study that shows how P-cycle configuration algorithms depend on the number of wavelengths serving in the network. Further, there is no research on deploying P-cycle-based server-centric DC networks. The main reason for wavelength dependency analysis is the increasing number of active wavelengths inside the fibers. In this paper, we propose a heuristic P-cycle approach that does not depend on the number of wavelengths. This paper is organized as follows. In Sect. 2.1, we discuss different data center networks and their characteristics. In Sect. 2.2, we focus on reliability analysis of large systems such as DC networks. This analysis will show that service failure is very much frequent in a large system. P-cycle network protection and its advantages and disadvantages are explained in Sect. 3. In Sect. 4, we describe the proposed algorithm and show how it can overcome the linear dependency problem common in existing solutions. In Sect. 5, we present our experimental study. Finally, Sect. 6 concludes the paper.

2   Related Work

2.1   Data Center Networks

A data center is a computing environment with large amounts of inter-connected resources such as computational and storage resources. A typical DC may have hundreds of thousands of servers. Data center resources interconnect using various data communication network topologies. These topologies are classified into two major categories: (i) switch-centric data centers and (ii) server-centric data centers. In switch-centric DCs, only server-switch and switch-switch connections exist (i.e., no server-server connections). Examples of switch-centric DCs include Fat-Tree and Flattened Butterfly. In server-centric DCs, most connections are server-switch and server-server connections. Examples of server-centric DCs include BCube, FiConn, and DCell [14]. In server-centric DCs, servers have more than one network interface card (NIC). Therefore, they can reroute incoming traffic back to the network. This is not possible in switch-centric DCs. The very basic DC topology is a hierarchical model such as the tree topology. In the tree topology, the end host servers connect to the leaves and the root would be the network connection switch. To make the DCs fault tolerant, multi-root and multi-path topologies like the Fat-Tree topology (Fig. 2) [1,7] emerged. In Fat-Tree, the servers just connect to the edge switches and the network uses the multi-root to route the intra- and inter-DC network traffic.

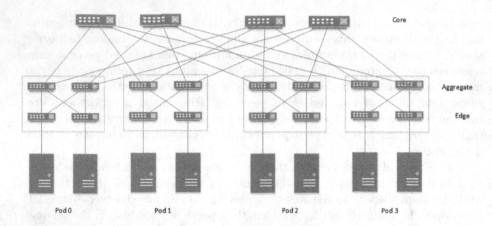

Fig. 2. Fat-tree network topology [1].

Switch-centric DCs may be two tier and three tier. Two tier DCs have leaf/spine [2] networks while three tier DCs consist of edge/aggregate/core switches. In the above mentioned two switch-centric DCs, a group of physical servers mount in a rack and connect to one edge switch named Top of Rack switch (ToR) and there are no server rerouting capabilities. These types of network architectures are typically expensive to deploy because these topologies scale up by inserting more levels of switches and higher levels need more powerful and more expensive switches.

In server-centric DCs, the servers are able to reroute the incoming traffic like edge switches and they utilize more than one NIC to connect to more than one switch or other servers. Hence, these architectures have mesh topologies and are suitable for the P-cycle network protection strategy. DCell [10] is one of the most used server-centric architectures. These architectures use a basic cell which includes switches and multi-port servers and recursively extend the number of servers in the network (Fig. 3).

DCell networks can use one or more servers to connect the cells. This recursive architecture deploys cheaper switches. This makes it low cost and highly scalable. The DCell architecture is highly scalable since a three level DCell with only eight servers in $DCell_0$ can accommodate $(8*9)*(72+1) = 5256$ servers. At the fourth level, the DCell topology can accommodate more than twenty seven million servers.

The most basic element in the DCell architecture is $DCell_0$ in which there are n servers which is usually less than eight, and one n-port switch. Then, the next construction recursion is $DCell_1$ which is created using $n+1$ $DCell_0$. Continuing this recursive process leads to exponential growth of the number of servers. For example if $n = 7$ for $DCell_0$, there will be $7*8 = 56$ servers in $DCell_1$ and $56 * 57 = 3192$ servers in $DCell_2$. Generally, if we consider each $DCell_k$ as a virtual node in $DCell_{k+1}$ then $DCell_{k+1}$ can be modeled as a complete graph. Hierarchical rerouting processes are performed to cope with any fault in this network. In this hierarchical process, DCell tries to reroute the traffic of the failed route in the same level DCell, if there is not a route able to handle the affected traffic, then DCell will try the next level recursively. One problem with this is the time to find the new path to reroute the traffic. The idea of using P-cycle can be performed to pre-configure the protection cycle to minimize the restoration time and extra bandwidth required. Figure 3 shows a $DCell_{0,1,2}$ using 2 servers in each basic cell.

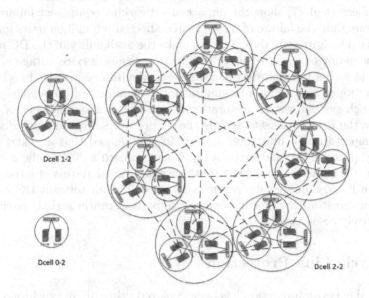

Fig. 3. $DCell_{0,1,2}$ network using $n=2$.

2.2 Reliability in Data Centers

Data center networks may have tens to hundreds of thousands of servers. As a result, they have a higher failure probability than systems with a few computing nodes. In reliability analysis, failure rate calculation is the most common technique to assess the availability of a system. Most manufacturers of servers and network devices provide the availability and reliability characteristics of their products. For example, Dell provides different availability and possible downtime per year for their products in [6]. Some basic parameters that help calculate the availability and possible outage time of a large system are Mean Time to Failure (MTTF), Mean Time to Repair/Restore (MTTR), and number of devices.

For data centers, availability is defined as the ratio between the expected uptime value of the system and the sum of the expected value of the up and down times as shown in Eq. 1.

$$A = \frac{E[uptime]}{E[uptime] + E[downtime]} \tag{1}$$

For example, if we use servers that have a MTTF of twenty years, then MTTF in hours is $20 * 365 * 24 = 175200$. If the MTTR is 1 h, then this means that the unavailability of one server is equal to $\frac{1}{175200+1} = 5.7 * 10^{-6}$ h per year. Assuming that there are one thousand servers in a DC, then the possible outage of the whole system would be $5.7 * 10^{-6} * 1000 * 3600 = 20.54$ s per year. If we add the possible outage value of the cabling, switches, air conditioning, power and other parts, we will have an even longer possible outage time.

Greenberg et al. [7] show the impact of networking equipment failure. They demonstrate that the failure of a core switch affected ten million users for about four hours. The impact of these failures make the availability of the DC network one of the major concerns of network operators. Since service outage is always probable in such a large hardware and software environment, it is always crucial to have a proper backup plan to guarantee the reliability of the whole system.

Although system service restoration is considered a key element of system reliability, the *time* it takes to restore the service in high speed networks is also equally important. To illustrate, a study in [15] showed that an extra 500 ms of latency (introduced inadvertently) in Google caused a 20% traffic reduction. Moreover, the same study showed that every additional 100 ms of latency costs Amazon a 1% loss in business revenue. As a result, fault tolerant DC networks and reducing restoration time are two very important concerns that are currently being actively researched.

3   P-cycle Link Protection

Ring-based network protection has been deployed primarily in synchronous optical networks (SONET) to transfer circuit-switched real time traffic such as voice. Two possible ring-based solutions are Unidirectional Path Switched Ring (UPSR) and Bidirectional Line Switched Ring (BLSR) [5]. Traffic multiplexers (MUX) and de-multiplexer (DEMUX) are used in these topologies to add/drop traffic to/from the ring. UPSR is a unidirectional network with two rings: one ring used as the working ring and the other as the protection ring (Fig. 4). In the case of BLSR, communication is bidirectional, which means that there are two rings for the working lines and also two rings for the protection lines (Fig. 5). This means BLSR uses four rings [5]. These topologies carry large amounts of traffic through a ring-based fiber network topology. Switching time in these topologies is very short because switching occurs in the optical layer. However, the problem with BLSR and UPSR is that backup bandwidth is not shared with working paths. They both need one hundred percent redundant resources as in the one-for-one protection.

Pre-configuration protection cycle (P-cycle) was introduced to achieve very low switching time and more shared backup bandwidth to protect the mesh topology network [8,9]. Rerouting traffic through alternate pathways is the technique this method uses to protect against failure. Afterwards, the concept was theoretically extended to other networks such as: WDM, MPLS, and IP [3]. The P-cycle idea was inspired by the ring-based network protection method which

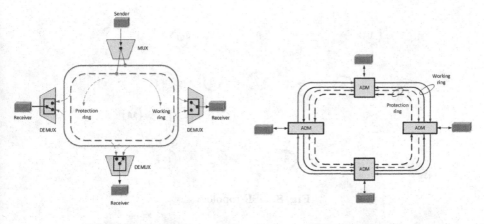

Fig. 4. UPSR [5]   **Fig. 5.** BLSR [5]

had been used for SONET ring networks. A P-cycle can switch to the backup path not only for on-cycle links, but also for straddle links as well which makes it highly efficient for mesh networks. Straddle links are the links that have both two end nodes on the P-cycle [3].

Figures 6 and 7 show how a P-cycle protects an on-cycle link and a straddling link respectively. To protect the on-cycle link failure, the traffic that was routed by a broken link reroutes over its pre-configured cycle. Hence, the pre-configured cycle needs the same amount of bandwidth as it was served before by the failed link. In order to recover from the straddle link failure, P-cycle divides the affected traffic into two halves and then sends them through the two parts of the pre-configured cycle (Fig. 7). Therefore, in case of straddle link protection, the P-cycle only needs to reserve half the amount of bandwidth that was served by the broken link.

There is still research in progress to improve P-cycle selection to achieve close to optimum value. In [3], Asthana et al. surveyed various methods to form network P-cycles. In [11], Guo et al. presented an improved genetic algorithm to find efficient P-cycle combinations. In [12], Ju et al. investigate the P-cycle deployment to find power efficient protection cycles. This work considered the NSF network (Fig. 8) and also the US backbone topology (Fig. 9). The authors studied the

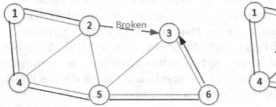

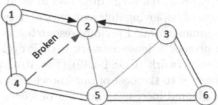

Fig. 6. On-cycle link protection   **Fig. 7.** Straddle link protection

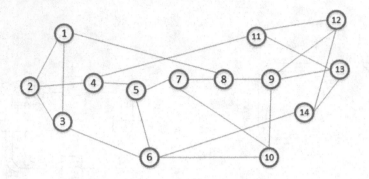

Fig. 8. NSF topology.

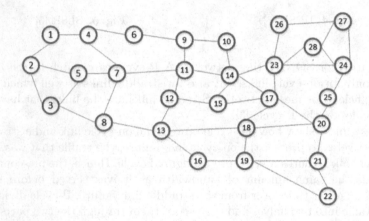

Fig. 9. US backbone topology.

power consumption of P-cycle under different traffic patterns and number of data centers. Deploying optical networks in DC networks is also another research area. In [13], Kabaciński et al. proposed four variants of optical data center network architectures. This work discusses only tree-based data center network topologies. Using P-cycle in tree-based DC network topologies leaves some links in the DC network unprotected.

Optical network utilization in cloud computing environments is another active research area. In [20], Yin et al. discussed the advantages and disadvantages of deploying different optical networks for both intra- and inter-data center communication. Previous research has shown that the extra capacity required to protect a dense network with P-cycle would be greatly reduced [18]. A European network (COST-239) (Fig. 10) was used as a benchmark dense network. However to the best of our knowledge, non of the previous research studies have considered increasing number of working wavelength in fiber links.

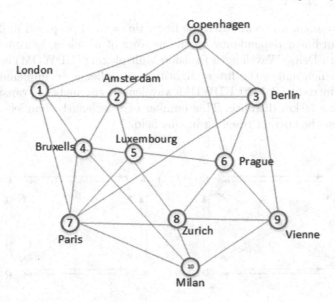

Fig. 10. COST 239 topology.

4   Proposed Approach (Min-Edge Efficient P-cycle)

Finding the optimum cycles to protect the entire network helps find the best place to consider the extra required wavelength within the network topology. Integer linear programming (ILP) is used to find the optimal redundant wavelengths [18]. Solving the ILP problem for dense mesh networks is computationally intensive. Therefore, different methods were proposed to find the most efficient P-cycles to consider pre-configured wavelengths. Some of the proposed methods result in a redundancy that is significantly higher than the optimum. For example, the pre-selection method filters the total cycle list. It is less intensive to compute but it results in more than optimum redundancy. In [21], Zhang et al. proposed a heuristic method to reach near optimum values. This method is an iterative method and it is not computationally intensive. In this method, the authors use unity-cycle as a unidirectional P-cycle whose capacity on every edge is one unit of wavelength. We therefore refer to their method as the unity cycle method. The unity cycle method calculates the Efficiency Ratio (ER in Eq. 2) of all cycles in each iteration. The P-cycle with maximum ER is considered as the most efficient unity cycle. This method achieves close to the optimum required redundant wavelength.

$$ER_k = \frac{\text{Number of wavelengths that can be protected by P-cycle number k}}{\text{Number of backup wavelengths needed to be stored in P-cycle number k}}$$
$$(2)$$

where $0 < k < N$ and N is the total number of possible P-cycles in the network topology.

One of the main problems with the heuristic method proposed in [21] is that it suffers from linear dependency on the number of wavelengths running in the network. Ultra Dense Wavelength Division Multiplexing (UDWDM) is a growing technology which makes the linear algorithm a challenge to implement. In [4], Ataie et al. introduced 1520 UDWDM wavelength channels to transmit about 32 Tbps over a 50 km distance. This number of wavelength channels will likely increase given the current research in this field.

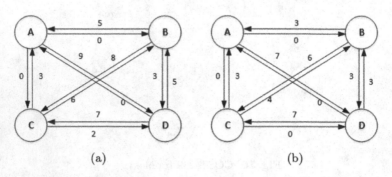

Fig. 11. Simple network to cover C-D as the minimum non-zero uncovered wavelength; the A-B-D-C cycle is chosen because it has the highest efficiency in Table 1. (a) Before (b) After covering by P-cycle.

Table 1. Efficiency ratio (ER) of cycles that cover the minimum weight edge of the simple network in Fig. 11.

Cycle	Clockwise	Counter-clockwise
A-B-C	-	-
B-C-D	$3/3 = 1$	-
A-B-D	-	-
A-C-D	$1/3 = .33$	-
A-C-D-B	$6/4 = 1.66$	-

In this paper, we propose a heuristic method that takes less time than the one proposed in [21]. Extensive experiments show that our approach does not depend linearly on the number of wavelengths. Figure 11 shows a simple network with ten unidirectional P-cycles. In our approach, we first use Eq. 2 in each iteration to calculate the ER of certain selected P-cycles. The P-cycle with the highest ER is selected as the most efficient P-cycle. Then, the uncovered wavelengths will be updated by removing the wavelength covered by the most efficient P-cycle in the current iteration. In the case of having multiple edges with the same minimum value or multiple P-cycles with the same maximum ER, the first one is selected.

Algorithm 1. Min Edge Weight P-cycle Algorithm

1: **procedure** MINEDGE(*Graph, CycleList*)
2:     **while** Uncovered wavelength ≠ 0 **do**
3:         $ME \leftarrow minEdge$ ▷ Find edge which has minimum non-zero weight. ME
4:         $FC \leftarrow$ Filtered cycles   ▷ Select only cycles that can protect the ME
5:         Calculate the ER of filtered cycles based on Equation 2.
6:         $MEC \leftarrow$ Select the most efficient cycle.   ▷ P-cycle with maximum ER.
7:         Remove covered wavelengths protected by MEC considering the weight of ME as reserved wavelengths on MEC.
8:     **end while**
9:     **return**
10: **end procedure**

Our algorithm uses the most efficient P-cycle to protect the non-zero minimum edge in each iteration to cover the whole network traffic.

Algorithm 1 demonstrates how our proposed min-edge efficient P-cycle algorithm works. Variable ME (in line 3) corresponds to the network edge that carries minimum non-zero wavelength traffic (weight). This edge in the current iteration of Fig. 11 is edge C-D which has weight 2 as the minimum non-zero weight. The second step is selecting the P-cycles that can protect the edge found in the previous step. These P-cycles in the current iteration of Fig. 11 are A-D-C, B-D-C, and A-B-D-C. The Efficiency Ratio (ER) of each one of these P-cycles is calculated as the number of protected wavelength divided by the number of stored backup wavelength (Eq. 2). This is the same ER as proposed in [21]. These values of the current iteration of Fig. 11 are presented in Table 1.

The efficiency of the P-cycle A-B-D-C is calculated as 1.66 which is the most efficient P-cycle. Therefore it will be selected in this iteration. Removing the protected wavelength by the selected P-cycle is the next step which is shown in Fig. 11(b).

In this scenario, it is assumed that all the optical nodes are able to convert the wavelength. Otherwise, wavelength continuity constraint needs to be considered in the optimization problem which is outside the scope of this paper.

5 Experiments

To evaluate our algorithm, we conducted a set of experiments using COST 239 as the network model (Fig. 10). We applied a uniform random traffic distribution. We assumed that full wavelength conversion is possible in all nodes. A random uniform traffic distribution pattern is considered where the number of wavelengths between any two nodes is selected from zero to n (both inclusive), where n is the maximum number of possible wavelengths passing through the network.

Figure 12 shows the redundancy required to cover the whole network versus cycle length using uniformly distributed traffic in the COST 239 network. Figure 13 shows the required processing time. It also shows that our approach

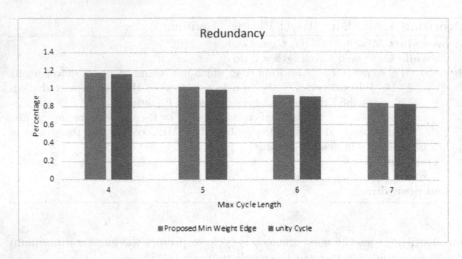

Fig. 12. Average required redundancy.

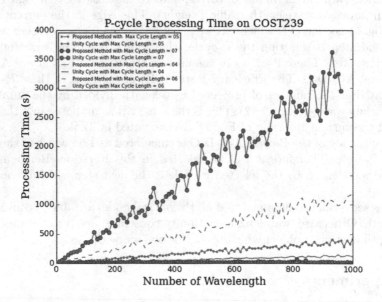

Fig. 13. Processing time on the European COST 239 benchmark network.

takes much less time than the unity cycle approach and that it achieves the same redundancy requirement. Figure 14 shows a closer look at the processing time of our solution. It shows that only increasing the cycle length increases the processing time but the processing time remains constant when the number of the required wavelengths increases.

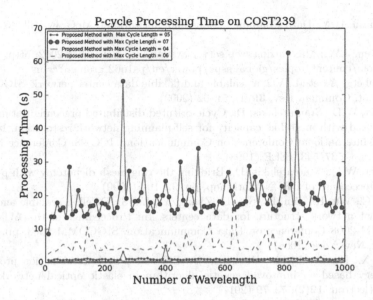

Fig. 14. Closer look at the processing time of the proposed approach.

6 Conclusion

The number of wavelength channels in fiber networks is increasing. This has a significant impact on the cost of computing P-cycles for those networks. Little research has been done to address this problem. In this paper, we propose the Min-Edge Efficient P-cycle computing approach, a new method that generates the same P-cycles that can be obtained using the unity cycle approach which are close to the optimum P-cycles. A significant improvement of the proposed approach is that its processing time does not depend on the number of wavelength channels. Also, our approach can be used in mesh data center networks such as DCell server-centric data centers. This, in turn, will make such networks more fault tolerant while requiring close to minimum redundant network resources.

References

1. Al-Fares, M., Loukissas, A., Vahdat, A.: A scalable, commodity data center network architecture. SIGCOMM Comput. Commun. Rev. **38**(4), 63–74 (2008)
2. Alizadeh, M., Edsall, T.: On the data path performance of leaf-spine datacenter fabrics. In: 2013 IEEE 21st Annual Symposium on High-Performance Interconnects (HOTI), pp. 71–74. IEEE (2013)
3. Asthana, R., Singh, Y.N., Grover, W.D.: P-cycles: an overview. IEEE Commun. Surv. Tutor. **12**(1), 97–111 (2010)
4. Ataie, V., et al.: Flex-grid compatible ultra wide frequency comb source for 31.8 Tb/s coherent transmission of 1520 UDWDM channels. In: OFC 2014, pp. 1–3, March 2014

5. Forouzan, B.A.: Data Communications and Networking. McGraw-Hill, New York (2012)
6. Graham, J.W.: Maximizing web server availability, November 2002. http://www.dell.com/content/topics/global.aspx/power/en/ps1q02_graham?c=us
7. Greenberg, A., et al.: Vl2: a scalable and flexible data center network. SIGCOMM Comput. Commun. Rev. **39**(4), 51–62 (2009)
8. Grover, W.D., Stamatelakis, D.: Cycle-oriented distributed preconfiguration: ring-like speed with mesh-like capacity for self-planning network restoration. In: 1998 IEEE International Conference on Communications, ICC 98. Conference Record, vol. 1, pp. 537–543. IEEE (1998)
9. Grover, W.D., Stamatelakis, D.: Bridging the ring-mesh dichotomy with p-cycles. In: Proceedings of DRCN Workshop, pp. 92–104 (2000)
10. Guo, C., Wu, H., Tan, K., Shi, L., Zhang, Y., Lu, S.: DCell: a scalable and fault-tolerant network structure for data centers. In: Proceedings of the ACM SIGCOMM 2008 Conference on Data Communication, SIGCOMM 2008, pp. 75–86. ACM, New York (2008)
11. Guo, X., Huang, J., Liu, H., Chen, Y.: Efficient p-cycle combination protection strategy based on improved genetic algorithm in elastic optical networks. IET Optoelectron. **12**(2), 73–79 (2017)
12. Ju, M., Zhou, F., Xiao, S., Zhu, Z.: Power-efficient protection with directed p-cycles for asymmetric traffic in elastic optical networks. J. Light. Technol. **34**(17), 4053–4065 (2016)
13. Kabaciński, W., Michalski, M., Rajewski, R., Żal, M.: Optical datacenter networks with elastic optical switches. In: 2017 IEEE International Conference on Communications (ICC), pp. 1–6. IEEE (2017)
14. Li, D., Wu, J.: FCell: towards the tradeoffs in designing data center network architectures. In: 24th International Conference on Computer Communication and Networks (ICCCN), pp. 1–8, August 2015
15. Munir, A., et al.: Minimizing flow completion times in data centers. In: 2013 Proceedings IEEE INFOCOM, pp. 2157–2165, April 2013
16. Provision Data Services: Data Center Downtime and Outages: Understanding the Costly Impact. http://provisiondataservices.com/news-events/data-center-downtime-outages-understanding-costly-impact
17. Rezgui, A., Noghani, K.A., Taheri, J., Mirzaeinia, A., Soliman, H., Davis, N.: SDN helps big data become fault tolerant, in big data and software defined networks. In: Taheri, J., Zomaya, A. (eds.) IET Book Series on Big Data, chap. 17, pp. 319–336. The Institution of Engineering and Technology, London (2018)
18. Schupke, D.A., Gruber, C.G., Autenrieth, A.: Optimal configuration of p-cycles in WDM networks. In: IEEE International Conference on Communications, ICC 2002, vol. 5, pp. 2761–2765. IEEE (2002)
19. Tzanakaki, A., Wosinska, L., Schares, L., Liu, H., Simeonidou, D.: Special issue on optical data center networks. IEEE/OSA J. Opt. Commun. Netw. **10**(7), 1–3 (2018)
20. Yin, Y., Liu, L., Proietti, R., Yoo, S.B.: Software defined elastic optical networks for cloud computing. IEEE Netw. **31**(1), 4–10 (2017)
21. Zhang, Z., Zhong, W.D., Mukherjee, B.: A heuristic method for design of survivable wdm networks with p-cycles. IEEE Commun. Lett. **8**(7), 467–469 (2004)

Toward Accurate and Efficient Emulation of Public Blockchains in the Cloud

Xinying Wang, Abdullah Al-Mamun, Feng Yan, and Dongfang Zhao[✉]

University of Nevada, Reno, NV 89557, USA
xinyingw@nevada.unr.edu, dzhao@unr.edu

Abstract. Blockchain is an enabler of many emerging decentralized applications in areas of cryptocurrency, Internet of Things, smart health-care, among many others. Although various open-source blockchain frameworks are available in the form of virtual machine images or docker images on public clouds, the infrastructure of mainstream blockchains nonetheless exhibits a technical barrier for many users to modify or test out new research ideas in blockchains. To make it worse, many advantages of blockchain systems can be demonstrated only at large scales, e.g., thousands of nodes, which are not always available to researchers. This paper presents an accurate and efficient emulating system to replay the execution of large-scale blockchain systems on tens of thousands of nodes. In contrast to existing work that simulates blockchains with artificial timestamp injection, the proposed system is designed to be executing real proof-of-work workload along with peer-to-peer network communications and hash-based immutability. In addition, the proposed system employs a preprocessing approach to avoid the per-node computation overhead at runtime and thus achieves practical scales. We have evaluated the system for emulating up to 20,000 nodes on Amazon Web Services (AWS), showing both high accuracy and high efficiency with millions of transactions.

Keywords: Distributed systems · Blockchains · Consensus protocols

1 Introduction

Blockchain, a decentralized and immutable database, has drawn a lot of research interests in various communities, such as security [9,22], database [2,14], network [16], distributed systems [30], and high-performance computing [1]. Although many existing blockchain frameworks [15,20] are open-source and offer docker images accessible in major cloud vendors (e.g., Google Cloud, Amazon Web Services (AWS), and Microsoft Azure), there are yet more challenges for blockchains to be widely adopted, such as (i) the lack of resources to carry out large-scale experiments and (ii) much, if not prohibitive, engineering effort to modify sophisticated production (despite open-source) systems to timely test out new ideas.

© Springer Nature Switzerland AG 2019
D. Da Silva et al. (Eds.): CLOUD 2019, LNCS 11513, pp. 67–82, 2019.
https://doi.org/10.1007/978-3-030-23502-4_6

To this end, multiple blockchain simulators were recently developed, two of the most popular ones being Bitcoin-Simulator and VIBES.

Bitcoin-Simulator [17] follows the same architecture and protocol of Bitcoin [7], the foremost application in cryptocurrency built upon blockchains. Users of Bitcoin-Simulator can specify various protocol and network parameters, such as the number of nodes and network bandwidth. The main goal of Bitcoin-Simulator is to study the trade-off between performance and security. Because of its design goal, Bitcoin-Simulator simulates the execution of a blockchain network at the block level rather than the transaction level. Bitcoin-Simulator does not provide a fine-grained control over the application, limiting its applicability for broader adoption. In addition, Bitcoin-Simulator simply inserts a series of static time stamps to simulate the proof-of-work (PoW) consensus protocol, which does not precisely characterize the behavior of real-world blockchain systems: for instance, Bitcoin dynamically adjusts the PoW difficulty and the nodes (as known as miners) usually complete the tasks in stochastic time intervals. Last but not least, Bitcoin-Simulator's network is built upon NS3 [26], a discrete-event network simulator, which limits the scalability on up to 6,000 nodes. Bitcoin network currently consists of more than 10,000 nodes [8], implying that Bitcoin-Simulator cannot simulate the entire network of Bitcoin as of the writing of this paper.

VIBES [28] extends Bitcoin-Simulator with the following improvements. First, VIBES supports a web-based interface for users to visually track the growth of the network. Second, VIBES improves the scalability of Bitcoin-Simulator by employing a fast-forwarding algorithm, which essentially designates a coordinator to control the events according to existing nodes' best guess on the block creation time. Such a centralized coordinator might be acceptable for a single-node simulator at small- or medium-scale, and yet could be a performance bottleneck for extreme-scale applications. Similar to Bitcoin-Simulator, VIBES takes the same approach of inserting time stamps to hypothetically carry out the PoW workload. Both Bitcoin-Simulator and VIBES are coarse estimators of real-world blockchain executions due to the lack of real PoW implementations or a decentralized architecture.

This paper presents **BlockLite**, the very first blockchain *emulator* with both high accuracy and high scalability. In contrast to Bitcoin-Simulator, BlockLite comprises a specific module to execute real PoW workload[1], supports fine-grained transaction management, and scales out to 20,000 nodes thanks to its efficient network communications built upon distributed queues along with PoW preprocessing that incurs negligible runtime overhead. Different than VIBES, BlockLite is fully decentralized with no single point of failure or performance bottleneck. It should be noted that even on a single node the decentralization philosophy of blockchains still holds for a blockchain *emulator* because each user-level thread is now considered as an individual node. Some preliminary results are currently under review in a short demo paper [29].

---

[1] Thus making it an *emulator* rather than a simulator.

The remainder of this paper is organized as follows. Section 2 reviews important literature of blockchain systems. We describe the system design of the proposed emulator BlockLite in Sect. 3. Section 4 presents the implementation details and the interface exposed to the users. We report the experimental results in Sect. 5, discuss some open questions in Sect. 6, and finally conclude the paper in Sect. 7.

2   Related Work

Several researches on blockchain are being under focus among the distributed computing community apart from the main stream blockchain systems like Bitcoin [7], Ethereum [15], and Hyperledger [20]. In order to mitigate the bottleneck with the storage a blockchain framework named Jupiter [18] is designed for mobile devices. Similarly, to alleviate storage bloating problem another framework [13] is proposed based on Network Coded Distributed Storage. To enable customization and enhancement in arbitrary scenarios Inkchain [21] is designed that is built with the flavor of permissioned blockchain based on Hyperledger.

Reliability and security in order to maintain data integrity is being considered another major concern for the distributed ledger technology. BigchainDB [6] is known to have all the features from database (i.e., indexing, querying structured data) and the blockchain properties (i.e., decentralization and immutability) while providing better fault tolerance. To improve the security at the Transport layer, Certchain [10] is proposed. Smart contract technology is leveraged in [19] to make sure the validity of data based on decentralized privacy preserving search scheme. Similarly, 2LBC [3] is designed to manage the data integrity in distributed systems based on leader rotation approach.

Distributed data provenance [11,12] has been another research attraction among the file system and database communities. Most recently, a consensus protocol called proof-of-reproducibility (PoR) [1] is crafted to manage distributed in-memory ledger for HPC systems in order to support scientific data provenance. For storage level provenance several I/O optimization techniques [11,12] for file systems are proposed. There is also an emerging trend for conventional workloads, such as high-performance computing and networking, to move to the cloud platforms [23,24,31,32]. Various solutions [5,25] are designed for the improvement of provenance in database transactions.

Though, a recent work namely SimBlock [4] focuses to develop a blockchain network simulator that supports changing node behavior on run time in order to investigate behavior of nodes; to the best of our knowledge, this paper presents a blockchain framework for the first time that supports emulation with very large scales of nodes in terms of user level threads along with the plug-in facility of custom components (i.e., ad-hoc consensus protocols) for domain specific applications.

3   System Design

The objective of BlockLite is to provide blockchain researchers and practitioners an easy-to-use and lightweight emulator to develop new components and evaluate new ideas, such as ad-hoc consensus protocols customized for domain-specific applications. To achieve that objective, BlockLite is designed to be deployed to a single node, with loosely-coupled components for flexible customization. In its infrastructure, BlockLite has implemented all the building blocks for a basic blockchain system. This section details how these common facilities are designed, the challenges we encounter, and the approaches we take to build up the emulator.

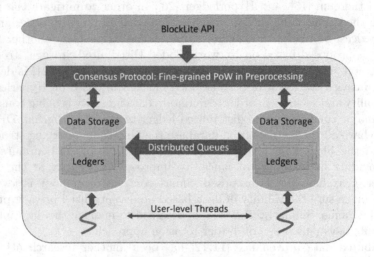

Fig. 1. BlockLite architecture.

The high-level architecture of BlockLite is illustrated in Fig. 1. While the interface, i.e., BlockLite API, will be detailed in Sect. 4, the infrastructure can be broken down into three categories: storage, computation, and networking. In the context of blockchains, they are usually referred to as *distributed ledgers*, *consensus protocols* (e.g., PoW), and *network communications*.

Distributed Ledgers. The transaction data of a specific blockchain are replicated, either fully or partially, in distinct files each of which is associated to a hypothetical node. The data, also called ledgers, could have been partially duplicated if the following two conditions are satisfied: (i) more than 50% of nodes have agreed on that the new block (of transactions) is valid and (ii) the current node (other than those nodes who have voted) does not process any request regarding the new block. Regardless of specific consensus protocols, a blockchain requires only 50% votes supporting the new block's validity.

Consensus Protocols. A basic proof-of-work protocol is implemented from scratch in BlockLite. In contrast to other simulators where the difficulty is *simulated* by time delay and timestamps, BlockLite, as an *emulator*, conducts the real PoW workload by solving the puzzle. The puzzles we define in BlockLite are similar to the Nakamoto protocol in Bitcoin [7] in the sense of comparing blocks' hash values against predefined thresholds. Nonetheless, BlockLite exhibits an additional feature that preprocesses PoW allowing for fine tuning of puzzle difficulty, which is detailed in Sect. 3.1.

Network Communications. It is one of the most challenging components to emulate the networking in BlockLite that is designed to be working on a single node. Fortunately, BlockLite is designed for emulating public blockchains that are based on PoW, which is compute-intensive rather than network-intensive[2]. Therefore, the real network impact for PoW-based blockchains lies in the network infrastructure's latency rather than bandwidth. BlockLite applies a statistical estimation of time delays for transmitting the messages between nodes, each of which is emulated by a user-level thread whose requests are buffered in a distributed queue. We will discuss the distributed queue in more detail in Sect. 3.2.

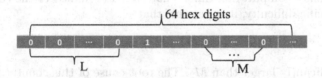

Fig. 2. Two-phase puzzle for efficient preprocessing of PoW in BlockLite.

3.1 PoW Preprocessing for Fine-Grained Calibration Across Heterogeneous Systems

One cornerstone of Nakamoto consensus protocol, or any PoW variants, is the puzzle-based winner selection:[3] the hash value of the (block of) transactions is compared against the predefined "small" number. Because BlockLite is designed to be running on an arbitrary node that can be heterogeneous case by case, we must provide an efficient yet flexible mechanism to ensure the compatibility across heterogeneous machines. To this end, we design BlockLite puzzles as follows. A puzzle's difficulty is expressed by two sub-fields, L and M, in the form of $L.M$ (assuming SHA256 [27] is used as the hash function): L indicates the required number of leading zeros in the 64-hex (i.e., 256-bit) hash value; M indicates the minimal number of zeros in the middle of the hash value.

---

[2] Private blockchains are indeed network-intensive due to the quadratic number of messages.

[3] As known as "leader" in the context of distributed systems.

Figure 2 illustrates how $L.M$ is constructed. The first part L is semantically equivalent to the Nakamoto protocol: checking whether a hash value is smaller than a predefined threshold is essentially the same to counting the number of leading zeros in the binary or hex form of the hash value. L is a coarse-level adjustment of difficulty because the same L might imply a wide spectrum of computation time, and this is exactly why Bitcoin dynamically adjusts the difficulty every 2016 blocks [7]. To address that, BlockLite introduces the M part to allow the system to check whether there are M zeros in the middle of the hash value satisfying the following conditions: (i) Any leading zeros in L are not considered; (ii) Tailing zeros, by definition, are counted towards M; and (iii) Zeros need not be continuous.

The benefit of the additional M-zero checking is that we can adjust the puzzle difficulty under the same meta-difficulty, i.e., same L but different M's. In addition, M is positively correlated to the puzzle difficulty: a larger M implies more computation time. To see this, we can think of a larger M representing a super-set of the sets of less zeros with smaller M's. As a consequence, a smaller M has a higher chance to meet the requirement—the difficulty is lowered.

While the flexibility is significantly improved, one limitation of this $L.M$ two-phase puzzle is that the two arbitrary difficulty numbers do not follow partial orders in terms of computation time. That is, if $T(\cdot)$ indicates the computation time of a specific difficulty, it is possible that

$$T(L_1.M_1) > T(L_2.M_2) \text{ and } L_1 < L_2,$$

if M_1 is significantly larger than M_2. The root cause of this counter intuition is that L and M are, essentially, incomparable. For instance, if L is much smaller than M, then finding out M zeros, despite from random positions, is still much harder than locating a few leading zeros. As an extreme case, if we have two setups as $L_1.M_1 = 1.63$ and $L_2.M_2 = 2.1$, obviously the former case is much harder where we will seek for a hash value with all 64 zeros, as opposed to finding a hash value with two leading zeros and another zero from any of the remaining 62 hex digits.

3.2 Optimization for Extreme-Scale Networking Through Distributed Queues

In contrast to existing blockchain simulators, BlockLite does not simply insert timestamps for the completion of PoW; instead, it solves the real puzzle to accurately *emulate* a real blockchain system. The downside of this approach is the cost and overhead for large-scale systems. For instance, Bitcoin has about 10,000 mining nodes as of January 2019 [8]. A single machine, despite its multi- or many-cores, is not able to efficiently emulate tens of thousands of nodes each of which works on a compute-intensive puzzle such as finding out a qualified hash value.

BlockLite overcomes the scalability challenge by delegating one node (thread) to solve the puzzle in a preprocessing stage and when the real application runs at a specific difficulty, the assigned nodes (or, threads) simply replicate the behavior of the delegation node. In doing so, BlockLite achieves the best of both worlds: real execution of PoW and low overhead (i.e., high scalability). Since the calibration is carried out in a preprocessing state, no runtime overhead is introduced.

The second technique taken by BlockLite to achieve high scalability is the usage of queue-based network communication. Specifically, we implement a priority queue who manages all the events in the order of their creation time. That is, the head of the queue always points to the earliest event, followed by later events each of which is requested by a specific node. Therefore, the queued events implicitly determine the orders of nodes completing their tasks (e.g., submitting transactions, solving puzzles, appending blocks), which significantly reduces the network traffic.

4   Implementation and Interface

BlockLite is implemented in Java with about 2,000 lines of code. We have been maintaining a website for the BlockLite project at https://hpdic.github.io/blocklite; the source code will be released to https://github.com/hpdic/blocklite.

Because users' machines are equipped with different resources, the very first step to deploy BlockLite is to calibrate the parameters in accordance to the system's specification. For instance, a throughput of 10 transactions per second might require 7.x difficulty on a high-end server with 32 cores, and the same throughput might require 4.x difficulty on a mainstream laptop with four cores. The calibration, also called PoW preprocessing, is to allow BlockLite to adjust the difficulty by considering factors input by users (e.g., expected throughput, consensus protocols) as well as system specification (e.g., number of cores, memory size).

When BlockLite runs for the first time, it generates a difficulty-time map between difficulty levels and the execution time. This map is implemented as a HashMap and is accessible to all the nodes. Whenever a node is waken up according to the consensus protocol, the node will consult with the difficulty-time map and replay the behavior with controlled randomness.

Specifically, the emulator starts by asking the user to specify the values of two parameters: MAX_DIFF and MAX_SUBDIFF. The emulator then goes on to repeatedly mine the blocks in a nested loop as shown in Algorithm 1. The complexity of the algorithm is $O(n^2)$ by observing the two levels of loops, one for the main difficulty and the other for the sub difficulty.

Algorithm 2 illustrates the mechanism of BlockLite to mine a specific block. The main difficulty mainDiff corresponds to L in Fig. 2, subDiff indicates the auxiliary difficulty corresponding to M, and miner() is the implementation method of mining. The overall complexity is therefore $O(n)$, where n indicates the number of attempts before we find out the qualified nonce number.

Algorithm 1. Calibration

```
 1: function RUNMILLSOFDIFFCULTS
 2:     mainDifficult ← 1
 3:     for i ∈ {0 ⋯ MAX_DIFF} do
 4:         subDiffcult ← 0
 5:         for j ∈ {0 ⋯ MIN_DIFF} do
 6:             Start Timer
 7:             powProof ← newProofWork(i, j);
 8:             mineBlock();
 9:             End Timer
10:         end for
11:     end for
12: end function
```

Algorithm 2. Mine Block

```
1: function MINEBLOCK
2:     nonce ← 0
3:     n ← mainDifficult + subDiffcultf
4:     target ← A string of ⌊mainDifficult⌋ 0's
5:     while !blockID.startwith(target) or countOfZero(blockID) <n do
6:         nonce ++;
7:         blockID ← calculateHash(lastBlockID + timeStamp + nonce + ...);
8:     end while
9: end function
```

BlockLite provides an easy-to-use interface for users to plug in application-specific components. Listing 4 illustrates a simplified code snippet of the interface with two core methods. Users can implement both methods to inject customized consensus protocols. For instance, `generateProof` solves the puzzle; in PoW, this means to check many nonce numbers until the hash value of the combined data satisfies the condition. Therefore, when the node wants to create a new Block, the program will call `mineBlock()` in block.java to solve the puzzle, i.e., select the appropriate difficulty to control the mining time according to the difficulty calibration map.

```
1  public interface Provable {
2      public boolean verifyProof(Block);
3      public String generateProof(Block);
4  }
```

Listing 1.1. BlockLite Plug-in Interface.

Both aforementioned methods take as input a `Block` object, whose fields are explained in Table 1. The class comprises all the necessary information for the system to manipulate the blocks and more important, the transactions—the dominant data format in blockchain-based applications. A more detailed declaration of the class can be found in the source code, which is open-sourced at the project website: hpdic.cse.unr.edu/blocklite.

Table 1. Block member variable.

Variable	Definition
blockID	ID of the block
creationTime	Creation time of current block
creatorID	Creation ID (Node ID) of current block
parentBlock	Parent block of current block
depth	Depth of current block
previousHash	Hash value of parent block
childList	Child list of current block
numChild	Numbers of current block children
txnList	Numbers of current block transactions
proof	Consensus protocol (Nakamoto by default)

5   Experimental Evaluation

5.1   Experimental Setup

We perform extensive experimental evaluation of BlockLite on AWS. We pick four different instance types, the processors of which represent a wide spectrum of CPUs from both Intel and AMD. Table 2 lists the instance types along with their processor specification.

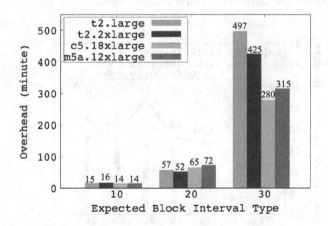

Fig. 3. Overhead of various instances.

The data we use for our evaluation are transactions in the same format of Bitcoin trades. Specifically, more than two million transactions are fed into the emulator for real-scale applications. We repeat all experiments for five times and report the average; we do not report the variance if it is unnoticeable.

Table 2. Different AWS instances used for evaluating BlockLite.

Instance types	CPU specifications
t2.large	2 Intel(R) Xeon(R) CPU E5-2686 v4 @2.30 GHz
t2.2xlarge	8 Intel(R) Xeon(R) CPU E5-2686 v4 @2.30 GHz
c5.18xlarge	72 Intel(R) Xeon(R) Platinum 8124M CPU @3.00 GHz
m5a.12xlarge	48 AMD EPYC 7571

5.2 Overhead

We report the overhead to find the map between the difficulty and the block-creation time in Fig. 3. Specifically, we build the maps of four VMIs for the following three example intervals: 10 min, 20 min, and 30 min. It should be noted that, however, these overheads are incurred only during the preprocessing stage and would not be applied to the real-time execution.

We can observe that the overhead increases at an exponential rate with respect to the intervals; take the t2.large instance for example, the overhead increases by 3.7× from 10 to 20 min and then increases by 8.7× from 20 to 30 min. Another observation is that these VMIs do not exhibit much difference in overhead at shorter intervals like 10 or 20 min; and yet, for longer interval like 30 min, the smaller instances (i.e., t2.large and t2.2xlarge) indeed incur much longer overhead (than c5.18xlarge and m5a.12xlarge). This phenomenon can be best explained by the fact that smaller VMIs are equipped with slower CPUs that need to solve the same puzzle in a longer time.

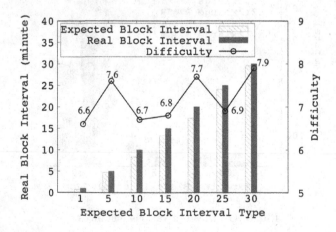

Fig. 4. Difficulty v.s. block creation time

5.3   Accuracy

Figure 4 shows the calibration map of the *m5a.12xlarge* instance. For practical time intervals, e.g., ten minutes or more, the emulated processing times are close to the expected time intervals. We also plot the preprocessing difficulties in the figure; the result suggests that most difficulty values range in between six and eight, covering mining time from 1 to 30 min.

   We then report the accuracy on various instance types in Fig. 5. The for sake of clarity, we do not plot the corresponding difficulty in the figure. As we can see from the figure, not all instance types exhibit the same accuracy; in our tested VMIs, the c5.18xlarge seems to achieve the highest accuracy except for the trivial case of 1- and 5-minute intervals.

5.4   Sensitivity

This section evaluates the sensitivity of BlockLite when deployed to various VMIs. Figure 6 shows the puzzle-solving time on four different instances with respect to practical difficulties from four to eight. For clarity, we only compare the main difficulty between VMIs in the figure (we will report sub difficulties later on). The figure clearly shows that smaller instances (t2.large, t2.2xlarge) take more time than the larger instances for all difficulties, which, again, can be explained by the different CPU performance on these instances.

   In Fig. 7, we report the puzzle-solving time of both main and sub difficulties. Indeed, the highest computation time appears on the top-right corner of the map in all cases, as that corner represents both the highest main difficulty and the highest sub difficulty; similarly the lowest value appears at the bottom-left corner. Nonetheless, we do observe different gradients from these four heat-maps. For instance, the largest instance (m5a.12xlarge) seems to have the most low-value cells (i.e., shorter puzzle-solving time).

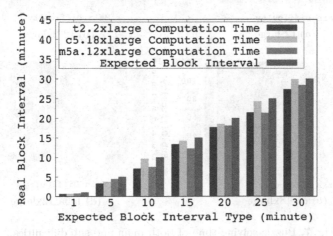

Fig. 5. Block creation rate with various instances type.

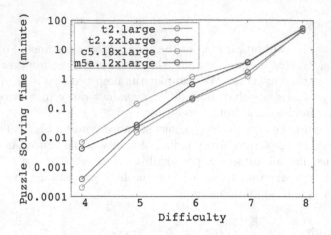

Fig. 6. Difficulty and puzzle solving time

5.5   Scalability

We tested BlockLite's scalability by emulating up to 20,000 nodes on the instance
with 48 AMD EPYC cores and 192 GB memory (m5a.12xlarge, see Table 2).
The workload is comprised of more than one million transaction data.

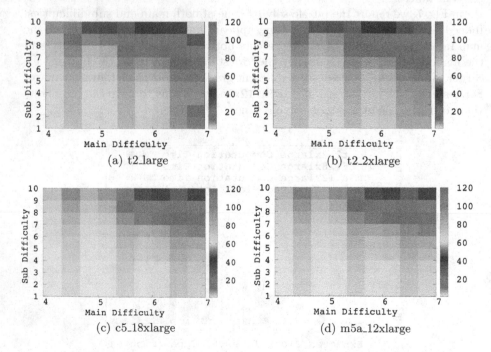

(a) t2_large

(b) t2_2xlarge

(c) c5_18xlarge

(d) m5a_12xlarge

Fig. 7. Puzzle-solving time of both main and sub difficulties.

Figure 8 shows BlockLite's real-time executions, along with memory footprint, on 5,000, 10,000, 20,000, and 40,000 nodes, respectively. The puzzle difficulty is set to one for the sake of fast demonstrations. We can observe that even at the real scale of Bitcoin—10,000 nodes, BlockLite can finish the emulation in 13 s with reasonable memory footprint of less than 4 GB.

5.6 Monetary Cost

This section evaluates the cost incurred at the cloud computing vendors when various CPU or instance types are selected. As we can see in Fig. 9, small instance t2.large incur the lowest cost in all intervals while the c5.18xlarge instance is the most costly one. This can be explained by the high unit price of the c5.18xlarge instance: although the execution time is comparable with the other large instance (m5a.12xlarge), the overall charge is higher because of the different unit price.

6 Discussion

There are a few optimizations that could have been applied to current BlockLite design, which are not supported at the writing of this paper. Although there are many more open questions to be answered, we list two of most interesting optimizations here in the following for the sake of limited space.

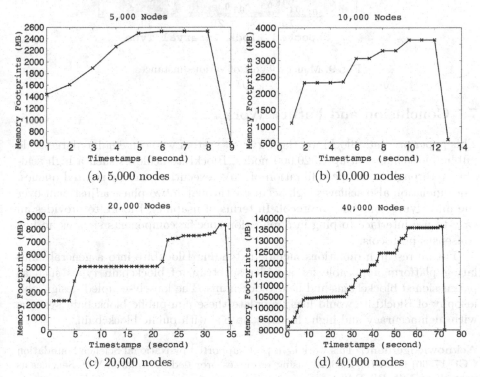

(a) 5,000 nodes

(b) 10,000 nodes

(c) 20,000 nodes

(d) 40,000 nodes

Fig. 8. Scalability and memory footprint of BlockLite.

One possible optimization to the current BlockLite implementation is to leverage the underlying multi- or many-cores in modern processors. It should be noted that in many computation-based consensus protocols, the workload is embarrassingly parallel. Therefore, we should be able to parallelize the proof-of-work (POW) protocols, which will be studied in our future work.

Another possible extension to this work is to implement an inter-node communication such that the emulator can be distributed over a cluster of nodes. This would further improve the adaptability of BlockLite if a single node is not capable of conducting the intensive computation expected by some large difficulties.

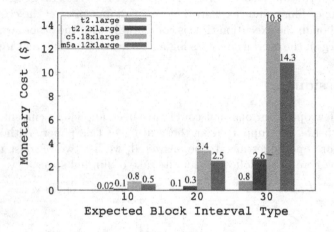

Fig. 9. Monetary cost of various instances.

7 Conclusion and Future Work

This paper presents BlockLite, the very first system who can emulate large-scale public blockchains on up to 20,000 nodes. BlockLite achieves such a high scalability through an offline calibration of PoW execution and distributed queues. The emulation also achieves high accuracy through a two-phase adjustment over the underlying consensus protocol. In terms of usability, BlockLite provides an easy-to-use interface to plug in application-specific components such as ad-hoc consensus protocols.

Future research directions include extending BlockLite into a general emulating platform applicable for a wider spectrum of blockchain types such as permissioned blockchains and field blockchains. The loosely-coupled design philosophy of BlockLite would likely emulate these non-public blockchain systems with high accuracy and high efficiency on par with public blockchains.

Acknowledgement. This work is in part supported by National Science Foundation CCF-1756013 and IIS-1838024 (using resources provided by Amazon Web Services as part of the NSF BIGDATA program).

References

1. Al-Mamun, A., Li, T., Sadoghi, M., Zhao, D.: In-memory blockchain: toward efficient and trustworthy data provenance for HPC systems. In: Proceedings of the 6th IEEE International Conference on Big Data (BigData) (2018)
2. Allen, L., et al.: Veritas: shared verifiable databases and tables in the cloud. In: 9th Biennial Conference on Innovative Data Systems Research (CIDR) (2019)
3. Aniello, L., Baldoni, R., Gaetani, E., Lombardi, F., Margheri, A., Sassone, V.: A prototype evaluation of a tamper-resistant high performance blockchain-based transaction log for a distributed database. In: 13th European Dependable Computing Conference (EDCC) (2017)
4. Aoki, Y., Otsuki, K., Kaneko, T., Banno, R., Shudo, K.: SimBlock: a blockchain network simulator. CoRR abs/1901.09777 (2019)
5. Arab, B.S., Gawlick, D., Krishnaswamy, V., Radhakrishnan, V., Glavic, B.: Using reenactment to retroactively capture provenance for transactions. IEEE Trans. Knowl. Data Eng. (TKDE) **30**(3), 599–612 (2018)
6. BigchainDB. https://github.com/bigchaindb/bigchaindb. Accessed 2018
7. Bitcoin. https://bitcoin.org/bitcoin.pdf. Accessed 2019
8. Bitcoin Scale. https://bitnodes.earn.com. Accessed 2019
9. Camenisch, J., Drijvers, M., Dubovitskaya, M.: Practical UC-secure delegatable credentials with attributes and their application to blockchain. In: Proceedings of the ACM SIGSAC Conference on Computer and Communications Security (CCS), pp. 683–699 (2017)
10. Chen, J., Yao, S., Yuan, Q., He, K., Ji, S., Du, R.: CertChain: public and efficient certificate audit based on blockchain for TLS connections. In: IEEE INFOCOM 2018 - IEEE Conference on Computer Communications (2018)
11. Dai, D., Chen, Y., Carns, P., Jenkins, J., Ross, R.: Lightweight provenance service for high-performance computing. In: International Conference on Parallel Architectures and Compilation Techniques (PACT) (2017)
12. Dai, D., Chen, Y., Kimpe, D., Ross, R.: Provenance-based object storage prediction scheme for scientific big data applications. In: IEEE International Conference on Big Data (BigData) (2014)
13. Dai, M., Zhang, S., Wang, H., Jin, S.: A low storage room requirement framework for distributed ledger in blockchain. IEEE Access **6**, 22970–22975 (2018)
14. Dinh, T.T.A., Wang, J., Chen, G., Liu, R., Ooi, B.C., Tan, K.L.: BLOCKBENCH: a framework for analyzing private blockchains. In: ACM International Conference on Management of Data (SIGMOD) (2017)
15. Ethereum. https://www.ethereum.org/. Accessed 2018
16. Eyal, I., Gencer, A.E., Sirer, E.G., Van Renesse, R.: Bitcoin-NG: a scalable blockchain protocol. In: Proceedings of the 13th Usenix Conference on Networked Systems Design and Implementation (NSDI) (2016)
17. Gervais, A., Karame, G.O., Wüst, K., Glykantzis, V., Ritzdorf, H., Capkun, S.: On the security and performance of proof of work blockchains. In: Proceedings of the 2016 ACM SIGSAC Conference on Computer and Communications Security (CCS) (2016)
18. Han, S., Xu, Z., Chen, L.: Jupiter: a blockchain platform for mobile devices. In: IEEE International Conference on Data Engineering (ICDE) (2018)
19. Hu, S., Cai, C., Wang, Q., Wang, C., Luo, X., Ren, K.: Searching an encrypted cloud meets blockchain: a decentralized, reliable and fair realization. In: IEEE INFOCOM 2018 - IEEE Conference on Computer Communications (2018)

20. Hyperledger. https://www.hyperledger.org/. Accessed 2018
21. Inkchain. https://github.com/inklabsfoundation/inkchain. Accessed 2018
22. Kosba, A., Miller, A., Shi, E., Wen, Z., Papamanthou, C.: Hawk: the blockchain model of cryptography and privacy-preserving smart contracts. In: 2016 IEEE Symposium on Security and Privacy (SP) (2016)
23. Li, T., Keahey, K., Wang, K., Zhao, D., Raicu, I.: A dynamically scalable cloud data infrastructure for sensor networks. In: Proceedings of the 6th Workshop on Scientific Cloud Computing (ScienceCloud) (2015)
24. Li, T., et al.: A convergence of key-value storage systems from clouds to supercomputer. Concurr. Comput.: Pract. Exper. **28**, 44–69 (2016)
25. Niu, X., et al.: Provenance-aware query optimization. In: IEEE 33rd International Conference on Data Engineering (ICDE) (2017)
26. NS3. https://www.nsnam.org/tutorials/NS-3-LABMEETING-1.pdf. Accessed 2019
27. SHA-256. https://en.bitcoin.it/wiki/SHA-256. Accessed 2018
28. Stoykov, L., Zhang, K., Jacobsen, H.A.: VIBES: fast blockchain simulations for large-scale peer-to-peer networks: demo. In: Proceedings of the 18th ACM/IFIP/USENIX Middleware Conference (Middleware) (2017)
29. Wang, X., Al-Mamun, A., Yan, F., Zhao, D.: BlockLite: a lightweight emulator for public blockchains. In: International Conference on Very Large Data Bases (VLDB) - Demo Track (2019, Under review)
30. Zhang, K., Jacobsen, H.: Towards dependable, scalable, and pervasive distributed ledgers with blockchains. In: 38th IEEE International Conference on Distributed Computing Systems (ICDCS) (2018)
31. Zhao, D., Mandagere, N., Alatorre, G., Mohamed, M., Ludwig, H.: Toward locality-aware scheduling for containerized cloud services. In: IEEE International Conference on Big Data (BigData), pp. 273–280 (2015)
32. Zhao, D., Yang, X., Sadooghi, I., Garzoglio, G., Timm, S., Raicu, I.: High-performance storage support for scientific applications on the cloud. In: Proceedings of the 6th Workshop on Scientific Cloud Computing (ScienceCloud) (2015)

Teleportation of VM Disk Images Over WAN

Oleg Zaydman$^{(\boxtimes)}$ and Roman Zhirin$^{(\boxtimes)}$

VMware, Inc., Palo Alto, USA
{ozaydman, rzhirin}@vmware.com

Abstract. As edge computing and hybrid clouds gain momentum, migrating virtual machines between datacenters is becoming increasingly important. Whether such migration is performed live or not, it starts with a full copy of a virtual disk over the network. This initial copy is consuming the bulk of the transfer time and network use. Improving this copy is the focus of our paper. While compression can somewhat help with this, we propose a novel technique, which we call *teleportation*. Teleportation assembles disk images directly at the destination from the pieces of other, unrelated disk images already present there. Since the data found at the destination doesn't have to be sent over, our prototype has achieved 3.4x increase in network throughput (comparing to compression).

Keywords: Deduplication

1 Introduction

Teleportation takes advantage of the fact that file systems align files inside a disk image on 4 KB block boundaries. We calculate a hash of each block in each disk image. If the same file (such as *ntdll.dll*) is present in two separate disk images, the hash of each block of that file would be present in the set of hashes of either disk image. Teleportation process is shown in Fig. 1.

Teleportation starts with the source endpoint calculating 256-bit cryptographic hashes of each block [❶] and sending them to the teleporter [❷]. The teleporter tries to find the block with the same hash among the blocks which belong to other disk images already present at the destination by doing a hash table lookup [❸]. If a matching block is found [❹], it doesn't need to be sent over the network, otherwise it is requested from the source [❺, ❻].

The biggest challenge in teleporter implementation is memory efficiency. The hashes we use are 32 bytes long. If we hash just one terabyte of disk image data and put all the hashes in memory, they would occupy 8 GB of memory. Instead of keeping hashes in memory, our implementation stores hashes in disk files, which we call *hash files*. Keeping hashes on disk allows us to use 9x less memory per cache entry. Hashes in the hash file follow the same logical order as blocks in the disk image, thus preserving locality of reference.

The most important insight we had when designing teleporter was that most files inside the disk image are not fragmented. Because of this, once the 1st block of a file (which we call *head*) got matched, in all likelihood, the sequence of blocks that follows

© Springer Nature Switzerland AG 2019
D. Da Silva et al. (Eds.): CLOUD 2019, LNCS 11513, pp. 83–98, 2019.
https://doi.org/10.1007/978-3-030-23502-4_7

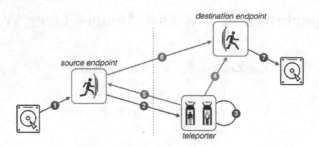

Fig. 1. Teleportation process.

would match too. This has two important implications. The first one is that it is sufficient to keep in memory information about the head of each file - the rest of the blocks of that file can be found by reading subsequent hashes from the hash file. By using this technique, teleporter started using 10x less memory. The second implication is that 2nd and subsequent blocks of the file can be matched with no extra disk I/O. This works because a unit of disk I/O is 4 KB, so every time teleporter performs a read from a hash file, 128 hashes are fetched into memory. As the result, teleporter performs very little disk I/O when the blocks do match. Teleporter detects file heads by analyzing content of each block.

When the blocks don't match, teleporter uses hash fingerprints to probabilistically reduce disk I/O. *Fingerprint* is a small 8-bit hash derived from the 256-bit hash of a block. Fingerprints are stored in memory inside the cache items instead of full hashes. When fingerprints don't match, there is no need to fetch hashes from the disk to compare, so most of unsuccessful disk I/O is eliminated.

As a result of the aforementioned design choices, we ended up with a hash matching system that performs matching with very few disk reads, while having a very small memory footprint. This matching system is a cornerstone of our design.

This paper makes the following contributions:

- Use of strong/weak head recognition (Sect. 2.3) for sequence discovery.
- Use of hash files to preserve referential locality for hashes stored on disk and reduce memory footprint (Sect. 2.5).
- Use of block sequences to reduce both the amount of disk I/O (Sect. 2.6) and memory footprint (Sect. 2.10).
- Novel space-efficient cache (Sect. 2.9) that combines cuckoo hashing with LRU-approximating cache replacement policy.
- Probabilistic cache admission policy (Sect. 2.10) that affects cache item's lifetime.
- Use of indirect addressing (Sect. 2.11) to reduce size of each cache entry by 7 bits.
- Alignment of sequences in the sequence cache on the 128-block boundaries to reduce disk I/O (Sect. 2.15).
- Novel cache coherence protocol (Sect. 2.16) that does not require notifying teleporter when destination blocks get modified.
- Use of grain table compression (Sect. 2.17) to reduce the memory footprint of the destination endpoint.

2 Design

Source endpoint is covered in Sects. 2.1–2.4, teleporter is covered in Sects. 2.5–2.15, and destination endpoint is covered in Sects. 2.16 and 2.17.

2.1 Parallelism

For both regular network copy and teleportation, it is important to perform major activities in parallel. For regular copy, these activities are reading, sending, and writing. For teleportation, there are two additional activities - hashing (done on the source endpoint) and matching (performed on the teleporter). We process blocks in batches and use the pipelining paradigm for parallelism (Fig. 2). There are dedicated threads for each activity, and each batch of blocks is processed in order by each thread.

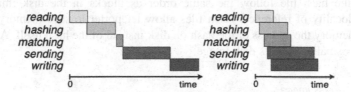

Fig. 2. Serial processing (left) vs pipelining (right).

2.2 Sparse Disks and Zero-Fill

Teleportation handles both flat and sparse disks [1]. In the case of sparse disk, source endpoint sends the sparse disk header and the grain table (a table of pointers to grains - units of allocated disk space) directly to the destination endpoint. Following that, source endpoint reads the disk in the logical grain order (effectively flattening it), and sends the hashes of the data to the teleporter. Destination endpoint receives the data in the flattened order, and uses the grain table to reconstruct the sparse disk. The teleporter is not aware whether the disk is sparse or flat. Hashes of zero-filled blocks are not sent to the teleporter. Information regarding zero-filled or unallocated blocks is sent as an array of bits. Such array is not only small to begin with, it compresses really well.

2.3 Head Recognition

The obvious way to identify file heads is to deploy a VM from the disk image, and install an agent (software to scan the file system) on that VM. We use a novel agent-less approach to identify file heads with high probability. One way to identify a file head is to examine first few bytes of the block. Files frequently incorporate file type metadata by storing a "magic number" at the very start of the file (for example, all the Windows executable files start with "MZ", all PDF files start with "PDF%", etc.). If we can find the first few bytes of a block in the known database of magic numbers (this can be a simple hash table lookup), we consider such block to be a *strong* file head. Another way to identify a file head is based on the observation that the size of most files is not an exact multiple of block size (4 KB). Because of this, most files end with one or more zeroes. We consider the block that has data, but ends with one or more zeroes to be a file tail, so the block right after that is a *weak* file head. Weak file heads exhibit higher rate of false positives. Information regarding strong and weak heads is sent to the teleporter as an array of bits.

2.4   Compression

The blocks which failed to teleport are compressed before being sent to destination and uncompressed upon arrival. This process further improves network throughput.

2.5   Hash Files

Hash file is a sequence of hashes of disk image blocks written to a disk file (Fig. 3). Hashes in the hash file follow the same order as blocks in the disk image, thus preserving locality of reference. Hash files allow teleporter to save memory by only storing in memory the address of the hash on disk instead of the hash itself. A hash file is 128 times smaller than its disk image.

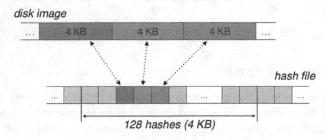

Fig. 3. Hash file.

2.6   Block Sequences

Block sequence is a sequence of blocks that matches between two or more disk images. It often (but not always) corresponds with a file inside a disk image.

Block sequence detection process is shown in Fig. 4. First, source endpoint sends a chain of hashes to the teleporter. Each incoming hash is looked up in the cache until a match is found in a hash file for one of the previously teleported files [❶, ❷]. At this point we can traverse forward both the chain of hashes received from the source and the hashes read sequentially from the hash file [❸]. We continue the traversal until a mismatch is found, thus identifying a sequence of blocks which qualifies for teleportation.

Once a match is found, block sequence can be identified very efficiently. Chain of hashes received from the source is fully in memory. Since a unit of disk I/O is 4 KB, every time teleporter reads from a hash file, 128 hashes are fetched into memory. As a result, block sequence identification works at amortized speed of 128 blocks per single 4 KB disk I/O.

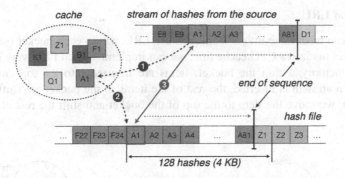

Fig. 4. Extending a match into a block sequence.

2.7 Cuckoo Hashing

We didn't want to use hash table collision resolution algorithm known as separate chaining, because it requires a pointer in each hash table entry, and we didn't want to waste memory on pointers. Instead, we have used an open addressing method of collision resolution known as cuckoo hashing [2]. Cuckoo hashing is shown in Fig. 5. In cuckoo hashing an item can go into one of two locations (determined by two separate hash functions). If both locations are full, item in one of them is kicked into its alternate location. This process is repeated until all the items are placed.

2.8 Cuckoo Hashing with Buckets

Cuckoo hashing works well until a load factor of roughly 49% is reached [3], after which insertions are starting to fail (when a maximum number of displacements was reached, but a vacant slot still wasn't found). In order to improve the load factor, we turn each location into a bucket (see Fig. 6) that can hold up to 4 entries. This enhancement supports load factors as high as 93%.

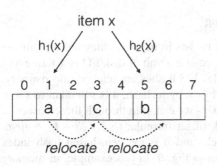

Fig. 5. Cuckoo hashing.

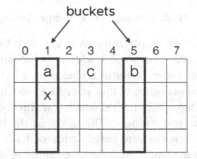

Fig. 6. Cuckoo hashing with buckets.

2.9   Cuckoo LRU

To turn cuckoo hash table into a cache, we use LRU within each bucket (see Fig. 7). Since a bucket fits into a CPU cache line, we can implement such LRU very efficiently by shifting memory within the bucket. Items are inserted into the top entry of the bucket. When an item is inserted, the rest of the items in the bucket are shifted down. On cache hit, we move the item to the top of the bucket and shift the rest of the items down.

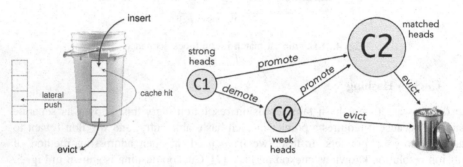

Fig. 7. Cuckoo LRU.   **Fig. 8.** Cache hierarchy.

2.10   Cache Hierarchy

Teleporter uses a hierarchy of three caches (Fig. 8). Only references to the blocks which were identified by the head recognition as a file head (either strong or weak) are added to any of the caches. Strong heads are added to the C1 cache, and weak heads are added to the C0 cache. When a match occurs in either C0 or C1, the cache item is promoted to a long-term C2 cache. When a match occurs in C2, the item is moved to the top of its bucket. When an item is evicted from C1, it is moved to C0 to prolong its lifetime. Cache sizing is discussed in Sect. 3.8.

2.11   Hash File and Disk Image Addressing

Hash files not only allow us to not store block hashes in memory, they aid in compact representation of a block address in memory. Because a unit of disk I/O is 4 KB, every time teleporter performs a read from a hash file, 128 hashes are fetched into memory. As a consequence of this, in order to lookup a block by its hash, it is sufficient to know the group of 128 hashes which contains the hash - we can scan through these hashes to find the one we need. This gives us the block offset formula: $(b * 128 + h) * 4096$, where b is the zero-based index of hash block, and h is the zero-based hash index within the block. Addressing example is shown in Fig. 9. In this example, in-memory address is "2", so we skip 256 hashes in the hash file and scan the next block of 128 hashes. Since the hash with index "1" in the block has matched, we can read the 257th block of the disk image to get the data.

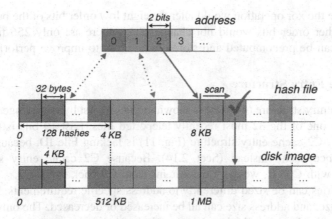

Fig. 9. Hash file addressing.

This approach allows a single bit to address as much as one megabyte of disk space ($2^1 * 128 * 4096$). C0 and C1 cache entries use 19 bits to address up to 256 GB of space. C2 cache entries use 24 bits to address up to 8 TB of space.

2.12 Probabilistic Fingerprints

As described in Sect. 2.6, once we find a match, we can process a sequence of blocks very efficiently. However, until we find a match, we would have to perform a disk read for each cache lookup. Teleporter avoids most of such disk I/O by using probabilistic fingerprints. *Fingerprint* is a small 8-bit hash derived from the 256-bit hash of a block. Fingerprints are stored inside cache items (see Sect. 2.13). When doing lookup, teleporter compares fingerprints first, and if they don't match there is no need to do disk I/O. Since an item can be placed in 8 possible cache locations (two buckets with 4 entries per bucket, Sects. 2.7 and 2.8), probability of a fingerprint collision is 3% ($8/2^8$).

Fingerprints are useful not just for reduction in disk I/O. They also help to implement cuckoo hashing. Cuckoo hashing relies on storing full keys in order to calculate an item's alternate location. Since we store fingerprints instead of full hashes, we utilize the partial-key cuckoo hashing technique [4] to figure out an item's alternate bucket index i_2 from the current bucket index i_1 and the fingerprint stored in this bucket:

$$i_2 = i_1 \oplus hash(fingerprint)$$

The xor operation ($\oplus$) allows to calculate bucket index i_1 from i_2 using the same formula. This allows to relocate an item between buckets without fetching full hash from the hash file. Fingerprint is hashed to help distribute the items more uniformly in the cache. If the fingerprint wasn't hashed, the items kicked out from nearby buckets would land close to each other in the cache. Since we use 8-bit fingerprints, the items kicked out from the bucket would be placed into buckets that are at most 256 buckets away, because the xor operation would alter the eight low order bits of the bucket index while the higher order bits would not change. Since there are only 256 fingerprints, their hashes can be precomputed and stored in an array to improve performance.

2.13   Cache Entry Structure

C0/C1 cache entry structure (4 bytes) is shown in Fig. 10. 1st byte is a fingerprint. Next 5 bits specify one of the 32 most recently teleported files. Last 19 bits is the address inside the file. C2 cache entry structure (Fig. 11) is lacking File ID, because it points into a sequence cache instead (Sect. 2.14). Because C2 cache entry structure is incompatible with C0/C1, we can't evict items from C2 back to C0/C1.

Cache entries can be sized differently to address specific requirements. Fingerprint size, file ID size, and address size can all be increased or decreased. The only limitation is that cuckoo bucket size (16 bytes in our design) must not exceed the cache line (typically 64 bytes). We chose our design to demonstrate that 4-byte entries are quite practical.

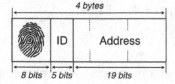

Fig. 10. C0/C1 cache entry.

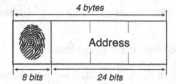

Fig. 11. C2 cache entry.

2.14   Sequence Cache

Sequence cache is an on-disk collection of all the block sequences ever matched for a given destination. Sequence cache consists of a hash file and a data file, and is backing C2 cache. The hash file is located on the teleporter, while the data file is located on the destination. In fact, data blocks are never sent to the teleporter, only directly from the source to the destination. Maximum size of the data file of the sequence cache (8 TB in our setup) is only limited by the amount of disk space addressable by the C2 cache entry (Sect. 2.11). However, most of the blocks in the data file would not use any extra space if destination uses deduplicating storage, because these blocks are also present in one or more disk images located on the destination. Copying matched data into sequence cache allows teleporter to stay performant even if the teleported files are modified or deleted (see Sect. 2.16).

Whenever items are evicted from the C2 cache, corresponding sequences are evicted from the sequence cache. In order to be able to do it, teleporter maintains a sequence bitmap file (each bit represents a sequence cache entry) with sequence starts set to "1".

2.15 Promotion Process

Once a match is found in C0/C1, we promote it to C2. After that we trace two block sequences forward until a mismatch is found. References to the first mismatched blocks are added to C1. Every strong head in the sequence is promoted to C2 as well.

Since C2 cache is backed by the sequence cache, every time a change is made to the C2 cache, corresponding change must be made to the sequence cache. Since promotion from C0/C1 is the only way to add entries into C2, data file of the sequence cache can be updated by copying data locally on the destination from the disk image pointed to by C0/C1.

When adding sequences to the hash file of the sequence cache, teleporter is trying to avoid cases when sequences cross a boundary between 4 KB hash file segments (128 hashes per segment), as this would generate extra reads during C2 matches. Instead, we maintain linked lists of gaps in the hash file - one list per gap size. If the sequence doesn't fit into the remainder of the segment, it is instead written to the beginning of the next segment, and the resulting gap is added to the linked list of the appropriate gap size. If the linked list corresponding to the sequence size is not empty, we fill the gap and remove the entry from the list. Since teleporter does not write sequences to hash file consecutively, it must communicate information about the gaps to the destination endpoint (together with the rest of the match info), so that data blocks could be written to the correct offsets in the data file of the sequence cache.

2.16 Handling Invalidated Blocks

Destination endpoint must be able to handle the case when one of the recently tele-ported files was modified (or even deleted) after teleportation. Note that this is not a problem if the data is reused as a result of a C2 match - in this case block data is copied from the sequence cache, where it couldn't be invalidated. The process that results from a C0/C1 match is shown in Fig. 12.

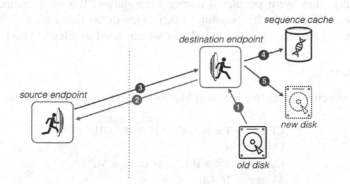

Fig. 12. Handling invalidated blocks.

Destination endpoint computes the hash of each block [❶] it was instructed to reuse, and compares the newly computed hash with the hash it received from the teleporter. If the hashes didn't match (or the file was deleted), destination endpoint requests block data from the source [❷, ❸]. When the data is received, destination endpoint writes it both to the sequence cache [❹], and to the disk image being teleported [❺]. Since most matches happen in C2, overhead of extra hashing in step [❶] is modest.

Note that no communication with the teleporter is required to handle invalidated blocks. When teleporter finds a match in C0 or C1, the matching hash is promoted to C2 (see Sect. 2.15). This is exactly what happens on the destination, whether the block data was invalidated or not.

Destination teleporter requests invalidated blocks in batches and uses the pipelining paradigm (see Sect. 2.1).

2.17   Grain Table Compression

Teleportation matches can come from 32 different recently-teleported sparse files, and keeping their grain tables in memory may consume hundreds of MBs. We have observed guest file systems frequently form long sequential or reverse-sequential ranges of grains. Source endpoint encodes grain tables as a sorted sequence of grain ranges before sending it to the destination endpoint. Such representation is typically hundreds of times more compact. Destination endpoint keeps this compact representation in memory for recently teleported files, and uses binary search when retrieving matched blocks.

3   Evaluation

We have developed a fully functional standalone teleportation prototype in Java and used it to transfer a library of disk images between two laptops using 1 Gbps network. We have placed 30 disk images on the source laptop; the destination laptop contained no disk images. All the caches on the destination (both in-memory and on-disk) were initially empty, they were populated during teleportation. We have compared teleportation vs compression when sending disk images to the destination. When using teleportation, we have compressed the blocks which failed to teleport (Sect. 2.4).

3.1   Platform

All our experiments ran on two identical MacBook Pro laptops using 1 Gbps network:

CPU:	1 x Intel Core i7 @ 2.5 GHz
Cores:	4
Caches:	256 KB L2 (per core), 6 MB L3
Memory:	16 GB
Storage:	1 TB SSD

Storage benchmark (done with Xbench):

Random 4K Read:	41.32 MB/sec (10,578 IOPS)
Sequential Read:	929.68 MB/sec
Sequential Write:	698.74 MB/sec

Note that the storage we tested with is quite slow. For comparison, VMware ESX is able to exceed one million IOPS for a single NVMe device, about 100 times faster than the storage we tested with.

3.2 Disk Image Library

We have obtained 30 thinly-provisioned disk images from another team. Images ranged in size from 4.7 GB to 18.8 GB (9.9 GB on average). We have mimicked real-life image distribution by the operating system (Fig. 13) and by the file system (Fig. 14). Average image size when flattened was 41.5 GB.

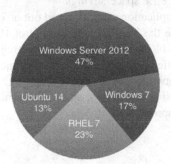

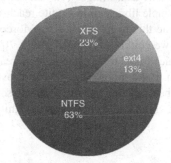

Fig. 13. Disk image library by the operating system.

Fig. 14. Disk image library by the file system.

3.3 Head Recognition

We have manually constructed the database of "magic numbers" based on one Windows and one Linux disk image. Checking for one or two zeroes at the end of a block worked poorly in practice due to an excessive number of false positives (for example, every block containing Unicode text at the end would end with a zero). We have experimentally determined that checking for 5 or more zeroes works well. In our experiments, head recognition reduced memory requirements by 90.4%, while reducing teleportation rate by only 5%.

3.4 Compression

The most commonly used compression algorithm DEFLATE [5] compresses at only 0.6 Gbps, which is too slow for our needs. We have used LZ4 compression algorithm [6]. LZ4 is compressing at the speed of 3.2 Gbps. We have only used 1 thread for compression, but have tested LZ4 compression running on 4 threads running in parallel, with linear increase in performance. LZ4 compression ratio is not as good as DEFLATE - it reduces the typical VM content by about 35%.

3.5   Network Throughput

Teleporter effectiveness depends on the rate of teleportation matches. Fortunately for us, this rate is exactly the same as the rate of storage deduplication for disk images - an area which was extensively studied before. Overlap between pairs of different installations of either Windows or the same distribution of Linux was studied in [7] - it turned out to be roughly 93% regardless of the OS. A different study [8] has applied deduplication to a set of 52 VM disk images (in VMware format) with different operating systems and application environments, and reported space savings of over 80%. Yet another study [9] has analyzed sets of VM disk images across 36 different tenants and concluded that applying deduplication across tenants has resulted in 80% savings. Finally, a VMware study [10] has applied deduplication to a randomly chosen set of 113 VM disk images (1.3 TB) and realized 80% space savings.

Our sample library didn't quite reach 80% deduplication rate, it maxed out at 75%. We attribute this to its small size. Moreover, since the head recognition is not 100% effective, we could only match about 70% of the blocks. However, compressing the blocks which failed to teleport have increased the effective teleportation rate (defined as "reduction in the amount of data sent over the network") up to 80.7% (see Fig. 15). This number includes the overhead of sending hashes, bit arrays, sparse file headers, etc. When compared to compression, this is an improvement of 3.4x.

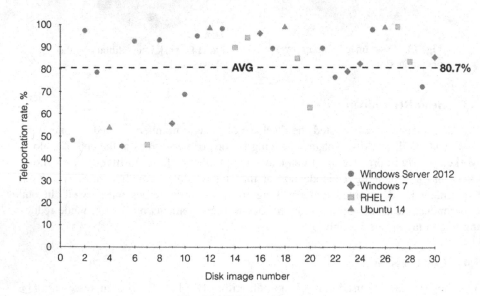

Fig. 15. Teleportation rate.

3.6   Hashing Performance

Out of 256-bit cryptographic hashes we chose BLAKE2 [11], because it is optimized for speed in software (as opposed to hardware). BLAKE2b is further optimized for 64-bit platforms. BLAKE2b operates at 7.12 Gbps, which was fast enough for our needs. We have only used 1 thread for hashing, but have tested BLAKE2b running on 4 threads in parallel, with linear increase in performance.

3.7   Disk I/O Amplification

Strong and weak heads combined represent approximately 10% of all blocks, the rest of the blocks are not looked up in the cache. First, let's look at the worst case - no blocks got matched. 3% of the unsuccessful lookups generate one unnecessary disk read. Since we lookup 10% of the blocks, completely unsuccessful teleportation would generate 0.3% read amplification. Next, let's look at the best case - all blocks got matched. In our experiments we have observed that the length of the average teleported sequence is 86 blocks (we are fairly confident in this number, as it strongly correlates with the average file size in the guest file system). Completely successful teleportation would generate $100/86 = 1.16\%$ read amplification.

In summary, teleporter produces between 0.3% and 1.16% read amplification, closer to the upper bound for datasets which teleport better and closer to the lower bound for datasets which teleport worse. Teleporter writes out hashes for every transferred 4 KB block, which is 0.78% write amplification.

3.8   Memory Footprint

Comparing to the conventional LRU implementation with double-linked lists, Cuckoo LRU (Sect. 2.9) allowed us to save three 8-byte pointers per cache entry. In combination with hash file addressing (Sect. 2.11), and 1-byte fingerprint replacing 32-byte hash, this allowed us to use 15x less memory per cache entry (4 bytes instead of 60 bytes).

The size of the short-term caches (C0, C1) is a largely driven by head recognition filtering out 90.4% of the hashes (see Sect. 3.3) and the fact that only teleportation failures (30%, see Sect. 3.5) remain in short-term caches. Teleporting 100 GB of disk image data would only fill 2.88 MB of short-term cache memory. Our prototype has used 4 MB for C1 and 12 MB for C0. Without the techniques we proposed, short-term caches would occupy $10 * 15 = 150x$ more memory.

Since the long-term cache C2 only contains sequences, its size is a factor of an average sequence length. In our experiments average sequence length was 86 blocks (Sect. 3.7), so in order to support 8 TB sequence cache (Sect. 2.14) using 93 MB for the C2 cache would be sufficient. Our prototype has used 16 MB for C2. Without the techniques we proposed, C2 cache would occupy $86 * 15 = 1,290x$ more memory.

Together, our caches have occupied $(1290 + 150)/2 = 720x$ less memory than a conventional implementation, or 32 MB instead of 23 GB. Such a dramatic decrease in memory footprint is what makes teleportation commercially viable.

3.9 Transfer Speed

Our test environment had atypically fast network (we used 1 Gbps LAN instead of a WAN), and atypically slow storage (see Sect. 3.1). In our experiments, teleportation has reduced network traffic enough that writing blocks to disk at the destination became a bottleneck and capped potential gains in copy time. We did teleportation in two phases. During the 1st phase ("network"), data stream that failed to teleport was written (while still compressed) to a delta file on the destination, and match info was written into a write-ahead log on the destination. During the 2nd phase ("merge"), teleported file was assembled from the delta file and the sequence cache. We have measured the network phase time separately from the total time. Network phase of teleporting our sample disk image library (Fig. 16, gray) was 4 times faster than a regular network copy. Full teleportation (Fig. 16, orange) was twice faster than a network copy and 24% faster than compression.

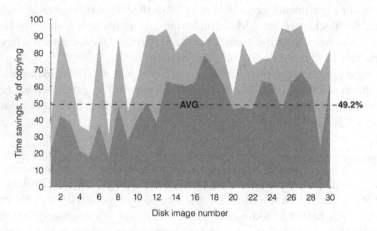

Fig. 16. Time savings: network phase (gray) and total (orange). (Color figure online)

We estimate that in a typical scenario storage is fast enough that even when sending several times less data over the network, network would remain a bottleneck. If this is the case, we expect teleportation to be up to 3.4x faster than compression and up to 5x faster than a regular network copy (see Sect. 3.5).

4   Related Work

Rsync [12] was one of the inspirations for us. Rsync starts with identifying two files a and b which are likely to be different versions of the same file. Rsync then hashes 4 KB segments of file a and uses a rolling checksum to find them in file b. Rolling checksum is guarding against inserting or removing bytes near the start of the file.

LBFS [13] builds on the ideas of Rsync and extends them to a file system. LBFS divides the files into variable-size chunks using Rabin fingerprints and indexes the chunks by hash value. LBFS is geared towards networks slower than 10 Mbps.

More recently, a number of papers [18–21] were written on the topic of using compare-by-hash to improve transfers of VMs over a WAN. To the best of our knowledge, we are the first to call attention to the memory footprint of such systems. The techniques we proposed allowed us to reduce the memory footprint by a factor of 720x (Sect. 3.8), while keeping disk I/O amplification (Sect. 3.7) under 2%.

Valerie Aurora has suggested in [14] that compare-by-hash should not be used for certain applications, such as file systems (but applications like Rsync are OK). Valerie's paper is using SHA-1 hash as an example. Rebuttal paper [15] was published specifically to addresses Valerie's concerns. Many papers [12, 13, 16, 19] were written with an explicit assumption to ignore cryptographic hash collisions.

We further address compare-by-hash concerns by using a stronger hash - 256-bit BLAKE2 [11] is 2^{96} times stronger than SHA-1. For the cache sizes we are proposing (up to 2^{28} entries), collisions in 256-bit hashes reduce teleporter reliability only down to 99.99999999999999999999999999992% (32 nines), which favorably compares to reliability guarantee of Amazon's AWS S3 of 99.9999999991 (11 nines) [17].

5 Conclusion

In this paper we have shown that teleportation can improve network throughput of VM transfers over WAN by a factor of 3.4x (when comparing to compression). In addition to the use cases of edge computing and hybrid clouds, teleportation would improve VM mobility across clusters and datacenters, large-scale load-balancing, hardware upgrades (including whole datacenter upgrades and datacenters with shared-nothing storage architectures), and disaster preparedness testing. Teleportation would also improve use cases when VMs are not transferred live, such as VM template distribution, onboarding and backup/restore.

References

1. VMware Virtual Disk Format 5.0. https://www.vmware.com/support/developer/vddk/vmdk_50_technote.pdf. Accessed 26 Dec 2018
2. Pagh, R., Rodler, F.: Cuckoo hashing. J. Algorithms 2, 122–144 (2004)
3. Erlingsson, U., Manasse, M., Mcsherry, F.: A cool and practical alternative to traditional hash tables. In: Proceedings of 7th Workshop on Distributed Data and Structures (2006)
4. Fan, B., Andersen, D.G., Kaminsky, M., Mitzenmacher, M.D.: Cuckoo filter: practically better than Bloom. In: Proceedings of the 10th ACM International on Conference on Emerging Networking Experiments and Technologies, pp. 75–88. ACM (2014)
5. Deutsch, P.: DEFLATE Compressed Data Format Specification version 1.3. https://tools.ietf.org/html/rfc1951. Accessed 26 Dec 2018
6. LZ4 - Extremely fast compression. http://www.lz4.org. Accessed 26 Dec 2018
7. Liguori, A., Van Hensbergen, E.: Experiences with content addressable storage and virtual disks. In: Proceedings of the First Workshop on I/O Virtualization (2008)

8. Jin, K., Miller, E.: The effectiveness of deduplication on virtual machine disk images. In: Proceedings of SYSTOR 2009: The Israeli Experimental Systems Conference (2009)
9. Nath, P., Kozuch, M., O'Hallaron, D., Harkes, J., Satyanarayanan, M.: Design tradeoffs in applying content addressable storage to enterprise-scale systems based on virtual machines. In: Proceedings of the 2006 USENIX Annual Technical Conference (2006)
10. Clements, A., Ahmad, I., Vilayannur, M., Li, J.: Decentralized deduplication in SAN cluster file systems. In: Proceedings of USENIX Annual Technical Conference (2009)
11. Aumasson, J.-P., Neves, S., Wilcox-O'Hearn, Z., Winnerlein, C.: BLAKE2: simpler, smaller, fast as MD5. In: Jacobson, M., Locasto, M., Mohassel, P., Safavi-Naini, R. (eds.) ACNS 2013. LNCS, vol. 7954, pp. 119–135. Springer, Heidelberg (2013). https://doi.org/10.1007/978-3-642-38980-1_8
12. Tridgell, A., Mackerras, P.: The Rsync algorithm. In: Technical Report TR-CS-96-05, Department of Computer Science, The Australian National University, Canberra (1996)
13. Muthitacharoen, A., Chen, B., Mazieres, D.: A low-bandwidth network file system. In: Proceedings of 18th ACM Symposium Operating Systems Principles. ACM Press (2001)
14. Henson, V.: An analysis of compare-by-hash. In: Workshop on Hot Topics in Operating Systems (HotOS) (2003)
15. Black, J.: Compare-by-hash: a reasoned analysis. In: Proceedings of the Systems and Experience Track: 2006 USENIX Annual Technical Conference (2006)
16. Quinlan, S., Dorward, S.: Venti: a new approach to archival storage. In: Proceedings of the USENIX Conference on File And Storage Technologies (FAST) (2002)
17. Amazon S3 Storage Classes. https://aws.amazon.com/s3/storage-classes/. Accessed 26 Dec 2018
18. Zhang, X., Huo, Z., Ma, J., Meng, D.: Exploiting data deduplication to accelerate live virtual machine migration. In: IEEE International Conference on Cluster Computing (2010)
19. Riteau, P., Morin, C., Priol, T.: Shrinker: improving live migration of virtual clusters over WANs with distributed data deduplication and content-based addressing. In: Jeannot, E., Namyst, R., Roman, J. (eds.) Euro-Par 2011. LNCS, vol. 6852, pp. 431–442. Springer, Heidelberg (2011). https://doi.org/10.1007/978-3-642-23400-2_40
20. Wood, T., et al.: CloudNet: dynamic pooling of cloud resources by live WAN migration of virtual machines. IEEE/ACM Trans. Netw. 23, 1568–1583 (2015)
21. Ha, K., et al.: You can teach elephants to dance: agile VM handoff for edge computing. In: Proceedings of the Second ACM/IEEE Symposium on Edge Computing (2017)

Live Migration of Virtual Machines in OpenStack: A Perspective from Reliability Evaluation

Jin Hao[1], Kejiang Ye[1(✉)], and Cheng-Zhong Xu[2]

[1] Shenzhen Institutes of Advanced Technology, Chinese Academy of Sciences,
Shenzhen 518055, China
{jin.hao,kj.ye}@siat.ac.cn

[2] Faculty of Science and Technology, University of Macau, Taipa, Macao,
Special Administrative Region of China
czxu@um.edu.mo

Abstract. Virtualization technology is widely used in cloud data centers and today's IT infrastructure. A key technology for server virtualization is the live migration of virtual machines (VMs). This technology allows VMs to be moved from one physical host to another while minimizing service downtime. The cloud providers usually use cloud operating system for virtual machine management. Currently the most widely used open source cloud operating system is OpenStack. In this paper, we investigate the reliability of VM live migration in OpenStack by increasing the system pressures and injecting network failures during the migration. We analyze the impact of these pressures and failures on the performance of VM live migration. The experimental results can be used to guide data center administrators in migration decisions and fault localization. Furthermore, it can help researchers to find bottlenecks and optimization methods for live migration in OpenStack.

Keywords: OpenStack · Virtual machines · Live migration · Reliability

1 Introduction

Cloud computing is a computing paradigm that provides virtualized computing resources to customers in the form of services over the Internet [1]. In typical cloud data centers, virtualization technology is usually used to achieve efficient resource utilization, faster configuration, lower power consumption, and higher service reliability. Currently, famous cloud service providers include Google, Amazon, Microsoft, Alibaba, and so on [2]. They all have their own cloud management platforms. Due to the expensive commercial licensing fee, small businesses usually choose OpenStack - an open source and free framework, to build their cloud platforms [3, 4]. Whether it is a large cloud computing provider or a small business, they usually use VM live migration technology to ensure the Quality of Service (QoS).

VM live migration is costly [5], which consumes both hardware resources and network bandwidth. Before the data center administrator performs VM migration, it is necessary to decide which VMs to migrate, how to reduce the migration cost and how to increase the migration success rate.

© Springer Nature Switzerland AG 2019
D. Da Silva et al. (Eds.): CLOUD 2019, LNCS 11513, pp. 99–113, 2019.
https://doi.org/10.1007/978-3-030-23502-4_8

Understanding the migration performance under system pressures and network failures is necessary to achieve the above goals. The total migration time depends on the activity of the VMs [6]. If the VM is very active and memory intensive, the migration process may take longer time to transfer the VM's state data. Different CPU usage, memory usage, and disk usage can result in different migration performance.

In this paper, we investigate the reliability of VM live migration in OpenStack by increasing the system pressures during the migration. We experimented with idle VMs and loaded VMs to find how much impact the system pressures have. In addition, the network can have a high impact on migration performance [7], so we also simulated several network failures such as packet delay, packet loss, packet duplication, and packet corruption to determine the impact of network failures on migration performance. The experimental results can be used to guide data center administrators in migration decisions and fault localization. Furthermore, it can help researchers to find bottlenecks and optimization methods for live migration in OpenStack.

The rest of this paper is organized as follows: Sect. 2 introduces the background and performance metrics of VM live migration, and summarizes the measurement methods; Sect. 3 describes our experimental testbed and test process; Sect. 4 presents the experiment results; Finally, we conclude the paper in Sect. 5.

2 Related Work

VM migration is the process of moving a VM from one physical machine to another. There are two different approaches for VM migration [8], static migration and live migration. In static migration, the VM is shut down at the source host. After the VM is moved to the target host, it will be restarted at the target host. In the whole migration process, the VM will keep running while moving the VM from the source host to the target host. One of the advantages of live migration is that the short downtime of the VM, which is close to zero [5, 9], guaranteeing the Service Level Agreements (SLAs).

In data centers, live migration facilitates load balancing, online maintenance and power management, which are summarized as below [2, 8]:

(i)   **Load balancing.** It can alleviate overloaded physical machines by migrating VMs to underutilized physical machines.
(ii) **Online maintenance.** Migrating VMs out from physical machines that are about to fail, the administrators can maintain or upgrade the hardware and software.
(iii) **Power management.** Concentrating VMs into a small number of physical machines can shut down unnecessary physical machines and save power.

During the last several years, researchers have implemented various live migration algorithms, such as pre-copy, post-copy [9, 10], etc. The original pre-copy technology has poor performance and the migration takes a long time. Jin et al. [11, 12] designed a feature-based compression algorithm that speeds up memory page transfers. Zhang et al. [13] used the similarity within VMs to remove duplicate pages during VM migration, which also speeds up migration. Huang et al. [14] used Remote Direct Memory Access (RDMA) to reduce the side effects of VM migration and improve migration performance. The post-copy technology firstly transfers the necessary VM states to the target host, which avoids the migration convergence problem of pre-copy [8]. This method can reduce the page errors that may occur after VM switching. Hines et al. [15] designed four optimization mechanisms to reduce page faults and total migration time: demand-paging, active pushing, prepaging, and dynamic self-ballooning. Shribman and Hudzia [16] designed three optimization measures to reduce the degradation of QoS caused by remote access to memory pages: RDMA, pre-paging and Linux Memory Management Unit (MMU) Integration.

In recent years, VM migration technology continues to evolve. Forsman et al. [17] designed an automatic VM live migration algorithm that enables automatic load balancing. Liu et al. [18] quantitatively predicted VM migration performance and energy costs, which can reduce migration costs. Ye et al. [19] considered different resource reservation mechanisms, then proposed corresponding optimization methods to improve migration efficiency. They also studied the live migration strategy of virtual machine clusters and proposed several optimization principles to improve the migration performance of the cluster [20]. Besides, they designed a profiling-based server consolidation framework that saves energy and reduces workload performance degradation caused by VM migration [22]. Beloglazov and Buyya [21] designed the OpenStack Neat framework for dynamic VM consolidation, which can be used to save energy. Sun et al. [23] focused on live migration of multiple virtual machines and proposed a hybrid migration strategy. Duggan et al. [24] proposed a live migration strategy for autonomous network perception, which is based on reinforcement learning and can improve the performance of cloud computing systems.

However, all of the above work focuses on the migration techniques or algorithm optimization. Different from the above work, we study the impact of system pressures and network failures on the live migration performance from the reliability perspective. The experimental results can guide the data center administrators to make better migration decisions, thereby improving migration efficiency in OpenStack.

3   Experiment Design

In this section, we introduce the testbed environment, including the hardware configuration of the physical machines, the network device, and the configuration of the virtual machines. We also present the simulation methods of system pressures and network failures. Then we select metrics for evaluating migration performance. In addition, the design of the benchmarking architecture will be also described. Finally, the entire experimental process will be explained.

3.1   Testbed

Our testbed is composed of four Dell SuperCloud R5210G10 physical servers, including one controller node, one storage node, and two compute nodes. The detailed configuration of the servers is shown in Table 1. Four servers are connected by a 1 Gbps switch. The operating system on the servers is Ubuntu Server 16.04 and the kernel version is 4.4.0–130-generic. OpenStack is deployed on the servers to perform live migration based on post-copy technique. The latest release of OpenStack is Rocky, here we choose the stable version which is named Queens [27]. OpenStack supports virtualization hypervisors such as KVM, QEMU, Xen, and VMware to manage VMs. We use KVM as the virtualization hypervisor in our experiment.

Table 1. Server specification

Server Model	Dell SuperCloud R5210G10
CPU	2x Intel XEONE5-2630V3 8core 2.40 GHz
Memory	64 GB DDR4 R-ECC 2133 MHz
Disk	4x 4 TB SATA 7200 rpm
NIC	1Gbps

OpenStack has five different default flavors (type templates): tiny, small, medium, large, and xlarge. Their vCPU, memory, and disk are gradually increased, as shown in Table 2. Note that the disk of tiny flavor is too small, so we changed the disk to 5 GB. Otherwise, we couldn't install Ubuntu Server 16.04 system in the flavor.

At first, we will test the performances of the live migration with different flavors in idle status. The results can help us find out the relationship between flavors and migration performances. Next, the small flavor will be used to do a series of experiments. The small flavor has 1 vCPU, 2G memory, and 20G disk. Ubuntu Server 16.04 with kernel version 4.4.0-130-generic has been installed in the VM.

Table 2. Default flavors

Flavor	vCPUs	RAM	Disk
tiny	1	0.5 GB	1 GB
small	1	2 GB	20 GB
medium	2	4 GB	40 GB
large	4	8 GB	80 GB
xlarge	8	16 GB	160 GB

During the migration, *stress-ng* is used to simulate system pressures on the VM [28]. System pressures are categorized by the resources consumed: CPU pressure, memory pressure, and disk pressure. We use *tc-netem* to simulate network failures on physical machines [29]. Network failures are classified into packet delay, packet loss, packet duplication, and packet corruption. The performance metrics of different system pressures and network failures during live migration are obtained through multiple experiments.

3.2 Metrics

To evaluate live migration performance, there are four typically metrics [8, 25, 26] for selecting: downtime, total migration time, migrated data amount, and service performance degradation. They cover the main performance metrics for live migration.

Downtime represents the time of service interruption. Total migration time represents the entire duration from the beginning to the end of the migration. Migrated data amount represents network traffic consumption. Service performance degradation indicates how the services running in the migrated VM are affected by the migration, which can be measured by throughput or response time.

This paper mainly focuses on the impact of system pressures and network failures on migration performance, which is from the system perspective. The first three metrics are used in this paper. We use the methods designed by Huang et al. [25] to measure the performance metrics.

Downtime. The VM is pinged during migration and the downtime is equal to the time the packet was lost [6].

Total Migration Time. Measures the duration by the OpenStack migration log.

Migrated Data Amount. Monitors the total amount of data transferred over the TCP port dedicated to migration.

3.3 Benchmarking Architecture

Our benchmarking architecture is shown in Fig. 1. Network File System (NFS) is installed in the storage node to store VM images and virtual disks, and all nodes share NFS. During the migration, the controller node keeps pinging the VM, controlling the interval of pings to get the downtime. It should be noted that VM live migration and performance testing occupy different network cards to avoid interference.

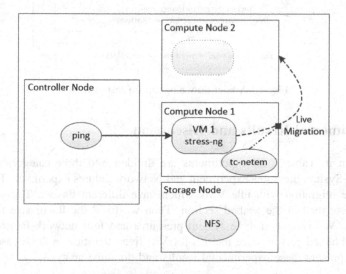

Fig. 1. Benchmarking architecture

3.4   Test Process

A complete test process consists of a number of iterations, as shown in Fig. 2. If the environment is ready, we start the VM. Then we configure and start *stress-ng* on the virtual machine when simulating system pressures. After that, we configure and start *tc-netem* in the compute nodes when simulating network failures. It should be noted that only one system pressure or network failure is simulated at one time, and other conditions remain the default. Next, we launch ping script to monitor downtime at the controller node. Meanwhile, we start *iptraf-ng* to monitor the amount of data transferred at two compute nodes. Once all the monitoring scripts are launched, we can start VM live migration. When the migration is completed, we record the tested performance metrics from measurement scripts and the above tools. Finally, we clean up the experimental environment so we can continue to do the next experiment.

In addition, we will repeat one experiment three times and choose the median value as the final performance.

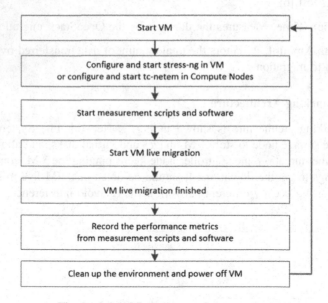

Fig. 2. A brief flow diagram for test process

4   Experimental Results and Discussion

As is shown in Table 3, all experiments are divided into three categories: Flavors experiment, System pressures experiment and Network failures experiment. Firstly, we perform live migration with idle VMs which have different flavors. The size of the flavors is described in the testbed section. Then we fixed the flavor size to do next experiments. We simulated three system pressures and four network failures. Meanwhile, we obtained performance metrics for VM live migration in these cases. In this section, we present these experimental results and do some analysis.

Table 3. Experiment categories

Category	Name	Brief Description
Flavors	Flavors	Live migration with different flavor sizes
System pressures	CPU pressure	Live migration with different CPU usages
	Memory pressure	Live migration with different Memory usages
	Disk pressure	Live migration with different write processes
Network failures	Packet delay	Live migration with different packet delay
	Packet loss	Live migration with different packet loss
	Packet duplication	Live migration with different packet duplication
	Packet corruption	Live migration with different packet corruption

4.1 Different Flavors

Figure 3 and 4 show the migration performance effects with different flavor sizes. As the size of the flavor increases, the total migration time increases. Tiny flavor has the longest downtime, and others have the downtime between 10 ms and 70 ms. It is because the tiny flavor's memory is too small to run Ubuntu Server 16.04, and the memory activity is very intensive. Note that the amount of migrated data also increases, and the data transferred into target machine is always 2 to 6 MB more than the data transferred out of source machine. It is because the migration may generate some additional data, such as packet retransmission data.

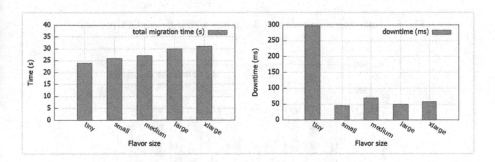

Fig. 3. Total migration time and downtime with different flavor sizes

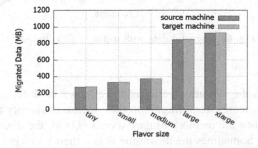

Fig. 4. Migrated data with different flavor sizes

4.2 System Pressures

CPU Pressure

The CPU pressure experiment and following experiments use the small type of flavor which has 1 vCPU, 2 GB memory and 20 GB disk.

Figure 5 and 6 illustrate the migration performance effects with different CPU usages. As the CPU usage increases, the total migration time does not change significantly. Downtime is generally between 200 ms and 400 ms after CPU usage is greater than 30%. The amount of migrated data doesn't change too much.

Note that there are some cases that OpenStack shows successful migration information, but the downtime is very long (greater than 600 s). As those cases happened very rarely, we consider the cases to be anomalies and will redo the experiment to remove these outliers.

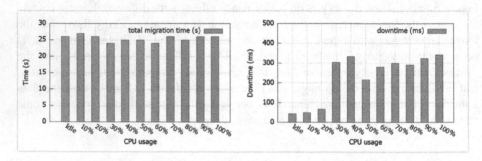

Fig. 5. Total migration time and downtime with different CPU usages

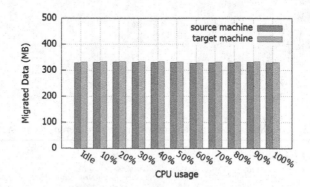

Fig. 6. Migrated data with different CPU usages

Memory Pressure

Figures 7 and 8 show the migration performance effects with different Memory usages. As memory usage increases, total migration time increases sharply and the downtime also keeps rising. When the memory usage exceeds 600 M, the downtime is generally between 3 s and 7 s. Sometimes the downtime is less than 1 s or greater than 30 s. We repeat the experiments for three times, Fig. 7 shows the median results of repeated experiments. The amount of migrated data also increases sharply, and the order of magnitude becomes GB. When the memory occupies 1600 MB, total migration time is longer than 1000 s, migrated data amount is larger than 120 GB, and the difference between the data transferred into target machine and the data transferred out of source machine is about 700 MB.

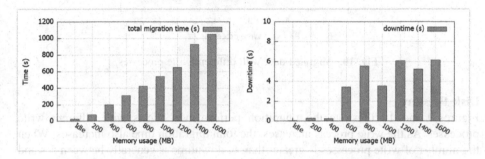

Fig. 7. Total migration time and downtime with different Memory usages

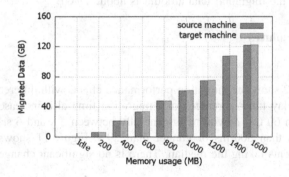

Fig. 8. Migrated data with different memory usages

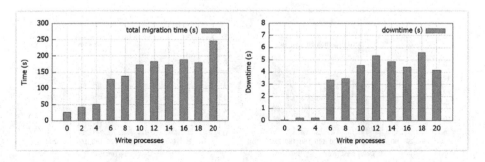

Fig. 9. Total migration time and downtime with different write processes

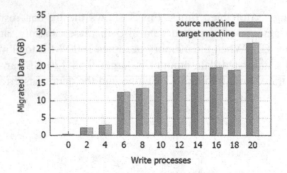

Fig. 10. Migrated data with different write processes

Disk Pressure

Figures 9 and 10 illustrate the migration performance effects with different write processes. As the write process increases, the total migration time also increases. When the number of write processes is greater than 6, downtime is generally between 3 s and 6 s. The amount of migrated data amount keeps increasing and the order of magnitude becomes GB. When the number of write processes is 20, the total migration time is about 250 s, and the migration data amount is about 27 GB.

4.3 Network Failures

Packet Delay

Figures 11 and 12 show the migration performance effects with different packet delay. As the packet delay time increases, total migration time also increases. When delay time is more than 60 ms, downtime is generally between 3 s and 6 s. Sometimes the downtime is less than 500 ms or greater than 20 s. Figure 11 shows the results of multiple experiments taking the median. There is no significant change in the amount of data migrated.

Besides, in packet delay experiments, the frequency of VM crashes (downtime greater than 600 s) is higher than CPU, memory, and disk experiments.

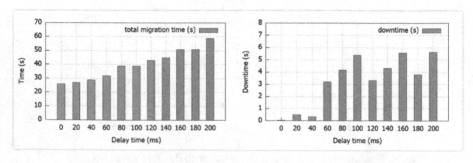

Fig. 11. Total migration time and downtime with different packet delay

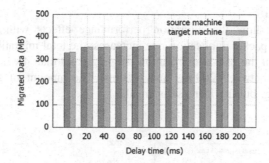

Fig. 12. Migrated data with different packet delay

Packet Loss

Figure 13 and 14 show the migration performance effects with different packet loss. As the packet loss rate increases, the total migration time and downtime also increases significantly. After the packet loss rate is greater than 6%, the downtime is generally greater than 10 s. When the packet loss rate is equal to 10%, the migration time is close to 400 s and the downtime is about 68 s. The amount of migrated data has not changed too much.

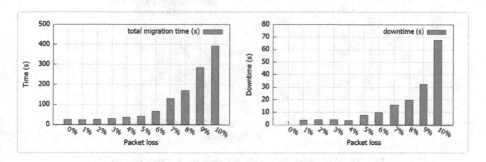

Fig. 13. Total migration time and downtime with different packet loss

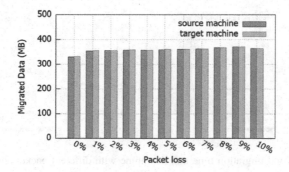

Fig. 14. Migrated data with different packet loss

Packet Duplication

Figure 15 and 16 show the migration performance effects with different packet duplication. As the packet duplication rate increases, the total migration time does not change much. When the packet duplication rate is greater than 40%, the downtime is slightly increased, between 200 ms and 600 ms. The amount of migrated data is gradually increasing, but the increase is small.

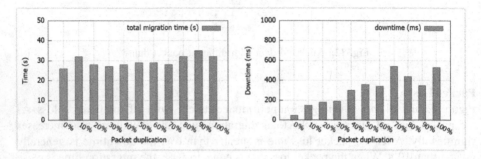

Fig. 15. Total migration time and downtime with different packet duplication

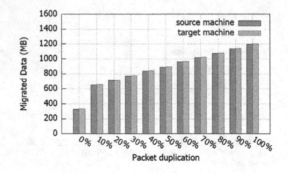

Fig. 16. Migrated data with different packet duplication

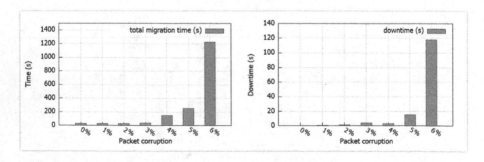

Fig. 17. Total migration time and downtime with different packet corruption

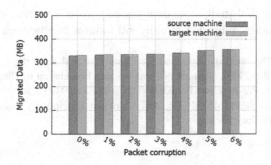

Fig. 18. Migrated data with different packet corruption

Packet Corruption

Figure 17 and 18 illustrate the migration performance effects with different packet corruption. After the packet corruption rate is greater than 3%, the total migration time will increase dramatically. The downtime is generally greater than 1 s, and the overall trend is upward. The downtime mutation occurs when the packet corruption rate is equal to 5% and 6%. There was no significant change in the amount of data migrated. When the packet corruption rate is equal to 6%, the migration time exceeds 20 min and the downtime is close to 120 s.

Moreover, in our experiments, when the packet corruption rate is greater than or equal to 7%, the migration failed. The migration has not been completed in 1600 s, and OpenStack will automatically cancel the migration. Another interesting phenomenon is that only 49152 port is used in normal migration. In the case of packet corruption, ports 49153-49216 are used to assist in data transmission.

5 Conclusion and Future Work

From the above results, we can make some suggestions to improve the efficiency of migration in OpenStack: (**I**) Selecting a smaller flavor can reduce migration time and migrated data amount. (**ii**) Basically, CPU usage is not a key metric in migration because it has little impact on migration performance. (**iii**) Selecting a VM with a small memory usage can reduce migration time, downtime, and migrated data amount. (**iv**) Selecting a VM with fewer disk write processes can reduce the migration time, downtime, and migrated data amount. (**v**) Packet delay will slightly increase migration time, with little impact on downtime and migrated data amount. (**vi**) Packet loss will dramatically increase migration time, with little impact on downtime and migrated data amount. (**vii**) Packet duplication will increase the amount of migrated data, and has little impact on migration time and downtime. (**viii**) When the package corruption rate is less than or equal to 3%, the impact on migration can be ignored. After the packet corruption rate is greater than 4%, the migration time and downtime will increase very sharply. When the packet corruption rate is greater than 7%, the migration will fail in our experimental environment.

In the future, we will study more complex migration scenarios, such as migration with non-shared storage, migration with hybrid failures injection, etc.

Acknowledgment. This work is supported by China National Basic Research Program (973 Program, No. 2015CB352400), National Natural Science Foundation of China (No. 61702492, 61572487), Equipment Pre-Research Foundation (No. 61400020403), Shenzhen Basic Research Program (No. JCYJ20180302145731531), and Shenzhen Discipline Construction Project for Urban Computing and Data Intelligence.

References

1. Mell, P., Grance, T.: The NIST definition of cloud computing, 1–3 (2011). https://nvlpubs. nist.gov/nistpubs/Legacy/SP/nistspecialpublication800-145.pdf
2. Choudhary, A., Govil, M.C., Singh, G., et al.: A critical survey of live virtual machine migration techniques. J. Cloud Comput. **6**(1), 23 (2017)
3. Sefraoui, O., Aissaoui, M., Eleuldj, M.: OpenStack: toward an open-source solution for cloud computing. Int. J. Comput. Appl. **55**(3), 38–42 (2012)
4. OpenStack Cloud (2019). http://www.openstack.org/
5. Voorsluys, W., Broberg, J., Venugopal, S., Buyya, R.: Cost of virtual machine live migration in clouds: a performance evaluation. In: Jaatun, M.G., Zhao, G., Rong, C. (eds.) CloudCom 2009. LNCS, vol. 5931, pp. 254–265. Springer, Heidelberg (2009). https://doi.org/10.1007/978-3-642-10665-1_23
6. Hu, W., Hicks, A., Zhang, L., et al.: A quantitative study of virtual machine live migration. In: Proceedings of the 2013 ACM Cloud and Autonomic Computing Conference, p. 11. ACM (2013)
7. Akoush, S., Sohan, R., Rice, A., et al.: Predicting the performance of virtual machine migration. In: 18th IEEE/ACM International Symposium on Modelling, Analysis & Simulation of Computer and Telecommunication Systems (MASCOTS 2010), pp. 37–46. IEEE (2010)
8. Zhang, F., Liu, G., Fu, X., et al.: A survey on virtual machine migration: challenges, techniques, and open issues. IEEE Commun. Surv. Tutorials **20**(2), 1206–1243 (2018)
9. Clark, C., Fraser, K., Hand, S., et al.: Live migration of virtual machines. In: Proceedings of the 2nd Conference on Symposium on Networked Systems Design & Implementation, vol. 2, pp. 273–286. USENIX Association (2005)
10. Hines, M.R., Deshpande, U., Gopalan, K.: Post-copy live migration of virtual machines. ACM SIGOPS Oper. Syst. Rev. **43**(3), 14–26 (2009)
11. Jin, H., Deng, L., Wu, S., et al.: Live virtual machine migration with adaptive, memory compression. In: 2009 IEEE International Conference on Cluster Computing and Workshops, pp. 1–10. IEEE (2009)
12. Jin, H., Deng, L., Wu, S., et al.: MECOM: live migration of virtual machines by adaptively compressing memory pages. Future Gener. Comput. Syst. **38**, 23–35 (2014)
13. Zhang, X., Huo, Z., Ma, J., et al.: Exploiting data deduplication to accelerate live virtual machine migration. In: 2010 IEEE International Conference on Cluster Computing, pp. 88–96. IEEE (2010)
14. Huang, W., Gao, Q., Liu, J., et al.: High performance virtual machine migration with RDMA over modern interconnects. In: 2007 IEEE International Conference on Cluster Computing, pp. 11–20. IEEE (2007)

15. Hines, M.R., Gopalan, K.: Post-copy based live virtual machine migration using adaptive pre-paging and dynamic self-ballooning. In: Proceedings of the 2009 ACM SIGPLAN/SIGOPS International Conference on Virtual Execution Environments, pp. 51–60. ACM (2009)
16. Shribman, A., Hudzia, B.: Pre-copy and post-copy VM live migration for memory intensive applications. In: Caragiannis, I., et al. (eds.) Euro-Par 2012. LNCS, vol. 7640, pp. 539–547. Springer, Heidelberg (2013). https://doi.org/10.1007/978-3-642-36949-0_63
17. Forsman, M., Glad, A., Lundberg, L., et al.: Algorithms for automated live migration of virtual machines. J. Syst. Softw. **101**, 110–126 (2015)
18. Liu, H., Xu, C.Z., Jin, H., et al.: Performance and energy modeling for live migration of virtual machines. In: Proceedings of the 20th International Symposium on High Performance Distributed Computing, pp. 171–182. ACM (2011)
19. Ye, K., Jiang, X., Huang, D., et al.: Live migration of multiple virtual machines with resource reservation in cloud computing environments. In: 2011 IEEE 4th International Conference on Cloud Computing, pp. 267–274. IEEE, 2011
20. Ye, K., Jiang, X., Ma, R., et al.; VC-migration: live migration of virtual clusters in the cloud. In: Proceedings of the 2012 ACM/IEEE 13th International Conference on Grid Computing, pp. 209–218. IEEE Computer Society (2012)
21. Beloglazov, A., Buyya, R.: OpenStack Neat: a framework for dynamic and energy-efficient consolidation of virtual machines in OpenStack clouds. Concurrency Comput. Pract. Experience **27**(5), 1310–1333 (2015)
22. Ye, K., Wu, Z., Wang, C., et al.: Profiling-based workload consolidation and migration in virtualized data centers. IEEE Trans. Parallel Distrib. Syst. **26**(3), 878–890 (2015)
23. Sun, G., Liao, D., Anand, V., et al.: A new technique for efficient live migration of multiple virtual machines. Future Gener. Comput. Syst. **55**, 74–86 (2016)
24. Duggan, M., Duggan, J., Howley, E., et al.: A network aware approach for the scheduling of virtual machine migration during peak loads. Cluster Comput. **20**(3), 2083–2094 (2017)
25. Huang, D., Ye, D., He, Q., et al.: Virt-LM: a benchmark for live migration of virtual machine. ACM SIGSOFT Software Eng. Notes **36**(5), 307–316 (2011)
26. Galloway, M., Loewen, G., Vrbsky, S.: Performance metrics of virtual machine live migration. In: 2015 IEEE 8th International Conference on Cloud Computing (CLOUD), pp. 637–644. IEEE (2015)
27. OpenStack Queens (2019). https://docs.openstack.org/queens/index.html
28. Stress-ng (2019). https://kernel.ubuntu.com/~cking/stress-ng/
29. Netem (2019). https://wiki.linuxfoundation.org/networking/netem

An Approach to Failure Prediction in Cluster by Self-updating Cause-and-Effect Graph

Yan Yu and Haopeng Chen[✉]

Shanghai Jiaotong University, Shanghai, China
chen-hp@sjtu.edu.cn

Abstract. Cluster systems have been widely used in cloud computing, high-performance computing, and other fields, and the usage and scale of cluster systems have shown a sharp upward trend. Unfortunately, the larger cluster systems are more prone to failures, and the difficulty and cost of repairing failures are unusually huge. Therefore, the importance and necessity of failure prediction in cluster systems are obvious. In order to solve this severe challenge, we propose an approach to failure prediction in cluster systems by Self-Updating Cause-and-Effect Graph. Different from the previous approaches, the most novel point of our approach is that it can automatically mine the causality among log events from cluster systems, and set up and update Cause-and-Effect Graph for failure prediction throughout their life cycle. In addition, we use the real logs from Blue Gene/L system to verify the effectiveness of our approach and compare our approach to other approaches using the same logs. The result shows that our approach outperforms other approaches with the best precision and recall rate reaching 89% and 85%, respectively.

1 Introduction

Cluster systems have been widely used in cloud computing, high-performance computing such as LANL, Hadoop, and Blue Gene/L. The usage and scale of cluster systems have shown a sharp upward trend. For example, in Blue Gene/L, the number of processors has reached 131,072 [1]. Bianca et al. [2] surveyed some cluster systems used for high-performance computing and found that the average failure rate is relatively high and that the average repair time is relatively long, it can be seen that the damage caused by failures is very huge. Therefore, the importance and necessity of failure prediction in cluster systems are obvious. We investigated a lot of related previous work and found that cluster systems logs are a very important resource for failure prediction, because they track the behavior of cluster systems by accurately recording detailed information, and that most approaches are based on the causality among log events.

However, we find that cluster systems logs are unstructured and complex and that logs format for different cluster systems is very different, which makes

The original version of this chapter was revised: typographical errors, references, and a figure were corrected. The correction to this chapter is available at https://doi.org/10.1007/978-3-030-23502-4_25

processing difficult, seriously affecting the efficiency of failure prediction. Even if we have got structured cluster systems logs, but we still face two huge challenges including event filtering and event mining. Event filtering is to filter out log events that are worthless for event mining. Event mining is to mine the causality among log events that can be used to set up and update Cause-and-Effect Graph(CEG). In addition, the most important task in our paper is failure prediction. The mechanism behind it is to reasonably infer on CEG of cluster systems. Although many researchers had proposed many approaches, some of them [5,7] suffer from the window-size restriction, making the expression of failure rule incomplete. As stated in [4,6,15], the time interval between a failure and its root cause may be unbounded. In recent research work, Fu et al. [6] proposed an approach without the window-size restriction, which can express complete failure rule to help us with failure prediction. However, Their approach is to set up a CEG in a cold-start manner, which means that it cannot automatically set up and update CEG in the entire life cycle of cluster systems.

Based on the above problems, we proposed two main objectives including eliminating the window-size restriction and replacing the cold-start manner with a hot-start manner under the condition of ensuring efficiency. To achieve them, we proposed an approach to failure prediction in cluster systems by Self-Updating Cause-and-Effect Graph(SUCEG).

Particularly, our paper makes the following contributions:

1. We proposed an approach to failure prediction in cluster systems by SUCEG, which can overcome the window-size restriction and automatically set up and update CEG in a hot-start manner in the entire life cycle of cluster systems.
2. We proposed a three-step SUCEG algorithm that can automatically mine the causality among log events and set up and update CEG, thereby improving our approach's ability to failure prediction.
3. We used the real logs from Blue Gene/L system to evaluate the effectiveness of our approach. The result shows that our approach outperforms other approaches with the best precision and recall rate reaching 89% and 85%, respectively.

The remaining parts of the paper are organized as follows. Section 2 reviews related work on failure prediction in cluster systems. Section 3 describes the framework of our approach and our SUCEG algorithm in detail. Section 4 evaluates the efficiency of our approach by using the real logs from Blue Gene/L system. Section 5 concludes our work.

2   Related Work

The main research hotspots of failure prediction in cluster systems contain four aspects. First, how to transform each unstructured log event from cluster systems into analyzable and usable structured data, that is, Log Parsing. Second, how to filter out log events that interfere with mining causality, that is Event Filtering. Third, how to dig out the causality between them from a huge amount of log events, namely Event Mining. Fourth, how to apply the causality to predict failures, namely failure prediction.

2.1 Log Parsing

Cluster systems logs are unstructured as shown in Fig. 1 and must be parsed before feeding them into mining models [16]. In recent years, researchers have proposed many log parsing algorithms. Jiang et al. proposed AEL [9], which uses clone detection techniques to abstract each log line to its corresponding execution event. He et al. proposed Drain [10], which is an online log parsing algorithm that can parse logs in a streaming and timely manner and uses a fixed depth parse tree, which encodes specially designed rules for parsing, accelerating the parsing process. Makanju et al. proposed IPLoM [11], which is a log parsing algorithm based on heuristics specially designed according to the characteristics of log messages. Salma et al. proposed MoLFI [12], which recasts the log message identification problem as a multi-objective problem, and it uses an evolutionary approach to solve this problem, by tailoring the NSGA-II [13] algorithm to search the space of solutions for a Pareto optimal set of message templates.

- 1117838570 2005.06.03 R02-M1-N0-C:J12-U11 2005-06-03-15.42.50.363779 R02-M1-N0-C:J12-U11 RAS KERNEL

INFO instruction cache parity error corrected

a. A log event from BG/L

2015-10-18 18:04:11,034 ERROR [RMCommunicator Allocator] org.apache.hadoop.mapreduce.v2.app.rm.RMContainerAllocator:

Container complete event for unknown container id container_1445144423722_0020_01_000012

b. A log event from Hadoop

Fig. 1. The example logs from cluster systems

2.2 Event Filtering and Event Mining

Event mining is critical for failure prediction. Obviously, only by accurately mining as much causality as possible, we can accurately analyze and deal with more failures. In additon, event filtering is an indispensable part before event mining. It can help us filter out log events that interfere with event mining to improve the efficiency of event mining. In recent years, researchers have proposed a large number of approaches for these two challenges.

In [17], Zheng et al. exploited the causality between failure events extracted from a huge amount of log events. They defined temporal and spatial redundancy log events as interference events, and remove these two types of log events from the sequence of log events, and then utilize a priori association rules to combine related events for event mining. However, Fu et al. proved that the causality between non-failure events and failure events is also very important. In [6,14], they extend the range of log events from failure events to failure and non-failure events and define repetitive events and periodic events as interference events. In order to mine the causality among log events, they remove these two types of events from the entire sequence of log events and then mine the sequence of frequently occurring log events. Unfortunately, the previous approaches for event mining are coarse-grained, so that they are highly likely to miss the causality between certain log events, limiting the efficiency of event mining. In [19,20],

Kobayashi et al. proposed a fine-grained mining approach built on the causal inference to detect causality of two given events in the network logs.

2.3   Failure Prediction

Failure prediction is of paramount importance to any cluster systems. Over the past years, many researchers have proposed a large number of techniques. Zheng et al. [3] proposed a failure prediction mechanism that can predict the time and location of a possible failure, which mainly discovers failure patterns by observing and counting log events, but they ignore an important feature that log events are usually interlaced. Chuah et al. [5] developed a diagnostics tool, FDiag, to extract log events as structured message templates and uses statistical correlation analysis to establish probable cause and effect relationships for failures, and they also present a diagnostics system called ANCOR [7] that applies TACC Stats data to identify resource use anomalies and applies log analysis to link resource use anomalies with system failures. However, [3,5,7] suffer from the window-size restriction, and can not reflect the integrity of failure behavior in cluster systems. As stated in [4,6,15], the time interval between a failure event and its root cause event may be unbounded.

Fu et al. [6] successfully solved the problem of the window-size restriction by extracting the causality among log events from the entire cluster systems logs. However, their approach is a way to set up a CEG in a cold-start manner, and can not automatically set up and update CEG in the entire life cycle of cluster systems. So we are looking forward to a more intelligent approach that can use log events generated by cluster systems to automatically set up and update CEG for failure prediction, which helps system administrators to manage failures and reduces the huge losses caused by them in cluster systems.

3   Framework Design

In this section, we will cover all the details of our approach. In III-A, we will describe our framework design, and the rest of this section will explain the details of all components, where we will focus on our SUCEG algorithm in III-D.

3.1   Framework Design

The framework design of our approach is shown in Fig. 2. It consists of five components including Log Parser, Event Identification, Cluster System Event Base(CSEB), SUCEG, Failure Prediction, where CSEB is used to store various types of log events generated by cluster systems. The details of all components will be described in the following subsections.

3.2   Log Parser

In order to facilitate the follow-up work, our first task is to get the structured representation of original log events. Our log parsing is based on the following two observations:

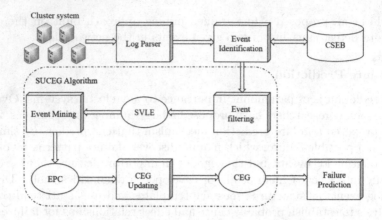

Fig. 2. Framework design of our approach

1. Different cluster systems logs meet their respective log format, allowing us to express these log events with multiple fields.
2. Each log event in cluster systems logs contains a special field describing itself, but this field often contains immutable and variable parts. We need to extract a more representative event description of this type of log event from this field.

Based on the above two insights, we can get a general structured representation of log events from cluster systems as shown below.

$$log\_event = \{field_i | i \leq n \ and \ i\epsilon N^*, template\} \tag{1}$$

where $\{field_i | i \leq n \ and \ i\epsilon N^*\}$ usually contain these messages such as time of occurrence, the location of occurrence, severity and event description, and template is a more representative event description of the type of log event.

The number of these fields is determined by the log format of cluster systems. Obviously, different cluster systems logs may have different structured representation. Figure 3 shows the structured representation of two log events in Fig. 1, where the log event from Blue Gene/L system is represented by eleven fields while the log event from Hadoop system is represented by seven fields.

Label	–
Timestamp	1117838570
Date	2005.06.03
Node	R02-M1-N0-C:J12-U11
Time	2005-06-03-15.42.50.363779
Node	R02-M1-N0-C:J12-U11
Type	RAS
Component	KERNEL
Severity	INFO
Description	instructuion cache parity error corrected
EventTempale	instructuion cache parity error corrected

Date	2015-10-18
Time	18:04:11,034
Severity	ERROR
Process	RMCommunicator Allocator
Component	Org.apache.hadoop.mapreduce.v2.app.pm.RMC ontainerAllocator
Description	Container complete event for unknown container id container_1445144423722_0020_01_000012
EventTempale	Container complete event for unknown container id container_*

a. A log event from BG/L   b. A log event from Hadoop

Fig. 3. The example of structured log events with multiple fields

In recent years, researchers have proposed many algorithms for parsing cluster systems logs. However, we found that the parsing efficiency of different algorithms is very different as shown in Table 1 [21]. For example, the accuracy of Drain [10] and LKE [18] parsing logs from Blue Gene/L is 0.963 and 0.128 respectively. The efficiency of log parsing will directly affect the efficiency of failure prediction, therefore, we will use the most appropriate log parsing algorithm for different cluster systems.

Table 1. The efficiency of different algorithms for various cluster systems logs

id	HDFS	Hadoop	Spark	Zookeeper	Openstack	BGL	HPC	Thunderbird
AEL	0.998	0.538	0.905	0.921	0.758	0.957	0.903	0.941
IPLoM	1	0.954	0.920	0.962	0.871	0.939	0.824	.663
LKE	1	0.670	0.634	0.438	0.787	0.128	0.574	0.813
Drain	.998	0.948	0.920	0.967	0.733	0.963	0.887	.955
MoLFI	0.998	0.957	0.418	0.839	.213	0.960	0.824	0.646

3.3 Event Identification & CSEB

In general, cluster systems will generate a huge amount of log events. However, the precondition for mining the causality among them is the ability to identify their tags. In our paper, the mechanism of event identification is described below. Assume that the structured representation of the jth log event generated by cluster systems is as follows.

$$log\_event_j = \{field_{ji} | i \leq n \ and \ i \epsilon N^*, template_j\} \quad (2)$$

We extract some important fields such as time of occurrence, the location of occurrence, severity and template to get its simplified representation shown below.

$$log\_event_j = \{time_j, \ location_j, \ severity_j, \ template_j\} \quad (3)$$

Here, $time_j$ is a standardized timestamp obtained from these time-related fields, $location_j$ is obtained from these location-related fields, $severity_j$ indicates the severity of log_event_j, which usually includes INFO, WARNING, ERROR, SERVER, FATAL and FAILURE.

Before describing our Event Identification, it is worth mentioning that we will also automatically establish CSEB, which is a relational database containing fields such as id, time, location, severity, template, and tag. The establishment of CSEB will be explained in Event Identification.

Our Event Identification determines the tag of a log event by matching it with these event entries in CSEB. We will use log_event_j as an example to describe the process of identification. There are two cases:

1. CSEB is empty, that is, CSEB does not have any event entries. In this case, we will store log_event_j in CSEB and set the corresponding tag to 1.

2. CSEB is not empty, that is, there are already some event entries in CSEB. In this case, we will match $location_j$ and $template_j$ of log_event_j with the corresponding fields of these event entries. There are two sub-cases:

   (a) If there is an event entry $event\_item$ in CSEB that satisfies the following two conditions:

$$event\_item.location == log\_event_j.location_j \tag{4}$$

$$event\_item.template == log\_event_j.template_j \tag{5}$$

Then, we assign tag of $event\_item$ to the log event:

$$log\_event_j.tag_j = event\_item.tag \tag{6}$$

Therefore the above-structured representation can be simplified to the following representation further:

$$log\_event_j = \{time_j, \ severity_j, \ tag_j\} \tag{7}$$

   (b) If there is no event entry in CSEB that satisfies the above two conditions, then we can get tag_j of log_event_j by the following formula:

$$log\_event_j.tag_j = tag_{max} + 1 \tag{8}$$

Where tag_{max} is the maximum value of tag in CSEB. At the same time, we need to store log_event_j and its tag_j in CSEB. Table 2 shows some event entries in CSEB of Blue Gene/L system which were obtained in our experiments.

Table 2. Some event entries in CSEB of Blue Gene/L

id	time	location	severity	template	tag
1	1117838840	R02-M1-N0-C:J12-U11	INFO	*instruction cache parity error corrected*	1
..	...	...	..	...	...
39796	1118543338	R06-M1-N6-C:J15-U01	INFO	** torus * error(s) (dcr * detected and corrected*	39796
39797	118543339	R07-M0-N8-C:J06-U01	INFO	*total of * ddr error(s) detected and corrected*	39797

3.4 SUCEG Algorithm

SUCEG algorithm contains three steps including Event Filtering, Event Mining, and CEG Updating and a global Counter. As mentioned earlier, it can automatically mine the causality among log events and set up and update CEG in the life cycle of cluster systems. Generally, cluster systems always perform various tasks concurrently for high performance, so that log events are always interlaced. How to mine the causality among them from such chaotic log events and to establish

Fig. 4. The interleaving situations of log events

and update CEG has always been a huge challenge for researchers. By observing different cluster systems logs, we find that the interleaving of log events is either caused by parallel execution of the same task or by parallel execution of different tasks. These two situations are shown in Fig. 4, where log events a, b, c are generated by task A, while log events x, y, z are generated by task B.

We will use the following Sequence of Log Events (SLE) as an example to illustrate how our algorithm handles these above situations. The last two steps of our algorithm will be started if and only if our Counter reaches a threshold N(our Counter will be cleared), therefore a total of N log events will be processed during the process of updating CEG.

$$SLE = \{log\_event_i | i \leq n \text{ and } i \epsilon N^*\}$$
$$log\_event_i = \{time_i, severity_i, tag_i\} \tag{9}$$

Event Filtering. The first step of our SUCEG algorithm is Event Filtering, which is designed to solve the log interleaving problem caused by parallel execution of the same task. Our Event Filtering relies on two key features including timestamp and tag of log events. Before describing Event Filtering, we need to understand some concepts we define. First, we introduce a threshold T, which is important for filtering repetitive events generated by the parallel execution of the same task. At the same time, we refer to each selected log event after filtering as Valuable Log Event(VLE) and put it into SVLE. The form of SVLE is as follows:

$$SVLE = \{VLE_i | i \leq n \text{ and } i \epsilon N^*\} \text{ where } VLE_i = \{time_i, tag_i\} \tag{10}$$

Starting with the first log event in SLE, we compare each log event with the log events in SVLE. If there is no log event in SVLE with the same tag or even if there are such log events, the time difference between it and the latest log event in SVLE with the same tag exceeds our threshold T, then we will save it to SVLE, otherwise, we will filter it out.

Event Mining. Previous event mining approaches are either based on the fixed-size window or based on Frequent Event Sequences(FES). However, they all mine the causality among log events at the granularity of event sequence, and cannot cope with the log interleaving problem caused by the parallel execution of different tasks mentioned above. In order to solve this problem, we proposed a fine-grained method of mining the causality among log events in the second step of SUCEG algorithm, which focuses on discovering the causality among two log events. We find two characteristics that cannot be ignored. First, two log events with causality always occur in sequence within a certain time range. Second, the parallel execution of tasks is random. Based on these two characteristics, we can know that if a task is executed frequently, only the log events generated by itself will appear more frequently, therefore we can use statistics to mine the causality among log events.

In the previous step, we got SVLE. First, we count the types of tags in SVLE and get Tag_Type as follows.

$$Tag\_Type = \{tag\_type_i | i \leq n \ and \ i\epsilon N^*\} \tag{11}$$

Second, for each tag type, we extract the event fragments within the threshold T from SVLE. For example, when the tag type is tag_type_i, we start with the first event in SVLE.

Once the event with tag_type_i is found, the event will be extracted along with the events occurring after it within the threshold T, and get the event fragments as follows.

$$EF_T = \{\{tag\_type_i : (ef_j | j \leq m \ and \ j\epsilon N^*)\} | i \leq n \ and \ i\epsilon N^*\}$$
$$ef_j = \{tag_{jk} | k \leq t \ and \ k\epsilon N^*)\} \tag{12}$$

Third, we count the number of occurrences of each event in the event fragments of each tag type and calculate the probability of their occurrence, leaving only events that exceed our defined threshold M and P1 respectively, and determine that there is the causality between these events and tag_type_i, and get a Causal Event Set(CES) as follows.

$$CES = \{\{tag\_type_i : (ces_j | j \leq m \ and \ j\epsilon N^*)\} | i \leq n \ and \ i\epsilon N^*\}$$
$$where \ ces_j = \{tag_{jk} | k \leq t \ and \ k\epsilon N^*)\} \tag{13}$$

Finally, we count the tag of the first event in all ces of each tag type tag_type_i. If the number of certain tags exceeds our defined threshold P2, then we will determine that tag_type_i has direct causality with them.

In this way, we get Event Pairs with direct Causality as follows, where f_j is the frequency.

$$EPC = \{(tag\_type_i, \ tag_j, f_j) | i \leq n \ and \ i\epsilon N^*, j \leq m \ and \ j\epsilon N^*\} \tag{14}$$

CEG Updating. CEG updating is the final step of our SUCEG algorithm, which is designed to set up and update CEG. CEG is a directed graph in which nodes represent event tags, edges represent a direct causal relationship between an event tag and another event tag and weight represents the frequency. Throughout the life cycle of cluster systems, we will continuously update CEG. In each process of updating, we will get the latest EPC through the above steps and utilize it to set up and update nodes, edges and weight of CEG.

3.5 Failure Prediction

Failure prediction is one of the most important tasks for cluster systems. In our framework, we perform real-time failure prediction based on CEG. Our failure prediction consists of four modules, namely Log Capturing module, Log Parsing module, Event Identification module, and Prediction module. Firstly, Log Capturing module will capture the latest log event generated by cluster systems in real time and transmit it to Log Parsing module. Then, it gets a tag through the processing of Log Parsing module and Event Identification module. Finally, according to the tag of the log event, we infer reasonably based on CEG to predict whether any failure event will occur in the near future.

4 Experiments

In this section, we will use our proposed approach to mine the causality among log events and set up and update CEG based on the real logs from Blue Gene/L system. At the same time, we will evaluate the effectiveness of our approach by comparing with previous approaches using the same logs. The information about the logs used in our experiment are shown in Table 3 and it can be downloaded in https://www.usenix.org/cfdr-data.

Table 3. The information about the logs from Blue Gene/L

Properties	Blue Gene/L
Size(decompressed)	732.2 MB
Record Count	474796
Days	215
Start Date	2005-06-03
End Date	2006-01-03

4.1 Experimental Scheme

We use the first three million rows logs as training set and the next one million logs as the testing set. The training set is used to simulate this process of establishing and updating CEG, and the testing set is used to evaluate the effectiveness of our approach.

In order to evaluate the efficiency, we use two important indicators used in most approaches, namely prediction precision and recall rate. Prediction precision refers to the ratio of the predicted correct quantity to the predictable quantity, and recall rate is the ratio of the predicted correct quantity to the total number of failures. A good prediction has a high value (closer to 1.0) for both prediction precision and recall rate. However, there is usually a conflict between them, therefore we need to make a trade-off between them.

In addition, we need to set a series of parameters including N, T, M, P1, and P2. The purpose of these parameters has been mentioned above. Our experiments were divided into lateral experiments and longitudinal experiments. In the lateral experiments, we will compare the precision and recall rate under different M to discuss the impact of M. In the longitudinal experiments, we will compare the precision and recall rate of under different P1 to discuss the impact of P1. All the parameters used in our experiments are shown in Table 4.

Table 4. Experiment parameters

Experiment Parameters	Value				
Number of log events	4519666				
Training set size	3000000				
Testing set size	1000000				
N	300000				
T	10				
M	2		4		6
P1	0.5	0.7	0.9	0.5	0.5
P2	0.5			0.5	0.5

The process of our experiments is described as follows. Firstly, we will feed these log events in the training set into our framework chronologically. Secondly, Log Parser will automatically parse each log event to get the corresponding structured representation. Thirdly, Event Identification will identify them and establish CSEB. Thirdly, our SUCEG algorithm will mine the causality among them, and establish and update CEG of Blue Gene/L system. Finally, we will use CEG to perform failure prediction on the testing set to evaluate the effectiveness of our approach.

4.2 EPC and CEG

According to the above experimental scheme, our framework performed 10 rounds of mining the causality among log events and updating CEG in each experiment. In each round of single experiment, we obtained a large number of EPC through SUCEG algorithm, then used them to establish and update our CEG. The number of EPC we mined and the number of failure types covered by CEG in our experiments are shown in Figs. 5 and 6 respectively. Note that the number of them is a cumulative result. From the below two figures, we can get the following three conclusions:

1. With the operation of cluster systems, the number of EPC mined by our approach and the number of failure types covered by CEG will gradually increase, indicating that our approach's ability to handle failures will be improved.
2. The parameter M and the parameter P1 have a very significant effect on mining EPC. As M increases, the requirement for mining EPC becomes more stringent, resulting in a sharp drop in the number of EPC. In addition, the smaller P1 is, the more interference events we may get, resulting in the same result.

3. The number of failure types covered by CEG also has similar conclusions as described above.

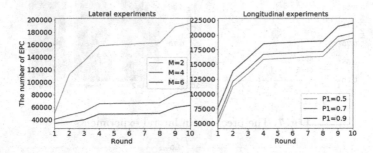

Fig. 5. The number of EPC

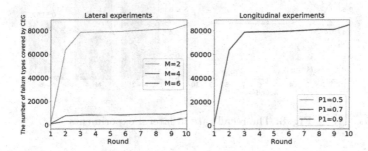

Fig. 6. The number of failure types covered by CEG

4.3   Failure Prediction

Different from other approaches, the most novel point of our approach is to use the hot-start manner instead of the cold-start manner to establish and update CEG. In order to evaluate the effectiveness of our approach, we use CEG obtained under different parameters to predict the failure events in the testing set. Figures 7 and 8 show the precision and the recall rate in our lateral experiments respectively. Figures 9 and 10 show the precision and the recall rate in our longitudinal experiments respectively. The left side of each figure is the result of using each updated CEG to predict failures, where the abscissa indicates the number of times the CEG is updated, the ordinate indicates the precision, and the right side of each figure is the average precision or the average recall rate.

In our lateral experiments, our average prediction precision is 87.03%($M =$ 2), 88.35%($M = 4$) and 87.78%($M = 6$), respectively, and our average recall rate is 83.72%($M = 2$), 81.85%($M = 4$) and 51.52%($M = 6$), respectively. In our longitudinal experiments, our average prediction precision is 88.34%($P1 =$ 0.5), 88.35%($P1 = 0.7$) and 89.02%($P1 = 0.9$), and our average recall rate is 83.72%($P1 = 0.5$), 84.01%($P1 = 0.7$) and 85.32%($P1 = 0.9$), respectively.

From the above results, we can draw the following conclusions:

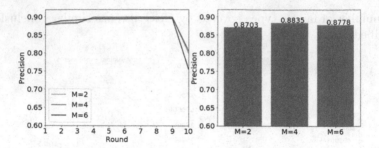

Fig. 7. The precision in lateral experiments

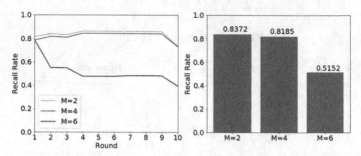

Fig. 8. The recall rate in lateral experiments

1. With the increase of M, the more stringent the requirement of mining causality is, the higher the reliability of EPC is, so the accuracy of fault prediction will be improved, and the callback rate will be reduced, which also verifies our previous statement. Since the average number of occurrences of each log event in the training set is no more than five, the situation of $M = 6$ is abnormal.
2. As mentioned above, increasing P1 can reduce the number of interference events, improving both the precision and the recall rate.

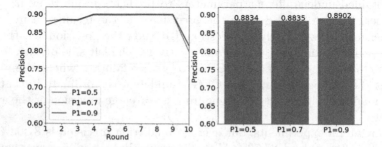

Fig. 9. The precision in longitudinal experiments

In addition, we compare our approach to other approaches using the same log as shown in Fig. 11. Here, "Dynamic" represents the work of Gu et al. [4], "Adaptive" represents the work of Gainaru et al. [8], and "LogMaster" and

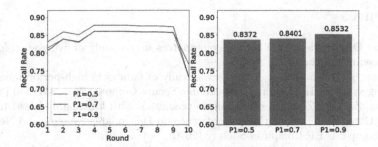

Fig. 10. The recall rate in longitudinal experiments

"CDG-Based" represent the work of Fu et al. [6,14]. Fortunately, the best prediction precision and recall rate obtained by our approach are 89% and 85% respectively, which outperform most approaches. In addition, our approach improves the recall rate by at least 10%.

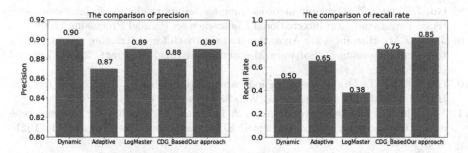

Fig. 11. The comparison between approaches

5   Conclusion

In our paper, we proposed an approach to failure prediction in cluster systems by SUCEG, which can overcome the window-size restriction and automatically set up and update CEG along with the entire life cycle of cluster systems. We also proposed a three-step algorithm SUCEG for mining the causality among log events and updating CEG. In addition, we used the real logs from Blue Gene/L system to validate the effectiveness of our approach and evaluate the efficiency of our approach by comparing it with other approaches. The results show that our approach outperforms other approaches. The best average prediction precision and average recall rate are 89% and 85% respectively.

Acknowledgement. This paper is supported by Project 213.

References

1. Adam, O., Stearley, J.: What supercomputers say: a study of five system logs. In: Proceedings of the DSN (2007)
2. Bianca, S., Gibson, G.A.: A large-scale study of failures in high-performance computing systems. IEEE Trans. Dependable Secure Comput. **7**(4), 337–350 (2010)
3. Zheng, Z., Lan, Z.: A practical failure prediction with location and lead time for Blue Gene/P. In: International Conference on Dependable Systems and Networks Workshops. IEEE Computer Society (2010)
4. Gainaru, A., Cappello, F.: Adaptive event prediction strategy with dynamic time window for large-scale HPC systems. In: SLAML. ACM (2011)
5. Chuah, E., Kuo, S.: Diagnosing the root-causes of failures from cluster log files. In: IEEE International Conference on High Performance Computing (2011)
6. Fu, X., Ren, R.: Digging deeper into cluster system logs for failure prediction and root cause diagnosis. In: IEEE International Conference on Cluster Computing (2014)
7. Chuah, E., Jhumka, A.: Linking resource usage anomalies with system failures from cluster log data. In: IEEE International Symposium on Reliable Distributed Systems (2013)
8. Gu, J., Zheng, Z.: Dynamic meta-learning for failure prediction in large-scale systems: a case study. In: International Conference on Parallel Processing (2008)
9. Jiang, Z.M., Hassan, A.E.: An automated approach for abstracting execution logs to execution events. J. Software Maintenance Evol. Res. Pract. **20**(4), 249–267 (2008)
10. He, P., Zhu, J.: Drain: an online log parsing approach with fixed depth tree. In: IEEE International Conference on Web Services (2017)
11. Makanju, A., Zincir-Heywood, A.N.: A lightweight algorithm for message type extraction in system application logs. IEEE Trans. Knowl. Data Eng. **24**(11), 1921–1936 (2012)
12. Makanju, A., Zincir-Heywood, A.N.: A search-based approach for accurate identification of log message formats. In: ACM SIGKDD International Conference on Knowledge Discovery and Data Mining (2009)
13. Deb, K., Pratap, A.: A fast and elitist multiobjective genetic algorithm: NSGA-II. IEEE Trans. Evol. Comput. **6**(2), 182–197 (2002)
14. Fu, X., Ren, R.: LogMaster: mining event correlations in logs of large-scale cluster systems. In: IEEE Symposium on Reliable Distributed Systems (2012)
15. Agarwal, M.K., Madduri, V.R.: Correlating failures with asynchronous changes for root cause analysis in enterprise environments. In: IEEE International Conference on Dependable Systems & Networks (2010)
16. He, P., Zhu, J.: An evaluation study on log parsing and its use in log mining. In: IEEE International Conference on Dependable Systems and Networks (2016)
17. Zheng, Z., Lan, Z.: System log pre-processing to improve failure prediction. In: IEEE International Conference on Dependable Systems & Networks (2009)
18. Fu, Q., Lou, J.: Execution anomaly detection in distributed systems through unstructured log analysis. In: IEEE International Conference on Data Mining (2009)

19. Kobayashi, S., Otomo, K.: Mining causality of network events in log data. IEEE Trans. Netw. Serv. Manag. **15**(1), 53–67 (2018)
20. Kobayashi, S., Fukuda, K.: Mining causes of network events in log data with causal inference. In: IEEE Symposium on Integrated Network and Service Management (2017)
21. Jieming, Z., Shilin, M.: Tools and benchmarks for automated log parsing. In: International Conference on Software Engineering (ICSE 2019) (2018)

Towards Decentralized Deep Learning with Differential Privacy

Hsin-Pai Cheng[1]([✉]), Patrick Yu[2], Haojing Hu[3], Syed Zawad[4], Feng Yan[4], Shiyu Li[5], Hai Li[1], and Yiran Chen[1]

[1] ECE Department, Duke University, Durham, NC 27708, USA
{hc218,hai.li,yiran.chen}@duke.edu
[2] Monta Vista High School, Cupertino, CA 95014, USA
pyu592@student.fuhsd.org
[3] Beihang University of Aeronautics and Astronautics, Beijing, China
haojinghu@buaa.edu.cn
[4] CSE Department, University of Nevada, Reno, NV 89557, USA
{szawad,fyan}@unr.edu
[5] Tsinhua University, Beijing, China
shiyu.li@duke.edu

Abstract. In distributed machine learning, while a great deal of attention has been paid on centralized systems that include a central parameter server, decentralized systems have not been fully explored. Decentralized systems have great potentials in the future practical use as they have multiple useful attributes such as less vulnerable to privacy and security issues, better scalability, and less prone to single point of bottleneck and failure. In this paper, we focus on decentralized learning systems and aim to achieve differential privacy with good convergence rate and low communication cost. To achieve this goal, we propose a new algorithm, Leader-Follower Elastic Averaging Stochastic Gradient Descent (LEASGD), driven by a novel Leader-Follower topology and differential privacy model.

We also provide a theoretical analysis of the convergence rate of LEASGD and the trade-off between the performance and privacy in the private setting. We evaluate LEASGD in real distributed testbed with poplar deep neural network models MNIST-CNN, MNIST-RNN, and CIFAR-10. Extensive experimental results show that LEASGD outperforms state-of-the-art decentralized learning algorithm DPSGD by achieving nearly 40% lower loss function within same iterations and by 30% reduction of communication cost. Moreover, it spends less differential privacy budget and has final higher accuracy result than DPSGD under private setting.

The original version of this chapter was revised: typographical errors were corrected. The correction to this chapter is available at https://doi.org/10.1007/978-3-030-23502-4_25
H.-P. Cheng, P. Yu, H. Hu and S. Zawad—Equal Contribution.

© Springer Nature Switzerland AG 2019
D. Da Silva et al. (Eds.): CLOUD 2019, LNCS 11513, pp. 130–145, 2019.
https://doi.org/10.1007/978-3-030-23502-4_10

1   Introduction

With data explosion and ever-deeper neural network structures such as *VGGnet* [1] and *Resnet* [2], distributed learning systems play an increasingly important role in training large-scale models with big training data sources [3–5].

Training time can be greatly reduced by dividing the data set into subsets and distributing them over different workers to train the model concurrently known as *data parallelism* [6]. Many modern machine learning systems extend the data parallelism concept from data center clusters to the server-client scenario, where clients help train a global model by iterating the model over their own private data sets.

Most distributed learning systems have centralized parameter server(s) to maintain a global copy of the model and coordinate information among workers/clients. However, such system topology is vulnerable in privacy because once the central server(s) is compromised, information of the entire system can be exposed [7]. Decentralized distributed learning systems are less vulnerable to privacy as the critical information such as training data, model weights, and the states of all workers can no longer be observed or controlled through a single point of the system [8], which greatly reduces the risk of privacy leakages. Moreover, decentralized systems are more robust to problems like communication bottleneck and single point of failure compared to the centralized design. Despite all these advantages over centralized topology, decentralized systems usually perform worse in convergence rate and are known to have higher communication cost due to the multi-way communication behaviors, especially the connection across the network is relatively intricate. In addition, most of the decentralized systems still can not guarantee deferentially privacy [9,10]. There are several recent works try to solve some of the above problems of decentralized learning systems. For example, DPSGD [9] focuses on improving communication efficiency and convergence rate of decentralized learning systems. However, it is not deferentially private. [8] is the recent work that considers both decentralized design and differential privacy. However, it is based on a simple linear classification task, not a good representation of the modern neural networks, which have much more complex and deeper structures. To this end, we propose a new algorithm called *Leader-Follower Elastic Averaging Stochastic Gradient Descent* (LEASGD), which provides differential privacy with improved communication efficiency and convergence rate. To improve both the communication and training efficiency while also facilitate differential privacy preserving, we propose a novel communication protocol that is driven by a dynamic leader-followerdesign. Workers with temporal better learning performance and can speedup the learning of followers to improve learning efficiency. The parameters are only transferred between the worker-follower pair, which significantly reduces the communication amount. To satisfy differential privacy, we follow the approach proposed in [11] to add stochastic noise on the information transmitted. We calibrate the noise scale by analyzing the sensitivity of the updating functions in our algorithm and further demonstrate the trade-off between accuracy and privacy theoretically. LEASGD adopts the insight of the *Elastic Averaging*

Stochastic Gradient Descent (EASGD) algorithm [12] by exerting the elastic force between the leaderand followerat each update. Inspired by [13], we use *moments accountant* to quantify the privacy budget which provides a tighter bound of privacy budget ϵ than the classical *Strong Composition Theorem* [14]. Additionally, we mathematically prove the convergence rate of LEASGD.

To conclude the comparison, we comprehensively evaluate our algorithm and compare it with the state-of-the-art approach DPSGD [9] on three main aspects: the convergence rate, the communication cost, and the privacy level. The theoretical analysis shows LEASGD converges faster than DPSGD after enough iterations. The experimental results on MNIST-CNN, MNIST-RNN, and CIFAR-10 show LEASGD achieves higher accuracy within the same iterations and within the same communication than DPSGD in the non-private setting. Also, it outperforms DPSGD by spending less privacy budget and reaching higher accuracy in the private setting.

2 Related Work

Decentralized Distributed Learning Algorithm. Different from centralized distributed learning algorithms, decentralized algorithms do not need any central entity. Every workers maintains its own copy of the training model and directly communicates with other workers. Many decentralized algorithms aim at solving distributed consensus problems [15–17], which is also the goal of our paper. Lian *et al.* [9] proposed DPSGD, which outperforms centralized algorithms by achieving the same convergence rate with lower communication complexity. All the decentralized algorithms mentioned above depend on a double stochastic matrix to organize the communication, which is hard to obtain and tune in real-life applications and they also do not implement their algorithms in a privacy-preseving setting. Moreover, adversarial attackers who reveal this matrix can easily obtain the model information by doing a simple linear combination, and even worse, to reveal the private data. Yan *et al.* [10] developed a scheme to prevent such attack, but the scheme depends on a specific communication topology. Our privacy-preserving scheme is not limited by any specific communication topology and we coordinate the communication in a random manner to reduce vulnerability.

EASGD. EASGD is first proposed by Zhang *et al.* [12] to solve the distributed consensus optimization problem. The basic idea is to let multiple workers pull a single master to the global optimum and the movement of model parameters is proportional to the distance between workers and master, which is so-called elastic force. They show EASGD can achieve final better accuracy than the DOWNPOUR [18] and other parallel algorithms and converge even faster in its momentum version EASGD. However, the communication topology in EASGD highly resembles a centralized one. The master in its algorithm plays a similar role as the central node. Moreover, they did not consider any privacy constraints in their algorithm.

Differential Privacy in Machine Learning *Differential Privacy* (DP), first proposed by Dwork, provides a specific quantitative method to measure and protect privacy [11]. It was then studied and applied to fields in *Machine Learning*. For instance, Kairouz *et al.* [19] studied utility and privacy trade-off of different mechanisms under local DP setting. Abadi *et al.* [13] proposed differential privacy SGD and suggested the moments accountant method to compute a much tighter bound of ϵ, δ privacy budget (which we also adopt in this paper) than classical strong composition theorem [14]. For distributed machine learning, Bellet *et al.* [8] proposed a completely decentralized and asynchronous algorithm to solve personalized optimization problem and also use DP in their privacy-preserving method. However, they did not compare with other parallel algorithms in the private setting and their experiment only focused on simple linear classification task and light-weight dataset, MovieLens-100K, rather than a more complex data set such as CIFAR-10 on which we conduct the experiment for our method. Furthermore, the model in their experiment is a simple p-dimensional vector. It is not clear whether their method could be applied for deeper neural networks, which we demonstrate in our experiments.

In [20], the basic idea of LEASGD is outlined and some preliminary analysis and evaluation results are present. The current extended version of this paper provides a more detailed description of the LEASGD approach, as well as a more comprehensive theoretical analysis and experimental evaluation.

3   Non-private Leader-Follower Elastic Averaging Stochastic Gradient Descent Algorithm

In this section, we introduce LEASGD in a non-private setting. The proposed algorithm includes both the model update at each worker and the communication protocol among workers. We start with the synchronous version (Algorithm 1) and then extend it to the asynchronous version (Algorithm 2), which is more commonly used in practice.

3.1   Problem Setting

Without loss of generality, we follow the problem setting of distributed decentralized autonomous learning in [10]. We assume there are m workers each with a set of local data S_i and $i \in \{1, 2 \dots \dots m\}$, which can only be accessed locally by worker i. To solve consensus problem, we assume all data sets S_i are homogeneous but can have different data distributions. Along the training process, each worker i computes a parameter vector w_t^i at each iteration t to represent the learning outcomes and then computes the corresponding loss function $f_t^i(w^i) = l(w_t^i, x_t^i, y_t^i)$ with the input x_t^i and given labels y_t^i. It is worth noting that fed data $\{x_t^i, y_t^i\} \subseteq S_i$. After learning from the data, each worker has two ways to contribute to the global learning progress: (1) Update its model parameters by local gradient descent; (2) Communicate with other workers to update each other's model parameters. To reduce the communication cost, communication is not always required at the end of each iteration. We define a communication interval τ to represent how many iterations between each update in our learning algorithm. When the training process is done, each worker has its own variation of the same model (i.e., performing the same task but with different trained model parameters w^i). This is quite different compared to the personalized distributed learning [8], where different workers have completely different models to solve personalized problems. It is also different from [9], where all workers have the same version of the model.

Given each worker has its own local version of the model, it is necessary to assemble all local models by averaging the loss function. We formulate it as an optimization problem as follows:

$$w^* = \{w^1, ..., w^m\}, \tag{1}$$

$$\underset{w^i \in \Omega}{argmin}\, \overline{F}(w, T) = \frac{1}{m} \sum_{i=1}^{m} f_T^i(w^i), s.t. \Omega \subseteq \mathbb{R}^n \, and \, T \in \mathbb{R}, \tag{2}$$

where T presents the predefined number of iterations in τ.

3.2   Decentralized Leader-FollowerTopology

To support the decentralized design, we categorize all workers into two worker pools - leaderpool with workers of higher loss function values and followerpool with workers of lower loss function values, see Fig. 1(a). The core idea is to let followersto pull so that better performing can guide the followersin the right direction to improve the learning. Specifically, we use an elastic updating rule to regulate the learning updates in each leader-followerpair as follows:

$$w_{t+1}^i = w_t^i - \eta g_t^i + \eta \rho(w_t^f - w_t^i) \quad and \quad w_{t+1}^f = w_t^f - \eta g_t^f + \eta \rho(w_t^i - w_t^f). \tag{3}$$

We use i to denote a leader; f is a follower; k is the categorization interval; ρ is elastic factor; g is gradient; and η is learning rate. Given learning is a dynamic process, the two worker pools are dynamically updated based on the learning progress. The pools are recategorized each $k\tau$ time interval. This protocol enables the convergence rate of our algorithm to have a limited upper bound, which will be discussed in detail in Sect. 5. To avoid over-fitting to one worker's model during the training process, we add the L2-normalization on the training loss function:

$$f_t^i(w^i) = l(w_t^i, x_t^i, y_t^i) + \lambda \parallel w^i \parallel_2 . \tag{4}$$

We also randomly pair the leaders and followers after each learning updates to avoid one follower's model having excessive influence on others. This randomization mechanism also benefits the privacy-preserving as randomized communication can confuse the attacker and make it more difficult to trace the information source.

Algorithm 1. Synchronous Follower Elastic Averaging Stochastic Gradient Descent Gradient Descent

---

1: **Require:** number of workers m, number of followers L, categorization interval k, communication interval τ, elastic factor ρ, learning rate η
2:
3: **for** $t = 1, 2, ..., T$ **do**
4:     **if** $t \bmod k\tau$ is 0 **then**
5:         **if** $t = 0$ **then**
6:             randomly select L followers $l_1, ..., l_L$
7:         **else**
8:             sort m based on loss f and select top L
9:             $l_1, ..., l_L = \underset{i=1,...,m}{argmax L}\, f_t^i(\omega^i)$
10:         **end if**
11:     **end if**
12:     **if** $t \bmod \tau$ is 0 **then**
13:         **for workers:** $i \in \{l_1, ..., l_L\}$ **do**
14:             local SGD updating
15:         **end for**
16:         **for workers:** $i \notin \{l_1, ..., l_L\}$ **do**
17:             randomly select a follower f from follower pool
18:             transmit parameter vector with f and do elastic updating
19:         **end for**
20:     **else**
21:         **for all workers:** $i \in \{1, ..., m\}$ **do**
22:             local SGD updating
23:          **end for**
24:     **end if**
25: **end for**

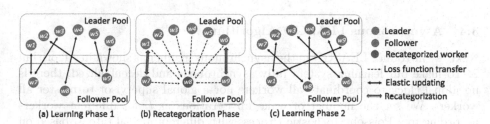

(a) Learning Phase 1   (b) Recategorization Phase   (c) Learning Phase 2

Fig. 1. The dynamic Leader-Followertopology. (a) shows the structure of leaderpool and followerpool. (b) shows a recategorization phase where one of the workers is elected as recategorized worker and gathers the latest loss function values from all other workers. (c) shows the new structure of leaderpool and followerpool after recategorization (note the randomization used for avoiding over-fitting).

3.3 Algorithm Hyperparameters

Next, we discuss in details of the hyperparameters in our algorithm.

Elastic factor ρ: This hyperparameter adjusts the exploration and exploitation trade-off in our learning algorithm. A large ρ represents more exploitation, which leads to a faster convergence rate at the beginning of training process especially in a convex case. However, workers can fall into a local optimum easily because the tight relations of the follower prevent them from further exploring the parameter space and this may compromise the final accuracy. On the the other hand, a rather small ρ leans towards exploration which could avoid this to some extent, but it also causes a much slower convergence rate and thus compromises the accuracy within the predetermined number of iterations. Selecting a well-balanced ρ is therefore important for the final accuracy.

Number of Followers L: Similar to ρ, this hyperparameter reflects learning aggressiveness. Small L enables more leaders to further explore the parameter space to improve the final accuracy. However, if L is too small, the communication between leaders and followers would increase. More importantly, workers with bad learning progress can be incorrectly categorized as leaders and thus could not receive help from workers with good learning progress, which can eventually result in worse final accuracy.

Categorization Interval k: It represents how frequently we recategorize and followers. A rather frequent categorization can ensure that and followersare timely identified. However, each categorization comes with a communication cost as the loss function values need to be collected and so a smaller k means higher communication cost. Our key insight here is that k can be set smaller at the beginning of the training process as workers' local models usually change more dramatically during that time and have more variance between them. As the training progresses, the loss function values tend to be more stable and we can decrease the recategorization frequency to reduce the communication overhead.

3.4   Asynchronous LEASGD Algorithm

Next, we introduce LEASGD in the asynchronous manner as shown in Algorithm 2. To make our learning system fully asynchronous and decentralized, there is no global clock to coordinate all workers nor a global supervisor to master all workers. We set the number of wake up iterations as t_i for different workers according to a Poisson Stochastic Process with different arrival rate λ_i based on local clock time t, that is $P[t_i(t + \triangle t) - t_i(t) = k] = \frac{e^{-\lambda_i \triangle t}(\lambda_i \triangle t)^k}{k!}$. The larger the λ_i, the more frequently the worker updates its model. Moreover, the worker pools also updated asynchronously as shown in Line 17–24 in Algorithm 2. Such mechanism may not guarantee all the leadersand followersare identified timely, but it reduces the communication cost of recategorization.

Note that the stochastic gradient descent in the algorithm can be replaced by other gradient descent optimization methods such as the mini-batch gradient descent without affecting the theoretical results.

Algorithm 2. Asynchronous Follower Elastic Averaging Stochastic Gradient Descent Algorithm

---

  1: **Require:** all workers have the same follower list F, this worker index w, current iteration t_i, communication interval τ, categorization interval k

  2:

  3: **if** w is a follower **then**

  4:     compute local SGD

  5: **else**

  6:     **if** $t_i \bmod \tau$ *is* 0 **then**

  7:         randomly select follower $f \in F$

  8:         transmit parameter vector to f and do elastic updating

  9:     **else**

10:         compute local SGD

11:     **end if**

12:     **if** $t_i \bmod k\tau$ *is* 0 **then**

13:     **for all** $f \in F$ **do**

14:         get f's loss function value l_f

15:         get w's loss function value l_w

16:         **if** find $l_f < l_w$ **then**

17:             recategorize all workers' follower pool by replacing f with w

18:             **break**

19:         **end if**

20:     **end for**

21:     **end if**

22: **end if**

---

4   Private-Preserving Scheme

In this section, we consider the privacy-preserving setting of the proposed algorithm. We first explain the notion of differential privacy, which serves as the theoretical foundation for our scheme. We then introduce our privacy-preserving scheme and how the privacy budget ϵ spent along the iterations.

4.1   Differential Privacy Model

Despite there is no direct exchange of raw data in the communication, the risk of leaking the data still exists when we transmit the parameter vectors. If the two consecutive transmitted vectors w_t^i and w_{t+1}^i are from same worker i, the attacker can easily derive the gradient by subtracting one vector from the other and due to the gradient g_t^i is proportional to the raw data x_t^i. More details about this type of attack can be referred to [10].

There are several methods proposed to preserve the privacy of distributed learning systems and prevent eavesdropping in the communication network. For example, Yan *et.al.* proposed a series of communication topologies to prevent the sensitive message from leaking to malicious workers [10]. In this work, we rely on a more general and flexible theory that does not depend on specific topology specified in the differential privacy theory in [11]. The basic property of differential privacy mechanism is that under a little perturbation of the input of the algorithm, the change of its output's probability distribution is within a limited bound. The specific definition is as below:

Definition 1. *A randomized mechanism $\mathcal{M}$ with domain $\mathcal{D}$ and range $\mathcal{R}$ satises (ϵ, δ)-differential privacy if for any two adjacent inputs D, $D' \in \mathcal{D}$ and for any subset of outputs $\mathcal{S} \subseteq \mathcal{R}$ it holds that*

$$Pr(\mathcal{M}(D) \in \mathcal{S}) \leq e^\epsilon Pr(\mathcal{M}(D')) + \delta. \tag{5}$$

When differential privacy applied in the machine learning, adjacent inputs D, D' refer two datasets that are only different at one training sample and the randomized mechanism $\mathcal{M}$ is the training update algorithm. In our setting we use elastic updating rule in Eq. 3. The factor ϵ in Eq. 5 denotes the privacy upper bound to measure an algorithm and δ denotes the probability of breaking this bound. The δ is generally set smaller than the reciprocal of the number of samples in the local data set S_i, which ensures that none of the samples can be revealed by the differential private attack.

4.2   Privacy-Preserving Scheme

The general idea to preserve differential privacy is to add noise on the output of the algorithm and the noise scale is based on the sensitivity of the output function as defined in [11].

Definition 2. *For $f : \mathcal{D} \to \mathcal{R}^d$, the $L2 - sensitivity$ of f:*

$$\triangle f = \max_{\mathcal{D}, \mathcal{D}_2} \parallel f(\mathcal{D}_1) - f(\mathcal{D}_2) \parallel_2 \tag{6}$$

for all $\mathcal{D}_1$, $\mathcal{D}_2$ differing in at most one element.

For different input data, Eq. 3 only differs in the gradient g_t^i part. In other words, the sensitivity of the updating rule of LEAGSD is same as the gradient g_t^i. Thus we use the similar scheme as the differentially private SGD algorithm in [13]. To limit the sensitivity of gradient, we clip the gradient into a constant C. The clipped gradient $\overline{g}_t^i = g_t^i / max(1, \frac{\|g_t^i\|_2}{C})$. Then, we add Gaussian noise on the clipped gradient

$$\tilde{g}_t^i = \overline{g}_t^i + \mathcal{N}(0, \sigma_2^2 C^2). \tag{7}$$

By using $\tilde{g}_t^i$ to replace g_t^i in Eq. 3, we obtain the differential-privacy preserving scheme of LEASGD as:

$$\tilde{w}_{t+1}^i = \tilde{w}_t^i - \eta \tilde{g}_t^i + \eta\rho(\tilde{w}_t^f - \tilde{w}_t^i) \quad and \quad \tilde{w}_{t+1}^f = \tilde{w}_t^f - \eta \tilde{g}_t^f + \eta\rho(\tilde{w}_t^i - \tilde{w}_t^f). \tag{8}$$

When we choose the variance of Gaussian noise $\sigma_2 = \frac{\sqrt{2ln(1.25/\delta)}}{\epsilon}$, we ensure that each communication step of LEAGSD is (ϵ, δ)-DP. Using the property of DP-mechanism in [14], the composition of a series of DP-mechanisms remains DP, which guarantees that for each worker i, its training algorithm $\mathcal{M}_i$ at each iteration is DP. To compute the total (ϵ, δ), we don't use the strong composition theory [14]. Instead, we use the moments accountant method [13], which provides a much tighter bound of ϵ to evaluate the privacy-preserving performance of our algorithm.

5 Analysis

5.1 Convergence Rate Analysis

In this section, we conduct a convergence rate analysis for Synchronous LEASGD in a strongly-convex case and also compare it with the DPSGD theoretically. Before we show the result of the convergence rate, we first introduce some assumptions held in the analysis.

Assumption 1. *These assumptions are held throughout the analysis:*
*1. **i.i.d. Assumption:** We divide our system into several sub-systems with only 1 follower and p leaders. And all the variables in these sub-systems are i.i.d.*
*2. **Correct Categorization:** Assume that since the categorization step in Algorithm 1 is implemented, the identity of all workers will not change until the next categorization*
*3. **Bounded Stochastic Gradient:** Assume that the variance of all the local gradients is bounded for any w for any workers from $1, ..., m$ and input x_t^i. There exist constant σ_1 such that*

$$E[g_t^i - \nabla f(w_t^i)] = 0 \quad and \quad E[\| g_t^i - \nabla f(w_t^i) \|^2] \leq \sigma_1^2. \tag{9}$$

*4. **Strongly Convex Condition:** We focus on the strongly-convex case in this analysis. Correspondingly, there exists $0 < \mu \leq L$ for all the loss functions described in Eq. 4, we have:*

$$\mu \| w_i - w_j \|^2 \leq \langle \nabla f(w_i), \nabla f(w_j) \rangle \leq L \| w_i - w_j \|^2 . \tag{10}$$

We define that

$$d_t = \frac{E \sum_{i=1}^{p} \| w_t^i - w^* \|^2 + E \| w_t^f - w^* \|^2}{p+1}. \tag{11}$$

Proposition 1 *(Convergence rate of Algorithm 1). If $0 \leq \eta \leq \frac{2(1-\beta)}{\mu+L}$ and $0 \leq \alpha = \eta\rho < 1, 0 \leq \beta = p\alpha < 1$, then we obtain the convergence of d_t as follows:*

$$d_t \leq h^t d_0 + (c_0 - \frac{\eta^2 \sigma_1^2}{\gamma})(1 - \gamma)^t (1 - (\frac{p}{p+1})^t) + \eta^2 \sigma_1^2 \frac{1 - h^t}{\gamma},$$

$$where \ 0 < h = \frac{p(1-\gamma)}{p+1} < 1, k = \frac{1-\gamma}{p+1}, \gamma = 2\eta\frac{\mu L}{\mu+L}, \tag{12}$$

$$and \ c_0 = \max_{i=1,...,p,f} \| w_0^i - w^* \|^2 .$$

Under the Assumption 1.1, we simplify our system by dividing it into several subsystems and each includes only 1 follower and p leaders. We assume that the convergence rate of each subsystem is same as that of the whole system. To obtain this convergence rate, we rely on the following theorem.

Theorem 1. Let $y_t = \frac{1}{p}\sum_{i=1}^{p} w_t^i$, $a_t = E \parallel y_t - w^* \parallel^2$, $b_t = \frac{1}{p}\sum_{i=1}^{p} E \parallel w_t^i - w^* \parallel^2$, $c_t = E \parallel w_t^f - w^* \parallel^2$, $\alpha = \eta\rho$, $\beta = p\alpha$, $\gamma = 2\eta\frac{\mu L}{\mu+L}$. If $0 \leq \eta \leq \frac{2(1-\beta)}{\mu+L}$, $0 \leq \alpha < 1$, $0 \leq \beta < 1$, then

$$b_{t+1} \leq (1 - \gamma - \alpha)b_t + \alpha c_t + \eta^2\sigma_1^2, \tag{13}$$
$$c_{t+1} \leq (1 - \gamma - \beta)c_t + \beta a_t + \eta^2\sigma_1^2. \tag{14}$$

Proof of Proposition 1: from the sorting rule and the Assumption 1.1, we can easily obtain the inequality relation of a_t, b_t, c_t and d_t

$$a_t \leq d_t \leq c_t \quad and \quad b_t \leq d_t \leq c_t \tag{15}$$

Applying (15) in (14) and iterating through t times, we have

$$c_t \leq (1 - \gamma)^t c_0 + \eta^2\sigma_1^2\frac{1 - (1 - \gamma)^t}{\gamma}. \tag{16}$$

Now replacing $d_t = \frac{pb_t + c_t}{p+1}$ in (13), (14) and using (15), we have

$$d_t \leq hd_{t-1} + kc_{t-1} + \eta^2\sigma_1^2. \tag{17}$$

Applying (16) in (17), we have:

$$d_t \leq hd_{t-1} + k(c_0 - \frac{\eta^2\sigma_1^2}{\gamma})(1 - \gamma)^{t-1} + (1 + \frac{k}{\gamma})\eta^2\sigma_1^2. \tag{18}$$

Iterating t times though this inequality, we have

$$d_t \leq h^t d_0 + k(c_0 - \frac{\eta^2\sigma_1^2}{\gamma})\frac{(1 - \gamma)^t - h^t}{1 - \gamma - h} + (1 + \frac{k}{\gamma})\eta^2\sigma_1^2\frac{1 - h^t}{1 - h}. \tag{19}$$

To simplify (19), we note that

$$k + h = 1 - \gamma, \tag{20}$$

$$\frac{1 + \frac{k}{\gamma}}{1 - h} = \frac{1 + \frac{\frac{1-\gamma}{p+1}}{\gamma}}{1 - \frac{p(1-\gamma)}{p+1}} = \frac{p + 1 + \frac{1-\gamma}{\gamma}}{p + 1 - p(1 - \gamma)} = \frac{p + \frac{1}{\gamma}}{1 + p\gamma} = \frac{1}{\gamma}. \tag{21}$$

So (19) can be rewritten as

$$d_t \leq h^t d_0 + (c_0 - \frac{\eta^2\sigma_1^2}{\gamma})(1 - \gamma)^t(1 - (\frac{p}{p+1})^t) + \eta^2\sigma_1^2\frac{1 - h^t}{\gamma}. \tag{22}$$

This concludes the proof.

Under this proposition, it implies that the average gap between all workers and optimum in a subsystem includes three parts, which could also be applied to the whole system based on Assumption 1.1. The first part is a shrinkage part of itself by a constant factor $0 < h < 1$, which shows a exponential decreasing relationship between the gap and iteration t. The second part is tend to be 0 with the increase of t. The third part is a inherent noisy part with the variance of $\eta^2 \sigma_1^2$. If we ignore the influence of the inherent noise on the gradient and extend $t \to \infty$, we can obtain an purely exponential decline of the gap, that is $E[d_{t+1}] \leq hE[d_t]$.

According to the convergence rate analysis in DPSGD [9], its convergence rate is $O(1/[(p+1)t])$ with our denotation in the strongly-convex setting. Compared with our $O(h^t)$ rate, the convergence rate of DPSGD is relatively slower when we extend the $t \to \infty$.

5.2 Privacy Trade-Off Analysis

In this section, we provide the trade-off analysis between the accuracy and privacy. Following the convergence rate analysis above, we can obtain the modified convergence rate of d_t after adding the extra noise as the only part that needs to be changed is the third part of Eq. 12. In the private setting, the noise is composed of two different parts. First, the inherent noise, which is the same as defined in Assumption 1.3. Second, the differential-privacy preserving noise, which is defined in the Eq. 7.

We assume that the two noise is independent of each other. Thus, the variance of the composed noise is the sum of the two independent noise variances and it satisfies $\sigma^2 < \sigma_1^2 + C^2 \sigma_2^2$. Finally, the convergence rate in the private setting is as below:

Proposition 2. *(Trade-off for privacy). With the limits held in the Proposition 1, we can obtain the convergence of d_t after adding the Gaussian Noise:*

$$d_t \leq h^t d_0 + (c_0 - \frac{\eta^2 \sigma^2}{\gamma})(1-\gamma)^t [1 - (\frac{p}{p+1})^t] + \eta^2 \sigma^2 \frac{1-h^t}{\gamma}$$

$$< h^t d_0 + (c_0 - \frac{\eta^2 \sigma^2}{\gamma})(1-\gamma)^t [1 - (\frac{p}{p+1})^t] + \eta^2 \sigma_1^2 \frac{1-h^t}{\gamma} + \eta^2 C^2 \sigma_2^2 \frac{1-h^t}{\gamma}.$$

$$(23)$$

According to this proposition, the extra trade-off for privacy is $\eta^2 C^2 \sigma_2^2 \frac{1-h^t}{\gamma}$ and when $t \to \infty$, this trade-off can be formulated as $\frac{\eta^2 C^2 \sigma_2^2}{\gamma}$. Note that this trade-off remains the same when p grows, which implies that our algorithm has stable scalability when applied in the private setting. In other words, despite the group of workers become larger, the noise in the communication is not accumulated to further compromise the performance. Additionally, this analysis is under the assumption of strongly-convex setting. In fact, when applied in a non-convex setting, the adding noise in an appropriate scale could improve the performance as the noise motivates workers to explore more space and it becomes easier for those workers in the local optimum to get out of it.

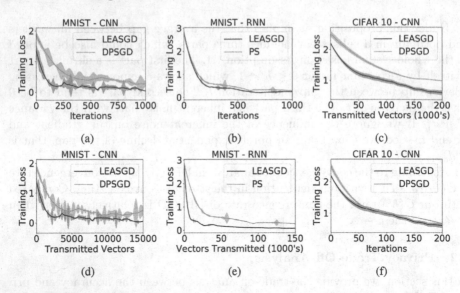

Fig. 2. Comparison between LEASGD, DPSGD, and PS. Training Loss VS Iterations for (a) MNIST-CNN, (b) MNIST-RNN, and (c) CIFAR 10. Training Loss VS Number of Transmitted vectors for (d) MNIST-CNN, (e) MNIST-RNN, and (f) CIFAR 10.

6   Experimental Evaluation

6.1   Experiment Setup

Non-private setting setup. In this setting, we perform experiments using MNIST-CNN, MNIST-RNN, and CIFAR-10. The structure of MNIST-CNN is a 3-layer Multi-layer Perceptron (MLP), and the MNIST-RNN has 32 hidden layers. For CIFAR-10, we use the ConvnetJS [21] as the model.

Private setting setup. In this setting, the neural network models and hyper-parameters are the same as in non-private setting. We test two algorithms of different worker sizes of $m = 5, 15$, respectively shown in Table 1. Additionally, we tune the elastic factor $\rho = 10$ for MNIST-CNN and $\rho = 100$ for CIFAR-10. For the private factors, we set Gaussian noise variance $\sigma = 4$, clipping constant $C = 4$, and fixed δ budget $\delta = 10^{-5}$.

6.2   Non-private Setting Comparison

Accuracy Comparison. We first conduct experiments on a cluster of 15 nodes to compare our LEASGD against DPSGD in the non-private setting form MNIST-CNN and CIFAR 10 models. For the MNIST-RNN model, we compare against Parameter Server (PS) as DPSGD does not support RNN models.

DPSGD has various communication topologies when communication matrix is set differently. We only test the ring topology for simplicity, which allows each worker to accept the information from two other neighbor workers. The training loss as a function of iterations is shown in Fig. 2(a)(b)(c), which demonstrate that LEASGD converges faster than DPSGD and PS at the beginning of the training process and also achieves a lower loss function at the end across all models.

Communication Cost. To quantitatively evaluate the communication cost, we track the average training loss of all workers with regard to the number of transmitted vectors as shown in Fig. 2(d)(e)(f). The results verify that LEASGD also outperforms DPSGD and PS in the efficiency of communication usage as within the same number of transmitted vectors, the loss function of LEASGD almost always under that of DPSGD and PS across all models.

Theoretically, in each iteration, LEASGD has less transmitted vectors compared to DPSGD and PS even though communication in LEASGD is two-way instead of one-way in DPSGD. In LEASGD, the number of transmitted vectors per iteration is $(m - L) * 2$ (14 in this experiment). In DPSGD, the number of transmitted vectors per iteration is the sum of numbers of neighbors of all workers, which is typically $2m$ (20 in this experiment) in a ring network.

Scalability. We also evaluate the scalability of LEASGD using MNIST-CNN and MNIST-RNN by varying the number of total nodes from 10 to 20 while keeping the percentage of leaders at 75%. The results are organized in Fig. 3, where we can see LEASGD outperforms PS across all cases. We also observe that the training loss becomes slightly worsen when the number of nodes increases, but the degrading speed becomes slower, i.e., the gap between 20 nodes and 15 nodes are much smaller than the gap between 15 nodes and 10 nodes. This indicates that LEASGD scales well.

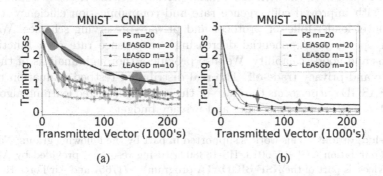

Fig. 3. Scalability of LEASGD (m is the total number of nodes).

6.3   Differential Private Comparison

In the private setting, we use the *moments accountant* to compute the totally spent ϵ and the adding noise scales are the same for two algorithms. As shown in Table 1, LEASGD achieves better accuracy with less ϵ than DPSGD. More importantly, the final accuracy of our algorithm does not vary greatly when the worker scale m increases. We believe this result benefits from two attributes of LEASGD: (1) the DP noise helps improve the accuracy by encouraging space exploration and helping workers trapped in local optimum to get out [22]; (2) the great scalability that prevents DP noise from accumulating when the worker scale expands.

Table 1. Private setting result of final accuracy and ϵ.

MNIST - CNN			CIFAR-10 - CNN		
Algorithm	Final accuracy	Total ϵ	Algorithm	Final accuracy	Total ϵ
LEASGD (m=5)	**0.97**	**4.183**	LEASGD (m=5)	**0.74**	**4.655**
DPSGD (m=5)	0.97	4.505	DPSGD (m=5)	0.71	4.925
LEASGD (m=15)	**0.97**	**4.651**	LEASGD (m=15)	**0.72**	**4.116**
DPSGD (m=15)	0.95	4.843	DPSGD (m=15)	0.68	4.56

7   Conclusion

In this paper, we propose a new decentralized algorithm LEASGD for training deep neural network with differential privacy. LEASGD ensures differential privacy with improved convergence rate and communication efficiency, thanks to the novel leader-follower protocol and privacy-preserving schemes. We theoretically prove its exponential decreasing convergence rate as a function of iterations and good scalability. We also provide a thorough analysis of the performance and privacy trade-off. The real distributed testbed evaluation results show LEASGD outperforms the state-of-the-art decentralized learning algorithm DPSGD in both convergence rate and privacy budget.

Acknowledgement. This work is supported in part by the following grants: National Science Foundation CCF-1756013, IIS-1838024 (using resources provided by Amazon Web Services as part of the NSF BIGDATA program), 1717657 and Air Force Research Laboratory FA8750-18-2-0057.

References

1. Simonyan, K., Zisserman, A.: Very deep convolutional networks for large-scale image recognition. In: ICLR (2015)
2. He, K., Zhang, X., Ren, S., Sun, J.: Deep residual learning for image recognition. In: IEEE Conference on Computer Vision and Pattern Recognition, pp. 770–778 (2016)

3. Abadi, M., Barham, P., Chen, J., Chen, Z., Davis, A., et al.: Tensorflow: a system for large-scale machine learning. In: Proceedings of the 12th USENIX Conference on Operating Systems Design and Implementation, OSDI 2016, pp. 265–283. USENIX Association, Berkeley (2016)
4. Dean, J., et al.: Large scale distributed deep networks. In: International Conference on Neural Information Processing Systems, pp. 1223–1231 (2013)
5. Xing, E.P., et al.: A new platform for distributed machine learning on big data. IEEE Trans. Big Data **1**(2), 1335–1344 (2015)
6. Poczos, B., Salakhutdinov, R., Smola, A.: Scaling distributed machine learning with system and algorithm co-design
7. Agarwal, N., Suresh, A.T., Yu, F.X.X., Kumar, S., McMahan, B.: cpSGD: communication-efficient and differentially-private distributed SGD. arXiv preprint arXiv:1805.10559 (2018)
8. Bellet, A., Guerraoui, R., Taziki, M., Tommasi, M.: Personalized and private peer-to-peer machine learning. In: AISTATS (2018)
9. Lian, X., Zhang, C., Zhang, H., Hsieh, C.J., Zhang, W., Liu, J.: Can decentralized algorithms outperform centralized algorithms? A case study for decentralized parallel stochastic gradient descent. In: Advances in Neural Information Processing Systems, pp. 5330–5340 (2017)
10. Yan, F., Sundaram, S., Vishwanathan, S.V.N., Qi, Y.: Distributed autonomous online learning: regrets and intrinsic privacy-preserving properties. IEEE Trans. Knowl. Data Eng. **25**(11), 2483–2493 (2013)
11. Dwork, C.: Differential privacy. In: Bugliesi, M., Preneel, B., Sassone, V., Wegener, I. (eds.) ICALP 2006. LNCS, vol. 4052, pp. 1–12. Springer, Heidelberg (2006). https://doi.org/10.1007/11787006_1
12. Zhang, S., Choromanska, A.E., LeCun, Y.: Deep learning with elastic averaging SGD. In: Advances in Neural Information Processing Systems, pp. 685–693 (2015)
13. Abadi, M.: Deep learning with differential privacy. In: Computer and Communications Security, pp. 308–318 (2016)
14. Dwork, C., Rothblum, G.N., Vadhan, S.: Boosting and differential privacy. In: Annual Symposium on Foundations of Computer Science, vol. 26(2), pp. 51–60 (2010)
15. Ram, S.S., Nedic, A., Veeravalli, V.V.: Distributed subgradient projection algorithm for convex optimization. In: IEEE International Conference on Acoustics, Speech and Signal Processing, ICASSP 2009, pp. 3653–3656. IEEE (2009)
16. Nedic, A., Ozdaglar, A.: Distributed subgradient methods for multi-agent optimization. IEEE Trans. Autom. Control **54**(1), 48–61 (2009)
17. Colin, I., Bellet, A., Salmon, J., Clémençon, S.: Gossip dual averaging for decentralized optimization of pairwise functions. In: Proceedings of The 33rd International Conference on Machine Learning, Proceedings of Machine Learning Research, PMLR, New York, vol. 48, pp. 1388–1396, 20–22 June 2016
18. Dean, J., et al.: Large scale distributed deep networks. In: Advances in Neural Information Processing Systems, pp. 1223–1231 (2012)
19. Kairouz, P., Oh, S., Viswanath, P.: Extremal mechanisms for local differential privacy. In: Advances in Neural Information Processing Systems, pp. 2879–2887 (2014)
20. Cheng, H.-P.: LEASGD: an efficient and privacy-preserving decentralized algorithm for distributed learning. CoRR, abs/1811.11124 (2018). (appeared in PPML 2018 Workshop – co-located with NeurIPS 2018)
21. Convnetjs. https://cs.stanford.edu/people/karpathy/convnetjs/demo/cifar10.html
22. Neelakantan, A.: Adding gradient noise improves learning for very deep networks. arXiv preprint arXiv:1511.06807 (2015)

Exploiting the Spam Correlations
in Scalable Online Social Spam Detection

Hailu Xu, Liting Hu$^{(\boxtimes)}$, Pinchao Liu, and Boyuan Guan

School of Computing and Information Science, Florida International University,
Miami, FL 33174, USA
{hxu017,lhu,pliu002,bguan003}@cs.fiu.edu

Abstract. The huge amount of social spam from large-scale social networks has been a common phenomenon in the contemporary world. The
majority of former research focused on improving the efficiency of identifying social spam from a limited size of data in the algorithm side,
however, few of them target on the data correlations among large-scale
distributed social spam and utilize the benefits from the system side.
In this paper, we propose a new scalable system, named SpamHunter,
which can utilize the spam correlations from distributed data sources to
enhance the performance of large-scale social spam detection. It identifies the correlated social spam from various distributed servers/sources
through DHT-based hierarchical functional trees. These functional trees
act as bridges among data servers/sources to aggregate, exchange, and
communicate the updated and newly emerging social spam with each
other. Furthermore, by processing the online social logs instantly, it
allows online streaming data to be processed in a distributed manner,
which reduces the online detection latency and avoids the inefficiency
of outdated spam posts. Our experimental results with real-world social
logs demonstrate that SpamHunter reaches 95% F1 score in the spam
detection, achieves high efficiency in scaling to a large amount of data
servers with low latency.

Keywords: Social spam detection · DHT-based overlay

1 Introduction

Online social networks (OSNs) have been an integral part of human life. More
and more people are acquiring the latest news, advertisements, social activities,
and breaking topics directly from the current popular OSNs such as Facebook,
Twitter, and WeChat. For example, a report said that the percentage of US
adults who primarily receive news and information from OSNs is as high as
62% [3]. However, the openness of widespread OSNs couple with massive spam
activities, which are damaging as they cause public panic and social unrest. For
example, in February of 2019, social users in Paris watched a lot of photos of
kidnappings on Facebook and videos of vans speeding away on Snapchat and

© Springer Nature Switzerland AG 2019
D. Da Silva et al. (Eds.): CLOUD 2019, LNCS 11513, pp. 146–160, 2019.
https://doi.org/10.1007/978-3-030-23502-4_11

Twitter, all of which hinted that the Roma (Gypsies) robbed children with vans in the suburbs of Paris [5]. Although the information proved to be wrong later, they brought serious consequences to the Roma and the whole society: dozens of young men wielding sticks and knives attacked a Roma camp and burned two vans, and tens of people were arrested. Another example is that one latest report said the global enterprise spam filter market was valued approximately USD 849 million in 2018 and is expected to generate around USD 2,675 million by 2026 [2]. And it pointed out that the increasing number of social spam is driving the enterprise spam filter market globally.

The unprecedented success of online social networks has created tremendous opportunities for the emergence and rapid spread of spam. By leveraging a large social user, social spam often dominates and influences social life in a short period of time and can reach every corner of the social world. Therefore, quickly detecting spam from large-scale social activities is an urgent need in the current situation.

Furthermore, as our observation, the spammers in the online social networks are not only active on a single platform, but are often active on different social platforms, by simultaneously manipulating dozens or hundreds of fake accounts. Naturally, the information published by these fake accounts is highly similar. This phenomenon has been pointed out by several former studies [28]. Spammers certainly desire to spread similar posts on different platforms to attract as many people as possible to target on these topics. A case study of social spam posts for multiple different news sites also demonstrates that spam posts show a high degree of similarity in content and topics during the same period of time and will immediately propagate from one site to another [1]. Therefore, this correlation between cross-platform social spam is a common phenomenon in the current social media world. Although there are not many direct relationships between users, geographic locations, creation purposes, and regions in these various groups or platforms, the spam contents are highly correlated within similar topics during the same period of time.

However, former studies rarely utilized the spam correlations to handle the large-scale social data from distributed data servers. They either focused on the algorithm side to achieve high accuracy in the detection [12,20,22,23,25], or the entire processing only targeted on a small size of dataset without the global view from similar data across large-scale data sources [7,9,26,30]. In this paper, to explore the efficient method in dealing with large-scale social data sources, we present a new social spam detection system, named **SpamHunter**, to take advantage of the spam correlation among distributed data sources for efficient large-scale social spam detection. SpamHunter implements multiple groups, where each group contains a DHT-based functional tree that jointly connecting multiple data sources (e.g., servers, datasets, etc.) to share the spam correlations (e.g., updated spam features) in a distributed manner. The DHT-based functional trees response to data delivery, spam identification, and correlation exchanges. Besides, the group-level coordination ensures multiple groups or clusters can instantly exchange and share the correlated features during the processing, that is, they collectively leverage the latest spam correlations to enhance the performance of spam detection.

This paper makes the following technique contributions:

- An *distributed* spam detection system named SpamHunter is presented that defend against social spam activities from large-scale social networks.
- The *scalable* DHT-based functional tree guarantees the orchestration and flexible management of a large amount of data sources.
- SpamHunter supports the use of the spam *correlations* among large-scale data sources to identify the latest spam activities and enables efficient online spam detection.

We outline the rest of this paper as follows: Sect. 2 presents the design and functional components of the system. Section 3 describes the detailed evaluation results with real-world social logs. Section 4 introduces the related works and we finally conclude this work in Sect. 5.

2 Design

In this section, we will introduce an overview of the SpamHunter system, describe the details of the functional components in the system, and outline the workflow for processing.

2.1 SpamHunter Overview

Figure 1 shows the designed architecture of the SpamHunter system. SpamHunter is built upon a peer-to-peer DHT-based Pastry overlay [17]. The overlay is utilized to orchestrate large-scale distributed social servers. As shown in the first step of Fig. 1, these data servers can be grouped by various kinds of features (e.g., geo-location, topic tags, or institutions), and the large amount of servers are connected to the DHT-based overlay. In the second step, SpamHunter creates a functional tree upon Pastry for each group, where nodes jointly route around a specific key (see details in Subsect. 2.2). The functional tree for each group will respond to the primary workload during processing, for example, data dissemination, spam detection, and results aggregation.

In the third step, SpamHunter deploys online social spam detection within the group management. In each group, SpamHunter manages the functional tree to fulfill the online social data processing. The root of the tree is responsible for the data/model dissemination and in charge of the entire workflow. The distributed leaf nodes will complete the processing of spam detection by following the root's instructions by coordinating the classified models. The root of the tree also aggregates the identified results from the following nodes, updates the spam dataset, and extracts the latest spam. Furthermore, as shown in the fourth step of Fig. 1, after the online spam detection, multiple groups in SpamHunter will periodically exchange and share the latest spam with others, so that all groups

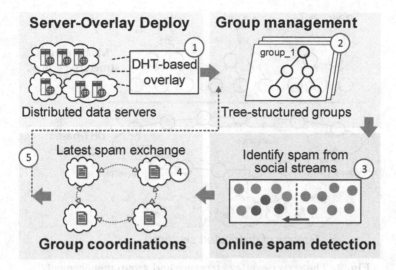

Fig. 1. The overview of the system design.

have a global view of the newest social spam and then utilize the correlated new spam in the continuing processing, as shown in the fifth step of the Fig. 1.

Next, we will introduce the system's functionality and implementations details. We first introduce the deployment of SpamHunter and the group management. Then we introduce the online social spam processing. Finally, we propose the group coordination and communication in enhancing the detection performance by leveraging the large-scale spam correlations.

2.2 SpamHunter Group Management

We first present the details of the overlay in SpamHunter. SpamHunter is built upon the peer-to-peer Pastry overlay [17], where each node has a unique 128-bit nodeId with a nodeId space ranging from 0–$2^{128} - 1$. Note that all nodeIds are evenly distributed, so that the deployment of nodes can be flexibly scaled to a large amount of instances. The message is the main link between nodes: nodes can route messages towards a specific key, for example, the key can be a target nodeId, a groupId, or a specific topic concatenates with a groupId. With the targeted key, messages can be routed to the node which nodeId is numerically closest to the key in $\lceil log_{2^b} N \rceil$ steps, where the default value of b is 4.

By leveraging Scribe [6], each node in SpamHunter can create a group by a groupId. Typically, the groupId is obtained by hashing (SHA-1) the name of the group with the name of its creator. Other nodes can randomly join a group by routing a JOIN message towards the groupId as the key, which enables flexible group membership. The nodeId of the rendezvous node in the group is closest in value to the groupId. Each group constitutes a functional tree which creates valid paths for the root to communicate with multiple layer nodes. The key idea is the use of a DHT-based application-level multicast tree [6] to propagate data/model

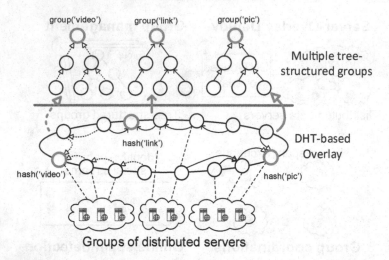

Fig. 2. The server-overlay structure and group management.

replicas through the tree path, which has the advantage of not maintaining N point-to-point connections for N leaf nodes. For example, assuming there are 7 nodes jointly work as group "*video*", if *hash* (video + creator name) equals to *EA34*, the node whose nodeId is closest to it, such like *EA34* or *EA35*, will serve as the root of the functional tree. The other six nodes will then subscribe to this tree and follow the root node. Due to the tree structure, the tree root can multicast the messages, instructions, or models to all leaf nodes in $O(logN)$ hops (Fig. 2).

SpamHunter Tree's Functions. SpamHunter creates multiple groups to support the scalability of social data processing. Each group constitutes as a functional tree, where the spam detection is fulfilled in this tree. As shown in Fig. 3, the group's functional tree mainly has four functions: *spam detection, aggregate function, spam extract*, and *external/inner tunnel*. We next present the details of these functions.

The *spam detection* is fulfilled by the coordination of the root and leaf nodes. In the group's tree, the tree root is in charge of the workflow of spam identification via the *inner tunnel* in root and leaf. The root of the tree will build a spam detection model by training the model using the training data set and then testing the model using the test data set. In addition, it manages the processing workflow by propagating instructions and models through the functional tree to the following branches and leaf nodes. By following the instructions of the tree root, the leaf nodes complete the pre-data processing and spam identification with the model. Details are presented in Subsect. 2.3.

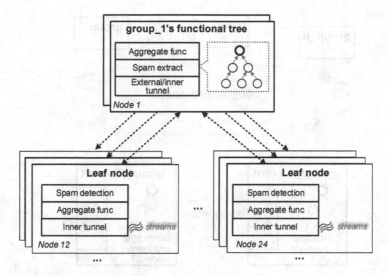

Fig. 3. The DHT-based functional tree.

The SpamHunter functional tree supports *aggregate function* during the processing to collect the interim results after spam detection. The tree branches and middle-level nodes are able to jointly work with the tree root to fulfill the aggregation. We next use an example to present it. After the local social spam classifications in the leaf nodes, batches of social logs are parsed as mappings from the content (*posts*) to categorical tag (*labels*), i.e., (*post_1*, 0) and (*post_2*, 1) in leaf nodes (here the tag 1 represents spam and the tag 0 represents non-spam). The leaf node will first filter out the identified spam data, (i.e., the social data has been detected as spam and marked with label 1), then sends the paired instances, e.g., (*post_i*, 1), to the upper layer via the *deliver tunnel*.

The third function supported in SpamHunter tree is the *spam extract*. After results aggregation, the tree root will accumulate the latest spam posts from the collected interim results and identify the prospected posts which are most highly be spam. For example, in a specific case, when 6 servers' interim results notify that the social post *post_k* as spam post, after the aggregation, the root will acquire the final votes for this post as (*post_k*, 6). The root node will extract this new identified spam post and join this post into the new training dataset, a set of data with identified spam and ham post which is used for creating spam models. After the default batch size, the root node will generate a new dataset consisting of latest spam posts and then periodically create a new spam model upon this dataset. After that, the tree root will disseminate the newly trained model to all following nodes in the continuing processing. Besides, when necessary, the tree root can multicast to its nodes within the group, to notify them to empty their sliding windows and/or synchronously start a new batch [29].

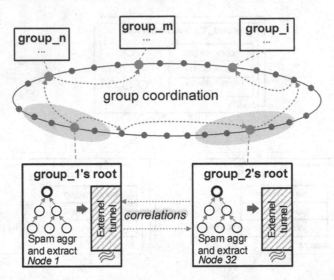

Fig. 4. The group coordination in the system. Group_1's root shares the spam correlations with group_2's root. Besides, the group_1's root communicates with other groups' roots via the overlay.

As shown in Fig. 4, after the date processing in the tree-level, the *external tunnel* ensures multiple groups' roots exchanging and sharing the latest spam posts at the runtime, which means that each group can leverage spam correlation to enhance its own processing and get better performance. As mentioned earlier, in order to allow distributed data servers to obtain a global view of spam information, SpamHunter allows the root of the group to send its aggregated spam to the roots of other peer groups. Details of data delivery among groups can be seen in Sect. 2.2. Each group's root can periodically update and exchange its extracted spam data with other groups.

SpamHunter ensures the entire spam detection in flexible processing granularity, including both globally large-scale data processing and locally distributed data processing. To support multiple processing targets, such as high latency sensitivity or good failure recovery, the functional tree is able to self-tune at the tree structure level by adjusting the tree fan-out element n, with achieving 2^n fan-outs per node.

Specifically, when the latency is the prime target of the users' defined applications, SpamHunter can customize the depth of functional tree by adjusting the fan-out element n. For instance, when 10^b (i.e., b = 4) nodes exist in the system, the original depth of the functional tree is $log_{2^b}(10^b)$. By adjusting the fan-out element from 4 (2^4) to 5 (2^5), the average depth of the tree can be pruned from 5 to 4. Consequently, the overall latency of root-to-leaf transmission will obtain 20% decrement.

2.3 Online Social Spam Detection

The SpamHunter leaf node is responsible for two functionality: (1) social raw log collection and normalization and (2) local spam detection. Each leaf node collects the social network logs (i.e., social posts, images, news, Tweets, and so on) from the distributed web servers. The leaf node can utilize the openly APIs (e.g., Twitter API, Facebook API) to collect the online/real-time streaming social logs. The logs will be collected from scripts and saved to the local server, which can be utilized next by the leaf node that connected to this server. Furthermore, the leaf node will pre-process and normalize the raw social logs into the same formatted separate set. The majority of posts contain URLs, typically, to confuse the malicious URLs, spammers will add white spaces and unicode characters into them [10]. This is a simple but effective way to bypass the filters that blacklist URLs only by simple string matching. Inspired by [10], we de-confuse URLs by removing whitespace padding and normalizing the encoded characters (e.g., "subsexvideo%26ip%3Dauto%26click%3D1" becomes "subsexvideo&ip=auto&click=1"). For social contents, specifically, we remove punctuation, tokenize each word, and remove stopwords. We extract the tf-idf values of the terms in each document. The tf-idf weight of the term represents the frequency at which the term appears throughout the document [32].

After the data collection, SpamHunter leaf node will first normalize the original data into unified formats. The SpamHunter leaf node extracts the posts' contents from the JSON formatted log. Then it divides these social data into same sized datasets for the local online spam detection. Next, the leaf node will utilize the trained spam model which is disseminated from SpamHunter root to complete the local data processing task. Original data which consists of unprocessed social logs without identified labels. After the spam classification with the trained model, an identified label will be created to each instance of the original social logs (here 1 presents spam and 0 presents non-spam). Besides, the SpamHunter leaf node will facilitate completing the results aggregation flow by sending intermediate results to the upper layers. Note that the leaf nodes will instantly process the collected social logs without long latency. Besides, they will follow the root's instructions to clean its slides and start new batches with the updated spam model.

The online social spam detection is completed by coordinating both tree-level and group-level. The tree-level processing has been presented before, we next introduce the group-level coordination in online processing, which primarily relies on group communications.

2.4 SpamHunter Group Coordination

The group communications in SpamHunter are responsible for the main function of spam correlated model update and data exchange among the entire detection. We fulfill the group communication by implementing diffusion broadcasting group. We now present the details of this functional component. SpamHunter group provides two major functions: *multicast* and *anycast*. *Multicast* is used to construct a hierarchical functional tree, which acts as a fundamental frame for scalability in SpamHunter. *multicast* allows messages or instructions can be delivered to all the members in one group. As presented before, any nodes can create a group in the overlay; and other nodes can flexibly join the group and then *multicast* messages from the rendezvous point to all member of the group along the functional tree.

Anycast can be used for group communications and model transmissions among multiple groups. It is implemented by the distributed depth-first search (DFS). Each node in the overlay (may in/out of group k) can *anycast* to the group k by routing a message towards the group k's groupId [17]. The convergence of local routing in Pastry guarantees that this message can highly reach a group member near the sender's nodeId. *Anycast* can also be used to serve the communications between multiple groups, such as exchanging the updated dataset and exploring the spam correlations among them.

SpamHunter supports group-level communications to allow multiple groups to exchange their updated models to enhance the final performances. Once a group finishes its whole processing in the leaf nodes, the root node aggregates the results that contain the newest spam information and then updates its model. Further, root nodes in groups exchange the updated models by disseminating their updated models to other peer-groups. Then all groups own the newest models from other groups and can utilize the new models in the continuing processing.

SpamHunter originally supports star group that allows each root of one group *anycasts* the updated model to other groups. Given a graph G with N nodes, one root needs to send $n - 1$ messages during one round time. In this case, SpamHunter group has to send out $m = 1/2 \times n \times (n - 1)$ messages which takes $O(n^2)$ time. To diminish the group communication latency, we design diffusion group in SpamHunter. We now present the details of this type of group communication.

The diffusion group communication lies in: each root node in a group holds a table where contains the model version and the original group, which denotes as a $<groupID, versionNum>$. The root within updated model in one group randomly chooses two other groups to disseminate the model with the new version number. The root of these two groups will check its model table to see if the current received model is the latest one. If the *versionNum* is larger than the value in the table, they will save the model and update the model table with the new version number. If not, they will return a message to the original group to notify they already own the newest one. These two roots will act as new propagators and begin to deliver the latest model to other groups. Finally, all groups' roots will receive the updated model and update their model tables. It's easy to refer that the number of rounds to propagate a single update model to all groups is $O(logn)$, where n is the number of groups in SpamHunter.

3   Evaluations

The experimental evaluation of the system is carried out with online real-world streaming data from social media. We utilize the data which is collected from Twitter streaming APIs [29]. We manually labeled the dataset for examining the performance of spam detection. These data were labeled based on the posts' URL, content, and Twitter official identifications. The dataset contains 60,000 posts which including of 43,897 ham posts and 26,100 spam posts. The application's purpose is to identify social spam posts, which produces predicted labels from online data streams via the system. Note that near 1'000,000 posts are used for evaluating the scalability of the system.

Experiments are conducted on a testbed of 10,000 nodes hosted by 10 servers. Each server has a 3.4 GHz CPU, 4G of memory and 30 GB hard drives. Our evaluations mainly answer the following questions:

- What are the performances of system metrics in the scale, such as the delivery and aggregation latency, functional tree construction latency, and runtime overhead (Sect. 3.1)?
- What are the performances of group coordination and online spam detection by utilizing the spam correlations (Sect. 3.2)?

3.1   System Performances with Scalability

SpamHunter achieves effective spam detection in large-scale online social data sources, therefore, scalability is a major part of the overall evaluation. To evaluate SpamHunter, we deploy the system with the nodes ranging from 1,000 to 10,000, which consists of ten groups (functional trees) in the cluster of servers.

SpamHunter implements functional tree to complete the local distributed social spam detection, which means that the functionality of the tree directly affects the final performance of the process. We first look at the tree paths in the group. The functional tree responses for the message routing, delivery, and communications between multiple layers of nodes, therefore, the average hops (steps) among node communication should affect the performances within scaling to a large amount of data sources. The evaluated average hops are shown in Fig. 5a. From this figure, we can see that the average hops between multiple layers of nodes are consistent when the system scales to large amount of nodes. The typical hops among the functional tree are around 2 to 3. This demonstrates that SpamHunter can flexibly and conveniently support large-scale data sources and servers, and can guarantee the total communication between servers/instances in a relatively small distance, which indicates the low latency in handling node interactions and communications.

The communication latency among SpamHunter is mainly from two parts: the delivery latency from the root and the aggregations latency from the leaf. The delivery latency refers to the root node of the functional tree disseminating the messages, data, spam model, and instructions to all following nodes. The aggregation latency generally refers to the root node aggregates the interim results (i.e., identified social spam posts) from the leaf nodes. The results of these two kinds of latency are shown in the Fig. 5b. From this figure, we can observe that when scaling the nodes to a large scale (up to 10,000), the latency is slowly increased with a few hundreds of milliseconds. This is reasonable since a large amount of nodes will cause part of delay in the message delivery and results aggregation. The difference between these two kinds of latency is usually from the delivered data size, for example, the delivered spam model is up to several megabytes, which causes the delivery latency is higher than the result aggregation latency.

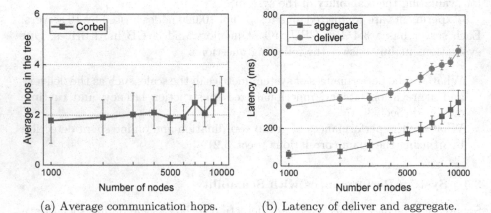

(a) Average communication hops.   (b) Latency of deliver and aggregate.

Fig. 5. The average hops of node communications, the latency of delivery and aggregation in the SpamHunter system. (a) represents the average number of hops when nodes communicate in the functional tree. (b) shows the average latency of delivery and aggregation in the functional tree, the delivery mainly refers to model dissemination and the aggregation mainly refers to the results aggregation.

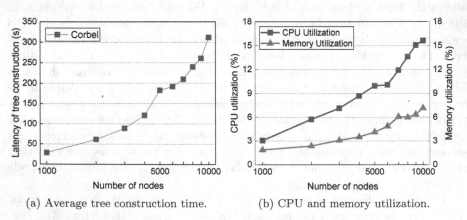

(a) Average tree construction time.   (b) CPU and memory utilization.

Fig. 6. The average functional tree construction time and the runtime overhead in CPU and memory. (a) represents the average latency when creating functional tree with different numbers of nodes in SpamHunter. (b) shows the runtime overhead of CPU and memory utilization.

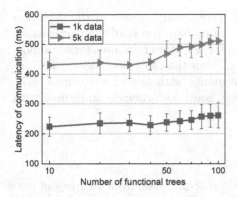

Table 1. Results of spam detection.

Model	F1	Precision	Recall
RF	0.951	0.951	0.951
SVM	0.942	0.945	0.944
RT	0.927	0.928	0.927
Logistic	0.859	0.866	0.855

Fig. 7. Group communication latency.

Moreover, we evaluate the latency in constructing functional trees with a different number of nodes. As shown in Fig. 6a, when the nodes scale from 1,000 to 10,000 (note that these are ten trees here, for each tree, the nodes scale from 100 to 1,000), the construction latency is linearly increased with the nodes' increment. The latency is usually from the hash of nodeId and the joining of the overlay. Note that the functional tree only needs to be built once at the beginning, and it will not cause other latency during the data processing.

Further, we evaluate the runtime overhead of the system in deploying the functionality. Results of the CPU and memory utilization are shown in Fig. 6b. The values of utilization present the overhead in one server and here they leave out the processing of spam detection since the data processing will periodically cost lots of computations and will make the overhead confusing in evaluating the functional tree's performances. From this figure, we can see that with the number of nodes scales to 10,000, the runtime overhead linearly increases by 16% in CPU and 7% in memory. It presents that SpamHunter achieves relatively lightweight overhead in guaranteeing the tree and group functions at runtime. And it can be beneficial for the large-scale data processing in the future.

3.2 Group Coordination and Spam Detection

SpamHunter supports multiple groups to exchange and share the latest spam posts with each other. In this subsection, we present the experimental results of group coordination and the performance of spam detection.

Figure 7 shows the latency of communication among multiple groups' roots. Here we use two sizes of dataset, with 1,000 and 5,000 posts separately. From the figure, we can see that the latency of communication is consistent with the increment of groups from 10 to 100. When deployed with a large number of groups, for instance, 100 groups, the average latency has linear increment. In general, the latency mainly depends on the size of the delivered data. When the root shares a large size of spam posts, it will incur longer latency.

Table 1 presents the performances of spam detection in SpamHunter. We implement several classical algorithms such like RF (Random Forest), SVM

(Support Vector Machine), RT (Random Tree), and Logistic in the detection with the labeled dataset. We present the major parameters of the performance including F1, Precision, and Recall, where the F1 score responses for an important factor in measuring the performance. From the table we can see the Random Forest (RF) achieves the best performance with the F1 score near 95%. This presents that SpamHunter can achieve good performances in dealing with the online real-world social spam data.

4   Related Work

There is a large body of studies that identified social spam from a variety of perspectives, such like from the view of follower/friend relationships [24], social accounts' behavior/activities patterns [18], and the review and user linguistic [21]. However, these studies are still limited to historical data of a certain size and are difficult to adapt to current online large-scale social data streams and applied to changing spam activities. Some recent applications had begun to integrate with scalable platforms for efficient processing [4,14,16,19]. For instance, a model within CELAR cloud platform is designed to catalog the distributed, dynamic and redundant cancer data [27]. Different from them, we consider to utilize spam correlations from various distributed data sources and achieve online social data processing.

Several prior studies had present the correlations between feature-similar social networks or social activities. Coviello et al. [8] found that online social network owes large-scale spillover where individual activities may ripple through whole social networks to generate large-scale synchrony. GSRank [15] demonstrated that the spam group presented strong correlation in their behaviors with the statistical validation. [13] presented the high correlation between social owner's comments and the followers' comments, and demonstrated that the user interactions also represent correlations. [11,31] presented that social influence now is a common phenomenon among social networks where highly connected users or central users of one group/activity will be the core disseminator of contents. Besides, more shared contents will get higher attention and propagation in a short period of time. Inspired by the correlations among large-scale data sources, we choose to apply the spam correlations from distributed data sources into traditional social spam detection and with achieving the large-scale online data processing in multiple data servers.

5   Conclusion

Social spam has become an inevitable part of the current social world. Various garbage activities surround people and cause huge negative impacts on both virtual and real life. In this paper, we present an online social spam detection system, named SpamHunter, which leverages the spam correlations among large-scale distributed data sources to enable efficient spam detection in a scalable manner. SpamHunter supports multiple groups to manage social data from various topics, areas, and geo-location. Each group forms a functional tree that guarantees flexible management across a large number of data servers/instances. Moreover, group coordination in SpamHunter allows multiple groups to exchange and share spam correlations from distributed data sources, enabling efficient processing with the latest social spam from online data streams. In future work, we will explore the deployment of extensions across multiple social platforms, which will build a unified platform for orchestrating social spam from a global view.

Acknowledgment. We gratefully thank the anonymous reviewers for their feedback that significantly improved the paper. We thank Florida International University School of Computing and Information Sciences for the travel award to present this work.

References

1. How fake news goes viral: a case study (2016). https://www.nytimes.com/2016/11/20/business/media/how-fake-news-spreads.html
2. Global enterprise spam filter market (2019). https://www.zionmarketresearch.com/report/enterprise-spam-filter-market
3. Allcott, H., Gentzkow, M.: Social media and fake news in the 2016 election. J. Econ. Perspect. **31**(2), 211–36 (2017)
4. Bhimani, J., Mi, N., Leeser, M.: Performance prediction techniques for scalable large data processing in distributed MPI systems. In: 2016 IEEE 35th International Performance Computing and Communications Conference (IPCCC) (2016)
5. Breeden, A.: Child abduction rumors lead to violence against roma in france, March 2019. https://www.nytimes.com/2019/03/28/world/europe/roma-kidnap-rumors-france.html
6. Castro, M., Druschel, P., Kermarrec, A.M., Rowstron, A.I.: Scribe: a large-scale and decentralized application-level multicast infrastructure. IEEE J. Sel. Areas Commun. **20**(8), 1489–1499 (2002)
7. Chen, C., Wang, Y., Zhang, J., Xiang, Y., Zhou, W., Min, G.: Statistical features-based real-time detection of drifted Twitter spam. IEEE Trans. Inf. Forensics Secur. **12**(4), 914–925 (2017)
8. Coviello, L., et al.: Detecting emotional contagion in massivesocial networks. PloS ONE **9**(3), e90315 (2014)
9. Gao, H., Chen, Y., Lee, K., Palsetia, D., Choudhary, A.N.: Towards online spam filtering in social networks. In: NDSS vol. 12, pp. 1–16 (2012)
10. Gao, H., Hu, J., Wilson, C., Li, Z., Chen, Y., Zhao, B.Y.: Detecting and characterizing social spam campaigns. In: Proceedings of the 10th ACM SIGCOMM Conference on Internet Measurement. ACM (2010)
11. Hodas, N.O., Lerman, K.: The simple rules of social contagion. Sci. Rep. **4**, 4343 (2014)
12. Hoefler, T., Barak, A., Shiloh, A., Drezner, Z.: Corrected gossip algorithms for fast reliable broadcast on unreliable systems. In: Parallel and Distributed Processing Symposium (IPDPS) (2017)
13. Jiang, J., et al.: Understanding latent interactions in online social networks. ACM Trans. Web (TWEB) (2013)
14. Kayes, I., Iamnitchi, A.: Privacy and security in online social networks: a survey. Online Soc. Netw. Media **3–4**, 1–21 (2017)

15. Mukherjee, A., Liu, B., Glance, N.: Spotting fake reviewer groups in consumer reviews. In: Proceedings of the 21st International Conference on World Wide Web. ACM (2012)
16. Pop, D., Iuhasz, G., Petcu, D.: Distributed platforms and cloud services: enabling machine learning for big data. In: Mahmood, Z. (ed.) Data Science and Big Data Computing, pp. 139–159. Springer, Cham (2016). https://doi.org/10.1007/978-3-319-31861-5_7
17. Rowstron, A., Druschel, P.: Pastry: scalable, decentralized object location, and routing for large-scale peer-to-peer systems. In: Guerraoui, R. (ed.) Middleware 2001. LNCS, vol. 2218, pp. 329–350. Springer, Heidelberg (2001). https://doi.org/10.1007/3-540-45518-3_18
18. Ruan, X., Wu, Z., Wang, H., Jajodia, S.: Profiling online social behaviors for compromised account detection. IEEE Trans. Inf. Forensics Secur. **11**(1), 176–187 (2016)
19. Salaria, S., Brown, K., Jitsumoto, H., Matsuoka, S.: Evaluation of HPC-big data applications using cloud platforms. In: Proceedings of the 17th IEEE/ACM International Symposium on Cluster, Cloud and Grid Computing (2017)
20. Sedhai, S., Sun, A.: Effect of spam on hashtag recommendation for Tweets. In: Proceedings of the 25th International Conference Companion on World Wide Web. pp. 97–98. International World Wide Web Conferences Steering Committee (2016)
21. Shehnepoor, S., Salehi, M., Farahbakhsh, R., Crespi, N.: NetSpam: a network-based spam detection framework for reviews in online social media. IEEE Trans. Inf. Forensics Secur. **12**(7), 1585–1595 (2017)
22. VanDam, C., Tan, P.N.: Detecting hashtag hijacking from Twitter. In: Proceedings of the 8th ACM Conference on Web Science. ACM (2016)
23. Viswanath, B., et al.: Towards detecting anomalous user behavior in online social networks. In: USENIX Security Symposium (2014)
24. Wang, A.H.: Don't follow me: spam detection in Twitter. In: 2010 International Conference on Security and Cryptography (SECRYPT), pp. 1–10. IEEE (2010)
25. Wang, D., Pu, C.: Bean: a behavior analysis approach of URL spam filtering in Twitter. In: 2015 IEEE International Conference on Information Reuse and Integration (IRI). IEEE (2015)
26. Xie, W., Zhu, F., Jiang, J., Lim, E.P., Wang, K.: TopicSketch: real-time bursty topic detection from Twitter. IEEE Trans. Knowl. Data Eng. **28**(8), 2216–2229 (2016)
27. Xing, W., Jie, W., Tsoumakos, D., Ghanem, M.: A network approach for managing and processing big cancer data in clouds. Clust. Comput. **18**(3), 1285–1294 (2015)
28. Xu, H., Guan, B., Liu, P., Escudero, W., Hu, L.: Harnessing the nature of spam in scalable online social spam detection. In: 2018 IEEE International Conference on Big Data (Big Data). IEEE (2018)
29. Xu, H., et al.: Oases: an online scalable spam detection system for social networks. In: 2018 IEEE 11th International Conference on Cloud Computing (CLOUD) (2018)
30. Xu, H., Sun, W., Javaid, A.: Efficient spam detection across online social networks. In: 2016 IEEE International Conference on Big Data Analysis (2016)
31. Zhang, J., Tang, J., Li, J., Liu, Y., Xing, C.: Who influenced you? Predicting retweet via social influence locality. ACM Trans. Knowl. Discov. Data (TKDD) **9**(3), 25 (2015)
32. Zhang, Y., Hong, J.I., Cranor, L.F.: Cantina: a content-based approach to detecting phishing web sites. In: Proceedings of the 16th International Conference on World Wide Web, pp. 639–648. ACM (2007)

Dynamic Network Anomaly Detection System by Using Deep Learning Techniques

Peng Lin[1,2], Kejiang Ye[1(✉)], and Cheng-Zhong Xu[3]

[1] Shenzhen Institutes of Advanced Technology, Chinese Academy of Sciences,
Shenzhen 518055, China
{peng.lin,kj.ye}@siat.ac.cn
[2] University of Chinese Academy of Sciences, Beijing 100049, China
[3] Faculty of Science and Technology, University of Macau, Taipa, Macao,
Special Administrative Region of China
czxu@um.edu.mo

Abstract. The Internet and computer networks are currently suffering from serious security threats. Those threats often keep changing and will evolve to new unknown variants. In order to maintain the security of network, we design and implement a dynamic network anomaly detection system using deep learning methods. We use Long Short Term Memory (LSTM) to build a deep neural network model and add an Attention Mechanism (AM) to enhance the performance of the model. The SMOTE algorithm and an improved loss function are used to handle the class-imbalance problem in the CSE-CIC-IDS2018 dataset. The experimental results show that the classification accuracy of our model reaches 96.2%, which is higher than other machine learning algorithms. In addition, the class-imbalance problem is alleviated to a certain extent, making our method have great practicality.

Keywords: Network anomaly detection · Deep learning · Attention · SMOTE

1 Introduction

Nowadays, due to the rapid development of Internet and cloud computing techniques, the number of global networked devices has become very large [1]. However, under such a large-scale network infrastructure, faults or attacks occur very frequently which bring a very bad experience to users and cause serious economic losses. In order to prevent network attacks, people often use firewalls as the first line of defense to ensure that the network works properly and use Intrusion Detection System (IDS) as the second line of defense to further improve system security.

IDS is a kind of network security device that monitors network traffics in real time and will alert or take proactive measures when an anomaly is detected. Abnormal network traffics refer to the network traffics that adversely affect the network, which deviate greatly from normal network traffics in pattern. The cause of abnormal network traffics can be the unreasonable network operation or external network attacks [2].

There are mainly three steps in IDSs. Firstly, IDS needs to track and collect the network flow data. Secondly, IDS needs to clean the raw data and convert them to the

© Springer Nature Switzerland AG 2019
D. Da Silva et al. (Eds.): CLOUD 2019, LNCS 11513, pp. 161–176, 2019.
https://doi.org/10.1007/978-3-030-23502-4_12

input-format needed for the next step. Finally, a classification engine is needed to identify the network traffics as normal or abnormal.

Among the above three steps, the most important one is the classification operation, which determines the detection performance of an IDS. The classification engine can be implemented by signature-based methods and anomaly-based methods. The former method implements the classification by comparing the network traffics with the signatures of the abnormal traffics that have been already defined, while the latter one generally learns the characteristics of abnormal traffics through some machine learning (ML) algorithms and then uses the trained ML model to make a judgment. Although the signature-based methods can achieve high accuracy and have a fast detection speed, it is powerless for identifying unknown network traffics. In contrast, the anomaly-based approaches are more flexible as well as having better generalization, and they perform well even in the face of the classification tasks on unknown network traffics [3]. Nowadays, with new network attacks emerging, an excellent network anomaly detection system should have the ability to discover unknown anomalies. The systems discussed above are refer to as *dynamic network anomaly detection systems*, which are usually implement by anomaly-based approaches.

In recent years, with the improvement of computing power and the outbreak of data volume, deep neural networks (or deep learning) have attracted people's attention again. The strong nonlinear fitting ability of deep learning techniques make them exhibit excellent performance in many fields [4]. Compared to traditional machine learning algorithms, deep learning techniques have a faster processing speed when dealing with big data and can learn the deep hidden representation of features with higher accuracy.

Some researchers have used deep learning approaches to detect network anomaly. Aksu et al. [5] compared the classification results of SVM and deep learning, and the results show that the deep learning method performed better. But they only studied the classification research on PortScan and normal network traffic. In the actual network environment, the network traffic's types are much more than two, which increases the difficulty of detection. Zhu et al. [6] used Convolutional Neural Network (CNN) to study the network traffics classification issue, but the accuracy obtained by the experiment is not high. And there are also some researches [7, 8] that use the outdated datasets such as KDD CUP99 [9] to do the experiments, which can no longer reflect the characteristics of today's network traffics.

To overcome the above challenges, this paper proposes a deep learning method to implement the dynamic IDS. The main contributions are as follows:

- We study the issue of multi-classification, which is more challenging and practical.
- An up to date dataset CSE-CIC-IDS2018 [10] is used in our experiment, which can reflect the characteristics of the latest network traffics.
- We use LSTM to establish our model, which has good performance in processing time-correlated sequences such as network traffics.
- We use the SMOTE, an over-sampling algorithm to get more samples and then optimize the loss function, which make some progress on the class-imbalance issue.
- Experimental results show that our method achieves an overall accuracy of 96.2%, which is higher than other machine learning algorithms used in the experiment.

The rest of this paper is organized as follows. We introduce the proposed methods in Sect. 2 and give the implementation details in Sect. 3. In Sect. 4, we conduct the network traffic classification experiments and analyze the experimental results. Section 5 introduces the related work and Sect. 6 concludes the whole paper.

2 The Method

2.1 Long Short Term Memory (LSTM)

LSTM is a special recurrent neural network structure, which is proposed to solve the problem of long-term dependence [11]. It adds the forget gate, input gate, and output gate to the standard Recurrent Neural Network (RNN). The forget gate lets the neural network forget the useless information, the input gate adds new content to the neural network and the output gate determines the final output of current node. Figure 1 shows the structure of a single LSTM cell.

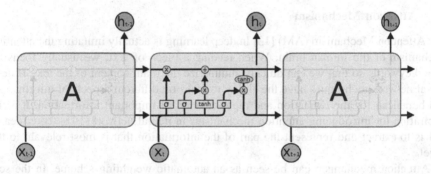

Fig. 1. Structure diagram of a single LSTM cell

The process of forward propagation of LSTM can be described by the following equation, where $h^{(t)}$ and $C^{(t)}$ are the two hidden states of the LSTM model, σ represents the sigmoid function, i, f and o are respectively the input gate, forget gate and output gate, W are weight matrices for different peephole connections.

Update the output of the forget gate:

$$f^{(t)} = \sigma\left(W_f * \left[h_{(t-1)}, x_t\right] + b_f\right)$$

Update the output of the input gate:

$$i^{(t)} = \sigma\left(W_i * \left[h_{(t-1)}, x_t\right] + b_i\right)$$

$$\widetilde{c}\,(t) = tanh\left(W_c * \left[h_{(t-1)}, x_t\right] + b_C\right)$$

Update cell's state:

$$C^{(t)} = f^{(t)} * C^{(t-1)} + i^{(t)} * \tilde{c}\,(t)$$

Update the output of the output gate:

$$o^{(t)} = \sigma\left(W_o * \left[h_{(t-1)}, x_t\right] + b_o\right)$$

$$h^{(t)} = o^{(t)} * tanh\left(C^{(t)}\right)$$

Classification engine is the most important part of the system, and we used LSTM to implement it. LSTM can not only learn the current network traffics, but also can remember previous network traffics' characteristics. When it comes to the network attacks, generally the attackers will carry out a series of continuous operations. So the current network traffic is normal or not strongly related to the previous network traffics.

2.2 Attention Mechanism

The Attention Mechanism (AM) [13] in deep learning is actually imitating the attention mechanism of the human brain. When reading a piece of text, we usually focus on some keywords so that we can quickly summarize the main content of the text. If deep neural network techniques have the ability to focus on different aspects of information, it is beneficial for the extraction and representation of important information. It is the inspiration for introducing attention mechanisms in neural networks. The core idea of AM is to extract and represent the part of the information that is most relevant to the target.

Attention mechanism can be seen as an automatic weighting scheme. In the scenario of anomaly detection, the role of AM is to calculate the impacts of each network traffic on the last network traffic. We can use the following formula to calculate the attention value of each flow:

$$\alpha_t = \frac{exp\left(u_t^T * u_w\right)}{\sum_t exp\left(u_t^T * u_w\right)}$$

Where u_w is the weight matrix and u_t represents the implicit representation of the LSTM hidden state (h_t) at time t, and u_t can be calculated by the following formula:

$$u_t = tanh(W_w h_t + b_w)$$

where W_w is the weight matrix and b_w is the bias. After obtaining the attention probability distribution value at each moment, the feature vector v that contains the network traffic information is calculated as follows:

$$v = \sum_t \alpha_t * h_t$$

Finally, we can use the *softmax* function to get the predicted label y:

$$y = softmax(W_v * v + b_v)$$

2.3   Smote

We have used the CICIDS2017 dataset to conduct an experiment on network traffics classification [14], but there was a serious class-imbalance problem in their experimental results. In their results, four of the eight categories have the precisions rate below 40%, and even three of them are close to 0. This is because in the IDS2017 dataset, the amounts of some categories are very small, the neural network cannot learn the characteristics of these categories well. In this paper, we experimented with the CSE-CIC-IDS2018 dataset and used the SMOTE [12] over-sampling algorithm to synthesize new samples for the small size classes. The principle of the SMOTE oversampling algorithm is as follows:

Let the size of a small size class be T, considering a sample i of the class, and its feature vector is $x_i, i \in \{1, \ldots, T\}$:

a. Find k neighbors of the sample x_i from all T samples of this small size class (For example, using Euclidean Distance), and denoted it as $x_{i(near)}, near \in \{1, \ldots, k\}$;
b. A sample $x_{i(nn)}$ is randomly selected from the k neighbors, and a random number ζ_1 between 0 and 1 is generated to synthesize a new sample x_{i1} as the following Equation: $x_{i1} = x_i + \zeta_1 \cdot (x_{i(nn)} - x_i)$;
c. Repeat step b. N times to synthesize N new samples: $x_{inew}, new \in \{1, \ldots, N\}$

2.4   Loss Function

In this paper, Adam gradient descent method is used to further optimize the model. In order to improve the efficiency, mini-batch algorithm is used for training. By calculating the gradient of the loss function, Adam can update the parameters of the model step by step, and finally reach convergence. The loss function we use is the cross-entropy function, which is defined as follows: $L = -\sum_i y_i' * log(y_i)$, where y_i' is the actual label of the sample while y_i is the label predicted by the deep neural network. We make some changes to the function, which enhances the accuracy of the classification on small size classes:

$$L' = - \sum_i w_i * y'_i * log(y_i)$$

We set different weights to each class. The weights of large size classes are setting smaller and the weights of small size classes are setting larger. If the samples of small size classes are classified incorrectly, the loss value of the system will increase rapidly so that the updating parameters of the neural network will be closer to the direction of small size classes. Note that the weights of small size classes cannot be the very large values, otherwise the system will tend to classify most of the samples into these classes, resulting in a very low overall accuracy.

3   Implementation

3.1   Dataset

We used CSE-CIC-IDS2018 as the experimental dataset, which was created by The Canadian Institute for Cyber-security (CIC) and Communications Security Establishment (CSE). The dataset includes seven different attack scenarios such as DDoS attack, Botnet attack, Infiltration attack, BruteForce attack, DoS attack, Web attack, and Heartleech (a type of DoS attack). By using the tool CICFlowMeter-V3, we can extract more than 80 features of the raw network data and save them as several csv files. Some of the features are listed in Table 1.

Table 1. Some features in CSE-CIC-IDS2018 dataset

Feature name	Description
fl_dur	Flow duration
tot_fw_pk	Total packets in the forward direction
tot_bw_pk	Total packets in the backward direction
tot_l_fw_pkt	Total size of packet in forward direction
fw_pkt_l_max	Maximum size of packet in forward direction
fw_pkt_l_min	Minimum size of packet in forward direction
fw_pkt_l_avg	Average size of packet in forward direction
fw_pkt_l_std	Standard deviation size of packet in forward direction

We compared the differences in sample sizes between CICIDS2017 and CSE-CIC-IDS2018, and the results are shown in Table 2. It can be seen that the sample sizes of the CSE-CIC-IDS2018 dataset have been comprehensively improved compared with the CICIDS2017 dataset, especially in the Botnet attack and Infiltration attack, which have increased by 143 times and 4497 times respectively. But the amount of samples for Web Attack is very small, only 928 samples are provided.

Table 2. Differences in samples of two datasets

	Normal	DDoS	PortScan	BOT	Inf	Web attack	BF	DoS
CICIDS-2017	1743179	128027	158930	1966	36	2180	13835	252661
CSE-CIC-IDS2018	6112151	687742	–	286191	161934	928	380949	654301

3.2 Pre-processing

In the original dataset, there are some features have little impacts on whether the traffic is abnormal or not, such as timestamps and IP addresses. The timestamp records the time when the anomalous network traffic occurred, which are of little help in training our neural network, so we removed this feature. In addition, as an anomaly detection system, we hope it can classify the network traffics according to their behavioral characteristics, and should not be biased against the IP address, so we also deleted the column of feature.

After completing the above works, we divide the dataset into training set, test set and validation set, which are 90%, 9% and 1% of the original data respectively. The training set is used for training, the validation set is used for rapid evaluation of the model during training, and the test set is used for final evaluation of the model. In addition, we noticed that there are too many normal network traffic samples in the dataset, which can easily affect the classification preference of the model. So we under-sampled the normal traffics and only took 2 million records randomly. Furthermore, we over-sampled the samples of Web attack and Infiltration attack by using SMOTE algorithm. Oversampling is only implemented in training set. After dividing the dataset, we shuffle the training set to ensure the loss value change smoothly during training.

3.3 Metrics

Three metrics are used to evaluate the performance of our experiment: Accuracy, Precision and Recall rate. Accuracy represents the proportion of correctly classified samples, and its formula is as follows:

$$Accuracy = \frac{TP + TN}{TP + FN + TN + FP}$$

In all samples classified as Category-A, the proportion of those really belong to Category-A is defined as precision. Generally, the higher the Precision, the lower the False Alarm Rate (FAR) of the system will be.

$$Precision = \frac{TP}{TP + FP}$$

Recall rate represents the proportion of all samples in Category-A that are eventually classified as A. Recall rate reflects the system's ability to detect anomalies. The higher it is, the more anomalous traffics are detected correctly.

$$Recall = \frac{TP}{TP + FN}$$

TP, FP, TN, FN represent True Positive, False Positive, True Negative and False Negative respectively.

3.4 Experimental Setup

Tensorflow [15] that runs on the Ubuntu 16.04 OS is used to build the deep neural network architecture. The server's CPU is Intel Xeon E5-2650 v4 with 48 cores and 128 GB of memory. In addition, 4 Nvidia Titan XP GPUs are used as the accelerator. The architecture of the deep neural network used in the experiment is shown in Fig. 2. We use two LSTM layers and three full connected dense layers to build our model, and add the attention mechanism to the LSTM.

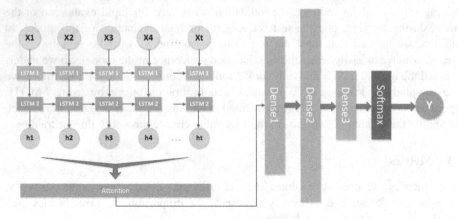

Fig. 2. Architecture of our model

4 Experiment

4.1 Performance

In this experiment, the hyperparameters that we need to optimize are: LSTM hidden nodes, flow length, batch size, learning rate and activation function. We carried out a lot of experiments, and found a set of optimal hyperparameters, which are as follows (Table 3).

Table 3. Best hyperparameters of DNN

Name	Value
LSTM hidden nodes	256
Flow length	10
Batch size	128
Learning rate	0.00005
Activation function	Relu

Under this hyperparameters setting, the best performance of the deep neural network is show in Table 4.

Table 4. Best performance of DNN

Class	Precision	Recall
0	0.93	0.99
1	1.00	1.00
2	0.99	1.00
3	0.93	0.17
4	0.95	0.98
5	0.98	0.99
6	0.30	0.98

And the confusion matrix of results is shown in Table 5.

Table 5. Confusion matrix

	Normal	DDoS	BOT	Inf	BF '	DoS	Web attack
Normal	190500 99.07%	15	234	111	370	348	207
DDos	196	67721 99.71%	0	0	0	1	0
BOT	26	0	28238 99.91%	0	0	0	0
Inf	11425	0	0	2563 17.12%	904	76	0
BF	361	0	0	4	36895 98.10%	352	0
Dos	393	1	0	0	377	63842 98.80%	0
Web Attack	2	0	0	0	0	0	90 97.82%

As can be seen from the above results, the overall performance of the classifier is very good. The average Precision and Recall rate are as high as 96%, reaching a practical level. Six of the seven categories have a Precision that more than 93%, and similarly there are six categories with a recall rate of over 98%.

In terms of Precision, the values for all categories have reached more than 93% except the web attack samples. Precision of web attack is only 27%, but the reason is obvious. Because the sample size of web attack is very small, the TP (True Positive) is limited to a very small value, therefore, even if a small amount of network traffics that don't belong to web attack category are classified into this category, the denominator of Precision's formula will increase rapidly, making it difficult to achieve a high Precision.

In terms of Recall rate, the classifier also performs well. There are six of the seven categories with a recall rate over 98%, indicating that most of the network traffics are correctly classified to the category that they belong. In other words, the system can detect most of the abnormal traffics. In addition, the classification performance of web attack greatly exceeded our expectations. After using the SMOTE algorithm and improved loss function, the Recall rate of web attack samples actually reached 98%, while it was 0 before the optimization. But we also found that the Recall rate of Infiltration samples which are processed by the same method with web attack was 17%, and it was only 6% higher than before. For this phenomenon, we guess that the pattern between web attack network traffics are similar. The new samples synthesized by SMOTE algorithm can well reflect the characteristics of this kind of traffics, so the neural network can fit them well. However, Infiltration is relatively rich in diversity. The new data synthesized by SMOTE algorithm cannot reflect the characteristic distribution of Infiltration well, so the effect is not greatly improved. In addition, we also find that most of the Infiltration samples are classified into the normal categories, which indicates that they are similar in patterns, thus it is difficult for neural networks to distinguish them.

Figure 3 shows the changes of Infiltration and Web attack before and after optimization on Recall rate.

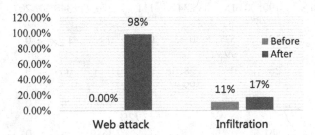

Fig. 3. Changes of recall rate before and after optimization

4.2 Influence of Hyperparameters

In the above experiments, we find that different hyperparameter settings have a great impact on the results of the model. Now let's explore the impacts of different hyperparameter settings, including LSTM hidden nodes, learning rate, flow length, and mini-batch size. We introduce F1-Score to evaluate the whole system, defined as follows:

$$F1Score = 2 \times \frac{Precision \times Recall}{Precision + Recall}$$

Hidden nodes of LSTM. We changed the values of LSTM hidden nodes from 64 to 128, 256, 384 and 512 respectively and fixed the other hyperparameters. Each experiment was done three times and then calculated the average value. Accuracy, Precision and Recall rate were recorded when the model converged. The experimental results are shown in Fig. 4. It can be seen that when LSTM hidden nodes are too few, the neural network cannot learn the network traffics' features very well, so its performance is not very good. With the increase of hidden nodes, the classification performance of model goes up. But when it reaches 256, the number of hidden nodes have little influence on the classification effect. Continuing to increase hidden nodes will not only prolong the training time, but also bring the risk of over-fitting. Thus, the best hidden nodes is 256.

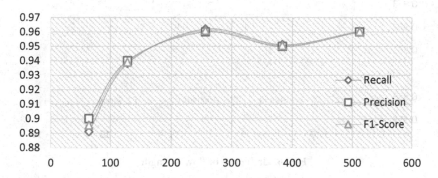

Fig. 4. Influence of LSTM hidden nodes

Learning Rate. Learning rate determines the speed of gradient descent so it plays a vital role in the training. We fix the values of other hyperparameters and then change the learning rates with logarithmic scales to 0.1, 0.01, 0.001, 0.0001 and 0.00001, respectively. We find that the best interval of learning is [0.0001, 0.00001], so we changed the learning rates again to 0.00001, 0.00003, 0.00005, 0.00007 and 0.00009 and repeat the experiments. The results are shown in Fig. 5. It can be seen that when the learning rate is 0.0005, the performance of the model is optimal.

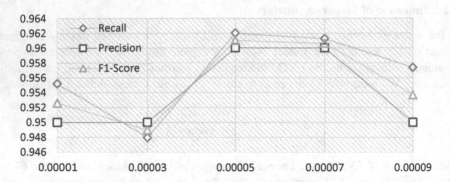

Fig. 5. Influence of learning rate

Flow Length. It is also important to choose the appropriate size of network traffics to train. Let the flow length be n, change the values of n to 6, 8, 10, 12, 14 respectively, and then do the experiments separately. The experimental results show the growth of n has no significant impact on the performance of the system, as shown in Fig. 6. When n is greater than 10, the classification performance can hardly be improved, so we set the flow's length to 10.

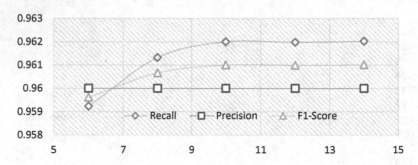

Fig. 6. Influence of flow's length

Batch Size. We also changed the batch size to 64, 128, 256, and 512 respectively and found when the batch size equals to 256, the classification performance is the best.

4.3   Comparison

In order to show the benefits of our method, we compared with some traditional machine learning algorithms, including: DecisionTree, GaussianNB, RandomForest, KNN, SVM. The experimental results are shown in Table 6.

Table 6. Comparison between ML methods

	Decision tree	Gaussian NB	Random forest	KNN	SVM	**Our method**
Precision	93%	66%	94%	94%	86%	**96%**
Recall	93%	55%	94%	94%	75%	**96%**
Accuracy	92.8%	55.4%	94.2%	94.2%	74.7%	**96.2%**

According to the results, we can know that the proposed method of this paper achieves both the highest Precision and Recall rate. The performance of traditional machine learning algorithms are also not bad. The Precision and Recall rate of Decision Tree, KNN and RandomForest algorithms both achieve more than 93%, but the classification effect of GaussianNB and SVM is poor, which have big gaps with the our method. In addition, we find that the training time of traditional machine learning algorithms is much longer than that of deep learning algorithm. For large volume data, the processing speed of traditional machine learning methods will become very slow. While the deep learning technique can quickly see the convergence of training results because of the mini-batch algorithm.

Based on the above experimental results, it can be concluded that the LSTM+AM model proposed in this paper achieves the best results. To further demonstrate the effectiveness of our model, we compared with other two deep learning algorithms: (1) using classical Multi-Layer Perception (MLP); (2) using LSTM without AM. The results are shown in Table 7.

Table 7. Comparison between other DL methods

MLP				LSTM			Our method		
	Pre	Rec	F1	Pre	Rec	F1	Pre	Rec	F1
Normal	0.88	0.99	0.93	0.94	0.93	0.93	0.93	0.99	0.93
DDos	1.00	1.00	1.00	0.85	1.00	0.92	1.00	1.00	1.00
BOT	1.00	1.00	1.00	0.99	1.00	1.00	0.99	1.00	0.99
Inf	0.93	0.19	0.31	0.74	0.23	0.35	0.93	0.17	0.93
BF	0.83	0.94	0.88	0.98	0.98	0.98	0.95	0.98	0.95
Dos	0.90	0.66	0.76	0.98	0.99	0.98	0.98	0.99	0.98
WebAttack	0.81	0.98	0.84	0.66	0.98	0.79	0.30	0.98	0.30
Average	0.91	0.90	0.89	0.93	0.93	0.93	0.96	0.96	0.93
Accuracy	0.904880			0.933332			0.961995		

From Table 7, we know that our method achieves the highest accuracy of 96.2%. The LSTM method is followed by an accuracy of 93.3%, and the accuracy of MLP is only 90.5%. The results show that: (1) LSTM method can indeed learn the previous network traffic information, and can effectively combine the characteristics of historical traffics to make classification. It can achieve better results than the classical multi-layer neural network; (2) AM can focus on those more valuable network traffics, which can help LSTM achieve better classification results.

5   Related Work

We summarized the related work of network anomaly detection into four parts [3].

- **Statistical:** Kruegel et al. [16] introduced a statistical intrusion detection scheme based on Bayesian network, which significantly reduces false alarm rate. Wang et al. [17] presented a payload-based anomaly detector called PAYL for intrusion detection. PAYL can model the normal application payload of network traffic in a fully automated, unsupervised and very efficient manner.
- **Rule-based:** Snort [18] is an open source network anomaly detection system (NIDS), which can analyze and record network data packets in real time. Users can discover various network attacks by performing protocol analysis, content search and matching. Scheirer et al. [19] reported a scheme that consider both syntax and semantics based approaches for dynamic network intrusion detection.
- **Machine Learning:** Boosting Trees (BT) has evolved from the application of boosting methods to Regression Trees, and has been successfully used in many IDS [20, 21]. An intrusion detection system using support vector machine (SVM) and feature selection method is proposed in [22].
- **Deep Learing:** Aksu et al. [5] compared the classification results of SVM and deep learning, and the results show that the deep learning method performs better. Zhu et al. used Convolutional Neural Network to study the network traffics classification issue, but the accuracy obtained by the experiment is not high so it lacks practicality.

6   Conclusion

This paper proposes a dynamic network anomaly detection system using deep learning method. We use LSTM to build the neural network model and incorporate attention mechanism to deal with time-correlated network traffic's classification issues. In order to solve the class-imbalance problem, we used the up to date dataset CSE-CIC-2018 to conduct our experiments, and used the SMOTE algorithm as well as the improved loss function to optimize the training process. The experimental results show that our optimization plays a very significant role. The final trained model achieved a very good result in traffic classification. The overall Accuracy of the system reached 96.2%, and the Recall rate of 6 categories reached 98%. We also compared our method with traditional machine learning methods and other deep learning approaches, and our model achieved the best results.

In the future, we are planning to use the raw data of network traffics so that deep neural networks can automatically learn their features instead of using the artificially extracted features, which can stimulate the maximum potential of neural networks.

Acknowledgment. This work is supported by China National Basic Research Program (973 Program, No. 2015CB352400), National Natural Science Foundation of China (No. 61702492), Equipment Pre-Research Foundation (No. 61400020403), Shenzhen Basic Research Program (No. JCYJ20170818153016513, JCYJ20170307164747920), and Shenzhen Discipline Construction Project for Urban Computing and Data Intelligence.

References

1. Ngu, A.H., et al.: IoT middleware: a survey on issues and enabling technologies. IEEE Internet of Things J. **4**(1), 1–20 (2017)
2. Gill, P., Jain, N., Nagappan, N.: Understanding network failures in data centers: measurement, analysis, and implications. ACM SIGCOMM Comput. Commun. Rev. **41** (4), 350–361 (2011)
3. Karatas, G., Demir, O., Sahingoz, O.K.: Deep learning in intrusion detection systems. In: 2018 International Congress on Big Data, Deep Learning and Fighting Cyber Terrorism (IBIGDELFT), pp. 113–116 (2018)
4. LeCun, Y., Bengio, Y., Hinton, G.: Deep learning. Nature **521**(7553), 436 (2015)
5. Aksu, D., Aydin, M.A.: Detecting port scan attempts with comparative analysis of deep learning and support vector machine algorithms. In: 2018 International Congress on Big Data, Deep Learning and Fighting Cyber Terrorism (IBIGDELFT), pp. 77–80 (2018)
6. Zhu, M., Ye, K., Xu, C.-Z.: Network anomaly detection and identification based on deep learning methods. In: Luo, M., Zhang, L.-J. (eds.) CLOUD 2018. LNCS, vol. 10967, pp. 219–234. Springer, Cham (2018). https://doi.org/10.1007/978-3-319-94295-7_15
7. Javaid, A., et al.: A deep learning approach for network intrusion detection system. In: Proceedings of the 9th EAI International Conference on Bio-inspired Information and Communications Technologies, pp. 21–26 (2016)
8. Dong, B., Wang, X.: Comparison deep learning method to traditional methods using for network intrusion detection. In: 2016 8th IEEE International Conference on Communication Software and Networks (ICCSN), pp. 581–585 (2016)
9. KDD Cup 1999 (1999). http://kdd.ics.uci.edu/databases/kddcup99/kddcup99.html
10. CSE-CIC-IDS2018. https://www.unb.ca/cic/datasets/ids-2018.html (2018)
11. Hochreiter, S., Schmidhuber, J.: Long short-term memory. Neural Comput. **9**(8), 1735–1780 (1997)
12. Chawla, N.V., et al.: SMOTE: synthetic minority over-sampling technique. J. Artif. Intell. Res. **16**, 321–357 (2002)
13. Chorowski, J.K., et al. Attention-based models for speech recognition. In: Advances in Neural Information Processing Systems, pp. 577–585 (2015)
14. Zhu, M., Ye, K., Wang, Y., Xu, C.-Z.: A deep learning approach for network anomaly detection based on AMF-LSTM. In: Zhang, F., Zhai, J., Snir, M., Jin, H., Kasahara, H., Valero, M. (eds.) NPC 2018. LNCS, vol. 11276, pp. 137–141. Springer, Cham (2018). https://doi.org/10.1007/978-3-030-05677-3_13
15. Abadi, M., et al.: Tensorflow: a system for large-scale machine learning. In: 12th USENIX Symposium on Operating Systems Design and Implementation (OSDI 2016), pp. 265–283 (2016)
16. Kruegel, C., et al.: Bayesian event classification for intrusion detection. In: Proceedings of the 19th Annual Computer Security Applications Conference. IEEE (2003)
17. Wang, K., Stolfo, S.J.: Anomalous payload-based network intrusion detection. In: Jonsson, E., Valdes, A., Almgren, M. (eds.) RAID 2004. LNCS, vol. 3224, pp. 203–222. Springer, Heidelberg (2004). https://doi.org/10.1007/978-3-540-30143-1_11
18. Roesch, M.: Snort: lightweight intrusion detection for networks. Lisa **99**(1), 229–238 (1999)
19. Scheirer, W., Chuah, M.C.: Syntax vs. semantics: competing approaches to dynamic network intrusion detection. Int. J. Secur. Networks **3**(1), 24–35 (2008)
20. Pfahringer, B.: Winning the kdd99 classification cup: bagged boosting. ACM SIGKDD Explor. Newsl. **1**(2), 65–66 (2000)

21. Levin, I.: Kdd-99 classifier learning contest: Llsoft's results overview. SIGKDD Explor. **1**(2), 67–75 (2000)
22. Li, Y., Xia, J., Zhang, S., Yan, J., Ai, X., Dai, K.: An efficient intrusion detection system based on support vector machines and gradually feature removal method. Expert Syst. Appl. **39**(1), 424–430 (2012)

Heterogeneity-Aware Data Placement
in Hybrid Clouds

Jack D. Marquez$^{(\boxtimes)}$ (iD), Juan D. Gonzalez (iD), and Oscar H. Mondragon (iD)

Universidad Autonoma de Occidente, Cali, Valle del Cauca 760030, Colombia
{jdmarquez,juan_davi.gonzalez,ohmondragon}@uao.edu.co

Abstract. In next-generation cloud computing clusters, performance of data-intensive applications will be limited, among other factors, by disks data transfer rates. In order to mitigate performance impacts, cloud systems offering hierarchical storage architectures are becoming commonplace. The Hadoop File System (HDFS) offers a collection of storage policies that exploit different storage types such as RAM_DISK, SSD, HDD, and ARCHIVE. However, developing algorithms to leverage heterogeneous storage through an efficient data placement has been challenging. This work presents an intelligent algorithm based on genetic programming which allow to find the optimal mapping of input datasets to storage types on a Hadoop file system.

Keywords: Hadoop · HDFS · Integer lineal programming ·
Genetic algorithm · Data placement

1   Introduction

As the amount of data generated by organizations is taking enormous proportions, more and more companies leverage Big Data analysis to drive business decisions [1,2]. The use of distributed file systems allows to reliably store this massive data and distribute storage and computation across very large clusters, facilitating scalability. In order to optimize the storage and retrieval of data, system software must provide efficient data placement mechanisms [3].

Modern distributed file systems commonly have large hybrid storage capacity through the combination of Solid State Drive (SSD) and Hard Disk Drive (HDD) disks. Data placement algorithms must be aware of these heterogeneous architectures in order to maximize the performance of applications using them. For example, applications with real-time requirements may benefit from using SSD instead of HDD, as disk data transfer rates have been identified as a bottleneck for such applications [4].

One of the most commonly used framework to process big data is Hadoop Apache software [5], which can run tasks that use and produce a large amount of data using a vast quantity of processing cores. Hadoop provides a distributed file system (HDFS) [6] and a framework that allows to analyze and process large amount of data using the MapReduce model [7].

© Springer Nature Switzerland AG 2019
D. Da Silva et al. (Eds.): CLOUD 2019, LNCS 11513, pp. 177–191, 2019.
https://doi.org/10.1007/978-3-030-23502-4_13

From version 2.3, Hadoop supports heterogeneous storage, which enables users to specify the type of storage (RAM_DISK, SSD, HDD, ARCHIVE) to use by setting storage policies (Lazy_Persist, All_SSD, One_SSD, Hot, Warm, Cold) to files and directories [4]. The selection of a storage policy impacts directly applications performance since it determines data locality and the data transfer rate offered to them [8]. We defined the problem of allocating different datasets to storage types resources as an Integer Linear Programming (ILP) problem and propose an intelligent algorithm based on Genetic Programming to solve it. Then, we contrast our genetic algorithm against other solutions, specifically Simplex, Generalized Reduced Gradient (GRG) and Evolutionary algorithms and show a comparison of the throughput achieved for each of them for different sizes of datasets by running each algorithm on a Hadoop cluster.

The contributions of this paper are (I) The formulation of the heterogeneous storage problem as an ILP problem. (II) The implementation of an intelligent algorithm based on genetic programming that solves the ILP problem allowing to find the optimal mapping of each dataset to storage types on a Hadoop file system. (III) A comparison of our solution against alternative algorithms. (IV) A new HDFS storage policy that allows using RAM_DISK without replication in other storage types. (V) A benchmark to test and evaluate data write and read throughputs in HDFS.

The rest of the paper is organized as follows. In Sect. 2, we present a brief background on Hadoop heterogeneous storage support and HDFS storage policies. In Sect. 3, we describe the problem and the proposed ILP model for data placement. Section 4 explains our proposed GA to solve the formulated ILP problem. In Sect. 5, we discuss the experiments performed to validate our model. In Sect. 6, we report related work. Finally, we conclude in Sect. 7.

2   Background

This section describes the main features of the Hadoop heterogeneous storage mechanisms and the HDFS storage policies that support our algorithm.

2.1   Hadoop Heterogeneous Storage Support

The heterogeneous storage support included in Hadoop 2.3 version changed the storage model from single storage to multiple physical storage media. This allows HDFS to adapt according to the characteristics of the data to store. HDFS supports the following storage types:

- ARCHIVE: archival storage is commonly used for heavy storage and for storing data that is accessed only rarely.
- DISK or HDD: hard disk drives are the default storage type.
- SSD: it is recommended to use solid state drives to store data that needs to be written and recovery with a higher intensity.
- RAM_DISK: this type of storage has the highest I/O performance, but the storage is non-persistent.

2.2   HDFS Storage Policies

HDFS storage policies allow managing different types of storage and the replication factor. As can be seen in the Table 1, Hadoop provides six different storage policies, based on the types of storage supported by HDFS and the combination of them. Block placement property defines the type of storage that will be used to locate the data blocks and its replicas (n). Fallback Storage for Creation property indicates what storage type will be used as an alternative in the case that the main storage type is not available. Fallback Storage for Replication property indicates what type of storage will be used for the replicas alternatively in the case that the main storage type defined for the replicas is not available [9]. HDFS provides the following policies:

Table 1. HDFS storage policies [9]

ID	Name	Block placement (n)	Fallback creation	Fallback replication
15	Lazy_Persist	RAM_DISK: 1, DISK: n-1	DISK	DISK
12	All_SSD	SSD: n	DISK	DISK
10	One_SSD	SSD: 1, DISK: n-1	SSD, DISK	SSD, DISK
7	Hot (default)	DISK: n	<none>	ARCHIVE
5	Warm	DISK: 1, ARCHIVE: n-1	ARCHIVE, DISK	ARCHIVE, DISK
2	Cold	ARCHIVE: n	<none>	<none>

- Lazy_Persist: this is the only one of the policies that allows to use the storage in RAM_DISK and combines it with the storage in DISK. Lazy_Persist always stores the data in RAM_DISK and replicates them in DISK regardless of the replication factor is 1. A replication factor greater than one impacts performance, since only one replica is stored in RAM_DISK while the rest of the replicas are stored in DISK [9].
- All_SSD: as the name implies, it stores all the replicas in SSD and uses the DISK storage as an alternative for creating data blocks and for replicas.
- One_SSD: this policy combines SSD and DISK. It stores one replica in SSD and the rest in DISK.
- Hot: when no policy is set, this is used by default. Both data blocks and replicas are stored on disk and there is no alternative for the storage of the blocks in case of a failure. For replicas, Archive is used as a fallback.
- Warm: Warm policy combines DISK and ARCHIVE. It stores one replica on Disk and the rest on file.
- Cold: Cold stores all replicas in ARCHIVE.

3 Modeling Data Placement on Heterogeneous Storage

In this section we describe the formulation of the problem of mapping input datasets to storage types on a Hadoop Distributed File System (HDFS). We formulate this as an Integer Linear Programming problem, which allows to minimize the time of placement of datasets on HDFS heterogeneous storage by leveraging storage policies.

3.1 Resource Constraints

We consider the problem of allocating N datasets (DS) to M different Storage Types (ST) in a Hadoop cluster. Each storage type has certain resource capacities including data write rate and storage capacity. Correspondingly, each dataset has a size. In any valid DS-to-ST allocation, the capacity constraint must be satisfied. That is, for each resource, the total capacity requested by all the DSs cannot exceed STs' storage capacity.

3.2 Optimization Objective

The optimization objective of our problem is to minimize the data placement time of the DS to the ST. The placement time may be affected by several contributors such as network technology, CPU, memory and storage throughput. For simplicity, we focus on the effect of storage throughput because it is the factor with impacts most data placement time [10]. HDFS storage policies play an important role here since they allow to define the storage types in which files will be stored.

3.3 Data Placement Model

Each one of the DSs to be stored is received from the application and moved directly to one of the STs. We develop an Integer Linear Programming model [11] for this problem which is considered as NP-Hard [12]. We define an objective function that includes the dataset size, the storage type data write rate, and the correct allocation as decision variable. We consider two types of constraints for this problem: storage capacity and the guarantee that each DS must be assigned to one ST. Table 2 describes the variables we use in our model.

Optimization Objective. Minimize

$$\sum_{j=1}^{M}\sum_{i=1}^{N}\frac{DSS_i}{B_j} \times X_{ij} \tag{1}$$

In our approach, the optimization objective is to minimize the data placement time of datasets to the available storage types. Each mapping time corresponds to the ratio between the dataset size (MB) and the allocated storage type data

Table 2. Problem model variables

Variable	Description
DS_i	i-th Dataset
DSS_i	i-th Dataset size
B_j	j-th Storage Type Data Write Rate
X_{ij}	Dataset i stored in Storage Type j
C_j	available storage capacity of the j Storage Type
M	Number of Storage Types
N	Number of Datasets

write rate (MB/s). The mapping of a dataset i to a storage type j is controlled by the binary variable X_{ij}, which indicates whether DS i is assigned to ST j, with $X_{ij} = 1$ if DS i is assigned to ST j and $X_{ij} = 0$ otherwise.

Constraints

$$\sum_{j=1}^{M} X_{ij} = 1, \quad \forall i \tag{2}$$

$$\sum_{i=1}^{N} DSS_i \times X_{ij} \leq C_j, \quad \forall j \tag{3}$$

(2) is the placement constraint, which ensures that each dataset should be assigned to exactly one ST.

(3) is the storage type capacity constraint. New allocated datasets size cannot exceed the current available storage of a storage type.

4 Solving the Optimization Problem Using Genetic Programming

Computational Intelligence (CI) often is used to address cloud computing resource allocation problems [13]. Our Optimization problem shows an ILP problem behavior and can be solved it using different algorithms such as Simplex [14], GRG [15], Evolutionary and Genetic Algorithms [16], among others. For this problem, we propose a Genetic Algorithm (GA) which is explained in next sections.

4.1 Chromosome Representation

One of the most important parts of a GA is the chromosomes representation. Each one of the "chromosomes" represents one individual or possible solution to the proposed problem [17]. In our case, each solution consists of a binary vector which represent the mapping of the datasets to any of the four storage types. In Fig. 1 there is an example where the file 1 and 3 are assigned to SSD, file 2 to RAM_DISK, and file 4 to ARCHIVE. In Fig. 1 the chromosome is shown as a matrix but in our algorithm, it is represented as a one dimension vector.

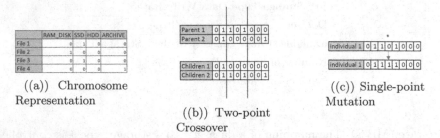

((a)) Chromosome Representation

((b)) Two-point Crossover

((c)) Single-point Mutation

Fig. 1. GA algorithm steps

The size of this vector is determined by the number of datasets to be placed. One dataset only can be placed in one storage type in order to satisfy the constraint (2). One storage type can store multiple datasets but without exceeding its capacity in order to satisfy the constraint (3).

4.2 Initialization

This is the first stage of the GAs. In this stage the initial population must be created. In our case the population is a number of chromosomes generated randomly. Here, the constraints have to be considered when creating possible solutions (i.e. chromosomes).

4.3 Fitness Function and Selection

The fitness function allows to measure the quality of the solution. Generally, this value is obtained using the objective function. In our case each of the solutions represents the X_{ij} values, therefore we have to multiply these values with the placement time, given by the quotient of the dataset size and the storage type bandwidth. The selection operation is the process in which the best solutions are selected from the population. In our case we are doing a elitist selection which consists in selecting two chromosomes that had the highest value on the fitness function.

4.4 Crossover and Mutation Operators

GAs are based in biological evolution, the crossover (Fig. 1(b)) and mutation (Fig. 1(c)) processes represent the steps in which new individuals, solutions or chromosomes are generated by mixing the best ones (parents) from the previous generation [18]. These new individuals are generated in each generation if the probability of crossover is bigger than the defined. The children usually tend to get a better value for the fitness function.

4.5 Genetic Algorithm Parameters

There is not a standard mechanism to calculate GA parameters [19]. Like conventional genetic algorithms, our chromosome parameters receive random initial values. We consider 100 chromosomes randomly created as initial population, a crossover probability of 0.9 and a mutation probability of 0.1. The number of generations was set to 1000.

5   Allocating Storage in a Hadoop Cluster

In the next sections we describe a number of experiments performed in order to validate our model, both using simulations and real hardware. First, we describe the experiment setup used for both kind of experiments. Next, we introduce a new storage policy that we propose in order to analyze the performance of RAM_DISK storage, which differs from the current Lazy_Persist policy in that it uses exclusively RAM_DISK storage. Then, we use our GA model to simulate the placement of datasets to storage and compare our results against alternative algorithms. Finally, in order to study the algorithms performance in a real HDFS environment, we executed some experiments on a cloud computing cluster running Hadoop.

5.1   Experiment Setup

We tested our GA algorithm and compare its performance against Simplex, GRG, and Evolutionary solutions. For that end, we performed experiments using different numbers of datasets as input, which are mapped to storage in a 5-node cluster with a hierarchical storage setup. We used the experiment setup described here to perform both simulated and real hardware experiments. For the latter, we configured our cluster on Chameleon Cloud [20], a large-scale cloud research configurable environment funded by National Science Foundation (NSF). Table 3 shows the experiment setup.

For the real hardware experiments, we used five Chameleon nodes, each one with two CPU, 67.6 GB RAM, x86_64 Platform Type, Intel Xeon 3.00 GHz Processor, 400 GB SSD and 2TB HDD. One of the nodes was configured as master and the rest as workers. Datasets are mapped exclusively to workers nodes. We allocate to HDFS only part of the worker nodes resources: 64 GB of RAM, 1 TB of HDD, and 250 GB of SSD from each node. The cluster architecture is shown in Fig. 2.

Table 3. Experiment setup

Parameter	Element
Number of datasets	15, 35, 50
Number of storage types	3
Total cluster RAM_DISK storage capacity	256 GB
Total cluster SSD storage capacity	1 TB
Total cluster HDD storage capacity	4 TB
RAM_DISK bandwidth	6600 MB/s
SSD bandwidth	2320 MB/s
HDD bandwidth	267 MB/s
Dataset size	$0 \leq \text{DSS} \leq 200\,\text{GB}$

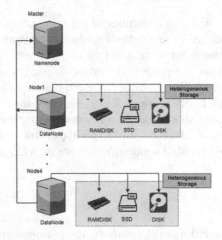

Fig. 2. Hadoop cluster architecture

5.2   A New HDFS Storage Policy

In order to get a sense of RAM_DISK storage performance it was necessary to implement a new storage policy. In HDFS, the only available storage policy that use RAM_DISK is Lazy_Persist and this policy always creates a replica on Disk, even if the replication factor is set as one. We named our new policy All_RAM and differs from Lazy_Persist in that it does not make replications on any other storage type. Table 4 describes All_RAM policy.

Table 4. All_RAM storage policy

ID	Name	Block Placement (n)	Fallback creation	Fallback replication
14	All_RAM	RAM_DISK: n	DISK	DISK

5.3 Using the Genetic Algorithm Model to Simulate Data Placement

Figure 3 shows the results of using the genetic algorithm model we describe in Sects. 3 and 4 to simulate the data placement of different numbers of datasets in a HDFS cluster, according with the experiment setup described in Sect. 5.1. Throughout the generations, the fitness value is getting better, this is because of the selection implemented method, elitism. This method ensures that the parents of each generation are going to be the best in order to likely get better children.

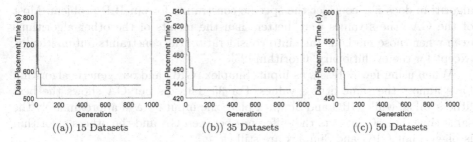

((a)) 15 Datasets   ((b)) 35 Datasets   ((c)) 50 Datasets

Fig. 3. Best fitness curves using elitism with a 0.9 crossover rate and a 0.1 mutation rate. The initial population is 100 chromosomes.

Each generation must accomplish the ILP problem constraints. In algorithms like simplex or GRG it is possible to explicitly include the constraints, but in the case of an Evolutionary algorithm and for our GA, mechanisms such as *penalization* have to be used in order to make sure that each of the chromosomes satisfies all the constraints. To accomplish that each chromosome satisfies the constraint (2) we have to guarantee that there always exist a storage type storing the dataset, even during the mutation process. Also, to achieve the fulfillment of constraint (3) we implement a penalty process, which sets a high penalization value in the objective function to the chromosomes that do not comply with the restriction. This penalty value is used to ensure that a bad chromosome is not going to be selected as a parent in the selection operation [21,22]. For all the test, the GA found the optimal value long before the generation number 1000. As shown in Fig. 3, for all the cases, the GA reached the equilibrium point before generation number 100.

Comparing Against Alternative Algorithms. Our purpose in this part is to evaluate the simulated data placement time achieved for alternative algorithms and compare against our GA algorithm results. The resulting data placement execution times are shown in Fig. 4.

Figure 4 shows that our GA outperforms the rest of studied algorithms. From that figure, we can see that the data placement times obtained for the generic evolutionary algorithm are significantly higher than the others, even though they have the same parameter values used for GA, this is because the evolutionary

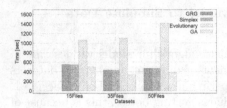

Fig. 4. Data placement execution time (s)

Table 5. Algorithms execution time (s)

	15 Files	35 Files	50 Files
GRG	5.2	50	46
Simplex	1.3	1.2	2.5
Evolutionary	37	34	34
GA	0.6	0.9	1.3

algorithm does not consider the specific constraints for our ILP problem. Most of the GA fitness values were better than the results of the other algorithms even when those methods take into consideration the constraints automatically, except for the evolutionary algorithm [23].

When using few datasets as input, Simplex, GRG and our genetic algorithm have almost the same fitness values. For 35 datasets our GA shows the best fitness value, while GRG and Simplex place the input data in approximately the same time. For 50 datasets the difference between GA and the others algorithm is bigger, but GRG and Simplex are still close.

Table 5 shows the time used for the algorithms under analysis to calculate the data placement allocations. GA was the fastest followed by the Simplex algorithm, while GRG and evolutionary take substantially more time to execute, especially for datasets with a higher number of files.

5.4   Placing Datasets into a Real HDFS Cluster

We wrote a synthetic benchmark which generates different numbers of datasets and load them to HDFS according to the allocation made by the algorithms. We performed two experiments using replication factors of one and three. We use replication factor 3 because this is the default replication factor to provide fault tolerance and is the most common replication factor in Hadoop clusters. Additionally, we experimented with a replication factor one in order to contrasts against our simulation results. We also compare these results with the ones obtained from the allocation of datasets using the default Hot policy, in order to evidence how the use of the studied algorithms and heterogeneous storage improve substantially the writing and reading throughput.

Testing Using Replication Factor 1. Figure 5 shows the writing and reading throughput obtained for each dataset, using a replication factor of 1. The GA algorithm shows the best writing and reading performance. Furthermore, it can be evidenced that the throughput using the Simplex and GRG algorithms are very similar. Finally, the Evolutionary algorithm throughput is the slowest of the four. It is inferred that the throughput changes substantially compared with the throughput obtained in simulation, due to the different processes that HDFS performs for the placement of the files. One of those processes is the division

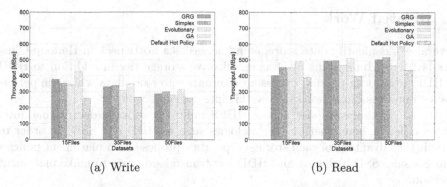

(a) Write   (b) Read

Fig. 5. Write and read throughput using replication factor 1.

of the files into blocks and the distribution of them through the cluster nodes.
Other factor that influences the disk writing performance is available cache.

Testing Using Replication Factor 3. Figure 6 shows the writing and reading throughput obtained for each dataset, using a replication factor 3. The data placement used in this test was different to the one used for the test with replication factor 1, because it was necessary to recalculate the size of the files to ensure that the files along with their replicas fit into the HDFS. As in the first test, the GA algorithm kept being the most efficient and the Evolutionary algorithm the slowest of the four.

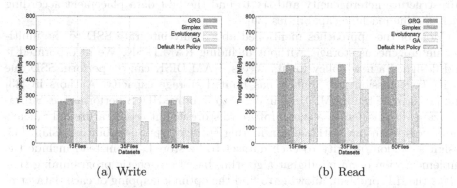

(a) Write   (b) Read

Fig. 6. Write and read throughput using replication factor 3.

In our datasets, as the number of files increases, the file sizes go smaller. Thus, the files belonging to the 50-files dataset are smaller than the files belonging the 15-files dataset. In the test with replication factor 3, it was possible to observe that HDFS is more efficient for big files. Figure 6 shows that for the dataset with 15 files the throughput was better than the dataset with 35 and 50 files.

6   Related Work

Several works identify data storage and access as a bottleneck in Hadoop Clusters [4, 24–27]. Integrating SSD as an effective storage tier in addition to HDD in HDFS, has been pointed out as an alternative to store data while the performance improves. Some works show this integration [25–30].

In [31], authors propose a new HDFS multi-tier storage design that integrates different heterogeneous technologies such as HDD and SSD. In order to exploit the advantage of each storage type, they propose data placement policies that consider SSD high cost and HDD low transmission rate to make placement decisions.

In [26], authors propose a dynamic data management system for Hadoop, allowing workloads that are expected to benefit from SSD to be able to use it as a cache for the HDDs too. They integrate in their data management system a component called Popularity Predictor, which is responsible for analyzing the number of accesses to different files in order to decide which files should be moved to SSD and get less access time to them.

Pan et al. [27], also propose a data access strategy for Hadoop. This strategy focuses in establish some categories for the tasks, taking into account data locality and available storage types. Both, different speeds of storage types and reduced access times thought data locality, allow reduce the applications execution time.

Other authors focused in managing the replication factor in order to guarantee the storage availability in HDFS [32]. Other techniques have been used to improve heterogeneous storage performance [4, 33], and some works consider infrastructure heterogeneity and try to find the best data placement according with specific machine capabilities [34].

Most of the approaches mentioned above only integrate SSD to the multi-tier heterogeneous storage, without including RAM_DISK. We incorporated it and designed a new policy for its access. RAM_DISK can outperform SSD due to its transmission rate, but it has limited storage capacity. Authors in [33] and [4], include the RAM_DISK in order to improve HDFS performance. Subramanyam [4] consider data temperature to store it, but temperature only means the access frequency without considering storage types capabilities. Islam [33] assign a random priority to each dataset to be stored. We instead include the implementation of an intelligent algorithm based on genetic programming that solves the ILP problem, allowing to find the optimal mapping of each dataset to storage types on a HDFS, taking in account the size of datasets and the write rate of storage types.

7   Conclusions and Future Work

In this paper we have shown how leveraging the Hadoop heterogeneous storage support in combination with intelligent algorithms to perform data placement can help to optimize the performance of applications by improving reading and writing rates in HDFS. All the studied algorithms outperformed the default hot storage policy used by HDFS, while our proposed GA solution showed the best results among all of them.

Genetic algorithms are not generally considered to work in a model with constraints. This is because the search or selection operators, crossover and mutation does not take into count constraints. Hence, there is no guarantee that if a parent chromosome satisfies the constraints the children will satisfy them as well. It is for this reason that some authors suggest not to work with GAs in problems with constraints [35]. We decided to tackle this by working with a penalization system which does not allow wrong chromosomes to be selected as parents due to its resulting fitness function value. This mechanism also provides faster solutions that chromosome repairing methods. As a result of this strategy, our proposed GA took less than 100 iterations to find the best value for our objective function even though it was configured to iterate 1000 times.

One direction for future work is to propose a complete model for data placement in HDFS clusters considering different characteristics of the input data such as arrival frequency, size, priority, among others; becoming a multi-objective optimization problem. Considering internal HDFS operations such as the division of the files into blocks and the distribution and replication of them through cluster nodes would make the model more accurate. Another direction for future work is to include in the model the monetary cost that generates the use of each one of the storage types as a criterion to decide mapping.

Acknowledgements. Results presented in this paper were obtained using the Chameleon testbed supported by the U.S. National Science Foundation.

References

1. Zhou, K., Fu, C., Yang, S.: Big data driven smart energy management: from big data to big insights. Renew. Sustain. Energy Rev. **56**, 215–225 (2016)
2. Li, H., Li, H., Wen, Z., Mo, J., Wu, J.: Distributed heterogeneous storage based on data value. In: 2017 IEEE 2nd Information Technology, Networking, Electronic and Automation Control Conference (ITNEC), pp. 264–271 (2017)
3. Bezerra, A., Hernandez, P., Espinosa, A., Moure, J.C.: Job scheduling in Hadoop with shared input policy and RAMDISK, pp. 355–363 (2014)
4. Subramanyam, R.: HDFS heterogeneous storage resource management based on data temperature, pp. 232–235 (2015)
5. Welcome to apache hadoop!
6. Shvachko, K., Kuang, H., Radia, S., Chansler, R.: The Hadoop distributed file system. In: 2010 IEEE 26th Symposium on Mass Storage Systems and Technologies (MSST), pp. 1–10 (2010)
7. Dean, J., Ghemawat, S.: MapReduce: simplified data processing on large clusters. Commun. ACM **51**(1), 107 (2008)
8. Xiong, R., Luo, J., Dong, F.: Optimizing data placement in heterogeneous hadoop clusters. Clust. Comput. **18**(4), 1465–1480 (2015)
9. Archival storage, SSD & memory

10. Yoon, M.S., Kamal, A.E.: Optimal dataset allocation in distributed heterogeneous clouds. In: Globecom Workshops (GC Wkshps), 2014, pp. 75–80. IEEE (2014)
11. Klein, D., Hannan, E.: An algorithm for the multiple objective integer linear programming problem. Eur. J. Oper. Res. **9**(4), 378–385 (1982)
12. Apers, P.M.: Data allocation in distributed database systems. ACM Trans. Database Syst. (TODS) **13**(3), 263–304 (1988)
13. Guzek, M., Bouvry, P., Talbi, E.G.: A survey of evolutionary computation for resource management of processing in cloud computing. IEEE Comput. Intell. Mag. **10**(2), 53–67 (2015)
14. Nelder, J.A., Mead, R.: A simplex method for function minimization. Comput. J. **7**(4), 308–313 (1965)
15. Lasdon, L., Waren, A.: Generalized reduced gradient software for linearly and nonlinearly constrained problems. Graduate School of Business, University of Texas at Austin Austin, TX (1977)
16. Coello, C.A.C., Lamont, G.B., Van Veldhuizen, D.A., et al.: Evolutionary Algorithms for Solving Multi-objective Problems, vol. 5. Springer, Boston (2007). https://doi.org/10.1007/978-0-387-36797-2
17. Gen, M., Cheng, R.: Genetic Algorithms and Engineering Optimization, vol. 7. Wiley, Hoboken (2000)
18. Srinivas, M., Patnaik, L.M.: Adaptive probabilities of crossover and mutation in genetic algorithms. IEEE Trans. Syst. Man Cybern. **24**(4), 656–667 (1994)
19. Chiroma, H., Abdulkareem, S., Abubakar, A., Zeki, A., Gital, A.Y., Usman, M.J.: Correlation study of genetic algorithm operators: crossover and mutation probabilities. In: Proceedings of the International Symposium on Mathematical Sciences and Computing Research, pp. 6–7 (2013)
20. About Chameleon | Chameleon
21. Gen, M., Cheng, R.: A survey of penalty techniques in genetic algorithms. In: Proceedings of IEEE International Conference on Evolutionary Computation, pp. 804–809. IEEE (1996)
22. Michalewicz, Z., Janikow, C.Z.: Handling constraints in genetic algorithms. In: ICGA, pp. 151–157 (1991)
23. Kolen, A.: A genetic algorithm for the partial binary constraint satisfaction problem: an application to a frequency assignment problem. Stat. Neerl. **61**(1), 4–15 (2007)
24. Li, H., Li, H., Wen, Z., Mo, J., Wu, J.: Distributed heterogeneous storage based on data value. In: 2017 IEEE 2nd Information Technology, Networking, Electronic and Automation Control Conference (ITNEC), pp. 264–271. IEEE (2017)
25. Krish, K., Anwar, A., Butt, A.R.: hatS: a heterogeneity-aware tiered storage for Hadoop. In: 2014 14th IEEE/ACM International Symposium on Cluster, Cloud and Grid Computing, pp. 502–511. IEEE (2014)
26. Krish, K., Iqbal, M.S., Butt, A.R.: VENU: orchestrating SSDs in Hadoop storage. In: 2014 IEEE International Conference on Big Data (Big Data), pp. 207–212 IEEE (2014)
27. Pan, F., Xiong, J., Shen, Y., Wang, T., Jiang, D.: H-scheduler: storage-aware task scheduling for heterogeneous-storage spark clusters. In: 2018 IEEE 24th International Conference on Parallel and Distributed Systems (ICPADS), pp. 1–9. IEEE (2018)
28. Krish, K., Wadhwa, B., Iqbal, M.S., Rafique, M.M., Butt, A.R.: On efficient hierarchical storage for big data processing. In: 2016 16th IEEE/ACM International Symposium on Cluster, Cloud and Grid Computing (CCGrid), pp. 403–408. IEEE (2016)

29. Kambatla, K., Chen, Y.: The truth about mapreduce performance on SSDs. In: 28th Large Installation System Administration Conference (LISA14), pp. 118–126 (2014)
30. Narayanan, D., Thereska, E., Donnelly, A., Elnikety, S., Rowstron, A.: Migrating server storage to SSDs: analysis of tradeoffs. In: Proceedings of the 4th ACM European Conference on Computer Systems, pp. 145–158 ACM (2009)
31. Kang, S.H., Koo, D.H., Kang, W.H., Lee, S.W.: A case for flash memory SSD in Hadoop applications. Int. J. Control. Autom. 6(1), 201–210 (2013)
32. Wei, Q., Veeravalli, B., Gong, B., Zeng, L., Feng, D.: CDRM: a cost-effective dynamic replication management scheme for cloud storage cluster. In: 2010 IEEE International Conference on Cluster Computing, pp. 188–196. IEEE (2010)
33. Islam, N.S., Lu, X., Wasi-ur Rahman, M., Shankar, D., Panda, D.K.: Triple-H: a hybrid approach to accelerate HDFS on HPC clusters with heterogeneous storage architecture. In: 2015 15th IEEE/ACM International Symposium on Cluster, Cloud and Grid Computing (CCGrid), p. 101. IEEE (2015)
34. Xiong, R., Luo, J., Dong, F.: Optimizing data placement in heterogeneous Hadoop clusters. Clust. Comput. 18(4), 1465–1480 (2015)
35. Coello, C.A.C., Montes, E.M.: Constraint-handling in genetic algorithms through the use of dominance-based tournament selection. Adv. Eng. Inform. 16(3), 193–203 (2002)

Towards Automated Configuration of Cloud Storage Gateways: A Data Driven Approach

Sanjeev Sondur and Krishna Kant[✉]

Temple University, Philadelphia, PA 19122, USA
{sanjeev.sondur,kkant}@temple.edu

Abstract. Cloud storage gateways (CSGs) are an essential part of enterprises to take advantage of the scale and flexibility of cloud object store. A CSG provides clients the impression of a locally configured large size block-based storage device, which needs to be mapped to remote cloud storage which is invariably object based. Proper configuration of the cloud storage gateway is extremely challenging because of numerous parameters involved and interactions among them. In this paper, we study this problem for a commercial CSG product that is typical of offerings in the market. We explore how machine learning techniques can be exploited both for the forward problem (i.e. predicting performance from the configuration parameters) and backward problem (i.e. predicting configuration parameter values from the target performance). Based on extensive testing with real world customer workloads, we show that it is possible to achieve excellent prediction accuracy while ensuring that the model is not overfitted to the data.

Keywords: Cloud storage gateway · Object store · Performance · Configuration management · Machine learning

1 Introduction

A Cloud Storage Gateway is an emerging concept in Cloud Storage Solutions; wherein the CSG application is installed on-premise and translates cloud storage object-store APIs such as SOAP or REST to the block I/O-based storage protocols such as SCSI, Fibre Channel, NFS or SMB.

Cloud Storage Gateway (CSG) concept was pioneered by Google [5], and subsequently offered by many leading industry vendors as a Cloud Storage solution. As shown in Fig. 1, CSG appliance connects the client applications running locally to an object store hosted in a remote cloud data center. Although the remote storage could be block based, it is almost universally object based due to many advantages of the cloud model. The advantage of CSG is that while the user data resides on the cloud storage devices, it makes the accesses appear locally going to a SCSI device.

© Springer Nature Switzerland AG 2019
D. Da Silva et al. (Eds.): CLOUD 2019, LNCS 11513, pp. 192–207, 2019.
https://doi.org/10.1007/978-3-030-23502-4_14

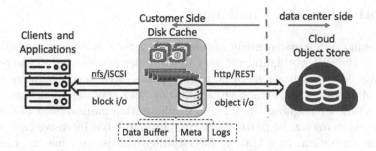

Fig. 1. Cloud storage gateway architecture.

Customers deploy CSG to expand storage capabilities of their local computing infrastructure. For example, a large video animation customer like Disney could work with hundreds of graphics files of size 1GB or more, a financial company may store a large number of fiscal records in medium size files (say 1–10 MB text files). The locally running business workloads would typically persist or retrieve a large amount of such data through the CSG. Since a single CSG may be used by many different business applications with different persist/retrieve patterns, a proper configuration of CSG is a very challenging problem.

Data center operators have a huge amount of operational data collected over time that can be exploited to understand the system configuration parameters and their influence on the operational behavior. We keep the discussion focused by studying the configuration challenges as pertaining to the customer side CSG system, and not the backend data center hosted cloud object store system in Fig. 1. We use a commercially available CSG available from a prominent market vendor. The main goals of our study are as follows:

- Design experiments to collect performance and configuration data for a large number of configurations of this CSG.
- Explore the use of suitable machine learning techniques to build models for solving the forward problem (predicting performance for given configuration parameters), and reverse problem (predicting certain configuration parameters based on target performance).
- Explore how the domain knowledge can be exploited to reduce the configuration space and enhance the accuracy of the predictions.

The key contribution of our work is to demonstrate that we can build robust models for relating user settable system and hardware parameters to the performance of cloud storage gateway and thereby *debugging* the configurations. Even in cases where such automated analysis fails to provide the optimal result, it is expected to yield configurations that are close to optimal and thus can be tuned further with far less effort and time than the prevalent manual approaches whose success entirely depends on the experience of the administrators. To the best of our knowledge, the prior work has predominantly considered performance as a function of workload parameters rather than the user tunable system parameters.

2 Motivation and Challenges

Proper configuration management of complex cyber-systems is a very challenging problem in the real-world, and yet very much under-appreciated in the research community. Misconfigurations in large enterprises often account for up to 80% of the malfunctions and attack vulnerabilities, and routinely consume days of engineer's time to diagnose and fix [10]. Configuration management of data center storage systems can be particularly complex and labor intensive task [3], and CSG is no exception. In addition, CSG configurations combine the complexities inherent in storage system configuration, cache configuration, unpredictable network traffic and the complexities of back-end cloud systems. Similar to other cyber-systems, CSG has many configuration parameters or "knobs" with little clarity on how to set them or what precise impact they have on the output end.

While working with the commercial vendor of a CSG product, we noticed that the most common problems were related to customer complaints about poor performance or I/O time-out errors. We invariably found that on further investigation that most of these complaints were a result of poor understanding of the workload (i.e. request streams) and the configuration parameters of the CSG. The main source of difficulties in configuration management are the numerous parameters with complex inter-dependencies that are mostly unknown or poorly understood with respect to their impact on the overall performance, availability or user experience [11].

This prompted our research into understanding the relationship between various parameters in the Cloud Storage Gateway environment. For example, there are few *uncontrollable* variables such as eviction rate, cloud storage response, internet throughput, etc. and some parameters under the user control such as: workload, hardware characteristics, cache configuration, etc.

It is well known that the storage system performance depends on the workload characteristics, deployed optimizations, and their specific configuration (See [3] & references therein). Configurations also "are often difficult and knowledge-intensive to develop, brittle to various environment and systems changes, and limited in capacity to deal with non-steady-state phenomena [7]."

Cloud storage gateway (CSG) is a relatively new paradigm in cloud storage solutions, and effective methods for its configuration management is largely unexplored.

3 Cloud Storage Gateway

Unlike the cloud storage services which they complement, CSGs use standard network protocols that integrate with existing applications and can also serve as an intermediary to multiple cloud storage providers. Increasingly, CSGs also provide many sophisticated services such as backup and recovery, caching, compression, encryption, storage de-duplication and provisioning. A CSG will typically serve multiple clients using a set of local storage devices (possibly a RAID but not necessarily) that is seen by the clients as a local block storage. All clients assigned to this local storage share the storage, although there might be some internal fine-grain storage allocation policies that are not revealed to the client. Each client will be allocated space for its data, metadata, and log files. The CSG can be viewed as two I/O layers (see Fig. 1): (i) front-end for local user I/O and (ii) the back-end for cloud storage I/O operations. At a minimum, the CSG will provide the ability of intelligently partitioning the space into data, metadata, and log files, and a suitable caching mechanism for each so that data transfers from the backend can be properly handled.

3.1   Characterizing the Behavior of a CSG

The performance and behavior of a CSG depends on the hardware platform architecture h (CPU, memory, storage, network, local I/O rate, etc.), workload characteristics k (incoming request rate/distribution, data writes/sec, data reads/sec, metadata reads/sec, metadata size, etc.) and application goals p. Application goal is predominately expressed as I/O performance (MBytes per sec). Generally, the application goals are achieved by: (a) most reads are satisfied locally (which is essential to match the higher I/O inject rate to the slower back-end rate), and (b) maintain and batch writes locally so as to make the writeback more efficient. These functions along with the management of meta-data files, rotating log files, garbage collection etc. are normal storage system attributes that affect the behavior of CSG. Furthermore, workload characteristics such as burstiness are also important. Workload and performance may be specified either directly in terms of resource requirements, or in more abstract terms such as priority, latency, or resource combination (e.g., a "small" vs. "medium" vs. "large" configuration). In any case, these are ultimately translated to individual system parameters, either explicitly or via policies.

It is easy to see that if the workload characteristics k, system configuration h and CSG configuration r are not matched, the end users would likely experience undesired performance p which is usually defined as the read and write rates supported with certain maximum latency and without any I/O timeouts. Read/write operations beyond the acceptable range or complete rejection is considered I/O failure. As workloads change over time (i.e. as i^{th} workload k_i deviates from initial assumed pattern k_i), the initial user-defined configuration r_i may no longer support the demands of new workload(s) and cause undesired end-user experiences.

A major issue in properly configuring the CSG is that *the vendors invariably do not reveal most of the internal details, and instead expose a limited set of administrator controllable configuration parameters to tune the system.* Often, these administrator controllable parameters are not even the actual configuration parameters, but merely some sizing controls or decision variables that affect multiple internal parameters. In other words, the knobs visible to the enterprise are rather fuzzy with little knowledge of what exactly they do. Of course, this is partly done to simplify the job of the administrator; a vendor willing to expose all raw knobs would invariably make them unusable. Thus the phenomenon of fuzzy knobs with little visibility is an essential characteristic of real systems and cannot be wished away! It alone precludes simple analytic models for characterizing performance of a component like CSG or fine-tuning it for very specific workload or hardware. With absence of any quantifiable, well-defined correlation or closed loop representation, configuration management is more an art than science.

3.2   Complexities in Configuration Control

Generally, as the size of the local storage (henceforth referred to as "cache") increases, we expect the CSG throughput to increase because more I/O can be handled locally. The benefit is entirely dependent on how well the caching mechanism keeps and prefetches "hot" data. Since the overall space available for caching is *shared* by multiple clients, there is interaction across clients. For example, giving more space for some clients hurts others, and the net effect is very complex to predict. This caching mechanism is hidden by the vendor and not controllable by the end-user, adding to the complexity of the configuration control. These comments apply to both data and metadata but with different effects. The metadata needs to be consulted for every I/O regardless of whether the corresponding data is in the cache or not. Depending on the workload and the granularity of access, metadata caching becomes more dominant than data caching. At the same time, metadata is generally much smaller than data, and thus it is much easier to provide generous amounts of storage for metadata. We explore the data cache vs. metadata size in our research through varied workload and configurations studies. The log size should have no influence on performance except that writebacks of the log would take up some backend I/O bandwidth. This initial description paves the way for understanding the complexity of configuring the CSG system.

Incorrect configurations could result in significant competition between the following three activities:

1. Eviction of modified pages requiring writeback to the backend object storage which is likely to experience high latency, limited I/O bandwidth due to network issues, and perhaps a significant write amplification due to the need to write the entire object.
2. Cache misses from client requests thereby requiring reading of backend object storage, which experiences similar issues as writebacks (e.g., significant read amplification and latency due to transfer of entire objects, for which the CSG need to make adequate room).
3. Local read/writes performed by the clients which are expected to be much more frequent and expect a low latency.

Note that the cache eviction is not complete until the write confirmation is received from the cloud storage, and the data must be kept in the cache until then. Consequently, a more aggressive eviction would only result in fewer entries in the cache to handle new data requests that must be fetched from the cloud. The CSG may also need to retry the *entire object* operation if unsuccessful. In addition to the whole object transfers on the backend, the transfer normally uses HTTP which adds considerable overhead. The varying size of the object could interfere with the SLA guaranteed to the user about upload/inject rates. We quantify SLAs based on local SCSI update traffic generated by the client, and any SLA violation is seen by the client as I/O timeout or errors. Note that increasing the cache size does not solve the writeback problem; in fact, it could even make it worse.

4   Configuration Problem Formulation

The CSG system in Fig. 1 serves as a 'disk cache' to buffer the incoming user request and match it with the cloud storage uploads (or downloads). User requests come over a SCSI bus at a high arrival rate λ_{in} (high throughput, high bandwidth, low latency) and the backend cloud storage presents a low eviction rate system λ_c (high latency/low bandwidth/higher error retries). Resource allocation for the disk cache needs to match the k_n incoming request streams and the service rates. We model CSG Controller of Fig. 1 as a queuing system. The incoming request stream k can be represented as:

$$k = f(ar, rs, rm) \tag{1}$$

where: k the request stream is a function of: ar the request arrival rate, rs the size of the request, and rm the metadata size. These request streams are characterized by the real world customer workloads as given in Table 2. Each of these requests consumes hardware and disk cache resource for servicing. Note in Fig. 1 that all n request streams share the same resource of CSG controller. There is no known functional relationship to analyze the queue behavior, and the controller has no user controllable factors to allocate resources per request stream. The relationship between the input stream, requested resource, queue and the disk cache is unknown. This leads us to conclude that there is no clear optimization or queuing technique that can model the serviceability of the incoming streams. For example, if the cache size is small and the eviction rate to backend cloud storage is high, then the system should be able to handle high requests. The converse means the requests will be dropped.

To add to this complex analysis, the CSG runs on a hardware platform characterized by core speed, number of cores, memory capacity, disk I/O capacity and network I/O throughput. Here, network I/O throughput represents the measurable I/O throughput to upload an object from the client system to the cloud storage. The hardware characteristics of the CSG platform is represented as:

$$h = f(cs, nc, me, m_{bw}, di, th) \tag{2}$$

where h the hardware characteristics is a function of: cs core speed, nc number of cores, me memory capacity, m_{bw} memory bandwidth, di disk I/O rate and th I/O throughput measured between the on-premise CSG and cloud object store. For example, one disk partition d_j on three independent disks has a better I/O rate compared to three individual partitions on one SCSI disk. Similarly a network card capacity of 10 Gbps would have better eviction rate than a network card capacity of 1 Gbps. Another evident characteristic is the performance boost from using a SSD versus a HDD disk. Again modeling the complex interactions between different these limited parameters and their relative effect on the *CSG disk cache performance* is unknown.

The disk cache is split into three distinct partitions: data buffer db, metadata md and log space ls (Sect. 3.2 & Fig. 1). These are bound by the total resource disk space available ds_{max}, such that:

$$ds_{max} \geq db + md + ls \tag{3}$$

Each of these parameters db, md, ls coupled with the request stream k influences the behavior of the system as explained earlier.

Finally, if the configuration r of the CSG is optimized on a given hardware h, the input stream/ workload k will experience a performance or service rate of p. We denote this performance as:

$$p = g(h, k, r) \tag{4}$$

denoting that the performance (or service rate) p depends on hardware characteristics h, service rate (or workload) k and CSG configuration r. Note that Eqs. 1, 2 and 4 is a multidimensional vector. Changing any one of the above parameters will affect the performance output p.

4.1   Research Questions

We define our research problem using a specific example relating to configuration challenge faced by a system administrator. Suggest a CSG configuration that satisfies the required performance p (10 MBps), given a specific hardware architecture h (2×1.2 GBps cores, 64 GB RAM, 1 GBps NIC card, 0.25 GBps network speed) and a workload w (5 concurrent users, 10 files, avg 5 GB size, upload time: 24 h). In general, we define the following:

1. $P = \{p_1, p_2, \cdots p_n\}$: performance constraints for each of the n applications, predominantly defined by expected I/O rate, e.g.: 100MBps min for both I/O write and reads.
2. $K = \{k_1, k_2, \cdots k_n\}$: workload characteristics for each of the n applications. We used real-world workload patterns observed from end customers of a commercial industry vendor (See Table 2), predominantly defined by average file size, number of files, users, sub-directory hierarchy etc.
3. $H = \{h_1, h_2, \cdots h_m\}$: m hardware characteristics, i.e. the machines running the CSG application, e.g.: core speeds, memory, local storage disk characteristics, network I/O bandwidth, etc.
4. $R = \{r_1, r_2, \cdots r_l\}$: l cloud gateway configurations each specified in terms of system configurations e.g.: 100GB data cache, 25GB log space, 50GB metadata space, 10 concurrent threads etc.

We can now ask two key questions:

Q.1 What should be the *cache configuration* to satisfy the 'k' request streams.
Q.2 What is the *maximum performance* from 'k' streams given certain cache configuration constraints (e.g. allocation of resources).

We are interested in a mechanism that draws a relationship between the workload characteristics K, system architecture H, configuration R, performance P and can *answer* the following.

1. Verify Configuration - given the system architecture, workload characteristics, and CSG configuration, determine if the performance constraints are met with a high probability.

$$[H_{new}, K_{new}, R_{new}] \Rightarrow P_{new} \text{ is satisfied} \tag{5}$$

In most cases, only a few parameters are new; however, because of the dependencies and nonlinear interactions, it may or may not be possible to exploit the unchanged parameters. This represents Q.2 of our discussion.

2. Configure - given the system architecture, workload characteristics, application goals and performance constraint, propose a configuration R_{new} that satisfies all the constraints. That is, given H_{new}, K_{new}, and P_{new} find R_{new}.

$$[H_{new}, K_{new}, P_{new}] \Rightarrow R_{new} \tag{6}$$

This problem is the reverse of the first problem and is substantially harder. As in the last problem, only a few parameters may be new but it may or may not be possible to exploit the unchanged parameters.

3. Predict - Based on a time series of performance data for a given configuration, with changing workload, predict if the current configuration is likely to fail.

$$[H_{old}, R_{old}] and [K_i, P_i], i = 1, 2, ... n \Rightarrow \text{Failure} \tag{7}$$

5   Solution Approach

As stated earlier, the complexity of the relationships between the user settable CSG parameters and the performance precludes a modeling or simulation based characterization. Therefore, we turn to machine learning based methods to learn various relationships along with our domain knowledge into the functioning of the CSG. Machine learning (ML) is, of course, no panacea; it often requires a significant amount of training data and the learned model may be "over-fitted", and thus may be unable to accurately predict behavior when the inputs (workload or configuration parameter values) are sufficiently different from those for the training data. We will address this aspect carefully in our analysis.

5.1   Feature Vector

The feature vector used to support our research is built from the above equations Eqs. (1, 2, and 3) and represented as below. We have included throughput (a.k.a performance in bytes/sec) in the feature vector. As explained earlier in Sect. 4, our work defines QoS and SLA in terms of latency. Any latency exceeding the limit is experienced as I/O time-out. We do not explicitly include latency in the feature vector since a configuration that leads to time-outs will be rejected right away and is not relevant for performance analysis. We discuss some tests that violated SLA and unacceptable latency in Sect. 6.3; these were attributed to wrong configuration choice for specific workload constraints. Learning configurations that cause time-outs (and thereby avoid them) is a reasonable goal, but much harder and beyond the scope of this work. Therefore, all our tests used in the analysis are for valid SLA conditions (Table 1).

There are many parameters relevant to CSG operation that could potentially affect the performance; however, it is neither possible, nor practical to consider them all. There is no escape from applying the domain knowledge to consider only those parameters that are likely to be controllable or relevant. One such

Table 1. Subset of feature vector supporting the problem.

ar	Request arrival rate	rs	Size of the request
rm	Request metadata size	cs	Core speed
nc	Number of cores	me	Memory capacity
m_{bw}	Memory bus bandwidth	di	Disk I/O rate
th	Network I/O throughput	db	Data buffer
md	Metadata	ls	Log size
p	System performance (measured as throughput)		

example is the ubiquitous use of NFS for users to mount the remote storage device (but still within the local data center boundaries). NFS has many mount options (rsize, wsize, etc.) that can be chosen for individual mounts. However, these parameters are invariably set at default values and unlikely to be changed. Similarly, although the storage interconnect speeds (PCI bus speed, SATA/SAS interface speed, etc.) are potentially important, their selection happens at a much more basic level (i.e., when deploying the storage device/system) rather than for performance optimization. Therefore, consideration of these aspects is beyond the scope of this paper.

5.2   Research Hypothesis

We use statistical machine learning, classification, and optimization mechanism to *learn* these relationships. Our prediction model is expressed as a function of the above feature vector. Let $\boldsymbol{x} = \{x_1, x_2, \ldots x_k\}$ denote the vector configuration parameter values. Let $\phi(\boldsymbol{x})$ denote the *hypothesized functional relationship* to be learned and $\gamma(\boldsymbol{x})$ is the true observed output for given values of the input $\boldsymbol{x}$.

We now have the basics to answer our research question Q.1 and Q.2 by using the above features and to accurately design our hypothesis $\phi(x)$ and output γ.

For a given workload, a service rate k_i, a set of constraints on hardware h_i and CSG configuration r_i, we *predict* the maximum performance p_i by the following hypothesis (i represents i^{th} variation).

Hypothesis:

$$\phi(ar, rs, rm, cs, nc, me, m_{bw}, di, th, db, md, ls)$$
$$\text{Output:} \quad \gamma() = p \tag{8}$$

Similarly, rearranging the features, and re-writing the hypothesis, we *predict* the data cache configuration r required to achieve a given performance p for a given workload (service rate) k under a set of hardware constraints h.

Hypothesis:

$$\phi(p, ar, rs, rm, cs, nc, m, m_{bw}, di, th)$$
$$\text{Output:} \quad \gamma() = (db, md, ls) \tag{9}$$

5.3   Classification Problem

In Eq. 8, we compute a single parameter p (performance) for a given set of constraints, and in Eq. 9, we compute multiple parameters db, md, ls (data cache size, metadata and log size). The former is called single label classification and the latter is called multi-label classification [6]. Computing a single label/parameter is relatively easier than computing three inter-related labels/parameters. For our end results, we predict performance, data cache size etc. as multiple classes (e.g. performance = {class 1, class 2, ...} or data cache size = { class 1, class 2, ... }). These are called multi-class prediction (for Eq. 8) and multi-class multi-label prediction (for Eq. 9). We will quantify this while discussing workload design and results in Sects. 6.2 and 8.

6   Implementation Details

6.1   Test Environment

Our test environment (Fig. 2) is comprised of (i) Dell PowerEdge R320 with 4 cores @ 1.8 GHz, 16 GiB memory, 3 ATA Disks- each of 500 GB and one 1 GB Ethernet interface (ii) Dell PowerEdge R730xd with 8 cores @ 2.1 GHz, 32 GiB memory, one SCSI disk of 5495 GB and one 1 GB Ethernet interface. Both servers have Ubuntu 14.04 with required tools and connected to local network. We used different hardware configurations to study the influence of cores, core speeds, disk, and memory configurations. On each of these servers, we partitioned the disk for several cache configurations. The server is connected to the HDD volumes on a remote cloud object store service, as NFS mounts. We used C++ and Python scripting tools for executing the workload and collecting metrics.

The algorithms were implemented in Python using *scikit-learn* [4] library. This tool gives both the algorithms, tuning parameters, cross validation and the associated metrics such as accuracy, prediction error, etc. For machine learning algorithm efficiency metrics, see [1].

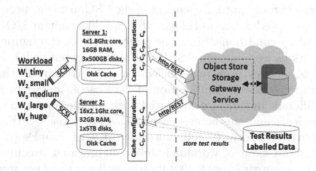

Fig. 2. Cloud storage gateway - test environment.

Once the test scripts were ready, the evaluation setup for each experiment involved partitioning the disks for various configurations, allocate cache/metadata size (see Table 3), connecting the newly configured server to data center object store and running the workloads and of course collecting the metrics. We ran over 100 different combinations of configurations/ workloads and collected the metrics (around 990 tests). Compared to the huge configuration space and vast research boundary, this limited tests gave us enough data points to validate our approach (see Sect. 8).

6.2   Workload Execution

Since there is no public domain workload data or readily available storage traces for CSG systems, we conducted our research using real world customer workload patters. We ran complete experiments on CSG platform from a commercial industry vendor and using workload characteristics as observed by real-world customers. This is shown in Table 2. Additional variants of workloads influencing meta-data size such as sub-directory depth and hierarchy were also used but are not shown in the table. File size and number of files followed a Zipf distribution with α of zero for maximum variance.

6.3   Metrics Collected

We executed workloads on different servers and various configurations, and collected metrics on execution time, meta-data time (e.g. to create sub-directories, open and close files etc.), throughput in bit/sec. Alongside the workloads we captured the configuration information

Table 2. Real world customer workloads.

Workload	Average file size	No. of files	No. of users	Total file size
Tiny	4 KB	10,000	25	1 GB
Small	256 KB	10,000	10	25 GB
Medium	1 MB	10,000	5	50 GB
Large	10 MB	1,000	5	50 GB
Huge	1 GB	200	2	400 GB

about the server (e.g. cores, core speed, memory, disk capacity etc.) and CSG cache configurations (i.e. data cache area, meta-data, log size). We captured the available network throughput independent of the CSG, using a special RESTAPI tool set. We attempted a few workloads that would result in I/O timeouts to study the boundary conditions. Since the performance or throughput metrics at boundary conditions were meaningless (i.e. zero throughput or IO timeouts), we discounted these metrics from our labeled data-set. We ran all the workloads on both servers for different combination of data cache/metadata size configurations. The different instances were tested both for the homogeneous case (all workloads identical) and the heterogeneous case (workloads with different file sizes and read/write ratios). To collect a wide range of samples (test-data), we ran over 100 combinations of workload and configurations, executed about 990 of test cases, i.e., approximately 9 10 different configurations per workload type. During the course of our experiments and data collection, we persisted over 8 million objects and populated over 5.5TB of cloud object store.

6.4   Data Pre-processing and Classification

For each experiment, we created the 'sample' using workload, configuration, compute servers characteristics, observed performance into the feature vectors as {2 cores, 1.2 GHz speed, 16 GB RAM, 100 GB cache, 50 GB metadata, 347 Mbps network I/O, 108 Mbps performance etc.}. We classified the discrete numbers into buckets to give us meaningful insight into the behavior of the gateway servers and configuration. For observed metrics, a discrete throughput data of 488175 bits/s and 21392622 bits/s was classified into bucket sets as throughput *class* 1 or throughput *class* 4. Similarly a configuration of cache data or metadata size of 450GB and 200 GB was classified as *class* 5, 4 and so on. Via such discretization, we classified the data into buckets as shown in Table 3. In terms of machine learning, this bucketization means that the regression problem is transformed into a classification problem.

7   Predicting Performance and Configuration

There are well proven algorithms in the field of machine learning and their applicability is specific to the data characteristics and domain [6]. Further, the efficiency and accuracy metrics of the algorithms depend on *both* the problem

Table 3. Metric Classification.

Metric	#Classes	Bucket size
N/W Throughput	10	unif (100 Kbps, 350 Mbps)
Performance	10	unif (100 Kbps, 350 Mbps)
Data cache	7	25, 50, 100, 200, 500, 1000, > 1000 GB
Metadata	5	25, 50, 100, 200 & 500 GB

domain and associated parameters like learning rate, regularization parameter, etc. We explored a wide range of ML algorithms to find the best fit for our problem domain. We found that Decision Trees fitted the relationship between the performance and configuration parameters with higher accuracy. Using statistical machine learning methods, Decision Trees tries to infer a split of the training data based on the values of the available features to produce a good generalization. The algorithm can handle both binary or multi-class classification problems. The leaf nodes can refer to either of the K classes concerned. It is basically an approximation function working on a multi-dimensional Cartesian space using piece-wise constant functions. Decision trees have been used in other storage metrics predictions such as [8] where authors exploit the trees for response time prediction of a single disk across different workload parameters. The reverse problem in Eq. 9, is a multilabel multi-class classification prediction, where in the end result includes multiple parameters: data cache and metadata configuration.

Our ML based solution approach is illustrated in Fig. 3. The working data-set is the used to train the ML Classifiers. We used two different algorithms and regression classifiers to predict (i) single label performance value and (ii) multi-label configuration parameters. The algorithms use a *sub-set* of data to train the respective model, using hypothesis in Eqs. 8 and 9. The resulting weights of the model is used to predict end result for a *new query*. The algorithm returns the predicted values, accuracy metric and root mean square deviation. We present the prediction accuracy, cross validation results and algorithm efficiency below.

8   Evaluation Results

The evaluation results should tell us how suitable our approach is to predicting the right performance (Eq. 8) <u>and</u> a right configuration (Eq. 9).

Preparing Cross Validation Data Set
    There are several ways in which the collected data can be split into the training set and the testing set to verify an algorithm for over-fit/under-fit (See Monte Carlo cross validation selection [9]). Towards this end, we first shuffle the data randomly and then divide it into three equal size buckets. We then use some part of each bucket for testing and use the rest of the bucket for training. We now consider two specific cases: (A) Use 90% of each bucket for training and the rest for testing, and (B) use 80% of each bucket for training and the rest for testing. For each case, we use only one bucket at a time, thereby giving three sub-cases in each case. These combinations are marked as suffix A.1, A.2, A.3, B.1, B.2, B.3 in the figures below.

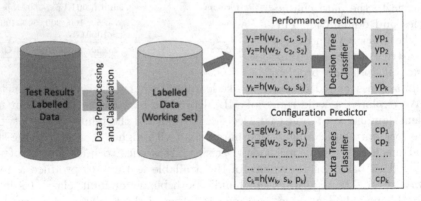

Fig. 3. Predicting performance and configuration.

Predicting Performance - Results
    The performance prediction efficiency is shown in Fig. 4. The bar-graphs have different sample size and *train vs. test* data ratios, as shown in primary (left side) y-axis labels. X-axis indicates the different test cases. For these test cases, the prediction accuracy is on secondary y-axis (right side). The results show that our solution has prediction accuracy around 95% for various combinations (or about 5% prediction error) and do not suffer from under-fit or over-fit. As stated earlier, we are not aware of other public studies on characterizing the relationship between configuration parameters and performance of CSG or other systems, and thus a direct comparison against prior results is not possible directly. However, we compare our results against results from similar techniques used in a different

storage context (e.g., performance vs. workload parameters). In particular, the study by Wang [8] using their CART-based models show a relative error between 17% and 38% for response time prediction. Using Inside-Out [2], Hsu reports a performance prediction error around 9%.

Predicting Cache Configuration - Results

The cache prediction efficiency is shown in Fig. 5. The bar-graphs have different sample size and *train vs. test* data ratios, as shown in primary (left side) y-axis labels. X-axis indicates the different test cases. For these test cases, the prediction accuracy is on secondary y-axis (right side). The results show that our solution has prediction accuracy around 75% for various combinations (or about 25% prediction error) and do not suffer from under-fit or over-fit. In cache prediction, we predict multiple parameters, i.e. data cache size, meta-data and log size. The reason for higher error is self-explanatory by the nature of complex multi-label multi-class parameter prediction with limited training data set.

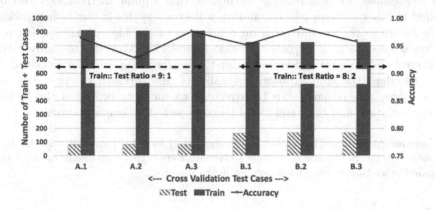

Fig. 4. Efficiency metrics for performance prediction.

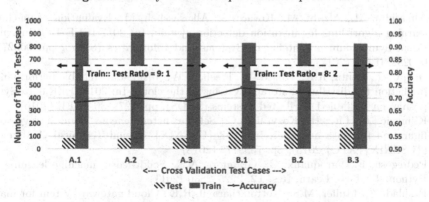

Fig. 5. Efficiency metrics for configuration prediction.

9   Conclusions and Future Work

In this paper, we present a methodology for the configuration and performance prediction of cloud storage gateway (CSG), which is an emerging system of crucial importance in providing scalable access to remote storage. Because of the large number of configuration parameters and inter-dependencies among them, modeling the influence of configuration parameters on the performance is a challenging problem. We show that machine learning techniques suitably aided by the use of domain knowledge can provide robust models which can be used for both the forward problem (i.e., predicting performance from the configuration parameters) and the reverse problem (i.e., predicting configuration parameters from the target performance).

We show that our models can provide performance prediction accuracies in the range of 5% without requiring large amounts of data. The prediction accuracies are worse when multiple configuration parameters are predicted, but still respectable (in 20% range). We believe that similar methodology can be applied to other systems as well, and we will examine this in our future work.

In future work, we will focus on robustness of the algorithms and extrapolation studies to look beyond test case boundaries. We plan to analyse the sensitivity cost to continuously monitor the performance and the workload in order to adapt the configuration gradually as the workload changes. Lessons learned from this research can be expanded to the auto-tuning of the hosted gateway solution and back end cloud based object store configurations.

Acknowledgements. This research was supported by NSF grant IIP-330295. Discussions with Dr. S. Vucetic of Temple University were highly valuable in devising the extended validation techniques presented in the paper.

References

1. Almseidin, M., Alzubi, M., Kovacs, S., Alkasassbeh, M.: Evaluation of machine learning algorithms for intrusion detection system. In: 2017 IEEE 15th International Symposium on Intelligent Systems and Informatics (SISY), pp. 000277–000282. IEEE (2017)
2. Hsu, C.-J., Panta, R.K., Ra, M.-R., Freeh, V.W.: Inside-out: reliable performance prediction for distributed storage systems in the cloud. In: 2016 IEEE 35th Symposium on Reliable Distributed Systems (SRDS), pp. 127–136. IEEE (2016)
3. Klimovic, A., Litz, H., Kozyrakis, C.: Selecta: heterogeneous cloud storage configuration for data analytics. In: 2018 {USENIX} Annual Technical Conference ({USENIX}{ATC} 2018), pp. 759–773 (2018)
4. Pedregosa, F., Varoquaux, G., Gramfort, A.E.: Scikit-learn: machine learning in Python. J. Mach. Learn. Res. **12**, 2825–2830 (2011)
5. Prahlad, A., Muller, M.S., Kottomtharayil, R.E.: Cloud gateway system for managing data storage to cloud storage sites, 2010. US Patent App. 12/751,953
6. Sorower, M.S.: A literature survey on algorithms for multi-label learning. Oregon State University, Corvallis **18**, 1–25 (2010)

7. Tesauro, G., et al.: Online resource allocation using decompositional reinforcement learning. AAAI **5**, 886–891 (2005)
8. Wang, M., Au, K., Ailamaki, A., Brockwell, A., Faloutsos, C., Ganger, G.R.: Storage device performance prediction with cart models. In: Proceedings of the IEEE Computer Society's 12th Annual International Symposium on Modeling, Analysis, and Simulation of Computer and Telecommunications Systems. (MASCOTS 2004). IEEE, pp. 588–595 (2004)
9. Xu, Q.-S., Liang, Y.-Z., Du, Y.-P.: Monte carlo cross-validation for selecting a model and estimating the prediction error in multivariate calibration. J. Chemom. J. Chemom. Soc. **18**(2), 112–120 (2004)
10. Xu, T., Zhou, Y.: Systems approaches to tackling configuration errors: a survey. ACM Comput. Surv. (CSUR) **47**(4), 70 (2015)
11. Yin, Z., Ma, X., Zheng, J., Zhou, Y., Bairavasundaram, L.N., Pasupathy, S.: An empirical study on configuration errors in commercial and open source systems. In: Proceedings of the Twenty-Third ACM Symposium on Operating Systems Principles, pp. 159–172. ACM (2011)

The Case for Physical Memory Pools: A Vision Paper

Heather Craddock(✉), Lakshmi Prasanna Konudula, Kun Cheng,
and Gökhan Kul

Division of Physical and Computational Sciences, Delaware State University,
1200 N DuPont Hwy, Dover, DE 19901, USA
{hcraddock,lkonudula,kcheng14,gkul}@desu.edu
http://delawaresec.com

Abstract. The cloud is a rapidly expanding and increasingly prominent
component of modern computing. Monolithic servers limit the flexibility of cloud-based systems, however, due to static memory limitations.
Developments in OS design, distributed memory systems, and address
translation have been crucial in aiding the progress of the cloud. In this
paper, we discuss recent developments in virtualization, OS design and
distributed memory structures with regards to their current impact and
relevance to future work on eliminating memory limits in cloud computing. We argue that creating physical memory pools is essential for
cheaper and more efficient cloud computing infrastructures, and we identify research challenges to implement these structures.

Keywords: Cloud computing · Memory · Operating systems ·
Virtualization

1 Introduction

The growth of cloud computing is fuelled by the rise of big data and the global
requirements for the inter-connectivity of computing resources. The cloud allows
for data and resources to be shared on demand to connected hardware devices,
reducing the need for reliance on purely local resources. According to the Data
Never Sleeps report, 1.7 MB of data is expected to be created every second for
every single person on earth by 2020 [6]. With such a vast amount of data being
generated, it is imperative that hardware and software architectures are modified
or created to manage modern requirements.

Virtualization plays a vital role in improving the utilization of distributed
resources, and consequently cloud computing. Currently, servers are capable
of hosting multiple operating systems (OS) with the help of multiple virtual
machines (VM) resulting in enhanced network productivity, recoverability, and
data migration. Virtualization works by combining hardware resources among
multiple VMs. It is a challenging task to run an unmodified operating system
on virtualized hardware. This led to development of several techniques to either

D. Da Silva et al. (Eds.): CLOUD 2019, LNCS 11513, pp. 208–221, 2019.
https://doi.org/10.1007/978-3-030-23502-4_15

modify the guest OS or combine application of virtualization techniques that help the system best use the available resources in a secure and efficient manner.

Despite developments in memory hardware that increase the availability of memory at lower cost, memory use and capacity is still limited by the ability of operating systems to manage the vast resources that are now available. It is particularly difficult to coordinate these memory resources over the cloud as the lack of systems and methods that have been developed to manage large, distributed memory is limiting.

The pervasiveness of the cloud makes it imperative to constantly improve cloud technologies and to understand the current state of cloud operating systems. This paper provides an overview of some recent innovations in operating system design, distributed memory management, and virtualization, while also noting where improvements may be further made upon these proposals. Suggestions are also made as to the future of cloud computing in general, and the direction in which future work may lie.

In this paper, we begin by discussing existing models and techniques, including operating system design proposals, improvements to memory virtualization, more efficient memory management, and memory protection methods in Sect. 2. We discuss the future direction of memory models for the cloud, with potential future work in operating system design, distributed memory, and virtualization, and also the direction of cloud computing in general in Sect. 3. We then conclude in Sect. 4.

2   Existing Models

2.1   Operating System Design

Operating system design is of paramount importance to any computing environment, but despite the increase in the popularity and necessity of the cloud there is little development in distributed OS design. Current models are outdated for cloud operations or ill-equipped to deal with the increased availability of resources. Vasilakis *et al.* [11] discussed a whole new OS design in a recent work, and Swift [10] suggested a technique for improving operating system memory management. Shan *et al.* [9] state that the direction of cloud computing leads away from monolithic servers and towards more disaggregated hardware components, and the authors propose a new operating system, LegoOS, that is designed for such a disaggregated system. LegoOS is the first operating system designed to manage these separate components and is a revolutionary method for approaching operating system design.

Revamping OS Design. Vasilakis *et al.* [11] state in their paper that in the 40 years since the original UNIX system was developed, new features or developments have just been stacked upon previous features, resulting in an overly-complex and unwieldy model. Having grown beyond the original simplistic intent, the model is not suitable for scaling or decentralization. The authors found four key issues:

1. Data Cataclysm: Distributed system developments require more than minor tweaks
2. Reliance on Commodity Hardware: Software must manage assurance on fault-intolerant hardware
3. Rise of the Personal Cloud: Original model is not designed for personal micro-clouds
4. Data Processing Shift: Data processing is now performed by ordinary people

The authors propose a distributed system design built from the bottom up. The design includes a large number of components such as file systems more tolerant to scaling, a new type of execution primitive, and sandboxing for software fault isolation. The system was designed based on a programming language, like UNIX is based on C, but the language does not yet exist. For this design to be proved to be useful, the design must be practically implemented using an adapted or created programming language. This system was important in beginning the discussion about revitalizing OS design. Finally, although the authors proposed automatic memory management as garbage collection to save on the bugs and vulnerabilities inherent in manual memory management, garbage collection can have its own issues; it can be difficult to analyze memory and performance, and this garbage collection only deals with memory resources and not all resources. These issues would need to be addressed in a practical implementation.

OS Design for Near Data Processing (NDP). The emergence of NDP architecture required a revision to the traditional memory structure. The proximity to the memory modules has proven to enhance the throughput and exhibit low power consumption. In NDP, however, heterogeneity and parallelism cannot be solely handled, hence requiring the support of OS support to deal with problems like locality, protection and low-latency. To address these issues, Barbalace et al. [5] proposed a new OS called Shadowgraphy based on a number of design principles. A multiple kernel OS design where CPU heterogeneity can be backed on the same machine, enabling the services and IO devices to interact individually in NDP and CPU while exhibiting the same protection and privileges across all kernels. NDP enforces user privilege protections across all the kernels, so applications running in the NDP processing unit can maintain different levels of user privilege. Scheduling is done locally at every kernel by tracking the data access pattern. Instead of moving the data, the code is moved. Data migration is made efficient by caching it in both hardware and software at different levels of the memory hierarchy. The CPU and NDP topology takes a new shape enabling a transparent environment for the users to review.

Barbalace et al. [5] state that it is time to redesign system software for NDP starting from the OS. They address the drawbacks of offloading while multiple applications are running; however, it isn't discussed how Shadowgraphy OS solves this issue. In order to achieve transparency for application developers, the system should both support asymmetricity in the processing units and should be able to provide multiple levels of OS interfaces. A new, multi-kernel, multi-server design should be considered to accommodate multiple users with concurrent accesses in the system.

Distributed Memory Techniques. Distributed Shared Memory (DSM) is a memory architecture that makes it possible to share computing tasks over multiple different hardware components. In DSM, separate physical address spaces can be logically addressed as if they were one space, and in this way multiple processing nodes with individual memory components can be connected over a network to create a larger pool of memory resources. There are many issues with current Distributed Shared Memory techniques that recent papers attempt to address.

Scalability in Data-Intensive Applications. Many systems in use for data-intensive applications are not easily scalable, particularly over the current hardware configuration of many nodes connected over a high-bandwidth network. To attempt to solve this problem, Nelson *et al.* [7] propose Grappa, a software distributed shared memory system for use over clusters to improve performance over data-intensive applications. Grappa's key improvement was the implementation of parallelism to ensure the use of maximum process resource while also disguising communication costs and message-sending latency. Although previous methods for implementing distributed shared memory relied on locality of data and caching to be able to scale effectively, implementing distributed computing in parallel allowed the authors to disguise the high-bandwidth network costs inherent in the hardware system. To create this scalable system, Grappa was designed with three key components:

1. Distributed Shared Memory - Allows access to data anywhere in the system, where local data can be exported to the global address space to be accessible to other cores. Operations are performed at the data's home node to prevent unnecessary retrieval or sending of data over the network, guaranteeing memory consistency and global order.
2. Tasking System - Multi-threading and work-stealing allow for functioning parallelism and load-balancing to better utilize system resources. All tasks are allocated to worker threads to execute, and threads performing long-latency operations yield their core so the processor can still be utilized.
3. Communication Layer - Smaller messages are aggregated into larger ones to limit the use of network bandwidth

Scalability in Grappa comes at the cost of fault-tolerance, as it was deemed cheaper to restart after failure than recover. This is an area for potential improvements. It may be interesting to explore in future how to improve the system so that recovering from failure is cheaper than restarting entirely. In addition, sending small messages using this method is somewhat limited by current hardware; Grappa should be revisited as hardware innovations could lead to improvements in network latency.

Improving Memory Access Speed. Improving the speed of memory access is always crucial in distributed memory. Constructing large-scale clusters with vast memory resources is cheaper now than it ever has been, but network latency is caused by separated hardware elements. [4] suggests methods to improve memory access speeds over clusters.

Memory access using TCP/IP protocol in cluster systems is slow. Existing techniques like Remote Direct Memory Access (RDMA) allow direct memory access from one machine into another without involving the OS, but to achieve this the NICs bypass the kernel and remote CPU providing direct access to data. FaRM utilizes one-sided RDMA reads and directly accesses the memory, enhancing the speed of message passing and thus improving the performance of the apps. FaRM allows lock-free reads which ensures that the transactions are in order and utilizing a single RDMA read.

RDMA allows high throughput and low latency. RDMA also achieves remote memory access through the NIC instead of the remote CPU which means that the I/O operations will not go through the CP. This may cause the CPU to lose control of the data in some cases. If a transaction occurs and there is a failure to determine if there is enough storage space for the transaction, there could be data loss or other serious error. This can be mitigated by reserving enough space in the preparation step, but there is room for improvement.

Server Load Imbalance. The RackOut memory pooling technique suggested in [8] utilizes direct access to improve access speeds across clusters. Novakovic *et al.* noted that server load imbalance limited performance. While most large-key value stores keep data in the memory of memory servers in order to provide both low latency and high throughput, skew limits performance capabilities and there are currently no methods to reduce the skew that do not involve incurring other overheads. As skew can cause load imbalance which correlates to poor utilization of data centers, the authors note that it was important to develop a system which could meet all of its objectives while managing load imbalance.

RackOut is implemented on a group of servers that have internal high bandwidth, a low-latency communication fabric, and direct access to other nodes' memory through one-sided operations. Using this method, nodes in the rack can access the memory of other server nodes without using the remote CPU, thus minimizing server load imbalance. Furthermore, as memory access within a rack is fast and data is only replicated when needed outside the rack, speed of memory access is improved and sharing operations between the nodes balanced the workload more evenly across the rack. The RackOut method is limited by the communication fabric latency, although technology is trending towards lower-latency fabrics. While this system discusses its scalability, the study was limited to research resources; it would improve on the theoretical nature of the paper for tests of this system to be conducted on larger or commercial-scale data centers.

Limited Discussion on Remote Memory. Without discussion of the issues facing areas of computing, it can be difficult to establish the direction of a field or the potential for future work. In [3], the authors enumerate a number of different areas in cloud computing that could face challenges as they believed that discussion on the subject was out of date. The idea of remote memory was proposed nearly 20 years ago when network technology made it difficult to find and implement remote memory solutions. Though current networks are a great deal faster than before, there is still limited discussion on efficiently realizing remote memory. There are still a number of challenges that we need to address, and some potential solutions:

1. Remote host crashes: (1) expose failures to the application by allowing it to provide failure handlers; (2) use replication or erasure coding to mask the failure through redundancy.
2. Slow or Congested Network: (1) prioritize network traffic and pre-allocate network bandwidth for remote memory; (2) give each application different regions of memory.
3. Virtual Memory Overheads: check and rebuild the subsystem of the virtual memory.
4. Virtual Machine Indirection: Based on the mechanisms of reducing virtual memory overheads, find ways for the hypervisor to extract information about applications.
5. Transparency Level: design the remote memory in different cases.
6. Sharing Model: Limit remote memory to private data, where sharing is prohibited.
7. Lack of Write Ordering Across Hosts: (1) DSM enforces ordering with appropriate protocols to solve the problem, although this is costly; (2) allow applications to use remote hosts for memory; (3) allow reordering for applications whose semantics support it.
8. Non-uniform latency: (1) use the existing operating system mechanisms for NUMA; (2) expose the memory speed to applications, which can use appropriate data structures and layouts to optimize the performance.
9. Remote Host Compromised: (1) encrypt the data in remote memory; (2) strengthen the security of the larger system to compensate for the larger attack surface.
10. Local vs. Cluster Memory: adopt a static allocation which reserves a reasonable amount of local memory and leaves the rest for cluster memory.
11. Remote Memory Allocation: centralize the problem by requiring allocations across the cluster to go through a host that manages memory.
12. Memory Placement: the simplest mechanism is to centralize the decision of placement.
13. Local Memory Management: the machine hosting the physical memory should manage it, but this may add overheads on modern RDMA-based NICs.
14. Control Plane Efficiency: use off-the-shelf solutions for control planes, although experiments testing their performance for this use are required.
15. Memory Metadata Overhead: manage remote memory in slabs that are much larger than the page size, so that the system need only keep one set of metadata for each slab.

Although [3] introduces a number of issues and the potential solutions, the authors overlook some key issues. Firstly, the authors do not deeply discuss security problems. When the data is stored in remote memory, not only do we need to consider the local machine security state, but we also need to think about the network and remote machine security. Implementation of suitable security measures may be more costly in terms of computing resources or finances; there are two possible ways to improve security: firstly, the remote machines may have the highest security priority because the bulk of the data is stored there; secondly, access and the network needs to be appropriately secured and protected; finally, distributing the data over a larger number of different remote machines with their own security could prevent an attack on one host from compromising the whole system.

2.2 Improving Memory Virtualization

Virtual memory plays a vital role in modern computing as it can deliver various benefits like improved security and increased productivity for programmers. The operating system and page table play a crucial role in memory management but can cause high execution-time overheads. As an attempt to solve the problem, Aguilera *et al.* [3] proposed a hardware/software co-design called Redundant Memory Mapping (RMM).

The paper proposes a hardware/software co-design called Redundant Memory Mapping (RMM). Range translation can map contiguous virtual pages to physical pages. The authors address the primary problem of using a page in their paper. A TLB miss can be overcome by using 124 range translations from the range table. The paper presented few evaluations showing that RMM works for all configurations and workloads.

Although RMM eliminates vast majority of page walks, using eager paging may increase latency, which in turn can induce fragmentation. Latency and fragmentation can have heavy impact on the performance. Implementing RMM also relies on additional hardware and software which may involve future development. Retrieving data in parallel during translation can be a potential solution to the stated problem. This allows storage of huge data sets with low-latency for real time data analysis.

2.3 Efficient Memory Management

Memory capacity is a key limitation in system design. The recent breakthrough 3D XPoint memory in non-volatile memory technology has given the world abundant memory capacity at much lower costs. These technologies provided memory in larger magnitudes than DRAM at lower power and prices. Existing system designs, however, are incapable of handling such large memories.

The essential design principle of Order(1) operations is proposed in [10] to manage vast memories. This principle aims to complete memory management operations in constant time, independent of the size of the operand. It applies a file-system technique to memory management. Instead of operating on individual pages, the operations are enabled on the whole file and thus providing Order(1) performance. It is less complicated to expose data directly to the programs instead of the kernel as the data already exists in the memory. Using the file systems to manage memory is convenient as they can maintain gritty meta data, and are capable of translating large addresses and handling large memories. In Towards O(1) memory, the memory layer above the files is removed and the user mode memory is allocated as files with tmpfs as a backup. Only the references to the files are counted, ignoring the references to pages. Memory can only be reclaimed when a process terminates or unmaps. Pointers are used to improve the efficiency in memory mapping through sharing between the processes. Overheads in tracking and cleaning bits is not required as the memory itself is too large which eliminates the need for swapping between disks. This system uses range translations to trim the cost of memory access.

Implementing Towards O(1) memory has its own limitations: operations that depend on page level mappings cannot be easily supported and are difficult to optimize; also, the system becomes complex when we try to store the volatile data in the persistent memory, breaking the isolation between user and kernel space and leading to memory leakages. In order to avoid this situation the memory should be zeroed before being reused.

2.4 Memory Protection

The emergence of large non-volatile main memories and rack-scale computers running large 'micro services' creates significant challenges for memory protection based solely on MMU mechanisms. Optimization for translation performance has put the protection at stake. Some challenges include stale locations leading to memory corruption, hypervisor calls, and nested pages.

Achermann et al. [2] propose Matching Key Capabilities(MaKC), a new architecture which is capable of scaling memory protection at both the user and kernel level. MaKC divides the memory hierarchies into equal sized blocks associated with Block Protection Key (BPK) and Execution Protection Key (EPK). Memory access is allowed only when there is a match between BPK and EPK, and blocked otherwise. HMACs (Hash Message Authentication Codes) ensure that messages cannot be forged nor manipulated in transit. The authors proposed that key matching could be implemented with protection tables that contain BPKs which the hardware can read and cache. Proposed MaKC has a capability-based system to handle authorization and protection in complex memory hierarchies. The MaKC approach also allows enabling huge pages without compromising the security of small page sizes.

MaKC has not been fully designed yet, and there are still decisions to be made on which features need to be implemented on the CPU-side or memory-side. Implementing MaKC could lead to some potential issues:

1. Storing large number of keys and HMACs can result in space overhead; in order to access them, one needs to enter supervisor state which can be expensive

2. The use of MaKC will add complexity
3. Using cryptographic keys in MaKC to authenticate the fingerprints could increase security management complexity
4. The model is proposed for fixed size blocks which may leave memory unused and thus poor memory management

3 Research Directions for Disaggregated Memory in the Cloud

In this section, we first make a case for physical memory pools. Then we discuss the potential improvements in OS design, distributed memory, and virtualization, as well as considerations regarding the direction of cloud computing as a whole.

3.1 Physical Memory Pools

We argue that the cloud systems need to migrate to a hardware resource disaggregation scheme that uses *physical memory pools*. A physical memory pool (PMemP) is a cluster of memory units that do not belong to any monolithic server, and can be demanded and used by connected monolithic machines on a need-based basis as seen in Fig. 1. This component is governed by a *governor* that prioritizes resource requests from participating servers, and allocates memory to these machines accordingly. An example of this approach in the literature is LegoOS [9] where networked *mComponents* are used as memory units. In this sense, an mComponent is a type of physical memory pool. There are four challenges that this hardware resource disaggregation scheme has to tackle: (1) Current OS architecture limitations (Sect. 3.2), (2) Plug-n-play use of the component (Sect. 3.3), (3) Adoption to existing virtual systems (Sect. 3.4), and (4) Network speed limitations to use memory as a networked device (Sect. 3.5).

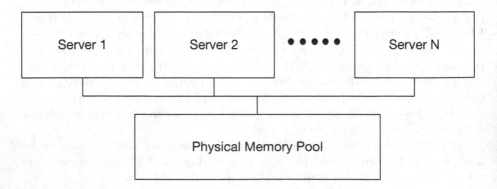

Fig. 1. Physical memory pool overview

Example. Java Virtual Machine (JVM) uses a memory space that is allocated to itself when a Java program is run on the system. The JVM users can define a minimum amount of heap memory as well as a maximum amount of heap memory for the program. Initially, the program is given the minimum amount. If the program requires more heap memory than this amount, JVM increases the allocated memory, up to the maximum heap amount [1]. We expect that the physical memory pools work as efficient and in a similar manner to this logic. To show how this would work on JVM, we designed the following simulation.

First, we create a `List`. In an infinite loop, in each iteration, we add 100 elements to the list, and randomly search for 100 elements by index in the list until we run out of memory. This enforces utilization of each part of the list, hence preventing the use of swapping function efficiently. When the system runs out of the initial heap memory, it has to make the next block of memory available, just like PMemPs would, as described in Sect. 3.1.

In the simulation run, we used an Apple MacBook Pro with 2.2 GHz Intel Core i7processor, 16 GB 2400 MHz DDR4 RAM, and 256 GB SSD. The OS is MacOS High Sierra 10.13.6, and we used Java 1.8.0. To show the efficiency of the mechanism and difference between block allocation and directly using maximum available heap memory, we compared initial allocations of 128 MB, 256 MB, 512 MB and 1024 MB, respectively, and maximum allocation of 1024 MB. The results can be seen in Fig. 2. We share all the code and documentation on GitHub[1].

Figure 2a shows the growth of the List over time. As expected, the runs with larger initial heap size reach to the maximum number of elements faster. However, the increase pattern is still comparable and the difference is due to the time JVM spends on adding new memory blocks and time spent on garbage collection before doing so. The garbage collection behavior can be better seen in Fig. 2b. The garbage collector runs more aggressively when nearing the initial heap size, but it still needs to add new memory blocks to be able to continue operating. In a memory resource disaggregation based system, this is the ideal behavior. The advantage of memory resource disaggregation is, instead of building monolitic servers with large memory sizes, we can share a common pool of memory accordingly.

3.2   OS Design

As in [11], OS design may be constrained by the availability of an appropriate language to code it. The OS should provide a transparent environment to the application developer which can allow users to inspect information about the platform, such as the topology of the CPU and NDP.

Future work may also include the design of a multiple-kernel, multi-server model that can allow concurrent access to multiple users on the system and

---

[1] Code repository located at https://github.com/PADLab/MemorySwapExperiment.

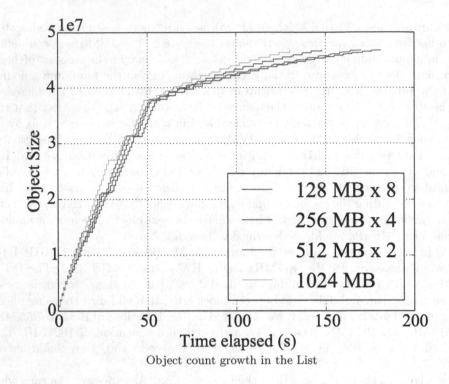

Object count growth in the List

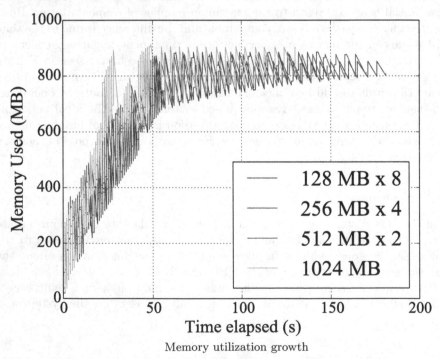

Memory utilization growth

Fig. 2. Comparison of allocation under varying memory configurations

support the asymmetricity in the processing units. A future cloud OS should be able to be as multi-functional and dynamic as possible to meet ever-developing requirements.

3.3 Distributed Memory

In distributed systems, networking hardware, address translation and NICs often act as performance bottlenecks to the system. To prevent this bottleneck, developments must continue to be made in the hardware that the discussed systems are designed upon. Meanwhile, these limitations could be curtailed by increasing the node processing and network capacity, building bigger and more capable nodes, aggregating multiple server nodes into larger entities, and implementing in-memory computing where the translations and data fetch can go hand in hand.

In systems such as Grappa proposed in [7], improving fault-tolerance is important, especially as systems are constantly being implemented on fault-prone hardware. Efforts must be made to design systems where recovering from faults is simpler than restarting.

3.4 Virtualization

Virtualization provides flexibility, scalability, and cost advantages to cloud computing. Although virtualization breaks the line between the hardware and the applications running on dedicated servers, adding a virtualization layer has downsides such as slashing the application performance, adding processing overheads for memory, translations and inducing security vulnerabilities in the system. To prevent these bottlenecks, the operating system should be considered as the principal design for virtualization. Temporarily, we can downsize these limitations by adapting towards in-memory computing and providing isolation between the kernel and user space.

In the future, range translations should pave the way for emerging workloads by utilizing in-memory computing, which can leverage the growth in physical memory to store huge data sets for low-latency and real-time data analysis.

3.5 Network

Using current network technology introduces some challenges that are still heavily researched. Firstly, network components and protocols include their own communication overheads. We believe that in a hardware communication focused environment this problem can easily be addressed, especially if the hardware network is isolated from the communication network. Secondly, network bandwidth limits the speed and it may not be as fast as a motherboard bus. It should be noted, however, that network technology has developed drastically in the last decade and this should soon become a minor issue.

3.6   Direction of Cloud Computing

There are a number of questions to contemplate:

1. How can system complexity be managed? With movement towards heavily interconnected microservices provided by a number of different service providers, it is important to maintain performance and security through all the different structures. There is also a strong degree of trust in these services, as other teams or companies may run vital infrastructure. It is important to find methods to maintain and ensure trust and reliability of outsourced services.
2. How can failure tolerance be guaranteed? Distributed systems are responsible for a number of critical societal components, and there is a huge reliance on the cloud for health, safety, productivity, business, and more. Ensuring network systems are failure-tolerant should be a top priority.
3. How can virtualization be improved and supported? Sharing resources between different and distant hosts is a key component of cloud computing, so how can operating systems continue to support more efficient virtualization of services and guarantee their security?
4. How can the environmental and financial impact of distribution be limited? Increased distribution leads to increased energy cost as giant data centers are always providing their services. Virtualization can help this as the resources can be used from many different physical locations. Potential work for the future may be in improving workload distribution on virtualized software so that the most demanding tasks are completed on the most energy-efficient hardware environments.

4   Conclusion

We discussed the contribution of a number of works that proposed methods of improving or innovating the cloud, from specific models such as LegoOS, Grappa, Shadowgraphy OS and RackOut to theoretical discussions of the issues cloud computing presents as in [3]. The core contribution of this paper lies in offering future research directions around the vision of independent physical memory pools that the servers in a data center can share based on their current need, and de-allocate when the resources are no longer needed.

Although some improvements or ideas for potential future work were suggested in this paper, the survey is by no means comprehensive; the consistent theme from the reviewed papers is that the discussion is only recently beginning and there is still so much to explore in the realm of cloud computing.

Acknowledgements. This material is based in part upon work supported by the funding provided by the State of Delaware to Delaware State University. Any opinions, findings, and conclusions or recommendations expressed in this material are those of the authors and do not necessarily reflect the views of the University or the State.

References

1. Tuning java virtual machines. docs.oracle.com. Accessed 22 Mar 2019
2. Achermann, R., et al.: Separating translation from protection in address spaces with dynamic remapping. In: HotOS (2017)
3. Aguilera, M.K., et al.: Remote memory in the age of fast networks. In: ACM SoCC (2017)
4. Hodson, O., Dragojević, A., Narayanan, D., Castro, M.: FaRM: fast remote memory. In: USENIX NSDI, 4 (2014)
5. Barbalace, A., Iliopoulos, A., Rauchfuss, H., Brasche, G.: It's time to think about an operating system for near data processing architectures. In: HotOS (2017)
6. James, J.: Data Never Sleeps 6.0. Technical report, Domo Inc, 06 2018
7. Nelson, J., et al.: Latency-tolerant software distributed shared memory. In: USENIX ATC (2015)
8. Novakovic, S., Daglis, A., Bugnion, E., Falsafi, B., Grot, B.: The case for rackout: Scalable data serving using rack-scale systems. In: ACM SoCC (2016)
9. Shan, Y., Huang, Y., Chen, Y., Zhang, Y.: Legoos: a disseminated, distributed OS for hardware resource disaggregation. In: USENIX OSDI (2018)
10. Swift, M.M.: Towards O(1) memory. In: HotOS (2017)
11. Vasilakis, N., Karel, B., Smith, J.M.: From lone-dwarfs to giant superclusters: rethinking operating system abstractions for the cloud. In: HotOS (2015)

A Parallel Algorithm for Bayesian Text Classification Based on Noise Elimination and Dimension Reduction in Spark Computing Environment

Zhuo Tang[1(✉)], Wei Xiao[1], Bin Lu[1], Youfei Zuo[1], Yuan Zhou[2], and Keqin Li[1]

[1] College of Information Science and Engineering, Hunan University,
Changsha 410082, Hunana, China
ztang@hnu.edu.cn

[2] College of Public Policy and Management, Tsinghua University,
Beijing 100084, China

Abstract. The Naive Bayesian algorithm is one of the ten classical algorithms in data mining, which is widely used as the basic theory for text classification. With the high-speed development of the Internet and information systems, huge amount of data are being produced all the time. Some problems are certain to arise when the traditional Bayesian classification algorithm addresses massive amount of data, especially without the parallel computing framework. This paper proposes an improved Bayesian algorithm INBCS, for text classification in the Spark computing environment and improves the Naive Bayesian algorithm based on a polynomial model. For the data preprocessing, this paper first proposes a parallel noise elimination algorithm, and then proposes another parallel dimension reduction algorithm based on Information Gain and TextRank computation in the Spark environment. Based on these preprocessed data, an improved parallel method is proposed for calculating the conditional probability that comprehensively considers the effects of the feature items in each document, class and training set. Finally, through experiments on different widely used corpuses on the Spark computation platform, the results illustrate that INBCS can obtain higher accuracy and efficiency than some current improvements and implementations of the Naive Bayesian algorithms in Spark ML-library.

Keywords: Big data · Naive bayesian classification ·
Parallel computing · Spark · Text classification

1 Introduction

With the rapid development of information society, the Internet has been widely used and currently has become the most important source of information. In particular, with the emergence of cloud computing and the big data era [1],

© Springer Nature Switzerland AG 2019
D. Da Silva et al. (Eds.): CLOUD 2019, LNCS 11513, pp. 222–239, 2019.
https://doi.org/10.1007/978-3-030-23502-4_16

the data generated from the Internet are rapidly growing with the index grade. These data have the following characteristics: large in amount, high in dimension, complex in structure and containing much noise, but widespread application prospects. Furthermore, most of the information and data stored on the Internet are text. How to organize, manage, and utilize these text data is a great challenge for the currently limited computing power, especially when confronts with a large amount of information that needs to be searched effectively, quickly and accurately by users for the Internet applications. The Spark platform [2], as the new generation of big data processing engine, supports a Resilient Distributed Datasets (RDD) model built on a in-memory computing framework. It allows users to cache data in memory, and to perform computation and iteration for the same data directly from memory. Based on the memory computing mode, the Spark platform can save the amounts of disk I/O operation time. Therefore, it is more suitable for machine learning algorithms with iterative computation.

This paper proposes an improved naive Bayesian classifier model based on the Spark platform (INBCS), which provides a new method to calculate the conditional probability and solve the above problems. INBCS uses TF-IDF weighting to obtain the probabilities of feature items belonging to a given class. It not only takes account of the respective proportions in feature items and the entire training set but also takes the impact of the proportion of documents into consideration, which contains the feature items in the training set. From the above, our contributions in this paper are summarized as follows:

1. A parallel method that removes noises in a data set running on the Spark platform.
2. A dimension reduction method for high-dimensional data in English and Chinese texts preprocessing.
3. An improved conditional probability applied in Naive Bayesian to improve the precision and accuracy.
4. A new memory prediction algorithm used in the *SpillWrite* operation of Spark's *Shuffle Read*.

The rest of the paper is organized as follows. Section 2 reviews the background and related work. Section 3 proposes an improved Multinomial Bayesian model, INBCS, and provides the formalization descriptions for this model. Parallel implementation of INBCS on Spark is developed in Sect. 4. Experimental results and evaluations are provided in Sect. 5. Finally, Sect. 6 presents the conclusion and future works.

2   Background and Related Work

Several machine learning and data mining algorithms have been proposed for text classification. The most popular methods include Naive Bayesian [3], support vector machines [4], decision trees, artificial neural networks, k-nearest-neighbor (k-NN) classification and association rules. The support vector machine model has been proven to be more accurate than most other techniques for classification, but the complexity of the algorithm is relatively high [5]. Compared to other algorithms, a decision tree is simple and easy to understand. However, its accuracy is unsatisfactory compared to other text classification algorithms, especially when the number of distinguishing features of documents becomes large. The k-NN algorithm is easy to implement and shows its effectiveness in a variety of problem domains. However, the computation will increase dramatically when the size of the training set grows large. Naive Bayes is based on an independence assumption for the features in a document. Although this assumption violates the natural language rules, after IR transformation [6], the results show that Naive Bayes classification can still perform surprisingly well [3]. Because Naive Bayes is efficient and easy to implement, this paper proposes an improved model INBCS for the text classification and improves its performance through noise diminution and dimension reduction, especially for various practical applications, such as spam filtering or news article classification.

Feature selection and reduction are extremely important phases in classification algorithms, and there have been multiple efforts to improve them in a variety of scenarios. Aghdam et al. [7] introduced a feature selection and reduction method using ant colony optimization. Shi et al. [8] considered test criteria, such as frequency, dispersion and concentration indices, and proposed an improved dimension reduction method and feature weighting method to make the selection more representative and the weighting of characteristic features more reasonable. Berka et al. [9] made another effort for the improvement of dimensionality reduction and introduced an algorithm that replaces rare terms by computing a vector that expresses their semantics in terms of common terms. Furthermore, due to the high dimensionality of data, Xu [10] proposed a dimension reduction method for the registration of high-dimensional data. Tao et al. [11] and Lin et al. [12] analyzed and proposed various improved classification algorithms for high-dimensional data based on dimension reduction. However, all the serial algorithms above achieved improved performance on small-scale data. When the scale and dimension of data become large, the effects of these algorithms would be reduced.

How to eliminate the noise in the text has always been a topic that must be considered in the text classification algorithm, too much noise in the text will not only increase the calculation amount of the processing, but also seriously affect the precision and accuracy of the classification. The researchers have made great progress in this area. For example, *RONG-LU LI* mentioned a method that based on text density and sample distribution can be used to eliminate noise data in the training data set, at the International Conference on Machine Learning and Cybernetics conference in 2003. In addition, how to classify text more quickly and effectively has also bothered people, so the concept of parallel and distributed computing has gradually become the focus of public attention. There are also many related researches on the implementation of text classification algorithms based on parallel computing platforms, such as, *Xiangxiang Chen* and *Kaigui Wu*'s paper presented at the 2010 MINS conference, which proposes a parallel distributed classification algorithm based on Mapreduce model to reduce computational time during large numbers of training process. At same time, *skender lgen Oul* introduced a fast Bayesian text classification method on the spark distributed platform, because the spark platform uses a distributed in-memory data structure to provide faster storage and analysis of data. Based on the previous research, this paper proposes a parallel algorithm for bayesian text classification based on noise elimination and dimension reduction in spark computing environment.

3   An Improved Multinomial Bayesian Model

3.1   The Naive Bayes Classifiers

The Bayes theorem describes the probability of an event, which is based on conditions that might be related to previous events. Naive Bayes classifiers are based on strong independence assumptions among all features in the samples. We define C as a set of predefined categories, which consists of m components as follows: $C = \{c_1, c_2, \cdots, c_m\}$. This paper defines $P(c_j|d_i)$ to denote the probability of a document d_i belonging to a class c_j. The classifier selects the class with the maximum probability as the result class, and the conditional probability $P(c_j|d_i)$ can be calculated by the Bayesian theorem as in Eq. (1):

$$P(c_j|d_i) = \frac{P(c_j)P(d_i|c_j)}{P(d_i)} \tag{1}$$

where $P(d_i|c_j)$ represents the distribution of documents in each class, and it cannot be estimated directly. We use this formula for text classification specifically. However, based on the *Naive Bayes Assumption*, the document d_i can be treated as a sequence SEQ_i with a set of independent words w_k. Therefore, the length of document d_i can also be regarded as the number of words in SEQ_i, and $P(d_i|c_j)$ can be calculated by Eq. (2):

$$P(d_i|c_j) = \prod_{k=1}^{n} P(w_k|c_j) \tag{2}$$

In Eq. (1), $P(d_i)$ represents the probability of a document d_i in the training data set. Because the values of $P(d_i)$ are the same for all the classes, we can ignore this probability when we compare $P(c_j|d_i)$ to other classes.

Because a Bayesian text classifier formalizes the distribution of words in a document as a multinomial, a document can be formalized as a sequence of words with the assumption that each word position is generated independently. Based on this, we assume that there are a fixed number of classes: $C = \{c_1, c_2, \cdots, c_m\}$ and that each of them has a fixed set of multinomial parameters. For a specific class c, the parameter vector is $\vec{V_c} = \{V_{c,1}, V_{c,2}, \cdots, V_{c,n}\}$, where n is the vocabulary size, $\sum_j V_{c,j} = 1$, and $V_{c,j}$ is the probability that word j appears in class c [6]. The likelihood of a document depends on the parameters of the words that appear in the document:

$$P(d|\vec{V_c}) = \frac{(\sum_j f_j)!}{\prod_j f_j!} \prod_j (V_{c_j})^{f_j} \tag{3}$$

where f_j denotes the frequency count of each different word in the document d. By assigning $P(\vec{V_c})$ as a prior distribution over the set of classes, we can acquire the minimum-error classification rule that selects the class with the largest posterior probability, as in Eq. (4):

$$L(d) = \arg\max_c \left[\log P(\vec{V_c}) + \sum_j f_j \log V_{c,j} \right] = \arg\max \left[h_c + \sum_j f_j W_{c,j} \right] \tag{4}$$

where h_c is the threshold term and $W_{c,j}$ denotes the weight of $class_c$ for $word_j$.

3.2   An Improved Naive Bayesian Text Classifier

To process the documents more efficiently, this section uses a Vector Space Model to represent the texts, which is often used in information filtering, information retrieval, indexing, and relevancy rankings. In INBCS, we formalize a set of documents as $\vec{d} = \{\vec{d_1}, \vec{d_2}, \cdots, \vec{d_i}, \cdots, \vec{d_n}\}$. For each item, $t \in (t_1, t_2, \cdots, t_m)$ denotes a set of feature items, and $tf_{i,j}$ counts the number of times that word j appears in the document $\vec{d_i}$. Thus, the texts can be represented as the matrix, where each row represents a specific document and each dimension of a column vector corresponds to a separate term feature. There are several different ways to compute the values of $tf_{i,j}$, which are also known as term weights. One of the best-known schemes is TF-IDF weighting.

For this method, we use a new variable to describe the word frequencies via a simple transform as in Eq. (5):

$$tf'_{i,j} = \log(tf_{i,j} + 1.0) \tag{5}$$

the transform in Eq. (5) has advantages when the number of features is zero or one, and it eliminates the effects of some large number of features. Another factor that would impact the classification decisions is the function words without actual meanings. This is because the function words normally do not contain specific information, which just increases the noise in parameter estimation. A heuristic transform in the information retrieval community, known as *inverse document frequency*, is widely used to discount terms by their document frequency [6]. A common way to do this is shown in Eq. (6):

$$tf''_{i,j} = tf'_{i,j} \log\left(\frac{N}{n_j + 1.0}\right) \tag{6}$$

where N represents the number of documents belonging to the training data sets and n_j represents the number of documents that contains $word_j$.

In practice, documents have strong word inter-dependencies. After a word first appears in a document, it is more likely to be there again. Because the Multinomial Naive Bayesian model assumes that the feature items in the document are independent of each other, it is harmful to the parameter estimation for long documents. This paper addresses this problem by normalizing the number of feature words. In practical terms, this paper uses a common IR transform [6] that has not been used with Naive Bayesian to eliminate the influence of word inter-dependencies. The formalization is shown in Eq. (7):

$$tf'''_{i,j} = \frac{tf''_{i,j}}{\sqrt{\sum\limits_{j=1}^{m}(tf''_{i,j})^2}} \tag{7}$$

where m represents the number of feature items in the ith document. Through combination and deformation for the above equations Eqs. (5), (6) and (7), we can obtain the following expression as Eq. (8):

$$tf'''_{i,j} = \frac{\log(tf_{i,j}+1.0) \times \log\left(\frac{N}{n_j+1.0}\right)}{\sqrt{\sum\limits_{j=1}^{m}\left[\log(tf_{i,j}+1.0) \times \log\left(\frac{N}{n_j+1.0}\right)\right]^2}} \tag{8}$$

Meanwhile, because the proposed model in this paper is based on the Multinomial Bayesian Model, according to Eq. (4), $P(\vec{V_c})$ is the priori probability of class c, which equals to the total number of words in class c divided by the total number of words in the training data set, and $W_{c,j}$ denotes the transformed posterior probability of word j in class c, which can be calculated via Eq. (9):

$$W_{c,j} = \log V_{cj} = \log P(w_j|V_c) \tag{9}$$

This model uses $P(w_j|V_c)$ to represent the probability of word j in the class c and uses variable n to count the total number of words in class c. $P(w_j|V_c)$ can be obtained from Eq. (10):

$$P(w_j|V_c) = \frac{N(w_j, V_c) + \delta}{\sum\limits_{j=1}^{n} N(w_j, V_c) + \delta|v|} \tag{10}$$

for this equation, $N(w_j, V_c)$ represent the TF-IDF weight of $word_j$ in class V_c as Eq. (7) specified, when $N(w_j, V_c) = 0$, it denotes that $word_j$ does not exist in class c. Because the accuracy of classification will be degraded in this case, this defect can be optimized by Laplace Calibration [13] with a simple implementation. In this manner, the value of feature items that do not exist in the class will be added to a coefficient to avoid the probability being equal to zero. In Eq. (10), as δ is the Laplace smoothing coefficient, we can set $\delta = 1$ to achieve this effect, and $|v|$ denotes the size of different words in the class c. However, the formula (10) does not take the number of words in all category into account. For instance, compared to the documents in category c_1, if a category c_r has more documents, or the document has more words, the probability of $P(w_j|V_c)$ will likely be higher than the value in c_1.

To address these above defects and shortcomings, we should consider the overall impacts of the proportions of feature words in documents, local classes, and training data sets. As an improvement, this paper introduces a comprehensive coefficient as an eclectic coefficient, as in Eq. (11):

$$P\left(w_j|V_c\right) = \left(\frac{N(w_j, V_c) + \delta}{\sum\limits_{j=1}^{n} N(w_j, V_c) + \delta|v|}\right)^{\alpha} \times \left(\sqrt{\frac{N(w_j, V_c) + \delta}{\sum\limits_{c=1}^{m}\sum\limits_{j=1}^{n} N(w_j, V_c) + \delta|v|}} \times \frac{T(w_j, V_c) + \delta}{\sum\limits_{c=1}^{m} T(w_j, V_c) + \delta|T|}\right)^{\beta}$$

(11)

where $\beta = 1 - \alpha$ and α takes the different values and have different impacts on $P(w_j|V_c)$. In this manner, the text classification has been changed into a problem of searching for the maximum probability value of Eq. (11). The bigger α is, the greater the local influence of feature items is. Therefore, our target is to find the optimal value of α to achieve the best classification performance through multiple training. $T(w_j, V_c)$ counts the documents that contain the feature w_j in the class c. As in Eq. (10), we also set $\delta = 1$ with $|T|$ as the average number of documents for each class in the training data set in Eq. (11).

3.3   Noise Elimination

Function words are ubiquitous and enormous in general documents, have no benefit on the document classification, and may even cause some serious influence on the classification results. In this section, we proposed a method to implement noise reduction based on *RDD* before data training. After the original input data set is uploaded to HDFS, the data path named as *datasetsPath* will be used as the input of the following preprocess function: *preprocess()*. If the *datasetsPath* is a directory, this algorithm will traverse it, and then continue recursively calling the function *preprocess()*. If the *datasetsPath* is a file, a parallel noise elimination process *removingFuncWords()* based on Spark will be executed to remove the meaningless function words in the original data set. In this function, firstly we read files from HDFS according to the specified data path to obtain a *HadoopRDD*, then, we spilt the very line of documents into different words by using the *map()* function to get a *MappedRDD*, secondly a *filter()* function will be applied to previous *FiltereddRDD*, to remove all words that appear in function words dictionary, finally a final *ProessedRDD* without function words will be returned. The specific process is shown in the Fig. 1.

The quality of the text in the training data set directly determines the result of the text classification. In practical applications, the construction of the training set inevitably produces noise samples. Besides some functional words which has simple structure contained in these samples, other kinds of words such as stop words, low frequency words, modal words... will also have a serious influence on the accuracy of the classification, because these words almost exist in

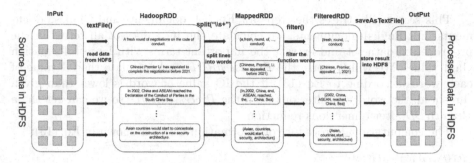

Fig. 1. The procedure of removing function words

all texts, and contain little information, and their function are too superficial to support the results of the classification. So we need to remove these words in each document of the training data set before text categorization, and then convert the remaining words into feature vectors. The processing of text noise is a very critical phase for text categorization, whose importance is self-evident. The DFRF (Document Frequency Ratio Filter) algorithm is a relatively simple algorithm with low computational complexity. It is mainly used for feature extraction and keyword filtering. The formula is as follows in Eq. (12):

$$DFRF\left(t, C_i\right) = \left\{ t \Big| \log_2 \left(\frac{S_{(i,t)}}{\sum\limits_{t=1}^{n} S_{(i,t)}} \times \frac{n_i}{N - n_i} \times \frac{C_{(i,t)}}{C'_{(i,t)}} \right) > \theta \right\} \tag{12}$$

where $S_{(i,t)}$ represents the amount of words t in class i, n_i represents the total size of articles in class i, and N represents the size of articles in the whole training set, and $C_{(i,t)}$ denotes the number of articles which contains the term t in class i, $C'_{(i,t)}$ denotes the total number of articles containing the word t in other classes, θ denotes the threshold, and only words whose $DFRF$ rates exceeds a certain threshold can be chosen. We can use this method to filter out the noise data in the text during the preprocessing stage.

3.4 Dimension Reduction

Information Gain (IG) has been widely used in machine learning and acts as a function to measure the amount of information obtained from category prediction by judging whether a feature term is present in a document or not. Because Chinese characters are connected to each other in the text and only the combination of characters can express complete semantics, IG is not suitable for reducing the dimensions of Chinese documents. In this section, we take a method based on IG through the maximum entropy model and TextRank [14] to extract feature items to reduce the dimensions for Chinese documents.

This section illustrates the steps for English documents and Chinese documents. For English documents, we calculate the IG values of all terms in the preprocessed data set and extract the important terms with large Information Gain values. We will traverse the *ProcessedRDD* and calculate the IG value of each words according to Eq. (13), if the IG value of word is lower than given threshold, the word will filter out from the *ProcessedRDD*, so we can get the a *ResultRDD* after dimensions reduction.

The computational procedure of Information Gains is shown in Eq. (13):

$$
\begin{aligned}
IG\,(t) &= H\,(C) - H\,(C|t) \\
&= -\sum_{i=1}^{m} P\,(C_i)\log_2 P\,(C_i) + P\,(t) \sum_{i=1}^{m} P\,(C_i|t)\log_2 P\,(C_i|t) + P\,(\bar{t}) \sum_{i=1}^{m} P\,(C_i|\bar{t})\log_2 P\,(C_i|\bar{t})
\end{aligned}
\tag{13}
$$

In Eq. (13), m is the number of classes in the preprocessed data set, $H(C)$ and $H(C|t)$ represent the original entropy of the system and the conditional entropy, respectively.

For the data sets of Chinese documents, this section implements the dimension reduction process through a retrieval algorithm based on the *Double Array Trie* data structure. *Double Array Trie* is essentially a deterministic finite automaton (DFA). Every node represents a state of automation, and the state transition among nodes depend on different Chinese character variables that are appended to the current *Double Array Trie*. When the end states in this DFA are reached, or the current state cannot transition to any other state, the retrieval is finished.

Based on *Double Array Trie*, we can use two arrays to store the actual data. One is named *base array*, in which every element represents the node of *Double Array Trie*. Another is named *check array* in which every element represents the previous state of the current state in this array. Equation (14) formalize the transfer from state s to state t:

$$
\begin{aligned}
base[s] + c &= t \\
check[base[s] + c] &= s
\end{aligned}
\tag{14}
$$

where variable c represents one or more input chars. The positions of Chinese characters in the *base array* should be depend on their Chinese encoding. If there are n words for which the first character is i, and the second characters of these n words are $a_1, a_2, \cdots, a_n$, respectively, then the positions of the second characters in the *base array* should be $base[i] + a_1, base[i] + a_2, \cdots, base[i] + a_n$. If the values of $base[i]$ and $check[i]$ are equal to 0 simultaneously, it denotes that the state does not exsit.

After completing the words net based on *Double Array Trie*, we use the *Viterbi* algorithm to generate a word graph. Algorithm 1 describes this processing.

Algorithm 1. Viterbi Segment Algorithm

Require:
  The words graph created by $DoubleArrayTrie$ algorithm, which is named $WordNet$;
Ensure:
  The list of shortest path of words graph;
  Receive the Vertex list of words graph:$nodes$;
  for $i = 1$ to $lenthof(nodes)$ **do**
    // The $nodeArray$ is the list that contains vertex
    $nodeArray = nodes[i]$;
    for $j = 1$ to $lenthof(nodeArrays)$ **do**
    // The $node$ is vertex
    $node =$ the jth element of $nodeArrays$;
    calculate the length of real word of node:$RWLength$;
    for $k = 1$ to$nodes[i + RWLength]$ **do**
      obtain $toVertex$: the j_{th} element of $nodes[i + RWLength]$;
      calculate the shortest path from $toVertex$ to $node$;
    end for
  end for
end for
create and return the list of shortest path depend on $nodes$.

3.5 Shuffle

The implementation of shuffle in Apache Spark consists of two kind of phase: *Shuffle Write* and *Shuffle Read*. In the *Shuffle Write* phase, the output of map task will be sorted by the partition id and key of record (key/value pair) in the memory buffer, when the capacity of buffer has arrived the threshold of memory, the intermediate data will be spilled into disk. In the *Shuffle Read* phase, the reducer tasks will fetch the corresponding intermediate data partly from different map nodes according to their own reducer id.

In the *Shuffle Write* phase, the input data is too massive to read into memory one time, it can only be loaded into memory partly, the result of calculation is stored in a data structure namely *Append only Map*, which is substantially a *data array* occupied with a continuous memory space. With the execution of map task, the capacity of *data array* will become bigger and bigger. Actually, there is a prediction process called *Maybe Spill Collection* before storing calculation result, which mainly predicts that whether this insertion will cause the out of memory (OOM) exception. Once this insertion is predicted to cause memory overflow, the *Spill Write* operation will be started up, and the data in *Append only Map* will be spilled into disk batch by batch, one batch may contain 10000 key/value pairs. After that, the *data array* in *Append only Map* will be cleared to leave more space for next round execution.

It can be seen from the above description that the prediction result of *Maybe Spill Collection* process determines the times of *Spill Write*, so how to predict memory overflow precisely is extremely important. However, the original prediction algorithm called *Moving average* algorithm is barely satisfactory.

This method only considers the latest and previous sampling of *Append only Map*, but the former samplings are all excluded which also have an significant effect on the estimated size of memory utilization of *Append only Map*. It also does not take the distribution of train data set into account, most data sets are not very uniform, especially for text data. So we apply a new algorithm called *Triple exponential smoothing* algorithm to predict memory capacity. Exponential smoothing is a rule of thumb technique for smoothing time series data using the exponential window function. It can make use of all the sampling results, the later the sampling is, the higher the weight will be. The every time of sampling sequence of *Append only Map* is represented by $\{x_t\}$ beginning at time t=0, and the output of the exponential smoothing algorithm is commonly written as $\{S_t\}$, which may be regarded as a best estimate of what the next memory size of *Append only Map* will be. The form of *Triple exponential smoothing* is given by the formulas Eq. (15):

$$\begin{cases} S_t^{(1)} = \alpha x_t + (1-\alpha)S_{t-1}^{(1)} \\ S_t^{(2)} = \alpha S_t^{(1)} + (1-\alpha)S_{t-1}^{(2)} \\ S_t^{(3)} = \alpha S_t^{(2)} + (1-\alpha)S_{t-1}^{(3)} \end{cases} \tag{15}$$

where the $S_t^{(1)}$, $S_t^{(2)}$ and $S_t^{(3)}$ represent the single, double and triple smoothed value of memory size of *Append only Map* for time t respectively, α is the smoothing factor, and $0 < \alpha < 1$. we can calculate the feature memory size of *Append only Map* after T times sampling as in Eq. (16):

$$\begin{cases} x_{t+T} = A_t + B_t + C_t T^2 \\ A_t = 3S_t^{(1)} - 3S_t^{(2)} + S_t^{(3)} \\ B_t = \frac{\alpha}{2(1-\alpha)^2}\left[(6-5\alpha)S_t^{(1)} - 2(5-4\alpha)S_t^{(2)} + (4-3\alpha)S_t^{(3)}\right] \\ C_t = \frac{\alpha^2}{2(1-\alpha)^2}\left[S_t^{(1)} - 2S_t^{(2)} + S_t^{(3)}\right] \end{cases} \tag{16}$$

where x_t is the latest sampling size of *Append only Map*, when $T = 1$, the x_{t+1} is the predicted memory size of *Append only Map* of next update.

4   Parallel Implementation on Spark

Figure 2 illustrates the steps of training and testing in INBCS based on the Spark computing framework, which are presented in detail as follow:

Step 1. Read the preprocessed data sets from HDFS into *parallelCollection RDD* using the *textFile* function.

Step 2. Organize the intermediate data in the form of keys/values from *parallelCollectionRDD*, where the keys are specified as an identifier that consists of the class and document names and the values are the contents of documents.

$$\{hello, morning, \cdots, apple\} \Longrightarrow \{class1/7834911 : hello, morning, \cdots, apple\}$$

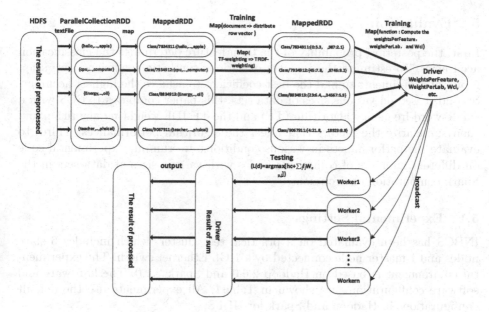

Fig. 2. The procedure of training and testing

Step 3. Transform the documents into distributed row vectors and convert the term frequency (TF) weight into the TF-IDF weight based on Eq. (8).

$$\{class1/7834911 : hello, morning, \cdots, apple\} \Longrightarrow \{class1/7834911 : 0 : 5.3,$$
$$1 : 7.8, \cdots, 987 : 2.1\}$$

Step 4. Calculate some necessary parameters that can be used as the input to the text classification model. These parameters include $WeightsPerFeature$, $WeightsPerLabel$ and $W_{c,i}$. They are described in detail as follows:

(1) $WeightsPerFeature$: a one-dimensional vector in which the elements represent the weights of each feature word. Because the length denotes the number of feature words in data sets, it can be obtained by accumulating all the feature vectors for each document.

(2) $WeightsPerLabel$: a one-dimensional vector in which each element represents the weight of all feature words in each class. The length of this vector equals the number of classes in data sets.

(3) $W_{c,j}$: the posterior probability of word j in class c, which can be calculated by Eq. (9).

Step 5. Broadcast the global variables to all worker nodes.

Step 6. Test each worker node to determine which class their document should belong to according to Eq. (4).

Step 7. Collect the testing results and output the final results.

5   Evaluation

First, the posteriori probability of the term feature determines the classification accuracies. To estimate the impacts of various synthetic coefficients, we set a group of experiments to find the best coefficient to achieve the highest accuracy. Second, based on various sizes of data sets, this paper compares INBCS with a single-word-frequency algorithm (TF) and the TF-IDF weighting algorithm and then summarize the factors that affect the algorithm performances. Third, to evaluate the performances in various conditions, we run our experimental code on different numbers of computing nodes with various sizes of data sets in the Spark computation environment.

5.1   Experimental Settings

INBCS has been evaluated on a practical test cluster, which includes 6 slave nodes and 1 master node connected by a 1-Gb Ethernet switch. The experimental environment is based on Hadoop 2.6.0 and Spark 2.1.0. The hardware and software configurations are shown in Table 1. All experiments use the default configurations in Hadoop and Spark for HDFS.

Table 1. The software and hardware configurations in the Spark cluster

The node type	Master	Slave
Software environment	Ubuntu 12.04, JDK 1.7, Hadoop 2.6.0, Scala 2.11.0, Spark 2.1.0	Ubuntu 12.04, JDK 1.7, Hadoop 2.6.0, Scala 2.11.0, Spark 2.1.0
CPU	4 cores, 2.7 GHz	4 cores, 2.7 GHz
Memory	8 G	8 G
Quantity	1	6

For comparison, this section selects the following four widely used corpora in text categorization: the *Reuters21578* (*R8*), *20Newsgroups* data sets, *SogouLab_Reduced* data sets, and *answer* corpus. The *Reuters-21578* Distribution 1.0 dataset consists of 12,902 articles and 90 topic categories from the Reuters newswire. We use the standard ModApte train/test split. *20Newsgroups* (20NG) contains messages across twenty different UseNet discussion groups. *R8* and *20Newsgroups* are English data sets, while the *SogouLab_Reduced* corpus and *answer* corpus are Chinese data sets.

5.2   Performance Analysis

In our experiments, we select approximately 60% of the preprocessed data as training data sets by a random sampling method and take the rest as the testing data sets. We can first acquire an optimal coefficient α from the Spark computing framework. This section compares the accuracies for the above four data sets with various values of α. In these experiments, we set $\alpha \in (0, 1)$, and the increment of the coordinate is 0.1. Figure 3 shows that the accuracies of these four data sets increase as the coefficient α varies from 0 to 0.9 and decreases as it varies between 0.9 and 1.0.

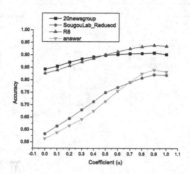

Fig. 3. The accuracies of different coefficient α

Because the time performances are usually related to the data quantities, the following experiments should estimate the execution time under the condition of different numbers of computing nodes with different sizes of input data sets. Using the same running environment from the above experiments, we choose the above four corpuses with size of 1 G, 5 G, 10 G, and 20 G.

As shown in Fig. 4(a) and (b), when the amount of data sets is 1 G or 5 G, the time consumption grows linearly as the number of computing nodes increases. This is because the Spark computing framework is based on memory computing. Each machine has 8 G memory; hence, a single computing node can load all the data sets into memory at once. Although the degree of concurrency of single node is lower than multi-node, the consumption time of the internal communication of the concurrent tasks is less than what the external nodes consume. Thus, this process can save a significant amount of communication consumption time among computing nodes. From these experimental results, when dealing with the small data sets, the performance of a cluster is usually lower than a single computing node with large memory.

As shown in Fig. 4(c) and (d), when the data size is 10 G or 20 G, with the increase of the number of machines, the processing time becomes less and less due to the limited memory capacity. In this situation, one machine cannot load all the data into memory. If there is only one node in the cluster, there will be many data exchanged between memory and disk. Meanwhile, the degree of concurrency is not high, which will lead to greater time consumption. Therefore, the time consumption by a single computing node is the largest. With an increasing number of nodes, the data sets can be distributed on more different nodes. After this, the increased number of nodes between clusters will yield increased

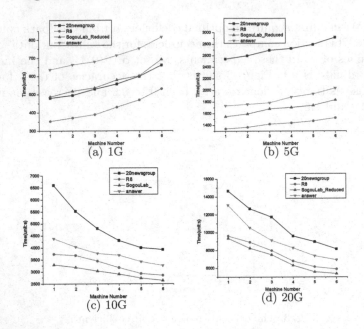

Fig. 4. Time consuming comparisons for INBCS in different dataset.

communication consumption. However, this is not the dominant factor of total time consumed. More nodes lead to a greater degree of concurrent tasks, and then the main factor in reducing the total time consumed is the higher degree of concurrency.

The experiments in Fig. 5(a) are all tested under a cluster with 8 nodes, and we also test the speedups of INBCS in different scales of the computing cluster. Figure 5(b) illustrates the speedups of INBCS with different corpus under the different node number of the cluster computing environment. From these results, we can easily draw a conclusion that the optimal speedup can be reached with 8 computing nodes in the experimental cluster. This is because the communication costs among the computing nodes usually increase as cluster scale increased. For the size of the input data in this experiment, eight computing nodes is an appropriate scale.

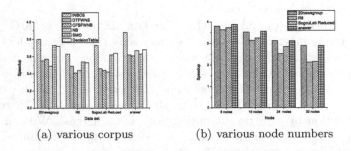

(a) various corpus   (b) various node numbers

Fig. 5. The comparison experiments for the speed up.

In this section, a group of experiments is designed to compare the standard naive Bayes (NB) to naive Bayes with decision tree-based feature weighting (DTFWNB) [15] and naive Bayes with CFS-based feature weighting (CFSFWNB) [16]. NB is regarded as the baseline.

All classification precisions were obtained by averaging the results from 8 separate runs of stratified 8-fold cross-validation. To further evaluate the performance of our proposed approaches over the standard baselines, the F1 values of classification are given in Table 2, which demonstrates that the competitive effects of INBCS are higher than NB, DTFWNB and CFSFWNB. The classification accuracies were obtained by averaging the results from 10 separate runs of stratified 10-fold cross-validation. From these results, INBCS can obtain satisfactory classification accuracies in these examinations.

Table 2. Classification F1 & Accuracy value comparisons

Dataset	F1				Accuracy			
	INBCS	DTFWNB	CFSFWNB	NB	INBCS	DTFWNB	CFSFWNB	NB
20news group	90.80%	86.47%	90.17%	86.79%	90.82%	87.69%	89.15%	86.79%
SogouLab Reduced	82.92%	82.83%	78.64%	78.34%	82.14%	81.15 %	76.15 %	78.58 %
R8	93.23%	93.46%	92.54%	90.68%	93.93 %	93.17 %	92.35 %	89.94 %
Answer	82.74%	82.64%	82.19%	81.48%	84.07 %	82.26%	82.47%	82.54%

To further validate the effectiveness of former proposed approach, INBCS is also compared with some other state-of-the-art methods that are not based on naive Bayes, such as SVMs using Sequential Minimal Optimization [17] and the Decision Tree [18]. In this experiment, INBCS is regarded as the baseline. Table 3 show the detailed comparison results in terms of classification accuracy, and AUC, respectively. To save time in running the experiments, we estimate the classification accuracy of each algorithm on each dataset by averaging the results from 5 separate tests of stratified 5-fold cross-validation.

Table 3. Classification Accuracy & UAC value comparisons

Dataset	Accuracy			AUC		
	INBCS	SVM	DecisionTree	INBCS	SVM	DecisionTree
20newsgroup	90.82	90.27	87.49	97.45	93.35	92.94
SogouLab Reduced	82.14	83.26	69.45	96.17	95.79	88.89
R8	93.93	97.65	89.82	99.34	98.74	97.64
Answer	84.07	88.68	72.45	93.48	92.48	88.49

6   Conclusion

The work in this paper are all based on the improvement of Naive Bayesian model. Besides the noise elimination and high dimensionality reduction, this paper also proposes an improved method for calculating the conditional probability that comprehensively considers the effects of the feature items in each document, class and training set. Experiments on Spark clusters with large amounts of data confirmed that the method proposed in this paper can achieve better accuracy, F1 values and other performance evaluation indexes for several popular corpora. From these efforts we can draw the following insights: 1. For natural language processing, especially for text classification, a higher quality training data set is essential for classification, so, the pre-processing of the text on the early stage is very important. 2. Parallel computing may improve the computational efficiency certainly, however, it is very important to choose the appropriate cluster size according to the amount of data set, since the communication and data transmission between multiple nodes may consume heavy times, therefore, we need find an optimal point between the data size and the cluster scale. Although the algorithm proposed in this paper can improve the classification accuracy and computational efficiency to a certain extent, but the classification result of Chinese text is not very satisfied, it may be caused by the complicated structure of Chinese text and word segmentation, so we will improve the model deeply to adapt it to different scenes in the future.

Acknowledgments. The work is supported by the National Natural Science Foundation of China (Grant Nos. 61572176, 61873090, L1824034), the National Key Research and Development Program of China (2018YFB1701401, 2017YFB0202201), China Knowledge Centre for Engineering Sciences and Technology Project(CKCEST-2017-1-10, CKCEST-2018-1-13, CKCEST-2019-2-13).

References

1. Gudivada, V.N., Baeza-Yates, R., Raghavan, V.V.: Big data: promises and problems. Computer **48**(3), 20–23 (2015)
2. Apache Software Foundation. Spark (2015). http://spark.apache.org
3. Pernkopf, F., Wohlmayr, M., Tschiatschek, S.: Maximum margin bayesian network classifiers. IEEE Trans. Pattern Anal. Mach. Intell. **34**(3), 521–532 (2012)
4. Bouboulis, P., Theodoridis, S., Mavroforakis, C., Evaggelatou-Dalla, L.: Complex support vector machines for regression and quaternary classification. IEEE Trans. Neural Networks Learn. Syst. **26**(6), 1260–1274 (2015)
5. Al-Mubaid, H., Umair, S.A.: A new text categorization technique using distributional clustering and learning logic. IEEE Trans. Knowl. Data Eng. **18**(9), 1156–1165 (2006)
6. Rennie, J.D.M.: Tackling the poor assumptions of naive Bayes text classifiers. In: Proceedings of the Twentieth International Conference on Machine Learning, pp. 616–623 (2003)
7. Aghdam, M.H., Ghasem-Aghaee, N., Basiri, M.E.: Text feature selection using ant colony optimization. Expert Syst. Appl. **36**(3), 6843–6853 (2009)

8. Shi, K., Jie, H.E., Liu, H.T., Zhang, N.T., Song, W.T.: Efficient text classification method based on improved term reduction and term weighting. J. China Univ. Posts Telecommun. **18**(18), 131–135 (2011)
9. Berka, T., Vajtersic, M.: Parallel rare term vector replacement: fast and effective dimensionality reduction for text. J. Parallel Distrib. Comput. **73**(3), 341–351 (2013)
10. Kim, S.B., Han, K.S., Rim, H.C., Myaeng, S.H.: Some effective techniques for naive bayes text classification. IEEE Trans. Knowl. Data Eng. **18**(11), 1457–1466 (2006)
11. Katz, S.M.: Distribution of content words and phrases in text and language modelling. Nat. Lang. Eng. **2**(1), 15–59 (2000)
12. Allison, B.: An improved hierarchical Bayesian model of language for document classification. In: International Conference on Computational Linguistics, pp. 25–32 (2008)
13. Meena, M.J., Chandran, K.R.: Naive Bayes text classification with positive features selected by statistical method, pp. 28–33 (2009)
14. Nie, Z., Zhang, Y., Wen, J.R., Ma, W.Y.: Object-level ranking: bringing order to web objects. In: International Conference on World Wide Web, pp. 567–574 (2005)
15. Hall, M., Hall and Mark: A decision tree-based attribute weighting filter for naive Bayes. In: Bramer, M., Coenen, F., Tuson, A. (eds.) SGAI 2006. Springer, London (2007). https://doi.org/10.1007/978-1-84628-663-6_5
16. Wang, S., Jiang, L., Li, C.: A CFS-based feature weighting approach to naive bayes text classifiers. In: Wermter, S., et al. (eds.) ICANN 2014. LNCS, vol. 8681, pp. 555–562. Springer, Cham (2014). https://doi.org/10.1007/978-3-319-11179-7_70
17. Platt, J.C.: Fast Training of Support Vector Machines Using Sequential Minimal Optimization. MIT Press, Cambridge (1999)
18. Kohavi, R.: The power of decision tables. In: Lavrac, N., Wrobel, S. (eds.) ECML 1995. LNCS, vol. 912, pp. 174–189. Springer, Heidelberg (1995). https://doi.org/10.1007/3-540-59286-5_57

On the Optimal Number of Computational Resources in MapReduce

Htway Htway Hlaing[1(✉)], Hidehiro Kanemitsu[1,2], Tatsuo Nakajima[1],
and Hidenori Nakazato[1]

[1] Waseda University, Tokyo, Japan
htwayhtwayhlaing@toki.waseda.jp, kanemitsuh@stf.teu.ac.jp,
tatsuo@dcl.cs.waseda.ac.jp, nakazato@waseda.jp
[2] Tokyo University of Technology, Tokyo, Japan

Abstract. Big data computing in the cloud needs faster processing and better resource provisioning. MapReduce is the framework for computing large scale datasets in cloud environments. Optimization of resource requirement for each job to satisfy a specific objective in MapReduce is an open problem. Many factors, e.g., system side information and requirements of each client must be considered to estimate the appropriate amount of resources. This paper presents a mathematical model for the optimal number of map tasks in MapReduce resource provisioning. This model is to estimate the optimal number of the mappers based on the resource specification and the size of the dataset.

Keywords: Big data · Cloud computing · Resource provisioning

1 Introduction

Large amount of the datasets are continuously produced from the web, scientific computing, social media, and IoT application. When input data is too large to handle by a single computational resource, the computation needs to be distributed across a massive number of machines to finish the job in the given time.

MapReduce library partitions the input data into a number of inputsplits. A map task reads an inputsplit and, the user-defined map function processes the inputsplit. The map function takes input key/value pairs and produces a set of intermediate key/value pairs. The intermediate key/value pairs are buffered in the memory of the mapper. When the amount of the data size reaches a threshold of the memory buffer, intermediate key/value pairs are written to the local disk and partitioned by hash function for reduce tasks. Reduce tasks read and sort intermediate data so that the data with the same key are grouped together. The key and the set of intermediate values are passed to the reduce function. The output data from the reduce function is appended to the final output file [1].

© Springer Nature Switzerland AG 2019
D. Da Silva et al. (Eds.): CLOUD 2019, LNCS 11513, pp. 240–252, 2019.
https://doi.org/10.1007/978-3-030-23502-4_17

Due to the flexibility, scalability, simplicity in scheduling and fault tolerance, MapReduce is increasingly used for large scale data processing such as personalized advertising and the other efficient data mining tasks. MapReduce programs are run in public cloud or private cloud. However, running the MapReduce program on the public cloud has become a realistic option for most users. In the public cloud environment, virtualization technique provides services for users to provision a virtual cluster or to release the cluster in a specified time. Users are responsible for determining the appropriate number of virtual machines to execute specific MapReduce tasks.

Optimal configuration for the map and reduce tasks may differ based on the type of application and the amount of input data. Running a MapReduce program in the cloud requires optimization for resource usage to minimize the cost or job finish time. In many research approaches, resource provisioning in MapReduce based on regression analysis such as profiling or sampling a number of parameters with test runs on small scale Hadoop clusters using sample datasets [2–4].

MapReduce performance models are designed to estimate job completion time based on job profile, size of input data and specification of resources [3, 4]. The job profile includes the application characteristics during all map and reduce phases of a MapReduce job. Any modifications of the MapReduce program or the underlying Hadoop framework are not necessary for profiling technique. However, test runs are necessary to estimate the number of resources using job profiles.

In MapReduce cloud services such as Amazon Web Services, customers can create MapReduce clusters to analyze large datasets by specifying required resources and submit MapReduce jobs and cloud service provider invokes virtual machines (VMs) to execute the jobs and the VMs are revoked by cloud service providers or released by customers after job completion. The cost of cloud service usage and performance of the specific job depends on the parameters chosen by users, such as the type of virtual machines, the number of virtual machines and the number of mappers per VM. Cloud service models can be generally classified as three approaches. In the first approach, the customer specifies the resource requirement for each job and the cloud service provider simply allocates the requested resources upon job arrival time [19, 20]. Customer manages each job for the efficient resource usage and, therefore it is lack of global resource optimization across jobs. In the second approach, customers specify the required resources for each job and cloud provider schedules the jobs [5]. Optimization is partly managed by the customer and partly managed by the cloud service provider. The cloud provider performs optimized resource management to finish the jobs in the specified time to meet the service requirements for the customers. Therefore, the opportunity for delay start is not provided for the jobs of the customer and each job is necessary to start immediately. Inefficient allocation of the resources to a job can result in higher cost for the cloud service provider. In the third approach, customers only require to submit the jobs and specify job completion time and, cloud service provider manages the resource requirements and allocation of resources [4].

However, all conventional resource provisioning models are on profiling technique, test runs and sampling. Such approaches are not realistic to apply for MapReduce resource provisioning system in practical use. Automatic provisioning approach can help solve the problems to reduce both customer's burden and cloud provider's burden. According to the best of our knowledge, our mathematical model is the first approach for the estimation of computational resources in the cloud environment.

In this paper, we propose a mathematical model to estimate the optimal number of mappers based on the resource specification and the size of datasets. This model can be used for both customer-managed and cloud-managed environments. The mathematical model is derived to find the number of map tasks from the phases of mapper to optimize resource provisioning in MapReduce. This paper is organized as follows. Section 2 presents our MapReduce performance model. The preliminary evaluation is shown in Sect. 3. Related works are described in Sect. 4. Section 5 summarizes the paper and describes future work.

2   MapReduce Performance Model

In this resource provisioning approach, computational nodes are assigned as mappers and reducers. Input data is distributed across mapper nodes in Hadoop File System (HDFS) and partitioned into equal-sized inputsplits. Mappers read inputsplits from HDFS, create key/value pairs of input records and process user-defined map function. Output data is partitioned and formatted by partitioning and serialization utilities of MapReduce. Output partitions are stored in the memory buffer of mappers. The buffer consists of two parts: accounting part that stores 16 bytes of metadata per record and serialization part that stores serialized map output records. When either of two parts fills up to threshold, the spill process begins to write data records to disk. If more than one spill file is created, all spill files are merged into a single output file. Thus, the total processing time for the map task includes time taken for read phase, map phase, collect phase, spill phase and merge phase. In a merged file on a mapper, several partitions are generated and evenly distributed to all reducers by using the hash function. A partition corresponds to the set of key/value, where all keys are the same. Reducer merges all partitions from mappers and writes to shuffle files. One shuffle file handles only one key. All shuffle files are merged into one input file for the reduce function. The reducer processes the input file and then writes the result on HDFS. Total processing time at reducer includes time taken for shuffle phase, sort phase, reduce phase and write phase. This paper presents the details of procedures at a mapper and estimation of the optimal number of mappers. Figure 1 shows the procedures of mapper and the notations for parameters of the equations are shown in Table 1.

Table 1. Notations

I, input data
N, number of inputsplit
I_i, i-th inputsplit
$|I_i|$, size of i-th inputsplit
C_I, constant for $|I_i|$
M, the set of mappers
m, number of mappers
M_k , k-th mapper
α_k^p, processing speed of k-th mapper
α_k^r, I/O read speed of k-th mapper
α_k^w, I/O write speed of k-th mapper
$R_{rec}^{in}(i)$, number of input records in i-th inputsplit
$w_{i,k}^{in}$, workload to process the k-th input record in I_i
$\overline{w}_{split}$, workload to generate an inputsplit
$T_{gen}(i,k)$, time to generate N inputsplits
$T_{map}(i,k)$, processing time of i-th inputsplit on k-th mapper M_k
$w_{i,j}^{in}$, workload of j-th input record in i-th inputsplit
$\overline{w}_i^{in}$, mean workload for each input record in I_i
$R_{rec}^{out}(i)$, number of output records in I_i
$\rho_{rec}(i)$, the ratio of the number of records between $R_{rec}^{in}(i)$ and $R_{rec}^{out}(i)$
W_{in}, width of each input record
W_{out}, width of each output record
$\overline{w}_i^{part}$, workload of partitioning the k-th output record from I_i
$\overline{w}_i^{ser}$, workload of serializing the k-th output record
$T_{ser}(i,k)$, serialization time of k-th output record
$T_{collect}(i,k)$, total time of collect phase
$R_{max}^{ser}(i)$, number of maximum serialization records
pSortMB, io.sort.mb
pSortRatio, Sorting ratio
pSpillRatio, Spill ratio
$|O_i|$, output size for I_i
$R_{max}^{acc}(i)$, maximum number of accounting records
$R_{spillb}(i)$, number of spill buffer records
$N_{spill}(i)$, number of spills
$|B_{spill}|$, spill buffer size
$|F_{spill}(i)|$, spill file size
$T_{spill}(i,k)$, total time for spill phase
N_{red}, number of reducers
$\overline{w}_{sort}$, workload to sort a record
$\overline{w}_{merge}$, workload to merge a record
$N_{max}^{spill}(i)$, maximum number of spill
N_{merge}, number of merges
$T_{merge}(i,k)$, merge time of of i-th inputsplit on k-th mapper M_k
$T_{map}^{total}(i,k)$, total processing time of i-th inputsplit on k-th mapper M_k
N_{opt}, optimal number of inputsplits
α_{ave}^*, average performance

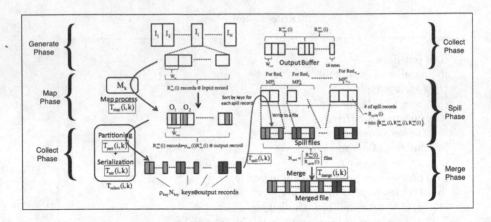

Fig. 1. Procedures at a mapper

2.1 Partitioning Input Data and Execution at Mappers

The input data is defined as $I = \{I_1, I_2, \ldots, I_N\}$ where I_i is the i-th inputsplit, $|I_i|$ is the size of I_i, and N is the number of inputsplits. In MapReduce, I_i is located on a local disk of a mapper in Hadoop File System (HDFS). The set of mappers is defined as $M = \{M_1, M_2, \ldots, M_m\}$. α_k^p, α_k^r, and α_k^w are the processing speed, I/O read speed, and I/O write speed of mapper k, respectively. Let the number of input records in I_i be $R_{rec}^{in}(i)$, and the workload to process the j-th input record in I_i be $w_{i,j}^{in}$. Since input data is divided into equal-sized inputsplits, $|I_i| = C_I, \forall I_i \in I$ for a constant C_I. If the workload to generate an inputsplit is defined as $\overline{w}_{split}$, the time to prepare N inputsplits is defined as

$$T_{gen}(i, k) = \frac{\overline{w}_{split}}{\alpha_k^p}\left(\frac{|I|}{C_I} - 1\right) = \frac{\overline{w}_{split}}{\alpha_k^p}(N - 1) \tag{1}$$

where $|I|$ is the size of input I.

The sum of the time to transfer inputsplit I_i, to read I_i, and to process the map task on mapper M_k is defined as

$$\begin{aligned}
T_{map}(i, k) &= \frac{C_I}{\alpha_k^r} + \frac{1}{\alpha_k^p}\sum_{j=1}^{R_{rec}^{in}(i)} w_{i,j}^{in} \\
&= \frac{C_I}{\alpha_k^r} + \frac{\overline{w}_i^{in} R_{rec}^{in}(i)}{\alpha_k^p},
\end{aligned} \tag{2}$$

where $\overline{w}_i^{in}$ is the mean workload to process each input record in inputsplit I_i.

2.2 Collect Phase

The number of output records for I_i from mapper M_k is defined as

$$R_{rec}^{out}(i) = R_{rec}^{in}(i) \times \rho_{rec}(i), \tag{3}$$

where $\rho_{rec}(i)$ is the ratio of the number of output records to input records. If the size of each input record is defined as W_{in}, the number of input records is $R_{rec}^{in}(i) = \frac{C_I}{W_{in}}$. Thus, (3) can be rewritten as

$$R_{rec}^{out}(i) = \frac{C_I \rho_{rec}(i)}{W_{in}}. \tag{4}$$

Let the workload to partition the output generated from I_i be w_i^{part} and their average be $\overline{w}_i^{part}$. Then the time of partitioning the output of I_i assigned to mapper M_k is defined as follows:

$$T_{part}(i, k) = \frac{1}{\alpha_k^p} \sum_{j=1}^{\frac{C_I \rho_{rec}(i)}{W_{in}}} w_{i,j}^{part} = \frac{\overline{w}_i^{part}}{\alpha_k^p} \frac{C_I \rho_{rec}(i)}{W_{in}}. \tag{5}$$

As for the serialization time, let w_i^{ser} be the workload to serialize the output from I_i assigned to mapper M_k and the mean workload to serialize the output records be $\overline{w}_i^{ser}$. Then the time for serialization is defined as follows:

$$T_{ser}(i, k) = \frac{1}{\alpha_k^p} \sum_{j=1}^{\frac{C_I \rho_{rec}(i)}{W_{in}}} w_{i,j}^{ser} = \frac{\overline{w}_i^{ser}}{\alpha_k^p} \frac{C_I \rho_{rec}(i)}{W_{in}}. \tag{6}$$

Thus, the total processing time in this collect phase can be derived by Eq. (5) + Eq. (6).

$$\begin{aligned} T_{collect}(i, k) &= \frac{\overline{w}_i^{part}}{\alpha_k^p} \frac{C_I \rho_{rec}(i)}{W_{in}} + \frac{\overline{w}_i^{ser}}{\alpha_k^p} \frac{C_I \rho_{rec}(i)}{W_{in}} \\ &= \frac{C_I \rho_{rec}(i)}{\alpha_k^p W_{in}} \left(\overline{w}_i^{part} + \overline{w}_i^{ser} \right). \end{aligned} \tag{7}$$

2.3 Spill Phase

In this phase, each output key/value pair is sorted and written to "spill" files. Spill phase starts when the output data (output records and accounting part) in the memory buffer exceeds the threshold value (e.g., $0.8 \times$ output buffer size). The size of each output records is $W_{out} = \frac{|O_i|}{R_{rec}^{out}(i)} = \frac{|O_i|}{R_{rec}^{in}(i)\rho_{rec}(i)}$, where $|O_i|$ is the output size for I_i.

The output buffer is divided into two parts: serialization buffer and accounting buffer. Each buffer stores its own serialization records and accounting records. The number of maximum serialization records in the output buffer can be defined as

$$\begin{aligned} R_{max}^{ser}(i) &= \frac{pSortMB \times 2^{20} \times (1 - pSortRatio) \times pSpillRatio}{W_{out}} \\ &= \frac{pSortMB \times 2^{20} \times (1 - pSortRatio) \times pSpillRatio}{|O_i|/\{R_{rec}^{in}(i)\rho_{rec}(i)\}}, \end{aligned} \tag{8}$$

where $pSortMB$ is "io.sort.mb" and therefore $psortMB$ is multiplied by 2^{20}.

16-byte data is written as metadata for each accounting record. The number of accounting records is defined as

$$R_{max}^{acc}(i) = \frac{pSortMB \times 2^{20} \times pSortRatio \times pSpillRatio}{16} \tag{9}$$

From (4), (8), and (9), the number of spill buffer records when spill is performed is defined as

$$R_{spillb}(i) = \min\{R_{max}^{ser}(i), R_{max}^{acc}(i), R_{rec}^{out}(i)\} \tag{10}$$

The number of spills is defined as

$$N_{spill}(i) = \left\lceil \frac{R_{rec}^{out}(i)}{R_{spillb}(i)} \right\rceil$$

$$\Leftrightarrow N_{spill} - 1 < \frac{R_{rec}^{out}(i)}{R_{spillb}(i)} \leq N_{spill} \tag{11}$$

The spill buffer size is defined as follows:

$$|B_{spill}| = R_{spillb}(i) \times W_{out}.$$
$$|F_{spill}(i)| = |B_{spill}|. \tag{12}$$

where $|F_{spill}(i)|$ is the spill file size. The total time for spill phase is defined as:

$$\begin{aligned}
T_{spill}(i, k) &= N_{spill}(i) \times \left\{ R_{spillb}(i) \log\left(\frac{R_{spillb}(i)}{N_{red}}\right) \times \frac{\overline{w}_{sort}}{\alpha_k^p} + \frac{|F_{spill}(i)|}{\alpha_k^w} \right\} \\
&= \left\lceil \frac{R_{rec}^{out}(i)}{R_{spillb}(i)} \right\rceil \left\{ R_{spillb}(i) \log\left(\frac{R_{spillb}(i)}{N_{red}}\right) \times \frac{\overline{w}_{sort}}{\alpha_k^p} + \frac{R_{spillb}(i)W_{out}}{\alpha_k^w} \right\} \\
&= R_{rec}^{out}(i) \left\{ \log\left(\frac{R_{spillb}(i)}{N_{red}}\right) \times \frac{\overline{w}_{sort}}{\alpha_k^p} + \frac{W_{out}}{\alpha_k^w} \right\} \\
&= R_{rec}^{out}(i) \left\{ \log\left(\frac{R_{spillb}(i)}{N_{red}}\right) \times \frac{\overline{w}_{sort}}{\alpha_k^p} + \frac{W_{out}}{\alpha_k^w} \right\},
\end{aligned} \tag{13}$$

where $\overline{w}_{sort}$ is the processing time to sort a record and $T_{spill}(i, k)$ is the total time to spill the records which exceed the threshold value. Thus, the time complexity is $O\left(R_{spillb}(i) \log\left(\frac{R_{spillb}(i)}{N_{red}}\right)\right)$, where $\log\left(\frac{R_{spillb}(i)}{N_{red}}\right)$ steps for the merging are needed for generating partitions in total. By applying (4) to (13),

$$T_{spill}(i, k) = \frac{|I_i|\rho_{rec}(i)}{W_{in}} \left\{ \log\left(\frac{R_{spillb}(i)}{N_{red}}\right) \times \frac{\overline{w}_{sort}}{\alpha_k^p} + \frac{W_{out}}{\alpha_k^w} \right\}. \tag{14}$$

2.4   Merge Phase

This phase is performed after the spill phase finishes. Both spill phase and merge phase are optional. The objective of the merge phase is to generate one output file from several spill files. The number of merges depends on the parameter of "io.sort.factor" which is the number of spill files to generate a new file. Thus, generally, the number of merges is

$$N_{merge}(i) = \left\lfloor \frac{N_{spill}(i)}{N_{max}^{spill}(i)} \right\rfloor (N_{max}^{spill} - 1) + N_{spill}(i) mod(N_{max}^{spill}(i)) - 1 + \left\lfloor \frac{N_{spill}(i)}{N_{max}^{spill}(i)} \right\rfloor$$

$$= \left\lfloor \frac{N_{spill}(i)}{N_{max}^{spill}(i)} \right\rfloor N_{max}^{spill} + \left(N_{spill}(i) - \left\lfloor \frac{N_{spill}(i)}{N_{max}^{spill}(i)} \right\rfloor N_{max}^{spill}(i) - 1 \right)$$

$$= N_{spill}(i) - 1. \tag{15}$$

The file read time for each spill file, the file write time for each spill file, and the number of records for merging into one records affect the time of the merge phase. By using (15), the time for merging is defined as

$$T_{merge}(i, k) = N_{merge}(i) \left(\frac{|F_{spill}(i)|}{\alpha_k^r} + \frac{|F_{spill}(i)|}{\alpha_k^w} + \frac{R_{spillb}(i)\rho_{rec}\overline{w}_{merge}}{\alpha_k^p} \right) \tag{16}$$

where $R_{spillb}(i)\rho_{rec}$ is the number of records in a spill file, and we assume that each single spill file is read and then written down to the merged file in one by one basis. By using (12), (16) is rewritten as follows:

$$T_{merge}(i, k) = (N_{spill}(i) - 1) \left\{ R_{spillb}(i) W_{out} \left(\frac{1}{\alpha_k^r} + \frac{1}{\alpha_k^w} \right) + \frac{R_{spillb}(i)\rho_{rec}\overline{w}_{merge}}{\alpha_k^p} \right\}$$

$$= (N_{spill}(i) - 1) \left\{ R_{spillb}(i) \left(W_{out} \left(\frac{1}{\alpha_k^r} + \frac{1}{\alpha_k^w} \right) + \frac{\rho_{rec}\overline{w}_{merge}}{\alpha_k^p} \right) \right\}. \tag{17}$$

2.5 Total Processing Time at a Mapper

Let the total processing time at a mapper M_k to process I_i be $T_{map}^{total}(i, k)$. Thus, we have

$$T_{map}^{total}(i, k) = T_{gen}(i, k) + T_{map}(i, k) + T_{collect}(i, k) + T_{spill}(i, k) + T_{merge}(i, k). \tag{18}$$

By developing (18), we have

$$T_{map}^{total}(i, k) = \frac{\overline{w}_{split}}{\alpha_k^p} \left(\frac{|I|}{C_I} - 1 \right) + \frac{C_I}{\alpha_k^r} + \frac{\overline{w}_i^{in} R_{rec}^{in}(i)}{\alpha_k^p}$$

$$+ \frac{C_I \rho_{rec}(i)}{\alpha_k^p W_{in}} \left(\overline{w}_i^{part} + \overline{w}_i^{ser} \right)$$

$$+ \frac{C_I \rho_{rec}(i)}{W_{in}} \left\{ \log \left(\frac{R_{spillb}(i)}{N_{red}} \right) \times \frac{\overline{w}_{sort}}{\alpha_k^p} + \frac{W_{out}}{\alpha_k^w} \right\}$$

$$+ (N_{spill}(i) - 1) \left\{ R_{spillb}(i) \left(W_{out} \left(\frac{1}{\alpha_k^r} + \frac{1}{\alpha_k^w} \right) + \frac{\rho_{rec}\overline{w}_{merge}}{\alpha_k^p} \right) \right\}. \tag{19}$$

At (19), if the system is homogeneous, total processing time at the mapper can be rewritten as

$$
\begin{aligned}
T_{map}^{total}(N,k) &= \frac{\overline{w}_{split}}{\alpha_{ave}^p}N + \frac{|I|}{N}\left\{\frac{N}{\alpha_{ave}^r} + \frac{\rho_{rec}(i)}{\alpha_{ave}^p W_{in}}\left(\overline{w}_i^{part} + \overline{w}_i^{ser}\right)\right\} \\
&+ \frac{|I|}{N}\frac{\rho_{rec}(i)}{W_{in}}\left\{\frac{\overline{w}_{sort}}{\alpha_{ave}^p}\log\left(\frac{R_{spillb}(i)}{N_{red}}\right) + \frac{W_{out}}{\alpha_{ave}^w}\right\} \\
&+ \frac{|I|\rho_{rec}(i)}{NW_{in}}\left\{W_{out}\left(\frac{1}{\alpha_{ave}^r} + \frac{1}{\alpha_{ave}^w}\right) + \frac{\rho_{rec}\overline{w}_{merge}}{\alpha_{ave}^p}\right\} \\
&- R_{spillb}(i)\left\{W_{out}\left(\frac{1}{\alpha_{ave}^r} + \frac{1}{\alpha_{ave}^w}\right) + \frac{\rho_{rec}\overline{w}_{merge}}{\alpha_{ave}^p}\right\} - \frac{\overline{w}_{split}}{\alpha_{ave}^p} \\
&= \frac{\overline{w}_{split}}{\alpha_{ave}^p}N + \frac{|I|}{N}\left\{\frac{1}{\alpha_{ave}^r} + \frac{\rho_{rec}(i)}{\alpha_{ave}^p W_{in}}\left(\overline{w}_i^{part} + \overline{w}_i^{ser}\right)\right\} \\
&+ \frac{|I|}{N}\frac{\rho_{rec}(i)}{W_{in}}\left\{\frac{\overline{w}_{sort}}{\alpha_{ave}^p}\log\left(\frac{R_{spillb}(i)}{N_{red}}\right) + \frac{W_{out}}{\alpha_{ave}^w}\right. \\
&+ \left. W_{out}\left(\frac{1}{\alpha_{ave}^r} + \frac{1}{\alpha_{ave}^w}\right) + \frac{\rho_{rec}\overline{w}_{merge}}{\alpha_{ave}^p}\right\} \\
&- R_{spillb}(i)\left\{W_{out}\left(\frac{1}{\alpha_{ave}^r} + \frac{1}{\alpha_{ave}^w}\right) + \frac{\rho_{rec}\overline{w}_{merge}}{\alpha_{ave}^p}\right\} - \frac{\overline{w}_{split}}{\alpha_{ave}^p} \qquad (20)
\end{aligned}
$$

where α_{ave}^* is the average performance for reading time, processing time and writing time of mappers.

If we define the optimal number of inputsplits as N_{opt}, it is obtained by differentiating equation (20) with respect to N. N_{opt} is the value of N when we have $\frac{dT_{map}^{total}(N,k)}{dN} = 0$. N_{opt} is derived as

$$
N_{opt} = \left[\frac{\alpha_{ave}^p |I|}{\overline{w}_{split}}\left\{\frac{1}{\alpha_{ave}^r} + \frac{\rho_{rec}(i)}{\alpha_{ave}^p W_{in}}\left(\overline{w}_i^{part} + \overline{w}_i^{ser}\right) + \frac{\rho_{rec}(i)}{W_{in}}A\right\}\right]^{\frac{1}{2}}, \quad (21)
$$

where

$$
A = \frac{\overline{w}_{sort}}{\alpha_{ave}^p}\log\left(\frac{R_{spillb}(i)}{N_{red}}\right) + \frac{W_{out}}{\alpha_{ave}^w} + W_{out}\left(\frac{1}{\alpha_{ave}^r} + \frac{1}{\alpha_{ave}^w}\right) + \frac{\rho_{rec}\overline{w}_{merge}}{\alpha_{ave}^p}. \quad (22)
$$

3   Preliminary Evaluation

In our MapReduce experiment, a program that estimates the value of Pi (π) using quasi-Monte Carlo method was tested to compare the performance with original approach. Hadoop MapReduce 3.0 is configured for 8 nodes cluster in cloud environment created by CloudStack. The π sample uses a statistical method to estimate the value of π. Random points are placed in a unit square which contains a circle. The area of the unit square is 1 and the probability of the points that fall within the circle are equal to the area of the circle, $\pi/4$. The value of π can be estimated by the value of $4R$ in which R is the ratio of the number of points inside the circle to the total number of points within the square. Mapper generates points in a unit square and counts the points inside and outside of the inscribed circle of the square. Reducer accumulates points inside and outside of the circle from the output of the mapper. If the sample of points is large, the estimation is better. The optimal number of map tasks is obtained after running the user program to estimate the value of π by varying the number of map tasks from 1 map task to 32 map tasks using 100×10^3 samples to 10×10^6 samples. The MapReduce program was tested on small scale cluster of 8 virtual machines with QEMU Virtual CPU built on Intel Xeon (R) CPU E5-1660 v4 @ 3.20 GHzx15 processor with 64 GB memory. The processing time for map tasks of the program is shown in Fig. 2.

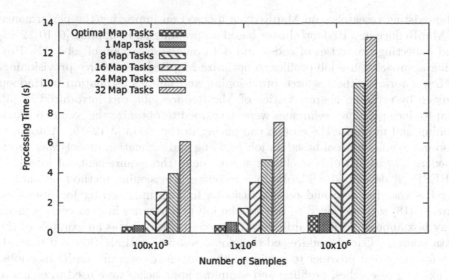

Fig. 2. Optimal processing time at the mappers

Optimal Number of Map Tasks with Various Samples		
10×10^3 samples	1×10^6 samples	10×10^6 samples
2	2	3

Fig. 3. Optimal number of map tasks

The program is tested for both single node Hadoop cluster setup and multinodes Hadoop cluster setup by varying input data size from 100×10^3 samples, 1×10^6 samples to 10×10^6 samples. Figure 3 shows the experimental result for the optimal number of map tasks when the various number of samples are processed and optimal number of map tasks is automatically figured out by the program. For resource provisioning, customers can choose the optimal number of map tasks to process 100×10^3 samples to 10×10^6 to estimate the value of π. The processing time of the optimal map tasks are significantly faster than that of the chosen number of map tasks in existing approach as shown in Fig. 2.

4   Related Works

The existing researches on MapReduce focused on improving the performance of MapReduce in a Hadoop cluster based on profiling and sampling [6–10,12,16] and collecting properties of codes and data on the execution of jobs [11]. Profiling approaches use job profiles to optimize MapReduce resource provisioning. A framework for the resource provisioning and failures estimation in Hadoop cluster by profiling characteristics of MapReduce jobs was introduced in [3]. MapReduce profiling techniques were developed to optimize the resource provisioning and minimize the cost of computing in the cloud [3,12–15]. Automatic resource prediction tool based on job profiling and estimation models was developed to provision the best cluster size to meet the requirements of jobs [17]. CRESP [2] developed a MapReduce resource provisioning method by analyzing the cost for map and reduce tasks to find optimal setting for resources. Bazaar [18] was developed to predict the job performance in data centers using gray box approach with MapReduce resource provisioning as an example of the data analytic. Cura [4] addressed the global resource optimization and scheduling for the cloud provider to minimize the customer costs in MapReduce jobs. In existing researches, profiling and sampling approaches were used to estimate the optimal number of resources with test runs. Profiling and sampling can incur overheads and increase processing time depending on the time for generating job profiles, the characteristics of data and resource specification. In our research, a mathematical model is derived to estimate the number of map tasks for both customer-managed and cloud-managed environment without profiling or sampling. Our research is to optimize resource provisioning in Hadoop MapReduce for both customers and cloud service providers in private and public cloud environments.

5   Conclusions and Future Work

This paper presents a mathematical MapReduce performance model for applying in both cloud-managed environment and customer-managed environment. In contrast to existing services, this approach can estimate the number of map tasks for resource provisioning in big data computing without test runs. Profiling or sampling is not necessary to find the optimal number of map tasks in this research. The required number of map tasks can be calculated based on the specification of resources and the size of input data. This research can improve performance of Hadoop MapReduce environment for cloud service provider and users. This research paper is on the mapper side to estimate the optimal number of map tasks. Future work and the extension of this research paper are on both map and reduce sides to estimate optimal number of mappers and reducers for the resource provisioning using MapReduce benchmarks with overall evaluation.

References

1. Dean, J., Ghemawat, S.: MapReduce: simplified data processing on large clusters. Commun. ACM **51**, 107–113 (2008)
2. Chen, K., Powers, J., Guo, S., Tian, F.: CRESP towards optimal resource provisioning for MapReduce computing in public clouds. IEEE Trans. Parallel Distrib. Syst. **25**(6), 1403–1412 (2014)
3. Verma, A., Cherkasova, L., Campbell, R.H.: Resource provisioning framework for MapReduce jobs with performance goals. In: Kon, F., Kermarrec, A.-M. (eds.) Middleware 2011. LNCS, vol. 7049, pp. 165–186. Springer, Heidelberg (2011). https://doi.org/10.1007/978-3-642-25821-3_9
4. Palanisamy, B., Singh, A., Liu, L.: Cost-effective resource provisioning for MapReduce in a cloud. IEEE Trans. Parallel Distrib. Syst. **26**(5), 1265–1279 (2015)
5. Sotomayor, B., Keahey, K., Foster, I.: Combining batch execution and leasing using virtual machines. In: Proceedings of the 17th International Symposium on High Performance Distributed Computing, pp. 87–96 (2008)
6. Jiang, D., Ooi, B.C., Shi, L., Wu, S.: The performance of MapReduce: an in-depth study. Proc. VLDB Endow. **3**(1–2), 472–483 (2010)
7. Babu, S., et al.: Towards automatic optimization of MapReduce programs. In: Proceedings of the 1st ACM Symposium on Cloud Computing, pp. 137–142 (2010)
8. Herodotou, H., Babu, S.: Profiling, what-if analysis, cost-based optimization of MapReduce programs. Proc. VLDB Endow. **4**(11), 1111–1122 (2011)
9. Wang, G., et al.: A simulation approach to evaluating design decisions in MapReduce setups. In: Proceedings of the IEEE/ACM International Symposium on Modeling, Analysis & Simulation of Computer and Telecommunication Systems, pp. 1–11 (2009)
10. Herodotou, H.: Hadoop Performance Models, Technical teport, CS-2011-05 (2011)
11. Agarwal, S., Kandula, S., Bruno, N., Wu, M.-C., Stoica, I., Zhou, J.: Re-optimizing data-parallel computing. In: Proceedings of the 9th USENIX Conference on NSDI, p. 21 (2012)
12. Kambatla, K., Pathak, A., Pucha, H.: Towards optimizing Hadoop provisioning in the cloud. In: Proceedings of the Conference on Hot Topics in Cloud Computing, pp. 156–172 (2009)
13. Morton, K., Friesen, A., Balazinska, M., Grossman, D.: Estimating the progress of MapReduce pipelines. In: Proceedings of the IEEE 26th International Conference on Data Engineering, pp. 681–684 (2010)
14. Tian, F., Chen, K.: Towards optimal resource provisioning for running MapReduce programs in public clouds. In: Proceedings of the IEEE 4th International Conference on Cloud Computing, pp. 155–162 (2011)

15. Popescu, A., Ercegovac, V., Balmin, A., Branco, M., Ailamaki, A.: Same queries, different data: can we predict runtime performance? In: Proceedings of the 3rd International Workshop on Self-Managing Database Systems, pp. 275–280 (2012)
16. Herodotou, H., et al.: Starfish: a self-tuning system for big data analytics. In: CIDR 2011, pp. 261–272 (2011)
17. Herodotou, H., Dong, F., Babu, S.: No one (cluster) size fits all: automatic cluster sizing for data-intensive analytics. In: Proceedings of the 2nd ACM Symposium on Cloud Computing, pp. 1–14 (2011)
18. Jalaparti, V., Ballani, H., Costa, P., Karagiannis, T., Rowstron, A.: Bazaar: enabling predictable performance in datacenters, Microsoft Res., Cambridge, U.K., Technical report MSR-TR-2012-38 (2012)
19. Amazon Elastic Compute Cloud (2018). https://aws.amazon.com/ec2/
20. Amazon Elastic MapReduce (2018). https://aws.amazon.com/emr/
21. Apache Hadoop (2018). http://hadoop.apache.org

Class Indistinguishability for Outsourcing Equality Conjunction Search

Weipeng Lin[1]([✉]), Ke Wang[1], Zhilin Zhang[1], Ada Waichee Fu[2],
Raymond Chi-Wing Wong[3], and Cheng Long[4]

[1] Simon Fraser University, Vancouver, Canada
{weipengl,ke_wang,zhilinz}@sfu.ca
[2] Chinese University of Hong Kong, Hong Kong, China
[3] Hong Kong University of Science and Technology, Hong Kong, China
[4] Nanyang Technological University, Singapore, Singapore

Abstract. Searchable symmetric encryption (SSE) enables a remote
cloud server to answer queries directly over encrypted data on a client's
behalf, therefore, relieves the resource limited client from complicated
data management tasks. Two key requirements are a strong security
guarantee and a sub-linear search performance. The bucketization approach in the literature addresses these requirements at the expense of
downloading many false positives or requiring the client to search relevant bucket ids locally, which limits the applicability of the method. In
this paper, we propose a novel approach CLASS to meet these requirements for equality conjunction search while minimizing the client work
and communication cost. First, we generalize the standard ciphertext
indistinguishability to partitioned data, called class indistinguishability,
which provides a level of ciphertext indistinguishability similar to that of
bucketization but allows the cloud server to perform search of relevant
data and filtering of false positives. We present a construction achieving these goals through a two-phase search algorithm for a query. The
first phase finds a candidate set through a sub-linear search. The second
phase finds the exact query result using a linear search applied to the
candidate set. Both phases are performed by the server and are implemented by plugging in existing search methods. The experiment results
on large real-world data sets show that our approach outperforms the
state-of-the-art.

Keywords: Searchable encryption · Equality conjunction search ·
Sub-linear search

1 Introduction

The current trend towards cloud-based Database-as-a-Service (DaaS) as an alternative to traditional on-site relational database management systems has largely
been driven by the perceived simplicity and cost-effectiveness. On one hand, the
sensitive and confidential nature of data requires that outsourced data need to be

© Springer Nature Switzerland AG 2019
D. Da Silva et al. (Eds.): CLOUD 2019, LNCS 11513, pp. 253–270, 2019.
https://doi.org/10.1007/978-3-030-23502-4_18

stored in encrypted form to preserve the privacy. On the other hand, outsourcing encrypted data precludes the client from delegating query processing tasks that depend on plaintext data information to the remote cloud server (or server for short), thus, induces inefficiency. Apparently, sending the whole encrypted data to the client for each query is impractical for most applications that deal with a large amount of data.

A promising solution to the above problem is *searchable symmetric encryption* (SSE) that allows the server to answer search queries directly over encrypted data on a client's behalf while protecting the confidentiality of plaintext data and queries, for example, in the sense of *ciphertext indistinguishability* [7,9]. Like most works [5,7,9], we focus on concealing plaintext data and queries but allow the disclosure of "access pattern", which refers to the set of (encrypted) records retrieved by each query as a result of granting the server the search capacity. For hiding access patterns, please refer to private information retrieval [25] and Oblivious RAM [21] techniques.

1.1   Motivation

A key challenge for SSE is dealing with two conflicting goals: a strong security guarantee, e.g., ciphertext indistinguishability (more details later), and a sub-linear search performance for computing a query. Ciphertext indistinguishability requires that the adversary cannot distinguish two *histories* of interacting with the system having the same trace that includes everything observed by the adversary during the interaction other than encrypted data and queries, such as the database size and the result size. Unfortunately, this level of indistinguishability is difficult to satisfy if we want the server to perform a sub-linear search that entails distinguishing the records that do not need to be searched from those that do.

In some practical scenarios, it suffices to maintain indistinguishability among a small number of individuals. For example, k-*anonymity* [22] ensures that each individual cannot be distinguished from $(k-1)$ other individuals, where k is a security parameter, which protects each individual by the indistinguishability within a group of size k. Another scenario is that not all individuals care about indistinguishability and indistinguishability is needed only for those who care. For example, suppose that *Alice* and *Bob* care about indistinguishability between them but *Cat* and *Dog* do not, it suffices to partition the domain into three classes $g_0 = \{Cat\}, g_1 = \{Dog\}, g_2 = \{Alice, Bob\}$ and enforce ciphertext indistinguishability *within* each class. On the other hand, such class indistinguishability would allow us to prune irrelevant classes for a query, which is impossible for the standard ciphertext indistinguishability.

Enforcing class indistinguishability is not new. The *bucketization* [11–13] can be considered as a construction of class indistinguishability. In this approach, records in the database are partitioned into buckets (i.e., classes) according to a specified partitioning of attribute domains and the records in a bucket are retrieved using the bucket id whereas plaintext data are encrypted using traditional techniques and stored on the server. To answer a query, the client first maps the query to relevant bucket ids using a local index and submits the bucket ids to the server. The server returns encrypted data according to the received bucket ids. The client recovers the query result after decrypting returned data and filtering false positives. Sub-linear search performance is supported by retrieving only the data in relevant buckets for a query.

However, bucketization suffers from two main drawbacks. One is that the client needs to search locally for relevant bucket ids for a query, referred to as query translation processing in [11–13]. This requires additional overheads on the resource limited client for storing and maintaining the translation information (i.e., the information for all buckets) for dynamic data, but the powerful server only needs to retrieve encrypted data through bucket ids computed by the client. Another drawback is that false positives are communicated to the client because they can only be filtered by the client. These are indicated by the boxes named "Search" and "Filtering" on the client side in Fig. 1(A). A finer bucket granularity will increase client's search work due to the increased number of buckets (especially for multi-dimensional data) whereas a coarser bucket granularity will increase the communication cost increased false positives. Since client resources and network bandwidth are limited, this approach's application will be limited.

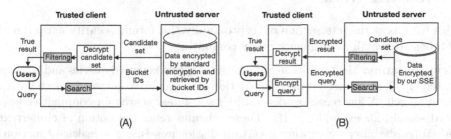

Fig. 1. (A) Bucketization [11–13]: The client searches for relevant bucket ids, the server returns all records in the buckets, and the client filters false positives; (B) Proposed scheme: The client encrypts the query predicate, the server searches for a candidate set and filters false positives, and the client decrypts the query result

1.2   Contributions

A preferred solution is pushing the "Search" and "Filtering" tasks to the server as in Fig. 1(B) where search for the relevant buckets and filtering of false positives are done by the server; the client only needs to encrypt the query and decrypt the query result. This approach calls for a new encryption scheme that would enable the server to perform search and filtering tasks. In this work, we present a novel scheme called CLASS to meet these requirements. We consider a relational database $\mathcal{D} = \{P_1, \cdots, P_{|\mathcal{D}|}\}$ containing $|\mathcal{D}|$ records with d attributes $\{A_1, \cdots, A_d\}$, where each A_t has a discrete domain $dom(A_t)$. A numeric domain can be discretized into a small number of intervals. We consider *equality conjunction queries* containing one or more equalities $A_t = v$ with $v \in dom(A_t)$, and $Att(Q)$ denotes the set of attributes on which a query Q has an equality. Each record has a unique record ID and $RID(\mathcal{D}, Q)$ denotes IDs for the records in $\mathcal{D}$ satisfying a query Q. Note that the database may contain other attributes that do not occur in any query. Our contributions are as follows.

- (Sect. 3) We formalize a relaxed notion of ciphertext indistinguishability, called *class indistinguishability*, that achieves a level of indistinguishability similar to that of bucketization.
- (Sect. 4) We propose a novel SSE scheme, called CLASS. CLASS is the first SSE scheme for equality conjunction queries that meets class indistinguishability and supports sub-linear search while pushing search and filtering tasks to the server as in Fig. 1(B). CLASS can be implemented by plugging in existing search methods without designing specialized methods.
- (Sect. 5) We formally prove class indistinguishability of CLASS.
- (Sect. 6) We present an empirical study to evaluate the practical efficiency of CLASS on large and real life databases. Our results show that CLASS outperforms the state-of-the-art.

2   Related Work

This work is at the intersection of cryptography (for formal security notion) and database (for high performance query computing).

Cryptography. Most works on SSE consider single keyword queries and a linear search [4]. [2,10] pioneered the construction of conjunctive keyword search with a linear search. A few recent works consider sub-linear search for conjunctive keyword search, for example, [5,15]. These schemes relax the notion of ciphertext indistinguishability by capturing certain disclosures (using a leakage function) caused by a sub-linear search process. One problem with these approaches is that it is a daunting task to capture the full extent of such low-level disclosures that are specific to the design of the index structure and the sub-linear search algorithm. In fact, the real-world consequences of such low-level disclosures are poorly understood, which was highlighted as an important open question [7,26]. Conjunctive keyword search is also studied based on Hidden Vector Encryption (HVE) [16], which suffers from prohibitive computation and communication costs.

Database. The research in database traditionally focused on scalability for large databases by adopting ad hoc security definitions. Examples are order preserving encryption [3] and distance preserving encryption [18], which makes indexing easy but discloses order and proximity information of plaintext. CryptDB [19] enables the DBMS server to execute SQL queries on encrypted data, using deterministic encryption for equality checks, group by, and equality-joins, and order preserving encryption for order checks. It is well known that deterministic encryption does not provide sufficient protection in practice. Asymmetric scalar-product preserving encryption (ASPE) [24] is suitable for designing a sub-linear search algorithm for equality conjunction search, but can not provide sufficient security [17]. Bucketization [11–13] provides a trade-off solution to security and sub-linear search performance. As discussed out in Sect. 1.1, this approach requires either significant client work or a high communication cost.

3   Proposed Security

In this section, we propose the notion of class indistinguishability. We consider the "honest-but-curious" adversary (i.e., the server) who follows all protocols honestly but may passively attempt to learn the plaintext information.

3.1   Classes

We assume that for an attribute A_t $(1 \leq t \leq d)$, the domain of A_t is partitioned into l_t disjoint *value classes*, $\{g_0^t, \cdots, g_{l_t-1}^t\}$. Typically, the class partitioning for each attribute is specified by the data owner and is public. In the following definition, we assume that the class partitioning for each attribute is given; we will discuss the specification of class partitioning after the definition. Given the class partitioning for every attribute, we can define the classes of records, queries, databases, and histories naturally as follows.

Definition 1. *Let $\{g_0^t, \cdots, g_{l_t-1}^t\}$ be the class partitioning for A_t, $1 \leq t \leq d$.*

- *A record class is a set of records $\prod_{t=1}^d g_j^t$, where g_j^t is a value class for A_t. In other words, a record class consists of all records P_i whose $P_i[t]$s are in the same value class for every attribute A_t.*
- *A database class consists of all databases $\mathcal{D}$ such that for any database $\mathcal{D}'$ in the class, there is a bijection η from $\mathcal{D}$ to $\mathcal{D}'$ such that for each record P_i in $\mathcal{D}$, P_i and $\eta(P_i)$ are in the same record class.*
- *A query class consists of all queries Q such that for any query Q' in the class, $Att(Q) = Att(Q')$ and for each $A_t \in Att(Q)$, $Q[t]$ and $Q'[t]$ are in the same value class.*
- *A history class consists of all histories $H = (\mathcal{D}, \mathcal{Q} = \{Q_1, \cdots, Q_m\})$ such that for any history $H' = (\mathcal{D}', \mathcal{Q}' = \{Q_1', \cdots, Q_m'\})$ in the class, $\mathcal{D}$ and $\mathcal{D}'$ are in the same database class, and for $1 \leq j \leq m$, Q_j and Q_j' are in the same query class.* □

Intuitively, a database class consists of all databases obtained by replacing each record with a record from the same record class; a query class consists of all queries obtained by replacing each specified value with a value from the same value class; a history class consists of all histories obtained by replacing the database with a database from the same database class and replacing each query with a query from the same query class. One extreme case is a singleton record class that contains a single record, which corresponds to a singleton value class on every attribute. Another extreme case is that there is a single class that contains all domain values for every attribute. In this case, all records (databases, queries, and histories) belong to the same class. Our class indistinguishability (Definition 3) ensures ciphertext indistinguishability for the members from the same class. Therefore, the size of value classes becomes a security parameter because a larger size leads to more members in a class that are indistinguishable from one another. The data owner can specify class partitioning through the size of value classes for each attribute. In this case, any grouping of value classes of the specified size suffices. In other cases, the data owner may want to group certain domain values into the same class, which can be done by enumerating the domains values in each value class.

In the rest of discussion, whenever it is clear from the context, we use the term "class" for any of record class, database class, query class, and history class.

3.2   Class Indistinguishability

Simply put, class indistinguishability is ciphertext indistinguishability of any two histories from the the same class. Formally, we can define this notion by a probabilistic game (or experiment) between an adversary and a challenger. We first borrow the definition of SSE from [7] as follows.

Definition 2 *(Symmetric Searchable Encryption (SSE) [7]). A SSE scheme is a collection of four polynomial-time algorithms (KeyGen, Enc, Enc_q, Search) such that,*

- *$K \leftarrow KeyGen(1^k)$: a probabilistic algorithm run by the client to initialize the secret key K for the scheme. The input is a security parameter k.*
- *$(\mathbf{I}, \mathbf{c}) \leftarrow Enc(K, \mathcal{D})$: a probabilistic algorithm run by the client to encrypt the database $\mathcal{D} = \{P_1, \cdots, P_{|\mathcal{D}|}\}$. The output is the ciphertexts $\mathbf{c}$ of records and the encrypted structure $\mathbf{I}$ for query testing.*
- *$\mathbf{t} \leftarrow Enc_q(K, Q)$: an algorithm run by the client to encrypt a query Q. The output is called the trapdoor for query testing.*
- *$X \leftarrow Search(\mathbf{I}, \mathbf{t})$: a deterministic algorithm run by the server to search for the records in $\mathcal{D}$ that satisfy Q with the input $\mathbf{I}$ and $\mathbf{t}$. The output is a set of record IDs.*

A SSE scheme is correct if for all $k \in \mathbb{N}$, for all K output by $KeyGen(1^k)$, for all $\mathcal{D} \subseteq \prod_{t=1}^{d} dom(A_t)$, for all $\mathbf{I}$ output by $Enc(K, \mathcal{D})$, for all $\mathbf{t}$ output by $Enc_q(K, Q)$, the output of $Search(\mathbf{I}, \mathbf{t})$ is the set of IDs for the records in $\mathcal{D}$ satisfying Q. □

One common technique for defining ciphertext indistinguishability is the probabilistic game [7]. We adopt this technique for defining class indistinguishability. Consider a history $H = (\mathcal{D}, \mathcal{Q} = \{Q_1, \cdots, Q_m\})$, which specifies a database and a sequence of queries. The *access pattern* induced by H is the tuple $\alpha(H) = (RID(\mathcal{D}, Q_1), \cdots, RID(\mathcal{D}, Q_m))$. The *search pattern* induced by H is the symmetric binary matrix $\sigma(H)$ such that for $1 \leq i, j \leq m$, the element in the i-th row and j-th column is 1 if $Q_i = Q_j$, and 0, otherwise. The *trace* induced by H is $\tau(H) = (|\mathcal{D}|, \alpha(H), \sigma(H))$. Two histories H_0 and H_1 have the same trace if there is a renaming ρ of RIDs such that $|\mathcal{D}_0| = |\mathcal{D}_1|$, $\alpha(H_0) = \rho(\alpha(H_1))$, $\sigma(H_0) = \sigma(H_1)$. For $b \in \{0,1\}$, let $|\mathcal{D}_b| = n$, $\mathcal{D}_b = \{P_{b,1}, \cdots, P_{b,n}\}$ and let $\mathcal{Q}_b = \{Q_{b,1}, \cdots, Q_{b,m}\}$.

Definition 3 (Class indistinguishability). *Assume that the class partitioning $\{g_0, \cdots, g_{l-1}\}$ is given for every attribute A_t. Let $SSE = (KeyGen, Enc, Enc_q, Search)$ and $\mathcal{A} = (\mathcal{A}_1, \mathcal{A}_2)$ be an adversary. Consider the following probabilistic experiment:*

$Ind_{SSE,\mathcal{A}}(k)$

1. $K \leftarrow KeyGen(1^k)$	8. *for* $1 \leq j \leq m$
2. $(st_\mathcal{A}, H_0, H_1) \leftarrow \mathcal{A}_1(1^k)$	9. $t_{b,j} \leftarrow Enc_q(K, Q_{b,j})$
3. $b \xleftarrow{\$} \{0,1\}$	10. *let* $t_b = (t_{b,1}, \cdots, t_{b,m})$
4. *parse* H_b *as* $(\mathcal{D}_b, \mathcal{Q}_b)$	11. $b' \leftarrow \mathcal{A}_2(st_\mathcal{A}, \mathbf{I}_b, t_b)$
5. *for* $1 \leq i \leq n$	12. *if* $b' = b$, *output* 1
6. $s_{b,i} \leftarrow Enc(K, P_{b,i})$	13. *otherwise output* 0
7. *let* $\mathbf{I}_b = (s_{b,1}, \cdots, s_{b,n})$	

subject to two restrictions: (i) H_0 and H_1 have the same trace, (ii) H_0 and H_1 are from the same class. $st_\mathcal{A}$ is a string that captures $\mathcal{A}_1$'s state after choosing the plaintext. We say that SSE ensures **class indistinguishability** *if for all polynomial-size adversaries $\mathcal{A} = (\mathcal{A}_1, \mathcal{A}_2)$,*

$$|\Pr[Ind_{SSE,\mathcal{A}}(k) = 1] - \frac{1}{2}| \leq negl(k) \tag{1}$$

where the probability is taken over the choice of b and the coins of KeyGen, Enc, Enc_q. We say that SSE ensures **strict class indistinguishability** *if*

$$\Pr[Ind_{SSE,\mathcal{A}}(k) = 1] = \frac{1}{2}. \tag{2}$$

$\square$

In the above game, the adversary chooses two histories H_0 and H_1 (line 2), and the challenger makes a choice $b \in \{0, 1\}$ uniformly at random (line 3) and encrypts the data and queries in H_b and return the result $\mathbf{I}_b$ and t_b to the adversary (lines 4–10). The adversary then guesses the value of b based on $\mathbf{I}_b$ and t_b (lines 11–13). $\Pr[Ind_{SSE,\mathcal{A}}(k) = 1]$ is the probability of the correct guess. Eq. (1) states that this probability is negligibly different from $\frac{1}{2}$, and Eq. (2) states that the adversary's guess is a random guess. Note the difference from ciphertext indistinguishability in [7]: the additional condition (ii) restricts H_0 and H_1 to be from the same history class, therefore, the indistinguishability is required only for the members from the same history class.

Remark 1. Class indistinguishability ensures that any two histories from the same class cannot be distinguished by the server given their ciphertexts and the search result (captured by traces). The standard ciphertext indistinguishability is the extreme case of a single value class containing all domain values of A_t for every attribute A_t, which produces the maximum number of histories in the class, thus, the maximum level of indistinguishability. This extreme class partitioning would lead to ineffective pruning in computing queries because the single class contains all records is relevant to every query. Class indistinguishability offers a trade-off between the level of indistinguishability and the effectiveness of sub-linear search through the specification of a more general class partitioning for each attribute, because classes containing no query result will not be searched.

The above definition considers a non-adaptive adversary in that all queries are chosen by the adversary before receiving any encrypted data or queries. In Sect. 5, we will show that our approach achieves class indistinguishability for an adaptive adversary as well.

4   Construction

In this section, we construct CLASS to meet two important goals: achieve class indistinguishability, and support a sub-linear search for equality conjunction queries through pushing the tasks of searching for relevant data and filtering false positives to the server as in Fig. 1(B).

4.1   Overview

At the high level, CLASS consists of two SSEs: $SSE_s = (KeyGen_s, Enc_s, Enc_{q,s}, Search_s)$ for $s \in \{1, 2\}$. The client encrypts each record P_i in $\mathcal{D}$ as $Enc(P_i) = (Enc_1(P_i), Enc_2(P_i))$ and uploads $Enc(\mathcal{D})$, i.e., the collection of $Enc(P_i)$, to the server. $Enc_1(\mathcal{D})$ and $Enc_2(\mathcal{D})$ denote the projection of $Enc(\mathcal{D})$ onto $Enc_1(P_i)$ and $Enc_2(P_i)$, respectively. At the query time, the client encrypts a query Q_j into $Enc_q(Q_j) = (Enc_{q,1}(Q_j), Enc_{q,2}(Q_j))$ and submits $Enc_q(Q_j)$ to the server.

The search for the query answer proceeds in two phases given in Algorithm 1. In the **Candidate Phase**, a sub-linear time $Search_1$ is applied to $Enc(\mathcal{D})$ to compute a candidate set $Cand$ that contains all records from the classes relevant to the query. This phase prunes all classes irrelevant to the query. In the **Filtering Phase**, a linear time $Search_2$ is applied to $Cand$ to filter false positives. The precision based (i.e., false positive free) $Search_2$ is expensive but is

---

Algorithm 1. $Search(Enc_{q,1}(Q_j), Enc_{q,2}(Q_j))$

Require: The server has $Enc(\mathcal{D})$
   Candidate Phase:

       $Cand \leftarrow Search_1(Enc(\mathcal{D}), Enc_{q,1}(Q_j))$

   Filtering Phase:

       $Results \leftarrow Search_2(Cand, Enc_{q,2}(Q_j))$

---

applied to the small candidate set *Cand*. These two phases correspond to the Search and Filtering in Fig. 1(B), respectively. With a small *Cand*, any existing SSE with a linear search such as [9,10] can serve as SSE_2. Therefore, our discussion below focuses on the construction of SSE_1.

4.2   Construction of SSE_1

Consider the class partitioning $\{g_0, \cdots, g_{l-1}\}$ for an attribute A_t, $1 \le t \le d$, where the domain values in each class g_y are arranged in any order. The intuition of our encryption scheme is modeling the equivalence of the domain values in the same class g_y by encoding each domain value into an angle and by exploiting the periodicity of circular functions sin and cos over such angles. Let v be the domain value v at the x-th position in the class g_y. We encode v by the angle computed by

$$\alpha(v) = y\frac{\pi}{l} + (x-1)\pi \tag{3}$$

where $1 \le x \le |g_y|$ and $0 \le y \le l - 1$. In other words, the class label y determines the initial angle $y\frac{\pi}{l}$ for the class and each next value in the class adds an additional angle π. To compute $\alpha(v)$, we need to choose an assignment of class labels to classes and the order of values in a class, but any such assignment and order will do. The next lemma follows because any two values from the same class have the same first term $y\frac{\pi}{l}$.

Lemma 1. *For any two values (v, v') in the domain of A_t, $(\alpha(v) - \alpha(v'))$ is a multiple of π if and only if v and v' are from the same class of A_t.*

Below, we construct each component of SSE_1. $KeyGen_1(1^{k_1})$ outputs the secret key $K_1 = M$, where M is a $(2d \times 2d)$ invertible matrix (i.e., $M^{-1}M$ is equal to the $(2d \times 2d)$ identity matrix) randomly chosen. The key size k_1 is implicitly specified by the data dimensionality d. If necessary, dummy attributes can be added to increase d. For simplicity, we omit K_1 in the following discussion.

Algorithm 2. $Enc_1(P_i)$

Require: The client has the secret key (M)

1. for $1 \le t \le d$
   (a) $\epsilon_{t,i} \xleftarrow{\$} [-U, -L] \cup [L, U]$, $(0 < L \le U)$
   (b)

$$I_i[t]_1 = \epsilon_{t,i} \sin(\alpha_t(P_i[t])) , \ \ I_i[t]_2 = \epsilon_{t,i} \cos(\alpha_t(P_i[t])) \tag{4}$$

2. $I_i = (I_i[1]_1, I_i[1]_2, \cdots, I_i[d]_1, I_i[d]_2)$
3.

$$Enc_1(P_i) = \frac{M^{-1}I_i}{|M^{-1}I_i|} \tag{5}$$

Algorithm 3. $Enc_{q,1}(Q_j)$

Require: The client has the secret key (M), $Att(Q_j) \neq \varnothing$

1. for $1 \leq t \leq d$
   (a) if A_t is in $Att(Q_j)$
      (i) $\mu_{t,j} \xleftarrow{\$} [-U, -L] \cup [L, U]$, $(0 < L \leq U)$
      (ii)

$$T_j[t]_1 = \mu_{t,j} \cos(\pi - \alpha_t(Q_j[t])) \quad , \quad T_j[t]_2 = \mu_{t,j} \sin(\pi - \alpha_t(Q_j[t])) \quad (6)$$

   (b) if A_t is not in $Att(Q_j)$

$$T_j[t]_1 = T_j[t]_2 = 0$$

2. $T_j = (T_j[1]_1, T_j[1]_2, \cdots, T_j[d]_1, T_j[d]_2)$
3.

$$Enc_{q,1}(Q_j) = \frac{M^T T_j}{|M^T T_j|} \quad (7)$$

Data Encryption. The detail of $Enc_1(P_i)$ is presented in Algorithm 2. Step 1 encodes each entry $P_i[t]$ into a pair $(I_i[t]_1, I_i[t]_2)$, where $\alpha(P_i[t])$ is the angle in Eq. (3) and $\epsilon_{t,i}$ is a noise randomly sampled from $[-U, -L] \cup [L, U]$ for t and i, $0 < L \leq U$. This (t, i)-specific noise is chosen independently for each record and each attribute. Step 2 assembles such pairs into a randomized $2d$-dimensional vector I_i. Step 3 blends all dimensions together using the private matrix M and produces $Enc_1(P_i)$ as a point on the $2d$-dimensional unit sphere centered at the origin. Note that the location of the point is randomized by the random noise $\epsilon_{t,i}$.

Query Encryption. Algorithm 3 gives the details for $Enc_{q,1}(Q_j)$. Step 1 encodes each specified $Q_j[t]$ into a pair $(T_j[t]_1, T_j[t]_2)$ using the angle $(\pi - \alpha_t(Q_j[t]))$, and encodes each unspecified $Q_j[t]$ into $(0, 0)$. Step 2 creates a randomized $2d$-dimensional vector T_j and Step 3 blends all dimensions together and produces $Enc_{q,1}(Q_j)$ as a randomized point on the $2d$-dimensional unit sphere centered at the origin.

Search Function. $Search_1$ computes the *candidate set* of the query Q_j, denoted by $Cand(Q_j)$, as the set of $Enc_2(P_i)$ such that $(Enc_1(P_i), Enc_2(P_i))$ is in $Enc(\mathcal{D})$ and $P_i[t]$ is in the same class as $Q_j[t]$ for every $A_t \in Att(Q_j)$. $Cand(Q_j)$ contains the query result and possibly false positives. The next lemma gives the computation of $Cand(Q_j)$. By "P_i is in $Cand(Q_j)$", we mean "$Enc_2(P_i)$ is in $Cand(Q_j)$".

Lemma 2. *If P_i is in $Cand(Q_j)$, $Enc_{q,1}(Q_j)^T Enc_1(P_i) = 0$. If P_i is not in $Cand(Q_j)$, $Enc_{q,1}(Q_j)^T Enc_1(P_i) = 0$ holds with an exceedingly small probability.*

Proof. From Eqs. (5) and (7), we have

$$Enc_{q,1}(Q_j)^T Enc_1(P_i) = \frac{T_j^T I_i}{|M^T T_j||M^{-1} I_i|} \tag{8}$$

where the superscript T denotes a transpose operation. $Enc_{q,1}(Q_j)^T Enc_1(P_i) = 0$ holds if and only if $T_j^T I_i = \sum_{t=1}^{d}(I_i[t]_1 T_j[t]_1 + I_i[t]_2 T_j[t]_2) = 0$. Since $T_j[t]_1 = T_j[t]_2 = 0$ for all A_t which are not in $Att(Q_j)$, from Eqs. (4) and (6), we have

$$T_j^T I_i = \sum_{A_t \in Att(Q_j)} \epsilon_{t,i} \mu_{t,j} \sin(\Delta_t) \tag{9}$$

where $\Delta_t = (\pi + \alpha_t(P_i[t]) - \alpha_t(Q_j[t]))$. If P_i is in $Cand(Q_j)$, $P_i[t]$ and $Q_j[t]$ are in the same class for every $A_t \in Att(Q_j)$, so Δ_t is a multiple of π (Lemma 1) and $\sin(\Delta_t) = 0$. In this case, $Enc_{q,1}(Q_j)^T Enc_1(P_i) = 0$ holds. If P_i is not in $Cand(Q_j)$, $P_i[t]$ and $Q_j[t]$ are not in the same class for some $A_t \in Att(Q_j)$, and Δ_t is not a multiple of π (Lemma 1), so $\sin(\Delta_t) \neq 0$. In this case, the chance that $T_j^T I_i = 0$ holds in a small probability because noises ϵ's and μ's are randomly chosen. □

From Lemma 2, the server can compute $Cand(Q_j)$ by computing the *hyperplane query* defined by $Enc_{q,1}(Q_j)^T V = 0$ for a $2d$-dimensional point V. Therefore, computing the candidate set is transformed into a hyperplane query in the ciphertext space, which enables any existing sub-linear methods for hyperplane queries to be deployed by the server, such as R-Tree [20], M-Tree [6] and halfspace queries [23]. As these methods are well studied, we do not further discuss their details.

Remark 2. It is interesting to compare our approach with the bucketization approach [11–13]. Our candidate set is similar to the result retrieved using the bucket ids of the query in bucketization. The difference is that bucketization requires the client to perform local search of bucket ids for a query, whereas the client in our approach only needs to encrypt the query. Bucketization requires the client to filter false positives, whereas our approach filters false positives by the server (through SSE_2). Finally, bucket ids in bucketization are static, thus, directly tell what records are in the same bucket, whereas our encryption functions are probabilistic thanks to fresh random noises for each encryption.

4.3 Constructing Class Partitioning

While we expect that the class partitioning $\mathcal{X}_t = \{g_0, \cdots, g_{l-1}\}$ for an attribute A_t is specified by the data owner, the class partitioning can also be constructed to minimize a cost metric for a given class size $|g_y|$, $1 \leq y \leq l - 1$, which is useful if the data owner has no preference except that each class must have a minimum size. Below, we give a construction of $\mathcal{X}_t = \{g_0, \cdots, g_{l-1}\}$ to minimize the number of false positives in the candidate set, thus, the search cost of the linear time $Search_2$.

The cost metric is minimized with respect to a chosen query workload. For simplicity, we consider only queries with a single equality. For each attribute A_t, the query workload is denoted by $\{Q_1, \cdots, Q_{|A_t|}\}$ where Q_j, $1 \leq j \leq |A_t|$, denotes the query with the single equality $A_t = v_j$. We assume that the frequency for Q_j, $1 \leq j \leq |A_t|$, denoted by f_j, is known. Let O_j, $1 \leq j \leq |A_t|$, be the number of records in the database $\mathcal{D}$ having $A_t = v_j$. Consider a value class $g_y = \{v_1, \cdots, v_\kappa\}$ for A_t. For a query Q_j, all records having a value $v_k \in g_y - v_j$ are false positives, so the cost of false positives is $Cost(g_y, Q_j) = \Sigma_{v_k \in g_y - v_j} O_k f_j$ (recall that each false positive is returned f_j times). The cost of false positives related to g_y for all queries is $Cost(g_y) = \sum_{v_j \in g_y} Cost(g_y, Q_j)$, and the cost of all false positives is $Cost(\mathcal{X}_t) = \Sigma_{y=0}^{l-1} Cost(g_y)$.

Definition 4 (Optimal κ-sized class partitioning). *Given a class size $\kappa > 1$ such that $|A_t|$ is divisible by κ and $l = \frac{|A_t|}{\kappa}$, $(O_1, \cdots, O_{|A_t|})$ and $(f_1, \cdots, f_{|A_t|})$ specified above, find a class partitioning for the attribute A_t, $\mathcal{X}_t = \{g_0, \cdots, g_{l-1}\}$, such that $Cost(\mathcal{X}_t)$ is minimized and all g_y have the size κ.*

This problem can be solved as an instance of the following *r-way equipartition problem* for which a branch-and-cut algorithm exists [14]: divide the vertices of a weighted graph $G = (V, E)$ into r equally sized sets, so as to minimize the total weight of edges that have both endpoints in the same set. To solve the optimal class partitioning problem, we can define the graph $G = (V, E)$ as follows: $V = \{1, \cdots, |A_t|\}$ and $E = \{(i, j) \mid 1 \leq i < j \leq |A_t|\}$, where for each edge $(i, j) \in E$, the weight $w_{(i,j)} = O_i f_j + O_j f_i$. Let $r = l = \frac{|A_t|}{\kappa}$. Intuitively, $w_{(i,j)}$ is the total number of false positives for queries Q_i and Q_j if i and j are grouped into the same class. It can be shown that $\mathcal{X}_t = \{g_0, \cdots, g_{l-1}\}$ is an optimal κ-sized class partitioning if and only if $\mathcal{X}_t$ is an optimal solution to the *r*-way equipartition problem for $G = (V, E)$.

5   Security Analysis

We formally prove that $SSE = (SSE_1, SSE_2)$ presented in Sect. 4 achieves *class indistinguishability* (Definition 3). In other words, the adversary can not win the probabilistic game defined in Definition 3 with significantly greater probability than an adversary who must guess randomly. Intuitively, this is achieved by the same probability of the records (queries) from the same class given the observed ciphertext of a record (query) produced by SSE_1 (as shown in Lemma 3) so that the adversary can not distinguish two histories in the probabilistic game which are restricted to the same history class.

Lemma 3. *(i) For any 2d-dimensional vector V, $\Pr[Enc_1(P_i) = V] = \Pr[Enc_1(P_i') = V]$ holds for any records P_i and P_i' from the same record class. (ii) For any 2d-dimensional vector V, $\Pr[Enc_{q,1}(Q_j) = V] = \Pr[Enc_{q,1}(Q_j') = V]$ holds for any queries Q_j and Q_j' from the same query class.*

Proof. We give a brief proof for (i) only; the proof of (ii) is similar. Since P_i and P'_i are from the same class, in Eq. (4), each $\alpha(P_i[t])$ and $\alpha(P'_i[t])$, $1 \leq t \leq d$, differ by a multiple of π according to Lemma 1. This means $\sin(\alpha_t(P'_i[t])) = \theta \sin(\alpha_t(P_i[t]))$ and $\cos(\alpha_t(P'_i[t])) = \theta \cos(\alpha_t(P_i[t]))$ where θ is either + or - sign. The random noises ϵ from the symmetric distribution would cancel the effect of θ, that is, for any (v_1, v_2), $\Pr[(I_i[t]_1, I_i[t]_2) = (v_1, v_2)]$ equals $\Pr[(I'_i[t]_1, I'_i[t]_2) = (v_1, v_2)]$. Therefore, $\Pr[Enc_1(P_i) = V] = \Pr[Enc_1(P'_i) = V]$.

In the following, we first show that SSE_1 ensures strict class indistinguishability and then show that SSE composed by SSE_1 and SSE_2 achieves class indistinguishability.

Theorem 1. SSE_1 *constructed in Sect. 4.2 meets strict class indistinguishability, i.e.,* $\Pr[\boldsymbol{Ind}_{SSE_1,\mathcal{A}}(k_1) = 1] = \frac{1}{2}$.

Proof. Consider two histories H_0 and H_1 chosen by the adversary in Definition 3. H_0 and H_1 are from the same class and have the same trace. The challenger randomly chooses $b \in \{0, 1\}$ to encrypt $(\mathcal{D}_b, \mathcal{Q}_b)$ with Enc_1 and $Enc_{q,1}$ and sends the results to the adversary. From Lemma 3, H_0 and H_1 are equally likely to be the underlying history based on the observed ciphertexts. This remains true even if the adversary is allowed to compute the candidate set $Cand(Q_{b,j})$, $1 \leq j \leq m$, because $Cand(Q_{0,j})$ and $Cand(Q_{1,j})$ have the same size. Finally, any index structure $\mathbf{I}$ constructed using $Enc_1(P_{b,i})$, $1 \leq i \leq n$, discloses no more information than $Enc_1(P_{b,i})$ does. So the adversary gains no advantage in guessing the value of b from accessing $\mathbf{I}_b$ and $\mathbf{t}_b$ computing the queries. $\square$

Theorem 2. *Let SSE_1 be constructed in Sect. 4.2 and let SSE_2 be any scheme meeting ciphertext indistinguishability (say [7]). Then $SSE = (SSE_1, SSE_2)$ meets class indistinguishability, that is,* $|\Pr[\boldsymbol{Ind}_{SSE,\mathcal{A}}(k_1, k_2) = 1] - \frac{1}{2}| \leq negl(k_2)$ *where k_2 is the security parameter of SSE_2.*

Proof. Consider the two histories $H_0 = (\mathcal{D}_0 = \{P_{0,1}, \cdots, P_{0,n}\}, \mathcal{Q}_0 = \{Q_{0,1}, \cdots, Q_{0,m}\})$ and $H_1 = (\mathcal{D}_1 = \{P_{1,1}, \cdots, P_{1,n}\}, \mathcal{Q}_1 = \{Q_{1,1}, \cdots, Q_{1,m}\})$, chosen by the adversary for SSE_1. Unlike SSE_1 alone, the adversary also has access to $Enc_2(P_{b,i})$ and $Enc_{q,2}(Q_{b,j})$, as well as $Cand(Q_{b,j})$, $1 \leq j \leq m$, computed by SSE_1. The ciphertext indistinguishability assumption of SSE_2 implies that the advantage in guessing the value of b from accessing $Enc_2(P_{b,i})$ and $Enc_{q,2}(Q_{b,j})$ is negligibly different from the probability $\frac{1}{2}$. This remains so even in the access to $Cand(Q_{b,j})$, $1 \leq j \leq m$, because $Cand(Q_{0,j})$ and $Cand(Q_{1,j})$ have the same size. Finally, this advantage is unaffected by running the game of SSE_1 because the adversary gains no advantage in the game of SSE_1 according to Theorem 1. $\square$

So far, we considered a non-adaptive adversary in Definition 3 where the adversary chooses all queries in the query sequences $\mathcal{Q}_0$ and $\mathcal{Q}_1$ before receiving the encryption of any record or query. An adaptive adversary can choose adaptively the next query pair $(Q_{0,j}, Q_{1,j})$ in the query sequences *after* receiving the encrypted records and encrypted queries for the previous queries

$\{Q_{b,1}, \cdots, Q_{b,j1}\}$. The strict class indistinguishability in Theorem 1 allows us to extend Theorems 1 and 2 to an adaptive adversary: the strict class indistinguishability implies that receiving the ciphertexts of previous queries does not give the adversary any advantage of guessing the value of b.

6   Evaluation

In this section, we evaluated CLASS presented in Sect. 4.

Data Sets. We used the **US Census data set** [1] which was collected from 2006 to 2011 with $d = 3$ categorical attributes: Race (237), PlaceOfBirth (531) and City (1134), with the domain size indicated in the bracket. $\mathcal{D}_{1M}$, $\mathcal{D}_{10M}$, $\mathcal{D}_{50M}$ and $\mathcal{D}_{100M}$, denote four samples containing the first 1, 10, 50, and 100 million records, respectively.

Queries. We generated a query pool $QW = Q^1 \cup \cdots \cup Q^d$ using $\mathcal{D}_{1M}$. For each integer $q \in [1, d]$, Q^q contains 100 q-equality queries generated as follows. Let Q^q_* contain all q-equality queries that have a non-empty result in $\mathcal{D}_{1M}$. Let Sel_Q denote the *selectivity* of a query Q, defined as the percentage of records in the data that satisfy the query. We picked 100 queries Q from Q^q_*. The probability of picking a query Q is modeled by the beta distribution $Beta(\alpha, \beta)$ of the selectivity sel_Q [8]. In general, with a fixed β a smaller α leads to a higher probability for a query with a smaller selectivity. We set $\alpha = 0.5$ and $\beta = 3$, which assigns a higher probability to a query having a smaller selectivity, modeling the typical scenario that more queries retrieve more specific information.

Competing Methods. For CLASS, we implemented the sub-linear method $Search_1$ for hyperplane queries by M-Tree [6] and the linear method $Search_2$ by Secure Index [9]. Since [9] deals with only single-keyword search, we convert equality conjunction queries to single-keyword search by treating each conjunction up to the maximum number of equalities in a query as a new keyword. We used the method in Sect. 4.3 to construct the class partitioning for each attribute for a given class size κ with the single equality queries Q^1_* as the input. By *default*, we set the class size as $\kappa = 6$, and the bounds for the noise interval as $L = 1000$ and $U = 1100$.

   We consider two baselines. We provide brief outlines of the baselines as follows to keep the paper self-contained. Please refer to the references for more details. The first baseline is OXT, the state-of-the-art sub-linear search for conjunctive keywords queries [5]. OXT uses a disk-resident data structure $TSet$ to locate the documents containing the least frequent keyword in the query, called s-term, and uses a RAM-resident data structure $XSet$ to filter the result using the remaining keywords in the query, called x-terms. The second baseline, denoted by SI, is Secure Index [9] applied to the full database following the same strategy of converting equality conjunction queries to single-keyword search as described above for $Search_2$ in CLASS. We wrote all codes in C++ and leveraged OpenSSL library to implement cryptographic primitives. We simulated both the server and the client by a Linux machine with a single Intel Core i7 CPU with 2.3 GHz and 16 GB RAM.

6.1   Setup Cost

At system initialization, there is a one-time *setup cost*. Here, we focus on the storage overhead. For $\mathcal{D}_{1M}$, the storage overhead of SI, CLASS and OXT are 16 MB, 139 MB and 1.2 GB, respectively. The storage overhead for other sample sizes scales up linearly. These structures were stored on the server side, thus, there is no client side storage overhead. Since these structures were generated by the client, they also represent the upload communication cost at setup. OXT uses most storage and SI uses least storage.

6.2   Query Cost

For each query, We focus on query computing time (averaged over the queries in QW). Note that we omit the comparison on communication cost because our method has the minimum communication cost by filtering false positives on the server side. Figure 2 reports query time in log scale vs four different data cardinality. For $\mathcal{D}_{100M}$, we could not get OXT's query time due to long database encryption time. In fact, OXT hides the entries on an inverted list by storing them in random locations on disk, which results in a large number of random I/O accesses during index construction and query process. As expected, the query time of SI grows linearly with data cardinality. However, SI took about 1000 s on $\mathcal{D}_{100M}$ which is too slow for large databases. It is clear that CLASS outperforms SI and OXT.

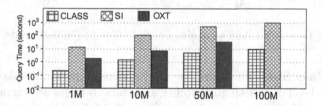

Fig. 2. Query time vs data cardinality

The efficiency of CLASS relies on the sub-linear Candidate Phase to reduce the search space of the linear Filtering Phase to a small candidate set. We measure this effectiveness by two metrics:

$$candidate\_size = \frac{|Cand|}{|\mathcal{D}|}, \qquad search\_size = \frac{|Test|}{|\mathcal{D}|}$$

where *Cand* denotes the candidate set computed by Candidate Phase and *Test* denotes the set of records that are searched in Candidate Phase to compute *Cand*. *search_size* measures the reduction of search space in Candidate Phase whereas *candidate_size* measures the reduction of search space in Filtering Phase. In all data sets tested, *candidate_size* is no more than 0.1% and *search_size* is no more than 4%. For example, the average total query time of CLASS on $\mathcal{D}_{50M}$ is less than 6 s. In the following, we study the effect of other factors to the efficiency of CLASS based on $\mathcal{D}_{50M}$.

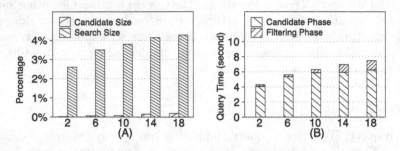

Fig. 3. Query time of CLASS vs value class size κ (50M Records)

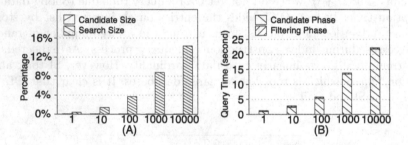

Fig. 4. Query time of CLASS vs nosize interval $(U - L)$ (50M Records, $L = 1000$)

Effect of Class Size. The class size κ of a class partitioning plays a role in balancing the level of indistinguishability and the sub-linear search performance. We studies the effect of the class size $\kappa \in \{2, 6, 10, 14, 18\}$ (x-axis) on query time. As shown in Fig. 3, a larger κ leads to larger *search_size* and *candidate_size* due to more data tested in Candidate Phase and more false positives in the candidate set *Cand*. Despite this trend, even for $\kappa = 18$, *Cand* is 0.2% of the full data set. This significantly reduces the time of Filtering Phase that is applied to the candidate set, as shown in Fig. 3(B). In all cases, the total average query time of the two phases is no more than 8 s. This study clearly shows that the sub-linear Candidate Phase is highly effective in pruning the search space.

Effect of Random Noises. Fig. 4 examines the impact of the interval $[-U, -L] \cup [L, U]$ for drawing random noises ϵ, μ in Enc_1 and $Enc_{q,1}$. We fixed the lower limit $L = 1000$ and varied the size $(U - L)$ (x-axis). A larger $(U - L)$ leads to more random noises injected, thus less effective indexed search in Candidate Phase as shown by the larger *search_size*. However, even with the maximum $(U - L) = 10000$, *candidate_size* remains very small, which suggests that restricting Filtering Phase to the candidate set is highly effective. In general, Filtering

Phase employs crypto primitives for producing the exact query result, therefore, it is more important to reduce the search space in this phase. Our two phase search exactly achieves this goal.

7   Conclusion

A key challenge of outsourcing data management is providing a provable security guarantee (e.g., ciphertext indistinguishability) while supporting a sub-linear search performance for dealing with large databases. The existing bucketization approach partially addresses this requirement at the cost of client performing search or increased communication cost of transmitting false positives. We proposed a novel SSE scheme, called CLASS, that provides a similar level of security to that of bucketization and pushes the work of search and false positive filtering tasks to the server. CLASS is a "framework" of sub-linear search through a two-phase search in which the search algorithms in both phases can be instantiated by existing methods.

Acknowledgments. This work was partially supported by a Discovery Grant from Canada's NSERC.

References

1. IPUMS US census data set. https://www.ipums.org
2. Ballard, L., Kamara, S., Monrose, F.: Achieving efficient conjunctive keyword searches over encrypted data. In: Qing, S., Mao, W., López, J., Wang, G. (eds.) ICICS 2005. LNCS, vol. 3783, pp. 414–426. Springer, Heidelberg (2005). https://doi.org/10.1007/11602897_35
3. Boldyreva, A., Chenette, N., Lee, Y., O'Neill, A.: Order-preserving symmetric encryption. In: Joux, A. (ed.) EUROCRYPT 2009. LNCS, vol. 5479, pp. 224–241. Springer, Heidelberg (2009). https://doi.org/10.1007/978-3-642-01001-9_13
4. Bösch, C.T., Hartel, P.H., Jonker, W., Peter, A.: A survey of provably secure searchable encryption. ACM Comput. Surv., 1125–1134 (2014)
5. Cash, D., Jarecki, S., Jutla, C., Krawczyk, H., Roşu, M.-C., Steiner, M.: Highly-scalable searchable symmetric encryption with support for boolean queries. In: Canetti, R., Garay, J.A. (eds.) CRYPTO 2013. LNCS, vol. 8042, pp. 353–373. Springer, Heidelberg (2013). https://doi.org/10.1007/978-3-642-40041-4_20
6. Ciaccia, P., Patella, M., Zezula, P.: M-tree: an efficient access method for similarity search in metric spaces. In: VLDB (1997)
7. Curtmola, R., Garay, J., Kamara, S., Ostrovsky, R.: Searchable symmetric encryption: improved definitions and efficient constructions. In: CCS (2006)
8. Falls, L.W.: The beta distribution: a statistical model for world cloud cover. J. Geophys. Res. **79**, 1261–1264 (1974)
9. Goh, E.J.: Secure indexes. IACR (2003)
10. Golle, P., Staddon, J., Waters, B.: Secure conjunctive keyword search over encrypted data. In: Jakobsson, M., Yung, M., Zhou, J. (eds.) ACNS 2004. LNCS, vol. 3089, pp. 31–45. Springer, Heidelberg (2004). https://doi.org/10.1007/978-3-540-24852-1_3

11. Hacigümüş, H., Iyer, B., Li, C., Mehrotra, S.: Executing SQL over encrypted data in the database-service-provider model. In: SIGMOD (2002)
12. Hore, B., Mehrotra, S., Canim, M., Kantarcioglu, M.: Secure multidimensional range queries over outsourced data. VLDB **21**, 333–358 (2012)
13. Hore, B., Mehrotra, S., Tsudik, G.: A privacy-preserving index for range queries. In: VLDB (2004)
14. Ji, X., Mitchell, J.E.: Branch-and-price-and-cut on the clique partitioning problem with minimum clique size requirement. Discrete Optim. **4**, 87–102 (2007)
15. Kamara, S., Moataz, T.: Boolean searchable symmetric encryption with worst-case sub-linear complexity. In: Coron, J.-S., Nielsen, J.B. (eds.) EUROCRYPT 2017. LNCS, vol. 10212, pp. 94–124. Springer, Cham (2017). https://doi.org/10.1007/978-3-319-56617-7_4
16. Li, M., Yu, S., Cao, N., Lou, W.: Authorized private keyword search over encrypted data in cloud computing. In: ICDCS (2011)
17. Lin, W., Wang, K., Zhang, Z., Chen, H.: Revisiting security risks of asymmetric scalar product preserving encryption and its variants. In: ICDCS (2017)
18. Oliveira, S.R., Zaiane, O.R.: Privacy preserving clustering by data transformation. In: SBBD (2003)
19. Popa, R.A., Redfield, C., Zeldovich, N., Balakrishnan, H.: CryptDB: protecting confidentiality with encrypted query processing. In: SOSP (2011)
20. R-Tree. https://en.wikipedia.org/wiki/R-tree
21. Stefanov, E., et al.: Path ORAM: an extremely simple oblivious ram protocol. In: CCS (2013)
22. Sweeney, L.: k-anonymity: a model for protecting privacy. Int. J. Uncertain. Fuzziness Knowl.-Based Syst. **10**, 557–570 (2002)
23. Wang, P., Ravishankar, C.V.: Secure and efficient range queries on outsourced databases using $\hat{R}$-tree. In: ICDE (2013)
24. Wong, W.K., Cheung, D.W.L., Kao, B., Mamoulis, N.: Secure kNN computation on encrypted databases. In: SIGMOD (2009)
25. Yi, X., Kaosar, M.G., Paulet, R., Bertino, E.: Single-database private information retrieval from fully homomorphic encryption. TKDE, 1125–1134 (2013)
26. Zhang, Y., Katz, J., Papamanthou, C.: All your queries are belong to us: the power of file-injection attacks on searchable encryption. Usenix (2016)

A Hybrid Approach for Synchronizing Clocks in Distributed Systems

Md Shohel Khan⊙, Ratul Sikder⊙, and Muhammad Abdullah Adnan$^{(\boxtimes)}$⊙

Bangladesh University of Engineering and Technology (BUET), Dhaka, Bangladesh
shohel.expo@gmail.com, ratulsikder121@gmail.com, abdullah.adnan@gmail.com

Abstract. The art of synchronizing clocks across a wide area network has got a new dimension when it comes to the reality of achieving the demand for high-accuracy synchronization; even for local or small computing systems. Before implementing any clock synchronization protocol, some important aspects must be considered. For example, communication latency- is it fixed or variable? Does there exist any reference clock in the system or not? In this paper, we have studied the standard and experimental protocols for synchronizing clocks over a geographically distributed network and implemented the features of the Network Time Protocol (NTP) combined with the timing signal of Global Positioning System (GPS) for synchronizing distributed system's clocks more accurately. Our proposed system can achieve higher clock synchronization accuracy compared to the traditional NTP clock synchronization protocol with the help of our designed decentralized GPS-based NTP servers.

Keywords: Clock synchronization · Reference clock ·
Distributed system · Communication latency · NTP · GPS

1 Introduction

Clock synchronization in a distributed system can be referred to clock recovery which is achieved by frequent synchronization in serial communication. The mechanism of implementing a clock synchronization system depends on which protocol we are going to implement. Clock synchronization protocols can be distinguished by several significant properties like logical vs physical time synchronization, external vs internal synchronization, a priori vs posteriori synchronization. Another important thing is the performance metrics behind the implementation of clock synchronization in a system. Precision, synchronization error, energy cost, memory requirement, implementation cost, fault tolerance, scalability, etc. are some of the most important performance metrics [14].

The problem of physical clocks is that these are subject to drift and only some precise atomic clocks have a very negligible drift. The difference between any two clocks is called skew. A token ring approach was proposed to solve the problem of synchronizing distributed system's clocks [8]. However, this system is unable to

© Springer Nature Switzerland AG 2019
D. Da Silva et al. (Eds.): CLOUD 2019, LNCS 11513, pp. 271–286, 2019.
https://doi.org/10.1007/978-3-030-23502-4_19

ensure high precision and scalability. On the other hand, the NTP (Network Time Protocol) is a widely used protocol and it provides microsecond precision whereas the PTP (Precision Time Protocol) provides sub-microsecond precision but this protocol requires PTP-enabled devices. Datacenter Time Protocol (DTP) offers nanosecond precision but it also requires DTP-enabled devices [9].

In this paper, we have proposed a decentralized GPS device-based approach over an NTP network to achieve relative improvements in clock synchronization accuracy compared to the traditional NTP protocol. Our objective is to minimize latency, cost and hardware dependency. According to our proposed mechanism, some low-layered strata computers are equipped with GPS time synchronizers. Relatively small UDP synchronization packets are sent over a secured channel to synchronize with GPS-enabled NTP's (GNTP) neighboring clients' clock. The selection for transforming a member of the network into GNTP solely dependents on the stratum number of that member, location of data centers and the accuracy over the cost factor.

For achieving our goal, we have developed an algorithm having the mechanism of comparing the values of the NTP server and the GNTP server's time accuracy to synchronize the clients' clock for higher precision. We first mapped the NTP nodes to find the positions which need to be transformed into GNTP and then we modified the clients and the servers to work with it. The *key contributions* of this work are to modify the NTP servers and the clients to handle the GPS enabled NTP node (GNTP) for neighboring devices' clock synchronization to achieve better accuracy. This includes the NTP network remapping, the appropriate nodes selection, and the synchronization of the neighboring nodes to the GNTP servers. We have also compared the regular NTP synchronization against our modified GNTP clock synchronization.

For testing and evaluating our proposed system, we have set up an appropriate scenario for the experimental analysis. Our system worked fine bearing the common characteristics of other WAN based clock synchronization. Comparing our system with the nationwide NTP clock synchronization servers, we have found a much better accuracy level with the presence of our proposed GNTP node. Both the drift and the RTT become smaller in our GNTP based clock synchronization system.

The rest of the paper is organized in the following sections. In Sect. 2, we briefly describe the existing works as well as the pros and the cons, and challenges of those works on clock synchronization in the distributed system. Section 3 explains our proposed model- a hybrid approach to synchronize distributed systems' clock more precisely than the traditional NTP clock synchronization. In Sect. 4, we have discussed the implementation of our proposed model, the modifications of the NTP server and the client. This section also includes the experimental analysis of the implemented system. Applications of our findings, discussions as well as concluding notes are addressed in Sect. 6.

2 Background Study

Clock synchronization plays an important role in establishing a distributed system. For example, if we consider a distributed and live e-auction, the system must know which bidder submitted their bid first for any of the two bidders. In a distributed system, at any moment, the values of all nonfaulty clocks should be nearly equal. If we could find out the difference between two clocks' values, then the result should be negligible. Sometimes knowing the order of the events is enough; this is known as logical time. But, in most of the other cases, the devices need to be synchronized accurately with respect to the physical time.

Every computer contains a hardware clock which operates by counting the oscillation of crystal. To keep track of the current time, the software clock of the computer uses the hardware clock. As the hardware clock varies over time, slowly the time information becomes inaccurate which results in different values of two different clocks at any point in time. This misdemeanor can lose up to 40 ms in every second [6] and the difference between the two clocks is known as their skew. To minimize the clock drifting a token ring approach was proposed where the clocks were synchronized both internally and externally [8].

There are several ways to synchronize the physical clock. If all the computers in a system are synchronized by an external source like UTC signal, then the method is considered as external synchronization. But internal synchronization doesn't require an external source. In this type of synchronization, the clocks in the different computers are synchronized with one another. Internal synchronization is used where time needs not to be necessarily accurate with respect to the precise UTC time [14].

Clock synchronization would be straightforward if the system had bounds on message transmission time. In that case, the lower and the upper bounds on the message transmission time were known. If a process sends a message to another process with its current time t, then the 2nd process sets its clock to

$$t + (min + max)/2 \tag{1}$$

and the skew is at most

$$(max - min)/2 \tag{2}$$

Where, *min* and *max* are the *lower* and the *upper* bounds of the message transmission time respectively.

Cristian's method [1] is another popular synchronization method and it does not depend on the preset lower and upper bounds of the message transmission time between two synchronizing nodes. Rather when a process P_1 requests current time from another process P_2, it calculates the Round Trip Time (RTT) of the request. When P_1 receives the current time from P_2, it sets its clock to

$$t + T_{round}/2 \tag{3}$$

Reference-Broadcast Synchronization (RBS) synchronizes clocks using physical-layer broadcasts called reference beacons [3]. The receiver nodes use arrival time for comparing and synchronizing their local clocks and achieved microsecond-level precision to an external time source.

Spanner uses TrueTime clock synchronization protocol for its geographically distributed datacenters. This industry-level high precision protocol guarantees logically incremental timestamps across the datacenters with high constancy. According to Spanner, if any event T_2 starts to commit after another event T_1 finishes committing, then the timestamp of T_2 must be larger than the timestamp for T_1 [2].

Generally, we assume that all the nodes are interconnected in a system, but this is not a permanent scenario. Sometimes the network is more complex; for example, each node knows only one or two of its neighboring nodes. In this case, achieving high precision in clock synchronization is very much challenging. Li et al. (2017), assume each clock as a node in the system [10] and based on different topological structures in a distributed system, they have designed three control algorithms for clock synchronization under three cases- with a reference clock, without a reference clock, and with a fixed communication delay in the networking system.

Madrigal and Tenor (2014) worked on two geographically distributed clock where one clock dwell in a device that is used to acquire sensor data and the other is in a computing system that is used to receive them [5]. They dealt with the problem of estimating the values of relative offset and the clock's rate. They have implemented their proposed method in remote control applications based on remotely transmitted sensor data. Reichman et al. (2015), have worked on a wireless mesh network that is non-centralized and non-hierarchical and has distributed synchronization process [13]. The synchronization process depends on the periodical transportation of messages with the timing data by all the nodes, and the timing messages can be re-transported to other nodes.

Sometimes it is sufficient to be aware of the order of the events. But, if we think of a large distributed system then we need some mechanisms to ensure synchronization in the first place. Park and Kim (2016) have introduced a method which is based on PALS (Physically Asynchronous Logically Synchronous) which is a complexity-reducing architectural pattern for a distributed system which allows the developers to design and implement logically synchronous applications [12].

Yong et al. (2015), have surveyed that the traditional clock synchronization solutions like IEEE1588 and NTP protocols depend on software-based synchronization along with message passing mechanism [16]. As a result, the processing time of software and message transmission delay gain the clock synchronization precision in milliseconds. But that is not an acceptable result where the precision requirement is much higher. To get rid of this situation and make the precision higher, they have introduced a physical clock signal at 1PPS (Pulse Per Second) and that was able to implement external clock synchronization decently. They have used FPGA (Field-Programmable Gate Array) hard logic to track and lock every 1PPS. Using these they have generated synchronization clock (S-Clock) and then the system has finally got higher precision and higher resolution clock in the local crystal clock domain.

Highly reliable and synchronous distributed system is essential for industrial applications. In these systems, the nodes synchronize them with the local clock. Vigner and Breuer (2013) have proved that instead of the local clock, the GPS timing signal can be more effective in terms of synchronization accuracy [15]. The distance between two master clocks can be up to 1000 km. Each master clock updates its time by catching the GPS signal through a GPS receiver. Then the master clocks communicate among themselves to make the system synchronous. We have also implemented a decentralized approach to synchronize the clock in a distributed system.

Clock synchronization protocols like Network Time Protocol and Precision Time Protocol are bounded by the disposition of the packet switching network. Lee et al. (2016) have presented Datacenter Time Protocol (DTP) that omits the data packets transmission and it can achieve nanosecond precision. It uses the physical layer of TCP protocol to implement DTP and it eliminates non-deterministic elements in synchronization protocol [9]. They showed a comparison between different protocols, and we have included our proposed protocol (GNTP) to the comparison table which is illustrated in Table 1.

Table 1. Comparison between different existing protocols with our proposed protocol [9]

Protocol	Precision	Scalability	Hardware requirements
NTP	us	Good	None
PTP	sub-us	Good	PTP-enabled devices
GPS	ns	Bad	Timing signal receivers, appropriate cables
DTP	ns	Good	DTP-enabled devices
GNTP	sub-us	Good	Timing signal receivers, cables

The application areas of clock synchronization are numerous. Some of the popular areas are- message delivery, cache consistency, active replication, GPS, GSM, CDMA and so on [7]. For many emerging applications and real-time systems in various domain like automation, smart power grid, etc., having a proper and precise clock synchronization mechanism is a prior condition. Lvesque and Tipper (2016) have surveyed the standard protocols and technologies for clock synchronization in a packet switched network to improve the accuracy when asymmetric delays are present [11]. Under variable channel delays, it is a challenging job but maintaining the cost-effectiveness, precision from microsecond to sub-microsecond is achievable.

3   Proposed Method

We propose a decentralized GPS device based approach over an NTP network to achieve improvements in clock synchronization accuracy compared to the traditional NTP infrastructure. We have considered the NTP's hierarchical architecture as a location-based circular layered design which helps to detect the more important geographic areas demanding greater clock synchronization accuracy. These areas could be equipped with a GPS enabled NTP server called GNTP server to achieve higher precision. A proper searching and routing model needs to be developed for implementing the GNTP servers. Our proposed method can be divided into three parts according to its relative domains: (i) NTP hierarchy conversion, (ii) GNTP selection, and (iii) synchronize nearby clocks with GNTP.

3.1   NTP Hierarchy Conversion

Network Time Protocol is the most used protocol for clock synchronization over a wide area network. NTP protocol generally delivers millisecond-level accuracy over WAN and microsecond-level accuracy over LAN. NTP uses a hierarchical structure and the time source is semi-layered. NTP creates a tree hierarchy and synchronizes all its node with each node's upper stratum layer. The top of the tree is called stratum-0; normally contains an atomic clock, GPS receiver, and other necessary circuits for achieving and maintaining the precise time. Stratum-0 is the time server for stratum-1 computers. Stratum-1 computers are the time servers for stratum-2 computers and so on. It is a server-client based approach where each node except stratum-0, acts as both server and client.

If we assume stratum-0 as the center of a circular NTP network and higher strata nodes as corresponding layers from the center then the overall network forms a circular structure. Stratum-1 devices form the perimeter of the first circular diagram; we can call the stratum-1 perimeter as layer 1 for the corresponding circle. In a similar fashion, we can imagine layer 2 consists of stratum-2 devices, layer 3 consists of stratum-3 devices and so on. The geographical location is considered forming these layers. Figure 2 illustrates this circular NTP network structure. The chronological, directional and geographical properties must be considered forming these layers. This means the circular layer shown in the Fig. 2 is not fully circular. Depending on the geographical coordinates, it becomes a circular type structure where physical locations are the elements of the circle. This circle with the circular layers is the reasoning building blocks of our proposed method.

3.2   GNTP Selection

GNTP is a new terminology used in this paper. It means GPS enabled NTP node. Any node in the NTP network having a GPS time receiver is considered as GNTP time server and thus we will find some additional accurate synchronizer for the network. As GPS time receiver has microsecond level precision, these GNTP servers also have this property (Fig. 1).

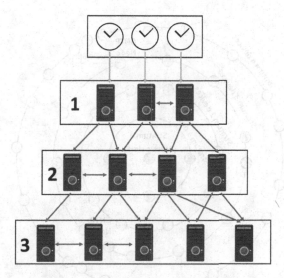

Fig. 1. A diagram showing the relationship between the various level of NTP hierarchy. The blue numbers are the stratum numbers; yellow arrows show direct connections, such as RS-232, while red arrows show networked connections [4]. (Color figure online)

There could possibly be some argument against this circular network visualization. The argument of considering a GNTP server as a stratum-0 device and imagining a new NTP network will simply be rejected because the GPS signal cannot be guaranteed to be available always because of the natural conditions. So, a GNTP node needs to synchronize its clock with its upper as well as the same layer devices rarely. Moreover, our proposed GNTP time server design does not involve an atomic clock. So, it can not be considered as a stratum-0 node.

The probability of generating more error to the clock synchronization accuracy on an NTP network is increased with respect to the increasing stratum number of the NTP network's nodes. This is due to the higher packet transmission delay, more middleman devices, long distance, etc. It means that the lower layers of the NTP tree having a high stratum number is prone to more clock synchronization error. NTP nodes can also use the nearby same stratum's nodes to synchronize its clock. It helps the nodes to fix some types of synchronization error but there is still some inaccuracy. By converting some nodes of the NTP network into GNTP, we can achieve more accuracy in the nearby nodes and the corresponding child tree. Here, child tree means the lower layered nodes which are connected to the GNTP node.

Selecting a node in the NTP network for the GNTP conversion is not a straightforward calculation. Whether a node will be selected for converting into GNTP or not, is solely depends on the cost to accuracy factor, the importance of a particular geographic area with respect to the expected accuracy level, etc.

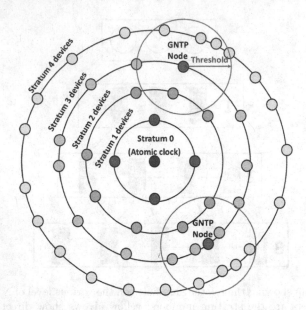

Fig. 2. A diagram showing the circular mapping of NTP hierarchy. The GNTP server can be installed on anywhere according to the demand.

3.3 Synchronize Nearby Clocks with GNTP

So far, we have proposed and discussed various factors of GNTP time server's design and goals. Our proposed GNTP is almost accurate regarding the atomic clock. Using these GNTP time servers to synchronize its nearby nodes, especially the nodes demanding more accurate time and the important systems which require more accuracy than traditional NTP synchronization, will improve the accuracy of the corresponding nodes and the accuracy of the child NTP nodes.

Now, the synchronization between our proposed server and client node is also an important factor in achieving higher precision. From our designing perspective and real networking system, this synchronization must be done over a wide area network such as the internet. For clock synchronization over the internet, NTP's original routing and transporting mechanism is well known and best suited for the purpose. So our GNTP server and client synchronization can be accomplished using the regular NTP protocol; only the timing information of the GNTP servers need to be fetched from the GPS receiver which is highly available. But a proper redirection and NTP server selection rules have to be enforced to each NTP client. The information about the GNTP servers and the relative distance information have to be kept by all the NTP clients. The next section will describe more about the implementation of the GNTP servers and the client nodes.

4   Implementation Details

Implementation of our proposed method in a real scenario needs to meet some challenges. The first challenge is transforming the right NTP nodes into GPS enabled NTP nodes or implementing new GNTP servers into the right position in the network. Eventually, it is the result of good NTP nodes mapping of the overall network and the synchronization demand. This includes re-configuring the existing servers and the clients, setting up the new rules and formations, etc. To achieve flexibility, it is possible to implement our proposed method in the software level only without the requirement of extra hardware except for GNTP servers. An extra server needs to be deployed as well for storing the GNTP servers' location which will in turns provide the nearest GNTP server(s) address to the requesting clients.

4.1   Implementing GNTP Info Servers

In our proposed method, the first challenge is to provide the nearest GNTP server's address to the clients. To keep the network simple and to achieve greater scalability, we have developed a global GNTP info server to provide the nearest GNTP server's address to the requesting clients.

A GNTP server is a global server which can be accessed by the clients on the network. This GNTP server stores the location information of every GPS enabled nodes in the corresponding network. Client node needs to send the request to the GNTP info server with its own location information to the GNTP info server in order to get the nearest GNTP server's address. The client location needs not to be highly accurate. The location retrieved from the client's very local router can be used for this purpose. In such type of request, our GNTP info server calculates the distance between client and GNTP servers and returns the IP address of the nearest GNTP server if any considering the distance threshold limit which can be configured according to the choice.

The other challenge regarding GNTP info server implementation is how each node of an NTP network knows the existence of a global GNTP info server address. This problem is resolved by a top to bottom approach for passing the GNTP info server's address from stratum-0 to stratum1, from stratum-1 to stratum-2, from stratum-3 to stratum-4 and so on. So, every node configured properly can know the address of the GNTP info server. On the other hand, to ensure the high availability of the GNTP info server, multiple distributed backup servers can be imposed.

4.2   NTP Nodes Mapping

In our proposed method, we have meant by *NTP nodes mapping* how we can achieve a circular mapping of NTP nodes, described in the previous section. Each NTP node maintains a file which will contain at least one or a few global servers (GNTP servers) of the corresponding NTP network that contains the address of the GNTP node. The principal job of this server is to provide the nearest GNTP

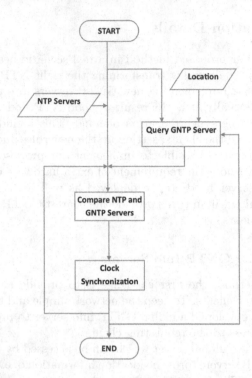

Fig. 3. Data flow diagram of the redesigned NTP client

server address to each NTP server as well as the client based on distance criteria. As GNTP is a static node and its address changes occasionally. New GNTP node is added infrequently as well. So, a typical NTP node will check for its nearby GNTP node in an infrequent fashion i.e. randomly two times per week. This will add very low pressure on those global servers (GNTP servers). Upon a successful GNTP discovery, its address will be locally stored by the corresponding node.

For the nearest GNTP calculation and mapping, each node must have its own exact or approximate geographical location which will be sent to the GNTP servers upon every GNTP discovery request. The GNTP servers must know its' location and update its' own address, and location to the global servers.

4.3   Modification to the NTP Servers and the Clients

We used custom UDP packets for our system's clock synchronization. The reference implementation of NTP protocol in the Java programming language is reused and modified according to our demand and structure. We first made our server program to work with GPS device, which delivered us the precise time information. We used this time information throughout our NTP server's system-wide clock. This time is also transmitted to the clients' machine according to the rules of NTP.

Result: Synchronize the client's clock
Input   : NTP Servers, Current Location, GNTP Info Server

while *Repeats in week* **do**
> $GNTPServers \leftarrow RequestGNTP(CurrentLocation)$;
>
> **while** *Repeats at synchronization frequency* **do**
> > $BestTimeServer \leftarrow Compare(NTPServers, GNTPServers)$;
> > Synchronize clock with $BestTimeServer$;
>
> **end**

end

Algorithm 1. Client Sync

On the other hand, our new modified NTP client checks for the nearest GNTP nodes at the beginning of its lifespan and it will continue checking for it twice per week at a random time. If a nearby GNTP client is found then it saves its address locally. When it comes to synchronization for the NTP client, it will check and compare the minimum delay among other NTP servers and GNTP servers. The server with the minimum delay is chosen and our NTP client synchronizes its clock with that.

We have developed a global server for storing the information about GNTP nodes. This global server's address is known by all nodes in an NTP network and this small information is passed in the top-to-bottom approach throughout the network. Our client request for GNTP nodes with its own location and in return it gets the closest GNTP server's information along with the distance between them. Depending on the distance threshold, defined by the system administrator, the client then decides to consider it or to go with the normal procedure of traditional NTP synchronization. We have summarized the concept through a data flow diagram in the Fig. 3.

Result: Return the best available time server
Input   : NTP Servers, GNTP Servers
Output: Best Time Server

$ServerAccuracyList \leftarrow NULL$;

foreach $NTP \leftarrow NTPServers$ **do**
> $ServerAccuracyList \leftarrow GetAccuracy(NTP)$;

end

foreach $GNTP \leftarrow GNTPServers$ **do**
> $ServerAccuracyList \leftarrow GetAccuracy(GNTP)$;

end

$SortAscending(ServerAccuracyList)$;

RETURN $ServerAccuracyList[FirstElement]$

Algorithm 2. Compare Time Servers

The concept shown in the Fig. 3 can be properly summarized in the Algorithms 1 and 2. Algorithm 1 shows how to synchronize the client's clock by finding the best available time servers. The best time server is found by comparing the NTP and the GNTP servers. The first loop repeats the procedure once or twice in a week: meaning that the discovery process of the nearby GNTP servers needs to perform merely. On the other hand, the second loop needs to repeat itself according to the required synchronization frequency. This generally varies from 5 to 10 s.

The Algorithm 2 shows the normal comparison procedure of the available time servers. This comparison depends on the NTP's *intersection algorithm* which is responsible to find the accuracy of any time server based on NTP protocol. After finding the accuracy of the available NTP and GNTP time servers, the best time server is returned to the Algorithm 1 and then the local system get synchronized its clock with the best time server.

5 Experimentation

We have set up an appropriate scenario for our experimentation. Setting up a full geographically distributed NTP network is challenging. Our proposed system's accuracy largely depends upon the availability of nearby GNTP nodes. Considering the situation, we have designed a similar structure for our experimentation. As expected, our experimental results show the basic characteristics of the clock synchronization system over a wide area network. Comparison of our work to the NTP, setting up the servers and the clients, etc are discussed below.

5.1 Setting up Servers and Clients

We have run our modified NTP server and client on Linux virtual server as well as a dedicated server. We used VirtualBox 5.2.18 as the virtualization platform. We used LinuxMint 19, a popular version of Linux distribution on our virtual machines and dedicated server for our testing. Our java programmes were run on OpenJDK 11 SDK. We have used two different networks for servers and clients to perform our experiments.

5.2 Experimental Results

From the resultant data of our proposed model, we have discussed four important graphs below. The performance and comparison are depicted with respect to different factors.

Offset vs Drift. We ran our designed clients and GNTP servers in different machines. The distance between the client and the GNTP server was about six kilometers. A dedicated workstation was used for time server with static

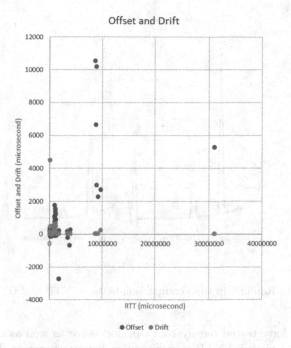

Fig. 4. A resulting graph showing offset and drift against RRT

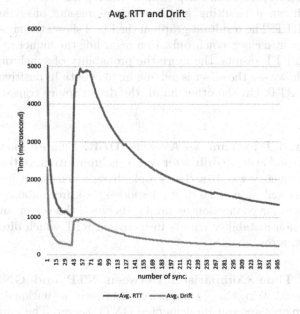

Fig. 5. Average RTT and drift- indicating connection stability.

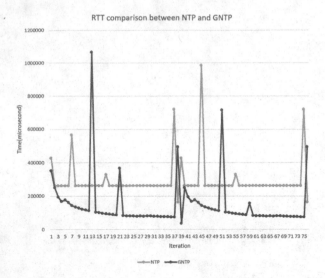

Fig. 6. Round trip time comparison between NTP and GNTP

IP address. We have tested our system's performance as well as have compared the results with a national NTP server. As the distance between the NTP server and client is greater, the round trip time is also higher.

We have drawn a resulting graph which represents offset and drift with respect to the RTT. The resultant graph in the Fig. 4 shows the non-deterministic nature of the error in clock synchronization regarding the higher round-trip time. The higher the RTT results, the more the probability of synchronization error. From the graph, we see the offset is getting higher (both in positive and negative axis) with the RTT. On the other hand, the drift is more consistent regarding RTT.

Average Round Trip Time vs Average Drift. Figure 5 shows the average round trip time and average drift after each synchronization. In the context, synchronization frequency was 10 s. The graph shows a consistent improvement on average RTT as well as average drift. A sudden peak from about 40th synchronization occurred for connection instability between the server and client. This type of connection instability results in increased RTT which directly increases synchronization error.

Round Trip Time Comparison Between NTP and GNTP. Figure 6 shows the round trip time comparison between a national NTP server (0.asia.pool.ntp.org) and our implemented GNTP server. The graph shows that the GNTP synchronization takes much lower RTT than the NTP. Lower distance results in lower RTT and greater synchronization accuracy as discussed earlier. The spikes in both the NTP and the GNTP's curves are result from connection instability, server's response time, etc. and it is a normal phenomenon in any kind of WAN-based communication.

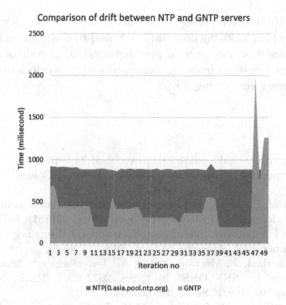

Fig. 7. Comparison of drift between NTP and GNTP servers

Comparison of Drift Between NTP vs GNTP Servers. As mentioned earlier, higher RTT is one of the main reasons for error in clock synchronization. The precision gets higher with respect to higher RTT as we have implemented a GNTP server closer to our client, the time inconsistency gets lower. As a result, the synchronization error has minimized and this improves the precision. Figure 7 shows the comparison of drift between a national NTP server (0.asia.pool.ntp.org) and our GNTP server.

6   Conclusion

We have implemented a hybrid method for synchronizing clocks in a distributed system which achieved better synchronization accuracy than the traditional NTP synchronization. Installing GNTP servers in more important regions according to the circular NTP hierarchy mapping with respect to the precision demand can decrease the synchronization error- that is a combined result of the lower RTT and the GNTP servers' higher accuracy. In a complex network, it is not always true that the observed nodes are interconnected; perhaps a node may only know its neighboring nodes. A global GNTP info server solves this problem in our work. Our proposed model is implemented and tested in some small-scaled geographically distributed virtual machines. Implementing and testing the system in a geographically large-scaled distributed real machines would led us to examine the existing and probably new factors on this domain more preciously. In the future, we have plans to extend this work in a large-scaled scenario and fine-tune the various threshold values according to the synchronization demand. Our work could be helpful where better clock synchronization accuracy is needed than the traditional NTP clock synchronization. Small to medium scaled distributed systems, embedded systems, peer to peer networking, as well as every personal computer, can get benefited from our proposed system as clock accuracy is more or less vital in every computing device.

References

1. Cristian's algorithm - wikipedia (2018). Accessed 24 Sept 2018
2. Brewer, E.: Spanner, truetime and the cap theorem. Google, Technical report (2017)
3. Elson, J., Girod, L., Estrin, D.: Fine-grained network time synchronization using reference broadcasts. ACM SIGOPS Oper. Syst. Rev. **36**(SI), 147–163 (2002)
4. Esham, B.D.: File:network time protocol servers and clients.svg - wikimedia commons, September 2007. Accessed 24 Sept 2018
5. Fernández-Madrigal, J., Martínez-Tenor, A.: Two-clocks synchronization for networked sensors. In: SENSORS, 2014, pp. 2022–2025. IEEE, November 2014. https://doi.org/10.1109/ICSENS.2014.6985431
6. Ganeriwal, S., Kumar, R., Srivastava, M.B.: Timing-sync protocol for sensor networks. In: Proceedings of the 1st International Conference on Embedded Networked Sensor Systems, pp. 138–149. ACM (2003)
7. Jerzak, Z.: Clock synchronization in distributed systems, September 2009. https://goo.gl/YvpQDv
8. Latha, C., Shashidhara, H.: Clock synchronization in distributed systems. In: 2010 International Conference on Industrial and Information Systems (ICIIS), pp. 475–480. IEEE (2010)
9. Lee, K.S., Wang, H., Shrivastav, V., Weatherspoon, H.: Globally synchronized time via datacenter networks. In: Proceedings of the 2016 ACM SIGCOMM Conference, SIGCOMM 2016, pp. 454–467. ACM, New York (2016). https://doi.org/10.1145/2934872.2934885, http://doi.acm.org/10.1145/2934872.2934885
10. Li, G., Niu, M.j., Chai, Y.s., Chen, X., Ren, Y.q.: A novel method of clock synchronization in distributed systems. Chin. Astron. Astrophys. **41**, 263–281 (2017)
11. Lévesque, M., Tipper, D.: A survey of clock synchronization over packet-switched networks. IEEE Commun. Surv. Tutor. **18**(4), 2926–2947 (2016, Fourthquarter). https://doi.org/10.1109/COMST.2016.2590438
12. Park, J., Kim, T.: A method of logically time synchronization for safety-critical distributed system. In: 2016 18th International Conference on Advanced Communication Technology (ICACT), pp. 356–359. IEEE (2016)
13. Reichman, A., Priesler, M., Wayer, S.: Distributed network synchronization. In: 2015 IEEE International Conference on Microwaves, Communications, Antennas and Electronic Systems (COMCAS), pp. 1–5. IEEE (2015)
14. Rollins, S.: Time synchronization (2015). Accessed 24 Sept 2018
15. Vigner, V., Breuer, J.: Precise synchronization in large distributed systems. In: 2013 IEEE 7th International Conference on Intelligent Data Acquisition and Advanced Computing Systems (IDAACS), vol. 1, pp. 226–230. IEEE (2013)
16. Yong, C., Hao, W., Xiaofeng, T., Wenbo, W.: Clock synchronization technology based on FPGA. In: 2015 IEEE International Conference on Communication Software and Networks (ICCSN), pp. 43–46. IEEE (2015)

JCallGraph: Tracing Microservices in Very Large Scale Container Cloud Platforms

Haifeng Liu[1,2]([✉]), Jinjun Zhang[1], Huasong Shan[1], Min Li[1], Yuan Chen[1],
Xiaofeng He[1], and Xiaowei Li[1]

[1] JD.com, Beijing, China
[2] University of Science and Technology of China, Hefei, China
{bjliuhaifeng,zhangjinjun1,huasong.shan,min.li,yuan.chen,
hexiaofeng,lixiaowei1}@jd.com

Abstract. Microservice architecture splits giant and complex enterprise applications into fine-grained microservices, promoting agile development, integration, delivery and deployment. However, monitoring tens of thousands of microservices is extremely challenging, and debugging problems among massive microservices is like looking for a needle in a haystack. We present JCallGraph, a tracing and analytics tool to capture and visualize the microservice invocation relationship of tens of thousands of microservices with millions of containers at JD.com. JCallGraph achieves three main goals for distributed tracing and debugging: online microservices invocation construction within milliseconds, minimal overhead without any significant performance impact on real-production applications, and application-agnostic with zero-intrusion to application. Our evaluation shows that JCallGraph can accurately capture the real-time invocation relationship at massive scale and help developers to efficiently understand interactions among microservices, pinpoint root-cause of problems.

Keywords: Microservice invocation graph ·
Distributed tracing system · Performance analysis and measurement

1 Introduction

Microservice architecture is increasingly embraced in enterprise in recent years due to its advantages and the advancement of container technologies [2–4,16, 20,25]. Compared to monolithic architectures, microservice paradigm breaks up complicated enterprise applications and software into smaller, modular, independent components communicating through lightweight mechanisms such as a HTTP RESTful API. Since the components can be developed and maintained independently, it allows better development agility, isolation, resilience and scalability. However, as the number of services continue to grow in microservice platforms, the communication between components becomes complex resulting

© Springer Nature Switzerland AG 2019
D. Da Silva et al. (Eds.): CLOUD 2019, LNCS 11513, pp. 287–302, 2019.
https://doi.org/10.1007/978-3-030-23502-4_20

in high maintenance cost. In particular, it is difficult to identify root causes when errors occur or diagnose performance bottlenecks as the interactions between microservices are too complex to trace.

At JD.com [10], the world's third largest and China's largest e-commerce site, we provide more than 8000 applications and approximate 34,000 microservices run on the cluster of 500,000 containers, and support over 250 billions of RPC-based microservice calls per day. A microservice typically interacts with hundreds or even thousands of other microservices, not to mention that these services are often deployed and executed across a large number of containers or machines for performance and reliability. Moreover, the interactions change dynamically when services evolve and are developed independently. Thus, it is difficult to trace the communications and detect the updated system behavior whenever a component is changed.

Existing distributed tracing systems, such as Google's Dapper [24], Mace [11], Stardust [19], X-Trace [6], Retro [13], Pivot Tracing [14], can be used to monitor and trace the timing and interactions of system components. Yet, they cannot be directly applied into our container-based microservice platform that has millions of service instances. At JD.com, we particularly focus on the following requirements and challenges that enable our system to effectively trace microservices at massive scale.

Firstly, how do we provide microservice level transparency while automatically tracing all applications in the microservice platforms without active involvement of upper level services and applications? A tracing system that requires input from upper level components is more fragile and takes significantly more efforts to encourage the adoption. Inspired by Dapper [24], our system adopts an approach of limiting the intrusion within the underlying middleware such as JSF, JMQ and JIMDB.

Secondly, how do we effectively capture all the critical points in both physical and logical invocation chains? We want to minimize the intrusion of our tracing system into the existing microservice middleware while guaranteeing to capture interesting and critical points in execution paths. A *physical* invocation chain represents an actual execution path whereas a *logical* invocation chain refers to a business logic flow. One logical invocation chain usually contains one or more physical invocation chain. It is also important to minimize the overhead of the tracing system in our microservice framework. If the overhead is not negligible, the adoption of the system would be significantly impacted as users are likely to turn them off. Finally, the tracing system should be scalable to support tracing of all microservices that run on millions of containers.

In this paper, we present JCallGraph, a distributed tracing system that tracks the interactions and timing information of microservices across systems and machines. The logical invocation chains captured are particularly important to JD.com as it helps develop and maintain complex business logic. JCallGraph addresses the challenges by only intruding the underlying middleware of the microservice platform, and eliminating the need to intrude applications. JCall-Graph also leverages sampling to dramatically reduce the overhead of the system. Efficient log transfer layer and in-memory storage layer are integrated to ensure real time analysis and visualization. JCallGraph provides better understanding of the system such as analyzing complex execution paths across microservices. Other functionalities include timing and bottleneck analysis, analyzing statistics of calling information or the entrance points, and analyzing the dependencies within an invocation chain.

In particular, our paper has contributions as follows:

- Distributed dynamic tracing to provide a holistic view of both physical and logical invocation chains for large-scale microservice-based applications in an enterprise cloud platform with millions of containers.
- Careful intrusion of core middlewares to eliminate active involvement of applications; short UUID, low rate sampling and high compression context to increase the performance and scalability of the system.
- Comprehensive stress tests in test environment and deployment in real production environment, and use cases from our experiences, demonstrating the effectiveness and efficiency of JCallGraph.

We outline the rest of this paper as follows. Section 2 introduces microservices in action at JD.com. Section 3 describes the design and implementation of JCallGraph. Performance evaluation results and use cases are in Sect. 4. Section 5 presents the related work and Sect. 6 concludes the paper.

2   Microservices in Action at JD.com

The microservice architecture and container techniques facilitate software development, maintenance and delivery. So far we provide 34,000 microservices deployed in 500,000 containers managed by JDOS [26], a Kubernetes-based datacenter operating system. Such a huge number of microservices invoke each other to serve various business units, e.g., JD Retails [10], JD Finance [8], JD Logistics [9] etc. It is hard to observe and monitor the microservice invocation relationship in such a large-scale real-production environment. Figure 1 shows part of microservice invocation graph at JD.com. This actual demand motivated us to design JCallGraph: a monitoring system for tracing and visualizing the microservice invocation relationship.

To manage and support the development of large-scale microservices effectively and efficiently, we develop JSF, an RPC framework supporting; JMQ, a distributed messaging and streaming platform; JIMDB, a journaled in-memory database compatible with Redis [17]. As shown in Fig. 2, each application consists of multiple microservices. These applications synchronously invoke microservices through JSF, asynchronously communicate with each other through JMQ, and retrieve and store data in JIMDB. All of the applications work together to perform e-commerce or other transactions at JD.com.

JCallGraph serves as a tracing and visualization tool to show the microservice invocation graph among various applications. The objective of JCallGraph is to construct the microservice invocation relationship graph in the large-scale container environments on the fly, at the same time, it requires minimal impact to applications in real-production environment.

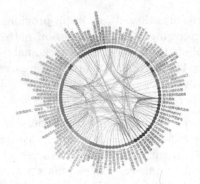

Fig. 1. Microservice graph at JD.com.

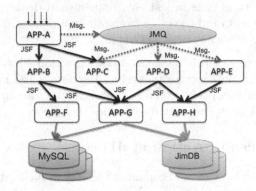

Fig. 2. An illustration of microservice invocation at JD.com. JSF as a synchronous framework, JMQ as an asynchronous messaging queue, JIMDB as a in-memory database.

3 Design and Implementation

3.1 Overview

To construct the invocation graph of microservices in the large-scale container environments, this greatest challenge is how to represent the invocation relationship, including the call flow and data flow. Previous work [24] uses end-to-end request flow tracing techniques to construct sequential and parallel activities in distributed systems. However, we have a unique requirement to fully comprehend the invocation relationship in our applications. For example, a customer purchases a product from JD Retails, pays through JD Finance, tracks the delivery using JD logistics. To monitor the performance of this business transaction, we need trace the real-time invocation graph among various microservices provided by several applications deployed across different machines and even across data centers. To this end, we not only need to construct the physical request-response flow as the previous work do, we also need to construct the logical microservice invocation graph, e.g., e-commercial order number.

Here, we use physical chain to trace the actual request flow among the applications, and logical chain to trace the business logic request chain for a special business requirement. All the logical and physical chains compose the complex microservice invocation graph at massive scale. Specifically, we design several identifiers (ID) to capture the microservice invocation graph. Specifically, we use two types of identifiers to represent the runtime invocation relationship for the applications and microservices: static identifiers (e.g., application ID, microservice ID) which are generated when the application and the microservice registered; and dynamic identifiers (e.g., global logical chain ID, RPC ID) which are generated during the runtime. In addition, since the invocation relationship is similar to a tree, we record the detailed structure of an invocation tree, such as the entry, parent, current node using these identifiers.

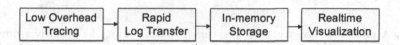

Fig. 3. Overview of JCallGraph's process pipeline.

Based on this idea, we design JCallGraph, including four components as shown in Fig. 3 (1) Trace Layer, tracing the invocation relationship in the middlewares (e.g., JSF, JMQ, JIMDB etc.); (2) Transfer Layer, transferring the traced invocation information to storages; (3) Storage Layer, storing the real-time data in JIMDB and offline analytic data in Elasticsearch[1] (4) Visualization and Analytics Layer, visualizing and deeply analyzing the microservices and their invocation relationship.

3.2 Tracing Microservices via Intruding upon Core Middlewares

JCallGraph's goal is to accurately construct microservice invocation graph at a lower cost without application intrusion. At JD.com, we use JSF, the microservice management platform to support over 250 billions of RPC-based microservice calls per day. To trace these invocation relationship, we add minimal critical tracing points in the core middlewares (e.g., JSF, JMQ, JIMDB), making zero code intrusion to thousands of applications and millions of microservices.

Primitives. JCallGraph's tracing layer provides several primitives to record the microservice invocation context, e.g., startTrace, endTrace, clientSend, serverRev, etc. We carefully place the primitives in the middlewares where it can record the request-response relationship among the microservices with minimal tracing points. Figure 4 depicts a concrete process to construct the invocation context using these primitives in the middlewares. Through the middleware (e.g., JSF, JMQ, JIMDB etc.), the front-end applications invoke startTrace to generate the global chain id and start a runtime invocation track; the upstream applications

---

[1] Elasticsearch. "https://www.elastic.co/".

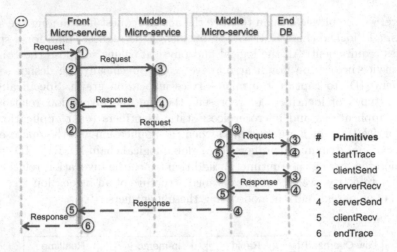

Fig. 4. A process to construct the invocation context using the primitives provided by JCallGraph. All the applications are unaware of the tracing process, since all the tracing points are in the middlewares.

invoke *clientSend* to record the start timestamp of the upstream application; once the downstream applications receive the request, they invoke *serverRecv* to record the start timestamp of the downstream application; after the downstream applications process the request, they invoke the *serverSend* to generate the downstream RPC id, record the end timestamp of the downstream application; once the upstream applications receive the response, they invoke *clientRecv* to generate the upstream RPC id and record the end timestamp of the upstream application; finally the front-end applications call *endTrace* to finish the specific runtime invocation track.

Tracing Invocations. The applications implement a RPC synchronous invocation by the interfaces provided by JSF. The invocation context is transferred during the process of the JSF, thus JCallGraph can restore the context of the synchronous invocation by plugging the primitives into the interfaces of JSF. For the asynchronous invocation, it involves the transparent transfer of the context among multi-threads. There are two cases as shown in Fig. 5: creating a new thread and requesting a thread from thread pools. JCallGraph intercepts the invocation context by adopting Java bytecode instrumentation technique [5] when JCallGraph's tracing primitives are called in the core middleware.

3.3 Low Overhead Tracing

To reduce the overhead in tracing layer and minimize the impact on the performance of applications, we adopt several specific techniques in the following.

Short UUID. We use unique identifier to record the entry, parent, current node in an invocation tree to record the runtime invocation relationship. Popular distributed systems such as OpenStack, Spark, and Hadoop use the universally

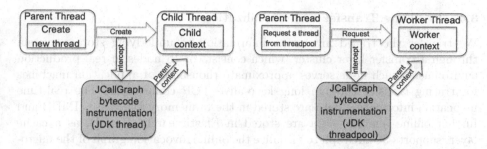

Fig. 5. Tracing the asynchronous invocation among multi-threads, including creating a new thread (left) and requesting a thread from the thread pool (right).

unique identifier (UUID), an 32 hexadecimal characters. However, 32 characters are too expensive for the tracing context, since it incurs more stress to the transfer and storage layer. Therefore, we use bit operations and cut down 32 characters into the 8 hexadecimal short UUID to uniquely represent these nodes of an invocation tree, which can dramatically reduce the overhead while still achieving similar low probability of conflicting identifiers as that by the traditional hexadecimal UUIDs with 32 bits. In our experiments, we observe that the likelihood of identifier conflict is one in a million, it is more than enough to distinguish all invocation chains since we can identify the invocation chain as long as all the RPC IDs in a runtime invocation chain is unique. Most importantly, the 8 hexadecimal short UUID can dramatically accelerate the tracing, transfer and visualization process.

Low Rate Sampling. Inspired by Dapper [24], to further reduce the impact on the applications, we use sampling. The difference is that we only sample successful invocation meanwhile recording all failure invocation. The benefit is that we can use very low sampling rate, but we still can guarantee the accuracy of constructing the normal invocation relationship. In our case the normal invocation is repeatable, once we miss some tracing, we can retry to guarantee the accuracy of constructing the invocation graph. We do not miss any failure invocation, which is useful for root-cause analysis. Various sampling rate impacts on the network traffic of transfer layer is available in Sect. 4.2.

All In-Memory. To eliminate the I/O contention between JCallGraph and the applications incurred by recording the call context, all the operations in tracing layer are in-memory, and we adopt an unlocked ring memory buffer to buff the traced context of the applications. Once the buffer is full, our policy is to drop these contexts to guarantee the efficiency of the applications, meanwhile we still can accurately construct the invocation graph through retrying.

3.4   Realtime Transfer and Visualization

We transfer the traced invocation information to underlying storage system through a transfer layer cluster, which consists of 16 nodes in real production environment, each node serves approximate thousands of application machines for tracing transfer through long keep-alive TCP connections. The real-time invocation information data are stored in the in-memory Database JIMDB and further offline analytic data are stored in Elasticsearch. JIMDB, as a cache layer, supports JCallGraph to visualize the online invocation graph of the microservices within milliseconds.

High Compression Context. In transfer layer, the main overhead comes from the additional network bandwidth consumption [18], which increases as the size of the messages increases which carry the information of invocation relationship. We represent the microservice invocation graph with the minimal context information. In particular, we effectively compress the invocation context by exploring the similarity between the contexts. In our cases, the same invocation chain typically shares the same context, and the invocation relationship is static for a specific application. Thus, we can achieve a very high compression ratio, usually 1/10 as observed in production environment. We observe that the actual message size is approximate 112 bytes for most of real-production applications, and using the message size can achieve the optimal throughput and resource utilization in our real-production environments. Detailed explanation can refer to our stress testing as shown in Sect. 4.2.

4   Evaluation and Experiences

4.1   Operation Data at JD.com

So far JCallGraph has been deployed in real-production environment for over than two years at JD.com, monitoring more than 8000 applications and approximate 34,000 microservices run on the cluster of 500,000 containers, tracing over 250 billions of RPC-based microservice calls per day.

Figure 6 shows the daily rates of real time microservice invocation amount and chain amount traced by JCallGraph in December 2018. All the transactions at JD (including JD Retails [10], JD Finance [8], JD Logistics [9] etc.) averagely trigger approximate 250 billions of microservice calls per day shown in the left. Using JCallGraph can effectively trace such massive scale microservice invocation relationship, around 500 millions of invocation chain amount per day as shown in the right.

4.2   Performance of JCallGraph

In this section, we evaluate the performance of JCallGraph from three key aspects through stress tests: the impact to applications caused by JCallGraph, the performance impact of various message size in log transfer layer, and the impact of various sampling rate.

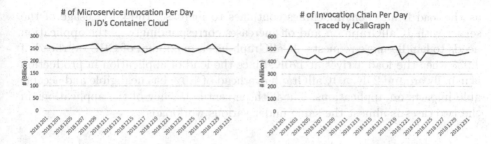

Fig. 6. One Month Operation Data in Dec. 2018. The transactions at JD.com averagely trigger approximate 250 billions of microservice calls per day shown in the left, JCallGraph records around 500 millions of invocation chain amount per day shown in the right.

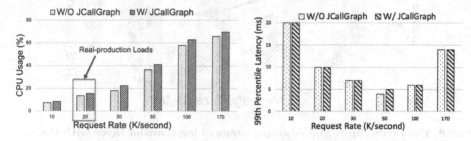

Fig. 7. Impact to applications under stress test when JCallGraph tracing is on and off. When the load of application is 20K per second, that is the usual load in our real-production environments, the around 1% overhead increase cause by JCallGraph has negligible impacts on applications. Meanwhile the 99th percentile latency of the applications in two scenarios is almost the same.

Impact to Applications Caused by JCallGraph. We first evaluate the impact to applications caused by JCallGraph via stress test in a test environment, where we deploy four client machines and one application server. Each machine is equipped with Intel(R) Xeon(R) CPU E5620 @ 2.40 GHz, 32 GB memory and 1 GB network. We use HP LoadGenerator [7] to generate the workloads of stress test in the client machines. We generate various workloads, the maximum workload did not go beyond 170K because we observe that the load of applications does not exceed more than 30K most of the time in real-production environment. We deploy one application in server machines to serve the requests from the clients, the application invokes middlewares (e.g., JSF) meanwhile the tracing primitives of JCallGraph are invoked in the middlewares. We compare the overhead of the server and 99th percentile latency of the applications in two scenarios: switching on and off the tracing of JCallGraph.

Figure 7 illustrates the average CPU usage of the server and 99th percentile latency of the applications, when the number of requests handled by the server increases from 10K to 170K and JCallGraph tracing is on and off, usages of other resources (e.g., memory) are omitted since they are almost the same. We see that as the load from client machines continues to increase, the CPU usage of the server with JCallGraph on and off increases correspondingly as the application needs to handle more requests. JCallGraph has a maximum of CPU overhead of 4.9% when the load arrives at 170K. Since the load of application in production is usually around 20K, a JCallGraph overhead of 1.9% has negligible and acceptable impacts on applications. The 99th percentile latency of the applications in the two cases is almost the same under various workloads.

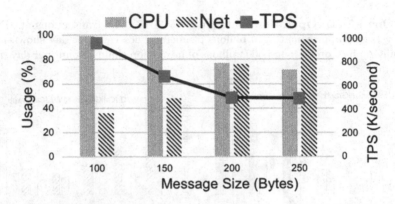

Fig. 8. The throughput and resource usage of log transfer layer with the various size of the message. It confirmed that the message size of 112 bytes, the actual message size in our real-production applications, can achieve the maximal throughput and resource usage environments.

Performance of Log Transfer Layer. We next study the performance of log transfer layer with the various size of the message carrying the information of traced microservice invocation relationships. In this experiment, we use one docker container as the transfer server and 50 docker containers as clients to send log messages. The server is equipped with 4 CPU cores, 8G memory, 50G disk and 10G ethernet.

Figure 8 illustrates how the length of messages impacts the throughput of log transfer layer and the resource usage. The y axis on the right refers to the maximum loads from clients which the server can sustain without losing any packages. We see that as the length of messages increases from 100 bytes to 250 bytes, the throughput of the transfer server decreases and the CPU usage drops from 99% to 72%. The reason is that as the messages size increases, the network bandwidth becomes the bottleneck in the real-production test environment leading to loss a lot of packages.

In real applications, the actual message size is around 112 bytes. Thus this result in Fig. 8 confirmed that the current context information and message size can achieve the maximal throughput and resource usage in our real-production environments.

Impact of Sampling Rate. We examine how the sampling rate reduces the number of packages sent per second, the network consumption as well as the burden of transfer server. In Fig. 9, we increase the client loads to report the number of packages sent by the application in log scale in various sampling rate from 1 to 4000. In all cases, we can successfully construct the normal invocation relationship. We see that the number of packages transferred without sampling compared with the number with sampling turned on is mostly proportional to the sampling rate. That means as the heavier the load the more network bandwidth consumption is saved.

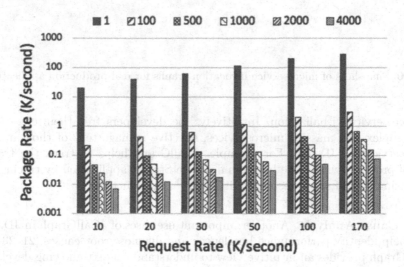

Fig. 9. Impact of sampling rate. Lower sampling rate can reduce the traffic pressure to the transfer layer.

JCallGraph uses different policy to record the invocation information for successful and failure microservice calling, and the accuracy of successful invocation context can be guaranteed by retry policy, thus we can use very low sampling rate to reduce the network pressure of transfer server.

4.3   Use Cases

In this section we share some use cases at JD.com, how JCallGraph helps developers to understand interactions among microservices, detect the problems and pinpoint the root-cause, analyse the dependencies of microservices.

Microservice Visualization. JCallGraph provides an interactive interface allowing users to visually explore the relationship across all microservices. Using the visualization, the developers can now then easily view the microservice invocation relationship. Figure 10 shows real-production application examples

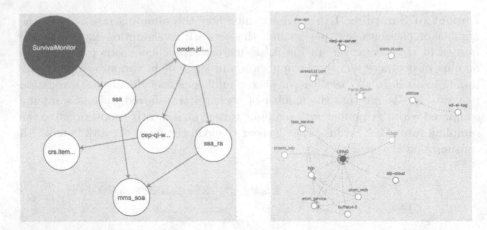

Fig. 10. Snapshots of microservice invocation graphs for real-production applications.

of microservice visualization. Intuitively, the developers free themselves from the complex and massive microservices, effective manage tens of thousands of microservices at JD.com. For example, JCallGraph helps to track the transition of products within the business flow of a Storm[2] application by tracing the processing flow of stock keeping unit (SKU)[3] of products.

Root Cause Analysis. Another important use cases of JCallGraph in JD.com is to help identify performance bottleneck and diagnose root causes [21–23,27]. JCallGraph provides an intuitive view to understand context allowing developer to quickly identify the location of errors with a meaning dynamic calling chain context. Figure 11 shows an example of invocation chain of an application where the exceptions occur and are marked as red. Note that the latency information is conveniently available showing that the top level exception takes around 50 ms. When an exception occurs, this call chain information can be easily accessed with the traceID that is injected into the application log. Based on this information, developers can quickly locate the corresponding portion of code and the runtime machine that produces the error and analyse why the error occurs under the current dynamic execution path.

Invocation Dependency Analysis. In addition to help identify root causes when exceptions or anomalies occur, JCallGraph offers various detailed analysis in terms of invocation dependencies and frequency analysis. We define two different types to represent the severity of dependency in JCallGraph, *strong dependency* and *weak dependency*. A call in an invocation chain has strong dependency when the call fails, all the subsequent calls can not be invoked, whereas a call

---

[2] Apache Storm. "http://storm.apache.org/".

[3] A stock keeping unit is a product or service identification code.

Microservice Name	Status	Latency
ShopGoodsService.getShopGoodsByParam	Success	7ms
SoService.checkReentrantSoMain	Success	5ms
WarehourseService.getWarehouse	Success	2ms
SoService.transportSo	Soft error	50ms
StockProcessServicd.occupySoStock	Soft error	5ms
DeptService.getDept	Success	1ms
SoService.addEcip2CloudTask	Success	8ms

Fig. 11. An example of root cause analysis. This figure shows errors of an invocation chain recorded by JCallGraph, we can further inspect the microservices with error and long latency to pinpoint the root cause.

L	Microservice Name	LR(%)	DR	CR	Note
0	Isv.EclpEdiOpenService.cancelSo	51.0	1.00	1.00	Strong dependency
1	Bbp.so.SoService.cancelSo	41.1	1.42	1.31	Strong dependency
2	Bbp.stock.StockProcess.Service.cancelSoStock	6.50	0.55	0.14	Strong dependency
1	Bbp.so.SoService.querySoMainByIsvSoNo	0.01	0.01	0.03	Weak dependency
1	Bbp.so.SoService.querySoMainByIsvSoNoPlus	0.01	0.01	0.04	Strong dependency
1	Bbp.so.SoService.addEclp2CloudTask	0.59	0.80	0.34	Weak dependency
1	Bbp.so.SoService.querySoMain	0.75	1.43	1.30	Strong dependency

Fig. 12. An example of invocation chain analysis. LR, DR, CR can be used to analyse the bottleneck, two types of frequency dependency as a caller and a callee. [L- level, LR - response time ratio, DR - dependency ratio, CR - calling ratio]

with weak dependency is the one when the call fails, some or all the subsequent calls are still invoked. Figure 12 marks strong and weak dependency in an invocation chain. Errors occur on calls with strong dependency are more severe than calls with weak dependency and usually have higher priority to be fixed.

Invocation frequency is another interesting insight for development and operation. We define two types of frequency dependencies in JCallGraph. One is the frequency as a callee in an invocation chain using the metrics of calling ratio

(CR), and the other is the frequency as a caller invoking other microservices in an invocation chain using the metrics of dependency ratio (DR). Figure 12 shows an example of invocation frequency analysis in an invocation chain. One successful use case of using invocation frequency analysis at JD.com is to plan the resource capacity. For example, JD.com launched its annual 6.18 Shopping Festival [1], we need to accurately estimate the usage frequency of microservices and plan the capacity and significantly improve the resource utilization while guaranteeing the performance of front-end on-line services during the period of annual 6.18 Shopping Festival.

Other Use Cases. There are other use cases of JCallGraph at JD.com such as entrance point and source analysis. Entrance point analysis identifies the first call in the calling chain where source analysis recognizes the callers and the callees of the current method. Entrance point analysis together with frequency analysis is used for capacity planning for shopping seasons or promotional sales days. As entrance points are the first call in the chain which can be invoked by frontend applications. It is easier to estimate the capacity from top to down following the chains. Source analysis is useful in that it helps developers to know exactly the upstream and downstream applications. Such information is used for new feature development and rolling updates.

5   Related Work

End-to-end request-flow tracing techniques are extensively implemented in distributed systems to support various performance monitoring tasks, such as Google's Dapper [24], Mace [11], Stardust [19], X-Trace [6], Retro [13], Pivot Tracing [14] etc. They gives us a lot of insights to design and implement JCallGraph to guarantee low overhead, such as sampling, trace points. However, they are not applied in such massive scale container environment.

OpVis [15] implements a monitoring and analytics framework in container environments to provide visualization and analytics, and DocMan [12] adopts the approaches such as distance identification and hierarchical clustering for detecting containerized application's dependencies, which are orthogonal and complementary to our works. JCallGraph, as the microservice monitoring platform at JD.com, provides a billion-scale invocation graph visualization as shown in Fig. 6 in Sect. 4.1, that is beyond the grasp of OpVis. More importantly, we can visualize the interactive microservices invocation graph in realtime, incur negligible overhead and not intrude applications, which can be practical in real-production industrial scenarios.

6   Conclusion

We presented JCallGraph, a tracing and analytics tool to visualize the microservice invocation graph for massive scale microservice platform in enterprise datacenter. Our evaluation and experiences at JD.com show that JCallGraph can accurately capture the real-time invocation relationship among tens of thousands of microservices in millions of containers, one of the largest Kubernetes clusters in real production in the world, while achieving minimal overhead without any significant performance impact on real-production applications, and zero-intrusion to the code of applications. We hope that sharing our practice with the massive scale tracing system will provide insights to solve the challenges of monitoring and managing tens of thousands of microservices in enterprise data-center.

References

1. JD.com's 6.18 Shopping Festival. https://www.fungglobalretailtech.com/news/jd-coms-6-18-shopping-festival-just-discounts/
2. Balalaie, A., Heydarnoori, A., Jamshidi, P.: Migrating to cloud-native architectures using microservices: an experience report. In: Celesti, A., Leitner, P. (eds.) ESOCC Workshops 2015. CCIS, vol. 567, pp. 201–215. Springer, Cham (2016). https://doi.org/10.1007/978-3-319-33313-7_15
3. Balalaie, A., Heydarnoori, A., Jamshidi, P.: Microservices architecture enables devops: migration to a cloud-native architecture. IEEE Softw. **33**(3), 42–52 (2016)
4. Bernstein, D.: Containers and cloud: from LXC to docker to kubernetes. IEEE Cloud Comput. **3**, 81–84 (2014)
5. Binder, W., Hulaas, J., Moret, P.: Advanced Java bytecode instrumentation. In: Proceedings of the 5th International Symposium on Principles and Practice of Programming in Java, pp. 135–144. ACM (2007)
6. Fonseca, R., Freedman, M.J., Porter, G.: Experiences with tracing causality in networked services. INM/WREN **10**, 10 (2010)
7. HP: LoadRunner. https://www.claudihome.com/html/LR/WebHelp/Content/Controller/toc_MainController.htm
8. JD: Finance. https://jr.jd.com
9. JD: Logistics. https://www.jdwl.com
10. JD: Retails. https://www.jd.com
11. Killian, C.E., Anderson, J.W., Braud, R., Jhala, R., Vahdat, A.M.: Mace: language support for building distributed systems. In: ACM SIGPLAN Notices, vol. 42, pp. 179–188. ACM (2007)
12. Liu, P., et al.: A toolset for detecting containerized application. In: 2018 IEEE 11th International Conference on Cloud Computing (CLOUD), pp. 194–201. IEEE (2018)
13. Mace, J., Bodik, P., Fonseca, R., Musuvathi, M.: Retro: targeted resource management in multi-tenant distributed systems. In: NSDI, pp. 589–603 (2015)
14. Mace, J., Roelke, R., Fonseca, R.: Pivot tracing: dynamic causal monitoring for distributed systems. In: Proceedings of the 25th Symposium on Operating Systems Principles, pp. 378–393. ACM (2015)
15. Oliveira, F., Suneja, S., Nadgowda, S., Nagpurkar, P., Isci, C.: OpVis: extensible, cross-platform operational visibility and analytics for cloud. In: Proceedings of the 18th ACM/IFIP/USENIX Middleware Conference: Industrial Track, pp. 43–49. ACM (2017)
16. Pahl, C.: Containerization and the PaaS cloud. IEEE Cloud Comput. **2**(3), 24–31 (2015)
17. RedisLabs: Redis. https://redis.io

18. Sambasivan, R.R., Shafer, I., Mace, J., Sigelman, B.H., Fonseca, R., Ganger, G.R.: Principled workflow-centric tracing of distributed systems. In: Proceedings of the Seventh ACM Symposium on Cloud Computing, pp. 401–414. ACM (2016)

19. Sambasivan, R.R., et al.: Diagnosing performance changes by comparing request flows. In: NSDI, 5, p. 1 (2011)

20. Sandoval, R., et al.: A case study in enabling DevOps using Docker. Ph.D. thesis (2015)

21. Shan, H., et al.: E-diagnosis: Unsupervised and real-time diagnosis of small-window long-tail latency in large-scale microservice platforms. In: Proceedings of the 2019 World Wide Web Conference on World Wide Web (2019)

22. Shan, H., Wang, Q., Pu, C.: Tail attacks on web applications. In: Proceedings of the 2017 ACM SIGSAC Conference on Computer and Communications Security, pp. 1725–1739. ACM (2017)

23. Shan, H., Wang, Q., Yan, Q.: Very short intermittent DDoS attacks in an unsaturated system. In: Lin, X., Ghorbani, A., Ren, K., Zhu, S., Zhang, A. (eds.) SecureComm 2017. LNICST, vol. 238, pp. 45–66. Springer, Cham (2018). https://doi.org/10.1007/978-3-319-78813-5_3

24. Sigelman, B.H., et al.: Dapper, a large-scale distributed systems tracing infrastructure. Technical report, Google, Inc. (2010)

25. Thönes, J.: Microservices. IEEE softw. **32**(1), 116 (2015)

26. TIG: JDOS: a kubernetes-based datacenter operating system. https://github.com/tiglabs/jdos

27. Zhang, S., Shan, H., Wang, Q., Liu, J., Yan, Q., Wei, J.: Tail amplification in n-tier systems: a study of transient cross-resource contention attacks. In: ICDCS (2019)

An Overview of Cloud Computing Testing Research

Jia Yao, Babak Maleki Shoja$^{(\boxtimes)}$, and Nasseh Tabrizi

East Carolina University, Greenville, NC, USA
jiasherryyao@gmail.com,
malekishojab16@students.ecu.edu, tabrizim@ecu.edu

Abstract. With the rapid growth in information technology, there is a significant increase in research activities in the field of cloud computing. Cloud testing can be interpreted as (i) testing of cloud applications, which involves continuous monitoring of cloud application status to verify Service Level Agreements, and (ii) testing as a cloud service which involves using the cloud as a testing middleware to execute a large-scale simulation of real-time user interactions. This study aims to examine the methodologies and tools used in cloud testing and the current research trends in cloud computing testing.

Keywords: Cloud testing · Cloud computing · Cloud services · Review

1 Introduction

Cloud computing has different characteristics which are varied based on the area of the providing service, but the most important ones can be categorized as follows.

- On-demand service: Customer can request for resources on a flexible short-term basis and get charged based on the utility of resources [3].
- Rapid elasticity: Customer can rapidly request for more resources or release unnecessary resources as needed [4].
- Virtualization: Customer can enjoy the portability and versatility of cloud when the lower level hardware is abstracted [4].
- High reliability: Customer can execute time-consuming operations on the cloud because the cloud is built to be fault tolerant [5].

The cloud services are usually classified into three major sections as infrastructure, platform and software, however, Testing-as-a-Service (TaaS) is recently known as a new and demanding type of service model.

- Infrastructure-as-a-Service (IaaS): Customer can acquire various computing hardware, including data storage, network devices, and processing power [1].
- Platform-as-a-Service (PaaS): Customer can access a set of developer environments, including operating systems, database, and web server [4].
- Software-as-a-Service (SaaS): Customer can access software applications through a client interface such as the web browser without the complexity of installations [4].

D. Da Silva et al. (Eds.): CLOUD 2019, LNCS 11513, pp. 303–313, 2019.
https://doi.org/10.1007/978-3-030-23502-4_21

- Testing-as-a-Service (TaaS): Customer can access test simulation environments and monitor complex program behaviors continuously [6].

Much research being conducted on cloud testing and most notable published studies include Testing Scope in Cloud, [7], cloud testing review [8], Integrated TaaS Platform for Mobile Development [9], A Systematic Mapping Study of Empirical Studies on Software Cloud Testing Methods [10], Research on Testing Software for Rapid Cloud Deployment [11], Cloud API Testing [12].

Cloud testing can have multiple interpretations: testing of cloud applications or testing as a cloud service. In general, Service Level Agreement (SLA) is a contract between cloud customer and cloud provider which describes the required quality of service (QoS) and the penalties for QoS violations. Adequate SLA monitoring can be of interest to both end users and cloud providers [13]. From the end user perspective, it is helpful to know which the best eligible cloud provider is, based on systematic testing of attributes such as reliability, performance, and security. Many researchers have investigated in this area. For example, Wagle et al. [14] proposed an evaluation model for ranking commercially available cloud providers using an ordered performance heat map. From the cloud provider perspective, it is important to monitor the health of the cloud system and to avoid the penalties for QoS violations. However, according to [15] testing of the cloud is a non-trivial task that requires continuous measurements of cloud application status and effective monitoring across multiple layers of the cloud stack.

As modern web applications are becoming more complex, traditional in-house testing also becomes insufficient in several ways. In-house testing facilities need to be carefully configured and maintained, and there is a significant amount of wastage when these facilities are in the idle state. Furthermore, as discussed in [4] in-house testing facilities are usually not powerful enough to simulate real-world concurrent user traffic. Due to the increasing awareness of testing as a cloud service, many businesses [16] have started to consider the trade-offs between keeping their existing testing facilities and migrating testing activities to the cloud. In fact, using the cloud as a testing middleware according to [2] promotes multi-scenario testing evaluation due to distributed testing and offers a large-scale simulation of real-time user interactions. In order to further understand the benefits of testing as a cloud service, it is useful to explore how testing environments are constructed in the cloud.

2   Cloud Services and Testing

This section describes some published methodologies on testing of cloud and testing as a cloud service, where the methodologies are categorized based on the type of testing, the type of cloud service, and the evaluation method. Table 1 lists the reference numbers of research papers according to the type of cloud service and the type of testing and Fig. 1 illustrates the breakdown of research papers according to the evaluation methods.

2.1 Types of Testing

Functionality. Testing: The key focus of functionality testing is to reveal deviations between software's intended and actual functionality. Gao et al. [17] developed a cloud-based testing as a service (CTaaS) system with a UI-layer, test space layer, and TaaS layer. Their system includes a pool of GUI-based test scripts from which cloud customers can select and obtain test simulation results after connecting to a GUI- based tool, such as Selenium. The approach that was suggested by Rosiello et al. [18] combines black box testing and the technique of fault injection. The authors introduce faults into the system under test by killing selected server threads and observing the output, e.g. the number of successful server responses, to see if there are any inconsistencies in system behavior.

Performance Testing. The key focus of performance testing is to determine software's responsiveness and effectiveness with numerical measurements. Nasiri et al. [19] described a multi-component framework consisting of an application analyzer to find the testable region in source code, a test case generator using SoapUI, and a cloud-based test executor. With this framework, they collected the mean execution times of activities in testing and discovered that the testbed startup time can be reduced by simultaneously initializing the system under test (SUT) master node and the test system machine.

A cloud-based testing as a service (CTaaS) system introduced in [17], includes a UI-layer, test space layer, and TaaS layer. The CTaaS includes a pool of performance test scripts, automatic test script generation using workflow graphs, and SaaS performance metrics collection using Amazon's EC2 CloudWatch APIs. The study was further supported by [20] declarative testing environment consisting of Crawl, a domain-specific language for defining performance test scenarios, and Crawler, a Java-based cloud engine for executing test scenarios and collecting the results. Others [13] created multi-module framework consisting of one design time module and four runtime modules. One of the runtime modules is responsible for computing response time, throughput, and reliability in order to detect SLA violations. The further study [21] of a mobile application testing framework that takes Android application as input, records application execution using a crawler, and output performance metrics of response time, throughput, and network latency.

A model-based approach was suggested by [22] for performance testing. The authors use a sequential action model to define the cloud services to be tested and a load model to define parameters such as test execution duration and number of simulated users. To this end, the further work [23] describes a framework to conduct performance testing on cloud applications. Their framework is based on identifying operational modes and actors, calculating occurrence probability of common operations, and measuring performance in terms of transaction time and page load time. Furthermore, Ghosh et al. [24] proposed three stochastic models (resource provisioning decision model, VM provisioning model, and run-time model) to describe the inner details of a cloud service. Based on these models, the authors also introduced formulas to calculate QoS metrics of job rejection probability and mean decision delay, which are indicators of system availability and response time.

Elasticity and Scalability Testing. The key focus of elasticity and scalability testing is to determine the cloud's adapting ability when the demand for resources changes. A perfectly elastic cloud can instantaneously scale resources up or down according to demand. However, as described in [25] in reality, there is always a delay between the time when a load change is detected and the time when resource configuration is changed accordingly. Further work on real-time elasticity testing by Albonico et al. [26] includes a framework with three different elasticity states (i) a scaling in the state when a resource is released, (ii) a scaling out state when a resource is acquired, and (iii) a ready state. For each elasticity state, they executed 2500 operations per second for a fixed period of time and recorded the number of operations that are successful. The authors used these recordings to identify problems during each elasticity state. Further research by Tsai et al. [27] reveals a framework that uses feature selection algorithms to identify bottleneck of an application and uses association rule to identify significant relationships between scalability and various parameters, such as a number of concurrent users.

Security Testing. The key focus of security testing is to reveal security leaks that make the software vulnerable to attacks. Cotroneo et al. [28] described a framework to identify the root cause of security alerts through a conceptual clustering approach. Their framework is valuable to testing because large volumes of security issues can be detected and classified automatically. Furthermore, an identity-based cloud data integrity checking protocol [29] that consists of six algorithms and can be used for auditing variable-sized data blocks. A framework described by [30] consists of a front-end module that uses the Model-View-Controller pattern, a test environment module that prepares tools and virtual machines, and a testing module that handles test scripts. To achieve security testing, the authors integrated Metasploit, a testing tool that offers security vulnerability scanning, into the test environment module.

A multi-component framework described by [31] consisted a test scheduler for allocating resources, a test controller for checking the status of security scanners, and several other components. The authors mentioned a set of security scanners, including IBM AppScan and HP WebInspect that can be used to identify vulnerabilities.

Automatic Testing. The automation of test case generation is another widely explored aspect of cloud testing. A framework proposed by [32] where semantic information in the form of Web Service Description Language (WSDL) is generated from source code and comments, event sequence graphs are generated from WSDL information, and test cases are generated from event sequence graphs. Further research conducted by [33] describes an architecture called Expertus to automate testing of large-scale applications in the cloud. Expertus uses two templates to generate and modify cloud resources and a multi-stage, XML-based code generator to systematically generate complex test scenarios. An interesting research work by [34] reveals layered parameterized tests that use layered symbolic execution (LSE) to dynamically automate test script generation. The LSE algorithm explores the path- based execution tree of an application and obtains inputs for testing by negating constraints in the path conditions. Based on cloud computing, [59] developed a multi-layered model of a software online testing platform which integrates IaaS and SaaS platforms as an automatic self-help service portal for users and operation maintenance portal for administrators.

2.2 Testing Cloud Service

Infrastructure as a Service. There are multiple articles published in this area each with its own unique and significant contributions. A declarative testing environment that can execute tests in multiple IaaS clouds was discussed by [20]. Others including [35] suggested using a third-party auditor to detect SLA violations of virtual machine CPU speed. The third-party auditor (TPA) must have its own timing functions and minimal communication overhead. Hence SLA violations can be detected by comparing the execution times on the cloud provider's virtual machine and on the TPA's virtual machine. Yet [29] describes a protocol for data integrity checking on IaaS cloud. The advantage of IaaS over traditional server was demonstrated [23] by deploying the same application on both infrastructures and comparing their performance under high load conditions. This was supported by a general description of IaaS cloud using three stochastic models [24], where some areas more than one of these cloud services are needed as in the autonomous neural network-based 3D positioning systems [55] which are very useful in rescue operations and need very reliable software and testing services.

Platform as a Service. Model-based approaches including [22, 34] that are used for testing enterprise PaaS cloud, are good at automating test script generation, making the testing process more efficient. Other proposed framework [34] that uses layered symbolic execution (LSE) algorithm to automate testing for PaaS applications.

Software as a Service. When testing SaaS pairwise testing, a form of black box testing, seems to be one of the best techniques [36, 58] to reduce the number of test cases when testing SaaS. Others [27, 28, 32] proposed framework to classify security alerts in SaaS cloud, automatically generate test cases that are based on Service Oriented Architecture, to test the scalability of SaaS applications [27]. Based on the MVC design pattern, [57] studied the construction and robustness testing of SaaS cloud computing data center.

Testing as a Service. According to [37] the testing of mobile applications is a complex task due to the rapidly increasing number of different devices, operating systems, runtime environments, and network providers. TaaS can effectively address these difficulties. Prathibhan et al. [21] proposed a mobile application testing tool that serves as an interface between the user's device and the cloud. Their tool systematically goes through a set of device emulators, where for each emulator, the execution of Android application is recorded as UI events, which are used to generate test scenarios. The proposed framework [37] consisted of multiple components: a cloud controller for administrative management, a hypervisor for virtual machine coordination, a mobile emulator manager for running different Android versions, a test automation manager for running GUI-based test cases was also implemented successfully.

In another study, the authors described a cloud-based framework [30] for conducting security tests on a set of mobile applications on the Android 4.0 OS. This work was further supported by [38] by the development of a framework for setting up large-scale emulator based mobile testing on the OpenStack cloud platform. The authors' framework is composed of a request loader for generating mobile service requests, a resource provisioning engine for running load balancing algorithms, a graphical service monitor for displaying resource utilization measurements and request processing time.

2.3 Evaluation Methods

Case Studies. Many authors have evaluated their methodologies by deploying their methodologies in real-world cloud systems or using real-world datasets as input. The authors selected Sunflow [19], an image rendering application, as the system under test (SUT) and FOSS-Cloud, an open source IT environment, as the runtime cloud provider. Others [17] selected OrangeHRM, an open source SaaS application as the SUT, and Amazon EC2 as the cloud infrastructure on top of which their TaaS system was built. Furthermore, the authors of [22] selected Olio, an open source social network application, as the SUT, and two public IaaS cloud providers, Amazon EC2 and Rackspace. Selection of OpenStack [13, 37] as the runtime cloud provider was an interesting approach. Mean response time was computed to detect related SLA violations and to determine the overhead of their proposed test system, the runtime cloud environment, and five mobile apps from Google Play Store. By inputting two datasets of security alerts generated from a production SaaS Cloud into their framework, the authors [28] evaluated the effectiveness of the framework for classifying alerts in the cloud.

The authors [30] describe selection of 100 mobile applications with varying vulnerabilities as input to their testing system and determined for their testing system correctly outputs the number of vulnerable applications, this work was further explored by [23] where, the authors selected a university-based social network application as the system under test and Azure Cloud as the runtime cloud provider. In a similar way others [26] selected Amazon EC2 as the runtime cloud provider and Yahoo Cloud Serving Benchmark, connected to MongoDB, as the system under test [33] selected a set of runtime providers, including Emulab, Amazon EC2, Open Cirrus, Wipro, and Elba, and a set of system of test, including RUBBoS, RUBiS, and Cloudstone. By deploying their framework on different cloud providers and for different systems, the authors [27] showed the richness of their solution to automated testing. Others [31] implemented their security testing system on the Microsoft SQL Server and used it to detect defects in 456 selected web applications.

Prototype Development. A prototype system developed by [32] has the typical features of online banking was used to show how well their testing framework adapted to the prototype system. Others [34] evaluated their work based on how quickly test cases can be generated on this prototype system by implementing a prototype system on a virtual machine that includes all necessary *PaaS components, such as language interpreter and operating system. They*

Formal Proof. To demonstrate the soundness of their proof, the authors used a formal proof [29] where, they proved that attacking their protocol through signature forgery has the same complexity as solving the RSA problem with large exponents.

Survey. Conducting a survey of an experienced QA tester team showed to be effective to determine the effectiveness of the authors [22] proposed CLTF framework. The tester respondents wrote down the time they need to test fifty cloud services separately using CLTF and using JMeter, a popular open source testing tool. Based on these responses, the authors proved that their framework is better than JMeter in terms of time cost.

Other Studies. Further studies were conducted in cloud computing including the introduction of a framework [56] to evaluate the risk involved in selecting a service provider, where the authors proposed a framework to evaluate the risk for various service providers in term of customers' priorities. This framework helps customers of the cloud services to choose the providers with the best Service Level Agreement.

3   Discussion and Results

The research papers reviewed in this paper were obtained from electronic databases and were selected based on the title, abstract, and conclusion. In general, there is an uneven distribution of research effort within the area of cloud testing. This is demonstrated in Table 1, where it shows distribution according to the type of cloud services and testing.

Table 1. Distribution according to cloud services and testing.

IaaS	Performance testing	[13, 20, 23, 24, 33, 35, 45, 47, 49, 52, 53]
	Elasticity & scalability testing	[25, 26, 40]
	Security testing	[29, 44, 51]
	Automatic testing	[33, 58, 59]
PaaS	Performance testing	[13, 19]
	Automatic testing	[34]
SaaS	Functionality testing	[23, 24]
	Performance testing	[13, 17, 19, 46]
	Elasticity & scalability testing	[17, 27, 46]
	Security testing	[28, 36, 60]
	Automatic testing	[32, 48, 59]
TaaS	Functionality testing	[17, 37]
	Performance testing	[17, 21, 38, 41–43, 50, 54]
	Elasticity & scalability testing	[17]
	Security testing	[30, 31]
	Automatic testing	[30, 31, 37]

From Fig. 1, it is clear that the majority of authors have demonstrated the usability of their proposals through real-world case studies indicating that real-world case study is the most convincing type of evaluation method in the research community.

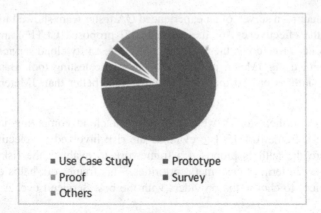

Fig. 1. Distribution of researches according to evaluation method

4   Conclusion

As the field of cloud computing evolves, more research is needed to address the new challenges in the testing of cloud application and testing as a cloud service. This study contributes to a better understanding of the current trend of cloud testing research. Especially, testing of Platform-as-a-Service is a subarea that needs more investigations. Right now, there is no standard toolset for cloud testing. For future work, it may be worthwhile to investigate the different aspects of various commercialized testing tools through a comparative study. Nachiyappan et al. [39] have already compared five publicly available cloud testing products in terms of their pros, cons, and pricing model. There are more available products that can be incorporated into a comparative study and more aspects that need to be considered, including the scripting environment and API support for each testing product.

Acknowledgement. This research is supported in part by grants #1560037 from the National Science Foundation.

References

1. Kuyoro, S.O., Ibikunle, F., Awodele, O.: Cloud computing security issues and challenges. Int. J. Comput. Netw. **3**(5), 247–255 (2011)
2. Fang, W., Xiong, Y.: Cloud testing the next generation test technology. In: International Conference on Electronic & Measurement, Chengdu, pp. 291–295 (2011)
3. Cai, J., Hu, Q.: Analysis for cloud testing of web application. In: International Conference on Systems and Informatics (ICSAI), pp. 293–297 (2014)
4. Inçki, K., Ari, I., Sözer, H.: A survey of software testing in the cloud. In: IEEE International Conference on Software Security and Reliability Companion, pp. 18–23 (2012)
5. Wang, W., Wang, B., Huang, J.: Cloud computing and its key techniques. In: IEEE International Conference on Computer Science and Automation Engineering, pp. 404–410 (2011)

6. Harikrishna, P., Amuthan, A.: A survey of testing as a service in cloud computing. In: International Conference on Computer Communication and Informatics, pp. 1–5 (2016)
7. Murthy, M.S.N., Suma, V.: Software testing and its scope in CLOUD: a detailed survey. In: International Conference on Innovative Mechanisms for Industry Applications, pp. 269–273 (2017)
8. Vilkomir, S.: Cloud testing: a state-of-the-art review. Int. J. Inf. Secur. **28**(17), 213–222 (2012)
9. Starov, O., Vilkomir, S.: Integrated TaaS platform for mobile development: architecture solutions. In: Proceedings of the Eighth International Workshop on Automation of Software Testing, pp. 18–19 (2013)
10. Al-Said, A.A., Brereton, P., Andras, P.: A systematic mapping study of empirical studies on software cloud testing methods. In: IEEE International Conference on Software Quality, Reliability and Security Companion (2017)
11. Chen, Y., Huang, J., Ji, X.: Research on testing software for rapid cloud deployment. In: International Conference on Electronics and Information Engineering (2017)
12. Wang, J., et al.: Cloud API testing. In: IEEE International Conference on Software Testing, Verification and Validation Workshops, pp. 385–386 (2017)
13. Grati, R., Boukadi, K., Ben-Abdallah, H.: A framework for IaaS-to-SaaS monitoring of BPEL processes in the cloud: design and evaluation. In: IEEE/ACS International Conference on Computer Systems and Applications, pp. 557–564 (2014)
14. Wagle, S.S., Guzek, M., Bouvry, P., Bisdorff, R.: An evaluation model for selecting cloud services from commercially available cloud providers. In: IEEE International Conference on Cloud Computing Technology and Science, pp. 107–114 (2015)
15. Alhamazani, K., et al.: An overview of the commercial cloud monitoring tools: research dimensions, design issues, and state-of-the-art. Computing **97**(4), 357–377 (2015)
16. Riungu-Kalliosaari, L., Taipale, O., Smolander, K., Richardson, I.: Adoption and use of cloud-based testing in practice. Softw. Qual. J. **24**(2), 337–364 (2016)
17. Gao, J., et al.: A cloud-based TaaS infrastructure with tools for SaaS validation, performance and scalability evaluation. In: IEEE International Conference on Cloud Computing Technology and Science, pp. 464–471 (2012)
18. Rosiello, S., Choudhary, A., Roy, A., Ganesan, R.: Combining black box testing with white box code analysis: a heterogeneous approach for testing enterprise SaaS applications. In: International Symposium on Software Reliability Engineering, pp. 359–364 (2014)
19. Nasiri, R., Hosseini, S.: A case study for a novel framework for cloud testing. In: International Conference on Electronics, Computer and Computation, pp. 1–5 (2014)
20. Cunha, M., Mendonca, N., Sampaio, A.: A declarative environment for automatic performance evaluation in IaaS clouds. In: International Conference on Cloud Computing (CLOUD), pp. 285–292 (2013)
21. Prathibhan, C.M., Malini, A., Venkatesh, N., Sundarakantham, K.: An automated testing framework for testing Android mobile applications in the cloud. In: International Conference on Advanced Communication Control and Computing Technologies, pp. 1216–1219 (2014)
22. Zhou, J., Zhou, B., Li, S.: Automated model-based performance testing for PaaS cloud services. In: International on Computer Software and Applications, pp. 644–649 (2014)
23. Cico, O., Dika, Z.: Performance and load testing of cloud vs. classic server platforms (case study: social network application). In: Mediterranean Conference on Embedded Computing, pp. 301–306 (2014)
24. Ghosh, R., Longo, F., Naik, V.K., Trivedi, K.S.: Modeling and performance analysis of large scale IaaS clouds. Futur. Gener. Comput. Syst. **29**(5), 1216–1234 (2013)

25. Brebner, P.C.: Is your cloud elastic enough?: performance modelling the elasticity of infrastructure as a service (IaaS) cloud applications. In: ACM/SPEC International Conference on Performance Engineering, pp. 263–266 (2012)
26. Albonico, M., Mottu, J., Sunyé, G.: Monitoring-based testing of elastic cloud computing applications. In: International Conference on Performance Engineering, pp. 3–6 (2016)
27. Tsai, W.T., Huang, Y., Shao, Q.: Testing the scalability of SaaS applications. In: IEEE International Conference on Service-Oriented Computing and Applications, pp. 1–4 (2011)
28. Cotroneo, D., Paudice, A., Pecchia, A.: Automated root cause identification of security alerts: evaluation in a SaaS cloud. Futur. Gener. Comput. Syst. **56**, 375–387 (2016)
29. Yu, Y., et al.: Cloud data integrity checking with an identity-based auditing mechanism from RSA. Futur. Gener. Comput. Syst. **62**, 85–91 (2016)
30. Tao, D., Lin, Z., Lu, C.: Cloud platform based automated security testing system for mobile Internet. Tsinghua Sci. Technol. **20**(6), 537–544 (2015)
31. Tung, Y.H., Lin C.C., Shan, H.L.: Test as a service: a framework for web security TaaS service in cloud environment. In: IEEE International Symposium on Service Oriented System Engineering, pp. 212–217 (2014)
32. Wu, C.S., Lee, Y.T.: Automatic SaaS test cases generation based on SOA in the cloud service. In: IEEE International Conference on Cloud Computing Technology and Science, pp. 349–354 (2012)
33. Jayasinghe, D., et al.: Expertus: a generator approach to automate performance testing in IaaS clouds. In: IEEE International Conference on Cloud Computing (CLOUD), pp. 115–122 (2012)
34. Bucur, S., Kinder, J., Candea, G.: Making automated testing of cloud applications an integral component of PaaS. In: 4th Asia-Pacific Workshop on System (2013)
35. Houlihan, R., Du, X., Tan, C.C., Wu, J. Guizani, M.: Auditing cloud service level agreement on VM CPU speed. In: IEEE International Conference on Communications (ICC), pp. 799–803 (2014)
36. Silva, A.C.D., Correa, L.R., Dias, L.A.V., Cunha, A.M.D.: A case study using testing technique for software as a service (SaaS). In: International Conference on Information Technology - New Generations, pp. 761–762 (2015)
37. Villanes, I.K., Costa, E.A.B. Dias-Neto, A.C.: Automated mobile testing as a service. In: IEEE World Congress on Services, pp. 79–86 (2015)
38. Tao, C., Gao, J., Li, B.: Cloud-based infrastructure for mobile testing as a service. In: International Conference on Advanced Cloud and Big Data, pp. 133–140 (2015)
39. Nachiyappan, S., Justus, S.: Cloud testing tools and its challenges: a comparative study. Big Data Cloud Comput. Chall. Procedia Comput. Sci. **50**, 482–489 (2015)
40. Ganis, G., Panitkin, S.: Evaluating Google compute engine with PROOF. In: International Conference on Computing in High Energy and Nuclear Physics (2013)
41. Hwang, G.H., Wu-Lee, C., Tung, Y.H., Chuang, C.J., Wu, S.F.: Implementing TaaS-based stress testing by MapReduce computing model. In: IEEE International Conference on Software Engineering and Service Science, pp. 137–140 (2014)
42. Gao, Q., Wang, W., Wu, G., Li, X., Wei, J., Zhong, H.: Migrating load testing to the cloud: a case study. In: IEEE International Symposium on Service Oriented System Engineering, pp. 429–434 (2013)
43. Malini, A., Venkatesh, N., Sundarakantham, K., Mercyshalinie, S.: Mobile application testing on smart devices using MTAAS framework in cloud. In: International Conference on Computer and Communications Technologies, pp. 1–5 (2014)
44. Kim, T., et al.: Monitoring and detecting abnormal behavior in mobile cloud infrastructure. In: IEEE Network Operations and Management Symposium, Maui, pp. 1303–1310 (2012)

45. Salah, K., Al-Saba, M., Akhdhor, M., Shaaban O., Buhari, M.I.: Performance evaluation of popular Cloud IaaS providers. In: International Conference on Internet Technology and Secured Transactions, pp. 345–349 (2011)
46. Gao, J. Pattabhiraman, P., Bai, X., Tsai, W.T.: SaaS performance and scalability evaluation in clouds. In: International Symposium on Service Oriented System Engineering, pp. 61–71 (2011)
47. Cotroneo, D., Frattini, F., Pietrantuono, R., Russo, S.: State-based robustness testing of IaaS cloud platforms. In: 5th International Workshop on Cloud Data and Platforms (2015)
48. Mathew, R., Spraetz, R.: Test automation on a SaaS platform. In: International Conference on Software Testing Verification and Validation, pp. 317–325 (2009)
49. Llamas, R.M., et al.: Testing as a service with HammerCloud. In: International Conference on Computing in High Energy and Nuclear Physics (2013)
50. Kuo, J.Y., Liu, C.H., Yu, Y.T.: The study of cloud-based testing platform for Android. In: IEEE International Conference on Mobile Services, pp. 197–201 (2015)
51. Ramachandran, M., Chang, V.: Towards performance evaluation of cloud service providers for cloud data security. Int. J. Inf. Manag. 36(4), 618–625 (2016)
52. Ye, L., Zhang, H., Shi, J., Du, X.: Verifying cloud service level agreement. In: Global Communications Conference, pp. 777–782 (2012)
53. Gonçalves, G.D., et al.: Workload models and performance evaluation of cloud storage services. Computer Net- works (2016). http://dx.doi.org/10.1016/j.comnet.2016.03.024. Accessed 2016
54. Yan, M., Sun, H., Wang, X., Liu, X.: WS-TaaS: a testing as a service platform for web service load testing. In: IEEE 18th International Conference on Parallel and Distributed Systems, pp. 456–463 (2012)
55. Hedayati, H., Tabrizi, N.: MRSL: autonomous neural network-based 3-D positioning system. In: International Conference on Computational Science and Computational Intelligence, pp. 170–174 (2015)
56. Yadranjiaghdam, B., Komal, H., Tabrizi, N.: A risk evaluation framework for service level agreements. In: IEEE International Conference on Computer and Information Technology, pp. 681–685 (2016)
57. Zhang, S., Liu, Z.: Research on the construction and robustness testing of SaaS cloud computing data center based on the MVC design pattern. In: 2017 International Conference on Inventive Systems and Control (ICISC), pp. 1–4. IEEE, January 2017
58. El Nagdy, A.M., El Azim, M.A., AbdelRaouf, A.: A new framework of software testing using cloud computing for banking applications. J. Softw. 12(8), 657–664 (2017)
59. Chen, J., Wang, C., Liu, F., Wang, Y.: Research and implementation of a software online testing platform model based on cloud computing. In: 2017 Fifth International Conference on Advanced Cloud and Big Data (CBD), pp. 87–93. IEEE, August 2017
60. Bhushan, K., Gupta, B.B.: Hypothesis test for low-rate DDoS attack detection in cloud computing environment. Procedia Comput. Sci. 132, 947–955 (2018)

A Robust Multi-terminal Support Method Based on Tele-Immersion Multimedia Technology

Ronghe Wang[1(✉)], Bo Zhang[1], Haiyong Xie[1], Dong Jiao[1], and Shilong Ma[2]

[1] National Engineering Laboratory for Public
Security Risk Perception and Control by Big Data (PSRPC),
Academy of Electronics and Information Technology, Beijing, China
wangronghe@buaa.edu.cn
[2] State Key Laboratory of Software Developing Environment,
School of Computer Science and Engineering,
Beihang University, Beijing, China

Abstract. In this paper, a multi terminal support method based on tele-immersion multimedia technology is proposed. This method provides two functions of synchronous request and asynchronous request, and it can dynamically download and decompress the material by the way of material sub-contracting and on-demand loading, which effectively avoids that the main thread is blocked because of too long request time and that browser crashes because of excessive memory footprint. The system excellently solves the problems of memory, storage and network communication in the development of cross WebGL platform, and optimizes the storage mode of memory, which realizes the high speed calculation and real-time processing of data. The system also integrates the system operation framework, and provides unified framework support for the development of the sub-systems of different platforms. Based on the framework, the secondary development can quickly complete the process development of the sub-system.

Keywords: Cloud rendering · Big data · High-concurrency ·
Real-time processing · Mobile computing

1 Introduction

In recent years, with the continuous development of cross platform technology and cross platform language, more and more software companies began to pay attention to the integration of software development department, and achieve that a set of code can run on multiple platforms by using the cross platform technology, which reduces the manpower, financial and time costs while maintaining the same platform software update progress.

With the rise of the browser 3D rendering technology WebGL technology, Unity engine WebGL cross platform compiler technology in the platform has initially reached the actual use requirements. It is of great significance to study the problems arising from the application of WebGL technology and give the corresponding solutions.

© Springer Nature Switzerland AG 2019
D. Da Silva et al. (Eds.): CLOUD 2019, LNCS 11513, pp. 314–323, 2019.
https://doi.org/10.1007/978-3-030-23502-4_22

Therefore, in this paper, a multi terminal support system based on Unity is proposed. First of all, this paper describes the overall architecture of the system, analyzes the problems faced in the development of cross WebGL platform, and then proposes the key middle-ware design method combined with the software engineering method. Finally, the system framework is proposed.

2 Related Work

The concept of cross platform is an important concept in software development, which is independent of operating system and hardware environment [1, 2]. In the field of mobile development, cross platform development technology has begun to become the first choice for many companies and developers [3–5].

At run time, it may appear the phenomenon of browser feign death or browser collapse [6–9]. It still needs to be improved in terms of hardware and software. March 2011, multimedia technology standardization organization Khronos released the WebGL standard specification R1.0 [10–13]. WebGL technology makes that the browser does not need any plug-ins to provide hardware graphics acceleration, thereby providing a high quality 3D experience [14].

Unity3D is developed by Unity Technologies. It is a multi-platform integrated game development tools [2]. In 2013, Unity global users have more than 1 million 500 thousand. Unity4.0 engine has been able to support ten platforms including MAC OS X [15], Android, IOS [16], and Windows etc. [17].

3 Overall Design of Multi-terminal Support System

The multi terminal support system is composed of the basic service component, the service middle-ware and the system operation frame. It is shown in the following Fig. 1.

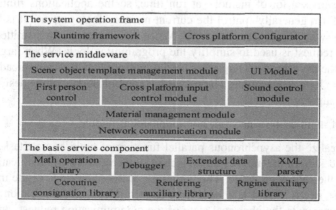

Fig. 1. The hierarchical structure of multi-terminal support system based on Unity

The main functions of each part are as following,

1. The basic service components: these components are the encapsulation of the basic functionality of the hardware abstraction layer and engine layer. They provide platform independent basic operating services for other parts and sub-systems in support system layer.
2. The service middle-ware: in this part, the same service in different platform subsystems are abstracted, and the general service middle-ware is implemented based on the interface provided by the basic service components.
3. Operation system: this part provides a unified operation framework for all subsystems running on different platforms. The system only needs to develop and improve the business function on the basis of the framework, without understanding the operation principle of the framework, so as to improve the code reuse rate, reduce the difficulty of development, and accelerate the development speed of the system.

4   Key Middle-Ware of Multi Terminal Support System

The multi terminal support system should be designed according to different characteristics of the target compiler platform, so it is necessary to take into account the characteristics of different platforms in the design process of support system middleware, so that the middle-ware can stably and efficiently run on all platforms. This section will elaborate on the design of the key middle-ware in the system.

4.1   Network Communication Module

1. Asynchronous network communication management design.

Network communication module provides support for the program on the WebGL platform to request the data packet resource in real-time and load it into memory. WebGL consumes a lot of memory at run time, so the applications running on the WebGL platform generally control the current memory footprint, and it is loaded into memory only when a packet is specified. When small packet is transmitted, the synchronization request is used to simplify the programming logic. When large packet is transmitted, the asynchronous request is used to prevent that the main thread is blocked because of too long request time. The network communication module design is shown in the following Fig. 2.

2. Design of main loop of network communication module.

In order to realize the asynchronous parallel function of multi request task, this paper presents the design of the main cycle flow chart of the network communication module as shown in the following figure. The main task of the main cycle of the module is to deal with the newly added and executing asynchronous communication tasks. The dotted line represents the abnormal state of the communication request, and the solid line represents the normal state of the communication request.

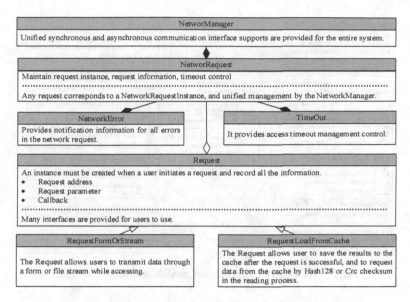

Fig. 2. The network communication module design

4.2 Material Management Module

1. The material management module architecture design.

The key idea of the design of material management module is two points:

(1) The dynamic loading material: all materials are stripped from the project, and the material is dynamically loaded in the program running. This method can effectively reduce the size of the compiled project, and ensure that the main program is quickly loaded by the browser to run, which improves the user experience.

(2) Material sub-contracting, on-demand loading: only when the program needs to be used, the material package is dynamically downloaded and decompressed. And when the package is no longer used, the release operation is performed immediately to save the resource space.

The material management module architecture design is shown in the following Fig. 3.

2. Asynchronous reading process design.

The Unity engine in the process of generating material package, usually through establishing citation association between materials to reduce the size of the material package, so when it comes to material package decompression, it must be processed after the relevant material package be downloaded to the local.

The flow chart of material package dependency check is shown in the following Fig. 4.

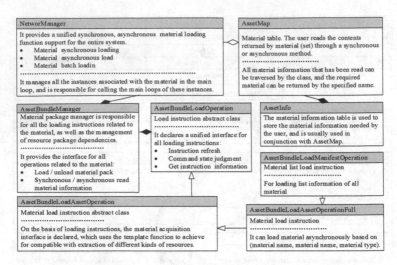

Fig. 3. The material management module architecture design

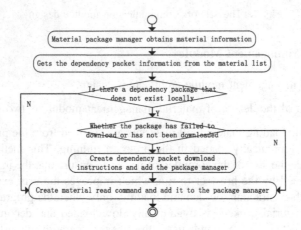

Fig. 4. The flow chart of material package dependency check

5 System Operation Framework

5.1 System Framework Design

The 3D scene in the rendering process feeds back in real-time based on user input, so it needs to have a main loop to momentarily process input data real-time. In addition, it is necessary to complete the initialization of the operating environment of the system before the main loop is started, and to release all resource information at the end of the main loop. Therefore, the system integrates the system operation framework, and provides unified framework support for the development of the sub-systems of different platforms. Based on the framework, the secondary development can quickly complete the process development of the sub-system. The system framework design is shown in the following Fig. 5,

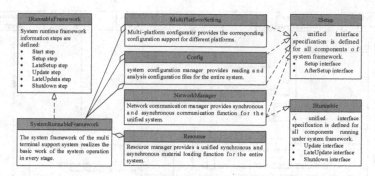

Fig. 5. The system framework design

In order to control the whole life cycle of the system, the system life cycle is divided into 6 stages as follows Table 1.

Table 1. The diagram of system operation phase division

System operation phase	Meaning
Master step	The main control phase of the system is responsible for the other phases of the system
Setup step	The system loads the configuration files phase in which each component is initialized
LateSetup step	After the system is loaded, the initial component is adjusted further
Update step	The main loop of the system, which is the main logic of the system
LateUpdate step	At the end of each system cycle, this phase is mainly processing a logical settlement and clearing parameters
Shutdown step	System shutdown phase, which is mainly used to release the system resources

In this paper, by dividing the system life cycle in detail, we give the running framework interface (IRunnableFramework) and realize the system running framework (System Runnable) based on the interface. As the underlying architecture, the system running framework will carry out some necessary operations in each stage to ensure that the system can complete the most basic operation. On this basis, the sub-system extends the framework of the system, and adds the necessary business logic to complete the development work. Sequence diagram of system operation process as show in the following Fig. 6.

At run time, any system of secondary development based on the framework follows the operation process shown above. First of all, Master step will complete engine's start work, and make the system into the Setup step and LateSetup step, respectively, to complete the configuration loading work of multi terminal support system and sub-system, then system enters main loop. Before receiving the shutdown request, the

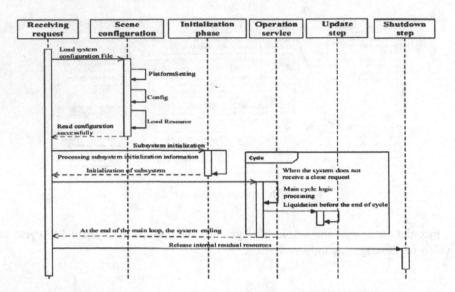

Fig. 6. Sequence diagram of system operation process

system will switch between Update step and LateUpdate step. The Update step mainly completes the works of scene rendering and interactive response. The LateUpdate phase performs the finishing process before the end of each loop. After receiving the closing request, the system will exit the loop and enter the Shutdown step to release all of the system's resources, and finally return to the Master step to end the entire program.

In the whole process, the Master step is responsible for switching between all steps of scheduling. In order to prevent that the main control work in this step is blocked because of the switch to other steps, the corresponding method in other steps is called by coroutines. This asynchronous logic processing method can ensure that the internal control work in the Master step is continuous.

5.2   Design of Main Loop Running State

In the realization of the main loop of the sub-system, the switching between different scenarios often occurs, so the system implements the optional main loop state components in the framework of the system, which is used to assist the sub-system to realize the state switch in the main loop. Interface information for the main loop state component as show in the follow Table 2.

When the system is in a certain state, the Update method and the LateUpdate method are called in each of the main loop. When the state switch occurs, the substituted state triggers OnExit method, indicating that the system is about to exit the state, and the new state will call the OnEnter method, indicating that the system is about to enter the state. The sub-system can be developed according to the business functional requirements of different main loop states, and can control the business logic code that is executed during the state operation and state switch.

Table 2. Interface information for the main loop state component

Method name	Meaning
OnEnter	Method for switching to this state
Update	When the state is the main state, the Update step of the system calls the method
LateUpdate	When the state is the main state, the LateUpdate step of the system calls the method
OnExit	This method is called when the end of the step

6 Conclusion

This paper analyzes the problems faced by the cross platform system based on Unity, and combines with the actual situation of WebGL platforms, such as program compatibility, stability, and reference of the development experience, to illustrate the work meaning of the development of cross platform support system. The support system adopts three layers design scheme. First, the Unity engine and the API related to the operating system are encapsulated as a basic service component layer, which provides platform independent service for the upper layer. Secondly, in the design process of business middle-ware, through the analysis of the problems of WebGL platform in network, memory and storage, this paper focuses on the design schemes of Network communication module and material management module in order to solve the problems of WebGL platform development. Finally, this paper summarizes and analyzes the characteristics of the system's operating life cycle, and proposes the design scheme of multi terminal support system framework in order to provide a unified framework for the development of the sub-system of different platforms.

Acknowledgement. We sincerely thank each one of the reviewer and editors' work to the paper. This paper is supported by National Key R&D Program of China 2017YFC0821603, Beijing NOVA Program of China (Grant No. Z181100006218041), The National Key R&D Program of China 2016YFC0800507.

References

1. Huang, B.R., Lin, C.H., Lee, C.H.: Mobile augmented reality based on cloud computing. In: International Conference on Anti-Counterfeiting, Security and Identification, pp. 1–5 (2017)
2. Liu, Y., Wang, S., Dey, S.: Content-aware modeling and enhancing user experience in cloud mobile rendering and streaming. IEEE J. Emerg. Sel. Top. Circuits Syst. **4**(1), 43–56 (2014)
3. Liu, Y., Wang, S., Dey, S.: Modeling, characterizing, and enhancing user experience in cloud mobile rendering. In: International Conference on Computing, NETWORKING and Communications, pp. 739–745. IEEE (2012)
4. Yao, D., Yu, C., Yang, L., et al.: Using crowdsourcing to provide QoS for mobile cloud computing. IEEE Trans. Cloud Comput. **1**(1), 1–1 (2015). https://doi.org/10.1109/TCC. 2015.2513390

5. Yin, Z., Yu, F.R., Bu, S., et al.: Joint cloud and wireless networks operations in mobile cloud computing environments with telecom operator cloud. IEEE Trans. Wireless Commun. **14**(7), 4020–4033 (2015)
6. Subrata, R., Zomaya, A.Y.: Artificial life techniques for reporting cell planning in mobile computing. In: Parallel and Distributed Processing Symposium. Proceedings International, IPDPS 2002, Abstracts and CD-ROM, p. 0203b IEEE (2015)
7. Kao, Y.H., Krishnamachari, B., Ra, M.R., et al.: Hermes: latency optimal task assignment for resource-constrained mobile computing. In: IEEE INFOCOM, pp. 1894–1902. IEEE (2015)
8. Wang, S.L.L., Tao, Y.H., Chen, L., et al.: Proceedings of the 12th international conference on advances in mobile computing and multimedia. Eur. Econ. Rev. **39**(5), 859–887 (2015)
9. Weigel, M., Lu, T., Bailly, G., et al.: iSkin: flexible, stretchable and visually customizable on-body touch sensors for mobile computing. In: SIGCHI Conference on Human Factors in Computing Systems, pp. 2991–3000 (2015)
10. Baccarelli, E., Cordeschi, N., Mei, A., et al.: Energy-efficient dynamic traffic offloading and reconfiguration of networked data centers for big data stream mobile computing: review, challenges, and a case study. IEEE Netw. **30**(2), 54–61 (2016)
11. Espeland, H., Beskow, P.B., Stensland, H.K., et al.: P2G: a framework for distributed real-time processing of multimedia data, pp. 416–426 (2016)
12. Lu, Y., Liu, Y., Dey, S.: Cloud mobile 3D display gaming user experience modeling and optimization by asymmetric graphics rendering. IEEE J. Sel. Top. Signal Process. **9**(3), 517–532 (2015)
13. Jakimovski, G., Karadimce, A., Davcev, D.: Multimedia content delivery between mobile cloud and mobile devices. In: Garcia Pineda, M., Lloret, J., Papavassiliou, S., Ruehrup, S., Westphall, C.B. (eds.) ADHOC-NOW 2014. LNCS, vol. 8629, pp. 3–11. Springer, Heidelberg (2015). https://doi.org/10.1007/978-3-662-46338-3_1
14. Anagnostopoulos, V., Sardis, E.: Cloud rendering a feasibility case study. In: IEEE International Conference on Cloud Computing Technology and Science, pp. 684–687. IEEE (2014)

15. Tian, W., Zhao, Y., Xu, M., et al.: A toolkit for modeling and simulation of real-time virtual machine allocation in a cloud data center. IEEE Trans. Autom. Sci. Eng. **12**(1), 153–161 (2015)
16. Powers, N., Alling, A., Osolinsky, K., et al.: The cloudlet accelerator: bringing mobile-cloud face recognition into real-time. In: GLOBECOM Workshops, pp. 1–7 (2015)
17. Garraghan, P., Perks, S., Ouyang, X., et al.: Tolerating transient late-timing faults in cloud-based real-time stream processing. In: IEEE International Symposium on Real-Time Distributed Computing, pp. 108–115. IEEE (2016)

CMonitor: A Monitoring and Alarming Platform for Container-Based Clouds

Shujian Ji[1,2], Kejiang Ye[1(✉)], and Cheng-Zhong Xu[3]

[1] Shenzhen Institutes of Advanced Technology, Chinese Academy of Sciences, Shenzhen 518055, China
sj.ji@siat.ac.cn
[2] University of Chinese Academy of Sciences, Beijing 100049, China
kj.ye@siat.ac.cn
[3] Faculty of Science and Technology, University of Macau, Taipa, Macao, Special Administrative Region of China
czxu@um.edu.mo

Abstract. Container technology has been recently recognized by the industry like Google and Alibaba as an emerging platform for building and deploying applications. Due to the high flexibility and low cost, more and more applications are beginning to use containers as the underlying resource abstraction platforms. In order to maintain the stability of the system and detect suspected abnormal events or operations, it is necessary to provide a monitoring and alarming mechanism for containers. In this paper, we design and implement a monitoring and alarming platform - *CMonitor* for the container-based clouds. It is built upon the interfaces provided by Docker containers. Specially, we added some new functions: (i) Integrated monitoring services. CMonitor not only monitors the basic resource usages of each container but also provides hardware-level and application-level monitoring services. (ii) Global topology view. CMonitor generates a global topology structure for containers by parsing network traffic among containers. (iii) Intelligent alarming mechanism. CMonitor contains several anomaly detection algorithms to identify abnormal behaviors in containers and then notifies an alarm to the users. (iv) Rich visualization functions. CMonitor records the runtime log for both system resources and application performance and generates tables and figures with advanced data visualization techniques. By using CMonitor, users can better understand the system runtime status and monitor potential abnormal events, making container-based clouds more stable, efficient and safe.

Keywords: Container · Monitoring · Alarming · Cloud computing

1 Introduction

Container technique is recently experiencing rapid development with the support from the industry like Google and Alibaba and is widely used in large scale production environments [1]. Container technique is also called operating-system-level virtualization, which allows multiple isolated user-space instances

D. Da Silva et al. (Eds.): CLOUD 2019, LNCS 11513, pp. 324–339, 2019.
https://doi.org/10.1007/978-3-030-23502-4_23

sharing the same operating system kernel and uses cgroups [2] to take control of the resources in the host. This provides functionality similar to a virtual machine (VM) but with a lighter footprint.

The Docker container is one of the mainstream containers as it solves many of the challenges of Internet services. The microservices provided by the Docker container can be executed on any supported container platform, which solves the problem of application portability. The emergence of containers and microservices based on container technology has led to a paradigm shift in the development and deployment of software applications. The granularity of application functionality becomes finer, and the scalability and resiliency become better, which brings additional challenges to the traditional monitoring solutions. It is important to understand the interdependencies between containers and to maintain dependability in large-scale container-based cloud environments. The monitoring tool should be able to provide graphical interfaces of application and resource metrics for each container, as well as an overview of the resource usages at the image level. Specifically, system monitoring services is also the foundation of many resource management solutions.

In order to enhance the stability of container-based clouds and detect any suspected abnormal events or operations, it is necessary to provide a monitoring and alarming mechanism for the container system. In this paper, we design and implement a monitoring and alarming platform - *CMonitor* for the container-based clouds. It is based on the some interfaces provided by the current Docker platform. We also add new functions:

- **Integrated monitoring services.** CMonitor not only monitors the basic resource usages of each container but also provides hardware-level and application-level monitoring services.
- **Global topology view.** CMonitor generates a global topology structure for containers by parsing network traffics among containers.
- **Intelligent alarming mechanism.** CMonitor contains several anomaly detection algorithms to identify any abnormal behaviors in containers and notifies the alarm to users.
- **Rich visualization functions.** CMonitor records the runtime log for both system resources and application behaviors and generates tables and figures with advanced data visualization techniques.

The rest of this paper is organized as follows. In Sect. 2, we introduce the related work. In Sect. 3, we describe the system architecture of CMonitor. In Sect. 4, we perform the performance evaluation of CMonitor. Section 5 concludes the whole paper.

2   Related Work

Currently, there are already several online monitoring tools developed for containers such as Docker stats [3], cAdvidor [4], Scout [5], etc. Docker provides built-in command monitoring for Docker hosts via the docker stats command.

Administrators can query the Docker daemon and get detailed real-time information about container resource consumptions, including CPU and memory usage, disk and network I/O bandwidth, and the number of processes running. Docker stats can only monitor a single host, and there is no graphic interface to collect data from multiple hosts. cAdvisor is originally developed by Google as a monitoring tool that collects, aggregates, processes, and exports information of running containers. cAdvisor has a web interface that generates multiple charts, but can only monitor one host. cAdvisor itself is not a complete monitoring solution, but it is often used as part of other monitoring solutions. Scout provides comprehensive data collection, filtering, and monitoring capabilities. But the commercial license fee is very expensive, that the standard package price for monthly use ranges from $99 to $299.

There have been many works focusing on cloud monitoring. Fatema *et al.* [6] surveyed monitoring tools revealing common characteristics and distinctions for clouds. Alhamazani *et al.* [7] also did a survey on commercial cloud monitoring tools and discussed the major research dimensions and design issues related to the development of cloud monitoring tools. Aceto *et al.* [8] analyzed and discussed properties of a monitoring system for the cloud, and described both commercial and open source platforms for cloud monitoring. Shao *et al.* [9] proposed a runtime model for cloud monitoring (RMCM), which gives an intuitive representation of a running cloud by focusing on common monitoring concerns. Zou *et al.* [10] designed a trusted monitoring framework, which provides a chain of trust that excludes the untrusted privileged domain, by deploying an independent guest domain for the monitoring purpose, as well as using the trusted computing technology to ensure the integrity of the monitoring environment.

Most recently, the cloud anomaly/fault has also attracted much attention. Sharma *et al.* [11] proposed a fault management framework - CloudPD for clouds which leverages a canonical representation of the operating environment to quantify the impact of resource sharing; an online learning process to tackle dynamism; a correlation-based performance model for higher detection accuracy; and an integrated end-to-end feedback loop to synergize with a cloud management ecosystem. Gunawi *et al.* conducted a comprehensive study of bug study in six popular cloud system [12]. CoMA [13] is a container monitoring agent that oversees resource consumption of operating system level virtualization platforms, primarily targeting container-based platforms such as Docker.

While our work CMonitor supports both monitoring and alarming functions for container-based clouds. This is also one of the very early work on the monitoring system for containers.

3   CMonitor Architecture

3.1   Design Challenges

LXC (Linux Container) is a kind of kernel virtualization technology that realizes the resource virtualization at the Linux operating system level. Docker encapsulates the underlying technology of LXC, implements resource isolation through namespaces, and implements resource restrictions through cgroups. The running mechanism of applications in Docker containers is different from that in hosts. Multiple containers may run many applications, sharing resources of one or more underlying hosts.

We firstly analyze the special challenges of monitoring the container in real time. In a traditional environment, most of the servers and applications we need to monitor are relatively static. While in a container-based cloud environment, the containers keep changing and are subject to more interference. Real-time monitoring of containerized environments can be more difficult. It is not possible to accurately understand what is happening inside a container by simply running a monitoring command such as *top* or *ps* on the host.

3.2   Performance Metrics

In order to achieve detailed monitoring information of the container, we collect the low-level resource metrics from CPU utilization, memory usage, block I/O and network I/O. As shown in Table 1, the metrics include fine-grained monitoring information.

Table 1. The description of per metric

	Metrics	Description
CPU Utilization	Total CPU Usage	Percentage of total cpu utilization
	CPU Usage by User	Percentage of user cpu utilization
	CPU Usage by System	Percentage of system cpu utilization
	Throttled CPU Time	the total CPU usage time throttled by the control group
Memory Usage	Total Memory Usage	Size of total memory usage
	RSS Memory Usage	Size of physical memory usage
	Cache Memory Usage	Size of cache memory usage
	Swap Memory Usage	Size of swap memory usage
Block IO	Total I/O Bytes	Bytes of total input/output
	Read/Written Bytes	Bytes of total read/written
	Sync/Async Bytes	Bytes of total Sync/Async
Network IO	Rx/Tx Bytes	Bytes of transportation/reception
	Rx/Tx Packets	Packets of transportation/reception
	Rx/Tx Errors	The error transmission /reception of packets
	Rx/Tx Dropped	The dropped transmission /reception of packets

CPU utilization includes Total CPU usage, CPU usage by the user, the CPU usage by system and Throttled CPU time. Knowing the CPU usage of containers can maximize the resource utilization of hosts. Lowering the CPU time of high-loaded containers can effectively ensure other services get the necessary resources.

Container memory usage includes Total memory usage, RSS memory usage, Cache memory usage, and Swap memory usage. Understanding the current operation and work plan is important for the memory usage of each container. According to the changes of Docker memory usage, we can improve the resource utilization by dynamically adjusting the capacity of containers.

Block I/O usage includes Total I/O bytes, read/written bytes and Sync/Async bytes. Docker container images consume additional host disk space and perform corresponding file reads and writes. Persistent Docker volumes also consume host disk space. Proper use of cleanup tools is important for the continued running of the Docker containers.

Network I/O includes Rx/Tx bytes, Rx/Tx bytes, Rx/Tx errors and Rx/Tx dropped. Docker containers will share a LAN within the same host. Focusing on container failures and lost packets can detect specific network failures of the host system. Especially for containers such as load balancers, the throughput of virtual networks is a big bottleneck.

3.3 Core Modules

Container monitoring is an extremely important part of the container management platform. Monitoring not only needs to get the running status of containers in real time but also needs to obtain the dynamic changes of the resources occupied by containers. We propose an architecture for CMonitor, including agents, server and client. The agent we designed can collect various monitoring data of containers on the host machines. Note that there are many monitoring metrics and the data amount is huge, the data collection of agents must be efficient. Besides, the same host machine can run dozens or even hundreds of containers with a large amount of data collection, sorting and reporting process must have low overheads. The Agent is deployed in each host running containers, and the monitored data is transferred to the server through the HTTP protocol.

The overall architecture design of CMonitor is shown in Fig. 1. The core modules are described as follows:

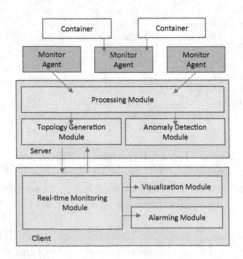

Fig. 1. The overall architecture and core modules of CMonitor

- **Monitoring Agent Module**. There are multiple nodes in a container cluster. Each node runs multiple containers. The monitoring agent of CMonitor is deployed on each physical node, which is responsible for collecting performance monitoring data such as CPU, memory, network, disk and so on. We develop the agent monitoring module based on libcontainer [14], which collects container data from the host proc [15], cgroups, and other system interfaces. The agent is encapsulated as a Docker image and exposes a port for external access to transmit monitoring data, and uses JSON technology to send the collected data to the server. The monitored data collection and reporting process does not go through the Docker daemon [16], so it does not burden daemon. The agent can set different configuration files for different host environments, and sends performance monitoring data to the server according to the predefined data transmission mechanism. This design allows the agent to customize the type of monitoring service and flexibly to adapt to the monitoring scenarios in different host environments.
- **Monitoring Server Module**. The monitoring server module is responsible for collecting, processing and analyzing the monitoring data. It includes three sub-modules.
  - Processing Sub-Module. The data processing sub-module pulls data collected by the agent through a specific port. Data preprocessing preserves important container operational status information through data categorizing and aggregating, removing meaningless noises. When the number of cluster nodes increases, the monitoring data amount becomes larger. This requires a concurrent processing mechanism.
  - Topology Generation Sub-Module. From the perspective of network traffic analysis, the entire system is visually observed by generating a topology of access relationships between containers. The topology generation sub-module updates the node and edge information by requesting the Processing sub-module. We use the a new data structure to store the topological relationships between each container and the operational performance metrics of containers. The topology generation sub-module then converts the original data structure into a new JSON format and transmits it to the real-time monitoring module through the HTTP protocol.
  - Anomaly Detection Sub-Module. This module is responsible for the normal and abnormal status monitoring. The simplest method for anomaly detection is the threshold-based detection. An alert will be issued if the usage limit exceeds the threshold. The abnormal information includes abnormal application behaviors, system faults, and other external attacks. The data is preprocessed by the Processing sub-module, and the anomaly detection sub-module can also configure other machine learning detection algorithms for further anomaly detection.
- **Client Machine Module**. Users can access the monitoring platform through the a Web interface. This module includes three sub-modules.
  - Real-time Monitoring Sub-Module. The real-time monitoring sub-module is responsible for further processing the data pulled from the server.

Then it forwards data to the visualization sub-module and alarming sub-module. CMonitor records the runtime log for both system resources and application performance.

- Report Visualization Sub-Module. The visualization module can collect the data sent by the real-time monitoring sub-module through a synchronous refresh. Then it visualizes various container topological relationships and operational metrics, and uses Echarts [17] to draw various types of charts.
- Alarming Sub-Module. This module is responsible for triggering the alert and notifying users with animation and sound. If the CPU and memory usage exceed the pre-set threshold value within a certain sampling period, the overload reminder function will be triggered and the system will send a notification to the administrator.

4   CMonitor Evaluation

The primary objective of the evaluate is to assess the validity of the collected metrics by CMonitor from various Docker containers. Validity means to the monitored data should reflect the real value. Considering the numerous metrics collected in the report regarding CPU, memory, network I/O, and block I/O, part of these metrics are selected for evaluation. We evaluate the effectiveness for user CPU utilization, system CPU utilization, memory utilization, and the number of bytes read and written to disk, where user CPU utilization and system CPU utilization refer to the percentage of execution CPU used. For all evaluations, Ubuntu 18.04 LTS and the Docker platform 1.35 have been used. The physical machine runs on Intel i5-8250U processor with 1.60 GHz and 2 GB of RAM with 2400 MHz.

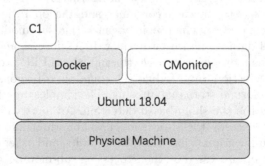

Fig. 2. Scenario 1, no workload is running in the host environment

To assess the accuracy of memory and CPU utilization metrics, three different scenarios were set up, with five rounds running. In scenario 1 (See Fig. 2), the Docker platform runs an empty container without any workloads, which presents

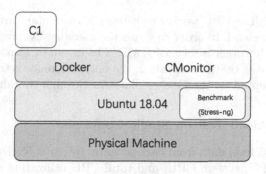

Fig. 3. Scenario 2, workload on host OS

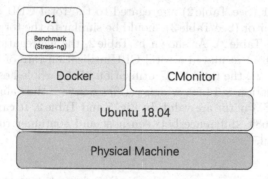

Fig. 4. Scenario 3, workload in container

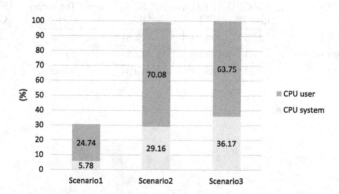

Fig. 5. CPU utilization is reported at host OS level by NetData in each scenario.

the baseline of CPU and memory usage for Docker execution. Scenario 2 (See Fig. 3) is similar to scenario 1, except for the fact that a workload generator is executed in the host OS. Stress-ng [18] has been used to generate load on both

CPU and memory. The CPU worker executes the maximum prime number addition to generate the load. In order to stress the memory, five workers are started, and the size of each worker is set to 400 MB. The layout of scenario 3 (See Fig. 4) is exactly the same as that of scenario 2, the only difference is that the Stress-ng process is implemented on the Docker platform through containerization.

4.1 CPU Workload Test on Single Container

We obtain the host level data from each scenario by using NetData [19]. Figure 5 shows the user CPU, system CPU, and total CPU utilization reported by Net-Data for each scenario. To determine that the measurements of the metrics collected by CMonitor are valid, we compare the data collected by NetData with collected by CMonitor in three scenarios, as shown in Figs. 5 and 6. The total CPU in scenario 1 (See Table 2) aggregated to the total CPU of the container reported by CMonitor (See Table 3) should be similar to the total CPU reported in scenario 3 (See Table 2). As shown in Table 2, the aggregation of two values (30.52% and 69.26%) results in a total CPU utilization rate of 99.78 %. In scenario 3 (See Table 2), the total CPU utilization of the whole host is 99.92% and the standard deviation is 14.89, which verifies whether the values of CPU metrics collected by CMonitor are valid. In Fig. 5 and Table 2, It can be determined that there is a 0.68% difference between host and container running the same Stress-ng workload.

Table 2. CPU utilization is reported by NetData in each scenario for Fig. 5. Total CPU is the aggregation of user CPU and system CPU. SD means standard deviation.

	CPU system (%)	SD CPU user (%)	CPU user (%)	SD cpu user (%)	Total cpu (%)	SD total CPU (%)
Scenariol	5.78	2.36	24.74	7.81	30.52	6.31
Scenario2	29.16	11.34	70.08	13.31	99.24	22.16
Scenario3	36.17	9.86	63.17	10.81	99.92	14.89

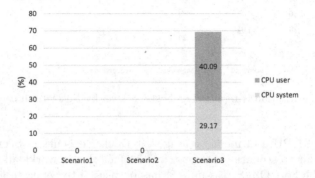

Fig. 6. Container CPU utilization reported by CMonitor

Table 3. CMonitor reports CPU utilization in each scenario for Fig. 6. There are no workload running in scenarios 1.

	CPU system (%)	SD CPU system (%)	CPU user (%)	SD CPU user (%)	Total CPU (%)	SD total CPU (%)
Scenario1	0	0	0	0	0	0
Scenario2	0	0	0	0	0	0
Scenario3	29.17	8.21	40.09	9.53	69.26	3.14

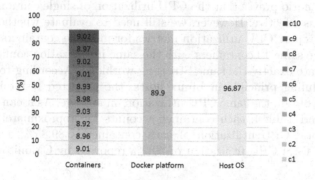

Fig. 7. Each container runs the same workload, generating the same CPU workload across all 10 containers, and CMonitor reports the total CPU utilization of the 10 containers and the value of the Docker platform. NetData reports the value for the host system.

Table 4. Total CPU utilization and standard deviation for Fig. 7.

Host OS		Docker platform		Containers		
Total CPU (%)	SD total CPU (%)	Total CPU (%)	SD total CPU (%)	Name	Total CPU (%)	SD total CPU (%)
96.87	4.61	89.9	5.32	c1	9.01	0.17
				c2	8.96	0.29
				c3	8.92	0.14
				c4	9.03	0.36
				c5	8.98	0.23
				c6	8.93	0.19
				c7	9.01	0.21
				c8	9.02	0.11
				c9	8.97	0.26
				c10	9.02	0.29

From Fig. 5 and Table 2, There is a slight difference in running the same Stress-ng workload on the local host and container. This difference may be due to errors in the data collected. Moreover, it can be seen from the test results of scenario 3 that running the same Stress-ng workload process and containerization can improve the CPU utilization of the system. The result is opposite when it comes to user CPU utilization.

4.2 CPU Workload Test on Multiple Containers

The above scenario proves that the CPU utilization of single container collected by CMonitor is effective. However, we still need to evaluate whether CMonitor can correctly report CPU utilization metrics for multiple containers. In the first evaluation, the same 10 containers with the same initialization configuration are used to generate exactly the same Stress-ng workload. According to the default process scheduling principle in Linux hosts, the expected result is that each container will obtain the same CPU utilization on average. As it can be observed from Fig. 7 and Table 4, each container accounts for approximately 9% of the CPU. The total CPU utilization of each container is 89.85%, approximately matching the total CPU utilization of 89.9% reported by CMonitor for Docker platform.

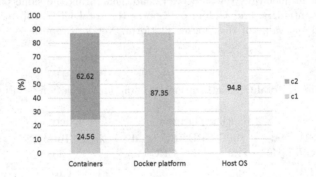

Fig. 8. The total CPU utilization of two containers running different Stress-ng workload configurations. CMonitor reports metrics for both containers and Docker platforms, respectively. NetData reports the values for the Host OS.

This result also shows that CMointor can independently collect CPU utilization of each container under the Docker platform. We also conduct the second evaluation to further determine the correctness of the collection metrics by running different Stress-ng workloads with the same initialized containers. As shown in Fig. 8 and Table 5, metrics collected by CMonitor show that one container uses 24.56% of the CPU and the other 62.62%. The total use of 87.18% for both containers is similar to the 87.35% CPU usage for the Docker platform.

Table 5. Total CPU utilization and standard deviation for Fig. 8

Host OS		Docker platform		Containers		
Total CPU (%)	SD total CPU (%)	Total CPU (%)	SD total CPU (%)	Name	Total CPU (%)	SD total CPU (%)
94.8	2.36	87.35	3.14	c1	24.56	1.13
				c2	62.62	0.96

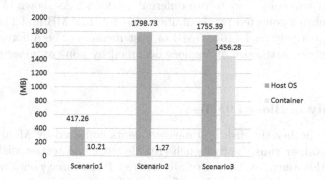

Fig. 9. Memory usage of the host OS and container in each scenario. Container memory usage is reported by CMonitor and host OS memory usage is reported by NetData.

Table 6. Memory usage and standard deviation for Fig. 9

	Host OS		Containers	
	Memory usage (MB)	SD memory usage (MB)	Memory usage (MB)	SD memory usage (MB)
Scenario1	417.26	13.24	10.21	0.32
Scenario2	1798.73	196.84	1.27	1.41
Scenario2	1755.39	266.31	1456.28	177.36

4.3 Memory Workload Test on Single Container

We analyze memory usage and collect the memory usage in three different scenarios. The values collected on memory usage for each scenario are shown in Fig. 9 and Table 6, which shows that the reported memory values fluctuate more than the CPU. The host memory usage in scenario 1 (417.26 MB) aggregating the container memory usage reported in CMonitor in scenario 3 (1456.28 MB) should be similar to the host memory in scenario 3 (1755.39 MB). There are approximately 118 MB differences in this example, which may be due to memory management in Linux system according to different usage scenarios.

4.4   Memory Workload Test on Multiple Containers

Testing memory load usage is the same as testing CPU usage for multiple containers and we also use CMonitor to evaluate multiple concurrently running container metrics. As can be seen from Fig. 10 and Table 7, the memory usage of each container is close to 150 MB, and the total memory usage of all 10 containers is 1524.25 MB. The memory usage of the host system is 1821.32 MB. The difference between the two values is 297.07 MB, which represents the memory of some processes in the operating system other than containers. In the second evaluation, we set two containers to run different workload. As shown in Fig. 11 and Table 8, CMonitor collected two containers using 431.35 MB and 1148.41 MB of memory, respectively, and 1764.85 MB of host memory. The difference between these two metrics is the size of memory occupied by non-container processes in the host.

4.5   Validity of Block I/O Test

To evaluate whether the disk I/O measurements collected by Monitor are reliable, the container runs the Sysbench [20] file workload to test disk reads and writes. For this purpose, the tests are written from three containers running simultaneously to disk. Sysbench configures different load workers and file sizes for each container. The first container runs two file load workers, and each worker writes 16 files with a total size of 300 MB to the host disk shared folder in a random write mode. The second container initiates a workload that the two workers have to write to the disk with a file size of 500 MB. The third container starts a worker to write 1000 MB to the disk folder. For each container, the number of bytes written by CMonitor is exactly correct. The first container takes around 90 s to write 600 MB to disk. The second and third containers take around 115 s to write 1000 MB to disk and the time each container writes files to disk is related to the number of worker loads in the container.

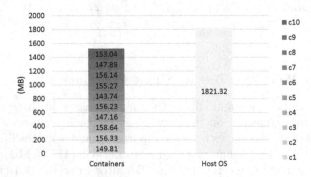

Fig. 10. Memory usage of 10 containers running the same process. CMonitor collects metrics for containers and NetData reports host values.

Table 7. Memory usage and standard deviations for Fig. 10

Host OS		Containers		
Memory usage (MB)	SD memory usage (MB)	Name	Memory usage (MB)	SD memory usage (MB)
1821.32	221.18	c1	149.81	31.24
		c2	156.33	24.56
		c3	158.64	19.21
		c4	147.16	26.11
		c5	156.23	17.98
		c6	143.74	26.77
		c7	155.27	34.19
		c8	156.14	25.23
		c9	147.89	17.73
		c10	153.04	26.39

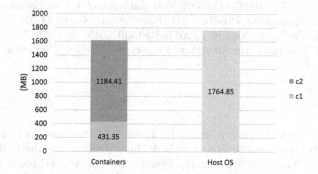

Fig. 11. Memory usage of two containers, where each container runs a different process. CMonitor collects metrics for containers and NetData reports host values.

Table 8. Memory usage and standard deviations for Fig. 11

Host OS		Containers		
Memory usage (MB)	SD memory usage (MB)	Name	Memory usage (MB)	SD memory usage (MB)
1764.85	214.62	c1	431.35	77.19
		c2	1148.41	145.78

5 Conclusion

As an emerging platform for building deployment applications, Docker has been recognized by the industry. More and more applications are starting to use Docker as the underlying resource abstraction platform. When users deploy their applications in the Docker platform, they want the container to be in good running condition on the Docker platform. This research is based on the basic functions of the current Docker platform, and designed a container monitoring application for distributed system. The contribution of this research is to propose a Docker container monitoring and alarming platform - CMonitor, which can help the operation and maintenance managers to control the security and performance of the container. In the experiment, we evaluate the CMonitor's effectiveness in collecting metrics including CPU utilization, memory usage and Block I/O for containers in different scenarios. From the evaluation, we know that CMonitor can accurately collect the running information of containers and has certain robustness.

Acknowledgment. This work is supported by China National Basic Research Program (973 Program, No. 2015CB352400), National Natural Science Foundation of China (No. 61702492), Equipment Pre-Research Foundation (No. 61400020403), Shenzhen Basic Research Program (No. JCYJ20170818153016513, JCYJ20170307164747920), and Shenzhen Discipline Construction Project for Urban Computing and Data Intelligence.

References

1. Soltesz, S., Pötzl, H., Fiuczynski, M.E., Bavier, A., Peterson, L.: Container-based operating system virtualization: a scalable, high-performance alternative to hypervisors. In: ACM SIGOPS Operating Systems Review, vol. 41, no. 3, pp. 275–287. ACM (2007)
2. cgroups (2019). http://man7.org/linux/man-pages/man7/cgroups.7.html
3. Docker (2019). https://aws.amazon.com/docker/
4. cadvisor (2019). https://github.com/google/cadvisor
5. Scout (2019). https://github.com/pingdomserver/docker-scout
6. Fatema, K., Emeakaroha, V.C., Healy, P.D., Morrison, J.P., Lynn, T.: A survey of cloud monitoring tools: taxonomy, capabilities and objectives. J. Parallel Distrib. Comput. **74**(10), 2918–2933 (2014)
7. Alhamazani, K., et al.: An overview of the commercial cloud monitoring tools: research dimensions, design issues, and state-of-the-art. Computing **97**(4), 357–377 (2015)
8. Aceto, G., Botta, A., De Donato, W., Pescapè, A.: Cloud monitoring: a survey. Comput. Netw. **57**(9), 2093–2115 (2013)
9. Shao, J., Wei, H., Wang, Q., Mei, H.: A runtime model based monitoring approach for cloud. In: IEEE 3rd International Conference on Cloud Computing (CLOUD), pp. 313–320. IEEE (2010)
10. Zou, D., Zhang, W., Qiang, W., Xiang, G., Yang, L.T., Jin, H., Hu, K.: Design and implementation of a trusted monitoring framework for cloud platforms. Futur. Gener. Comput. Syst. **29**(8), 2092–2102 (2013)

11. Sharma, B., Jayachandran, P., Verma, A., Das, C.R.: CloudPD: problem determination and diagnosis in shared dynamic clouds. In: 2013 43rd Annual IEEE/IFIP International Conference on Dependable Systems and Networks (DSN), pp. 1–12. IEEE (2013)

12. Gunawi, H.S., et al.: What bugs live in the cloud? A study of 3000+ issues in cloud systems. In: Proceedings of the ACM Symposium on Cloud Computing, pp. 1–14. ACM (2014)

13. Jimenez, L.L., Simon, M.G., Schelén, O., Kristiansson, J., Synnes, K., Åhlund, C.: CoMA: resource monitoring of Docker containers. In: International Conference on Cloud Computing and Services Science: 20/05/2015-22/05/2015, vol. 1, pp. 145–154. SCITEPRESS Digital Library (2015)

14. libcontainer (2019). https://github.com/docker/libcontainer

15. proc (2019). https://www.tldp.org/LDP/Linux-Filesystem-Hierarchy/html/proc.html

16. Daemon (2019). https://docs.docker.com/v17.09/engine/reference/commandline/dockerd/

17. Echarts (2019). https://ecomfe.github.io/echarts-doc/public/en/index.html/

18. Stress-ng (2019). https://github.com/ColinIanKing/stress-ng/

19. Netdata (2019). https://github.com/netdata/netdata

20. Sysbench (2019). https://github.com/akopytov/sysbench

CPR: Client-Side Processing
of Range Predicates

Shahram Ghandeharizadeh[(⊠)], Yazeed Alabdulkarim, and Hieu Nguyen

Computer Science Department, University of Southern California, Los Angeles, USA
{shahram,yalabdul,hieun}@usc.edu

Abstract. Range predicates are important to diverse application workloads. A system may process range predicates using either a server-side, a client-side, or a hybrid of these two solutions. This study presents CPR, a client-side solution that caches the result of range predicates and looks up their results. This implementation provides strong consistency and supports alternative write policies. It is embodied in a flexible framework named RangeQP that provides the hybrid solution. We quantify strengths and limitations of CPR when compared with the server-side solution.

1   Introduction

Range predicates are essential to diverse applications ranging from data science [8,20] to online transaction processing systems [24] and social networking [7]. They are included in popular benchmarks such as TPC-C's Stock-Level transaction and YCSB's Workload E.

A system may process range predicates using either a server-side, a client-side, or a hybrid of these two solutions. The server-side solution uses a data store with an order preserving index structure [6,14] and may employ materialized views [8]. Example index structures include B+-tree [6] and skip-lists [14], LSM-Tree [16] used in storage managers such as Google's LevelDB [12] and WiscKey [15], skip-lists in MemSQL, Bw-tree [14] in Microsoft's Hekaton, and BzTree [5] for the emerging NVM.

Surprisingly, there has been very little work on client-side processing of range predicates [1,2,19]. The primary contribution of this study is one such solution named CPR. CPR is a caching layer that augments an existing data store. It requires the application to cache and look up the result of range predicates. It may combine multiple cache entries together when a predicate overlaps them. Our evaluation shows CPR is superior to its server-side alternative in two cases. First, with read heavy workloads consisting of range predicates with a *small* result set. Second, with write heavy workloads when the cache is configured with abundant amount of memory in the write-back mode [10].

CPR is embodied in a framework named RangeQP that is a hybrid of the server-side and client-side solutions. RangeQP may use CPR with either a SQL or a NoSQL data store. Given a workload with a mix of range predicates with

© Springer Nature Switzerland AG 2019
D. Da Silva et al. (Eds.): CLOUD 2019, LNCS 11513, pp. 340–354, 2019.
https://doi.org/10.1007/978-3-030-23502-4_24

varying sizes, RangeQP employs either CPR or the data store for processing the predicates with the objective to enhance performance.

This study reports on an implementation of CPR using MySQL and MongoDB. Figure 1a compares the performance of each data store by itself (server-side) and using the CPR solution (client-side). The workload consists of range predicates with small result sets that CPR is ideal for processing. The y-axis of Fig. 1 shows CPR's percentage improvement in throughput when compared with the sever-side solution, i.e., the data store by itself. The x-axis of this figure is the percentage of scans (range predicates) in the workload, varying the workload from write-heavy to read-heavy. With a write-heavy (10% scan) workload, CPR enhances performance of MySQL (MongoDB) by almost 4x (2x). With a read-heavy (99% scan) workload, CPR provides more than 2x increase in system throughput with both data stores. CPR is superior for write-heavy workloads because its cache is configured with the write-back policy. In these experiments, the server-side implementation uses Solid State Disk, SSD. The reported percentage improvements provided by CPR would be higher if the mass storage device was a hard disk drive, HDD. Figure 1b shows the overhead of CPR in the form of additional memory required for buffered writes and log records for recovery from a failure. This overhead is a function of writes that constitute a workload.

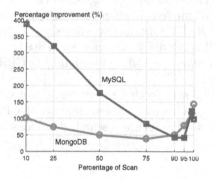

(a) Observe improvement when compared with MySQL and MongoDB.

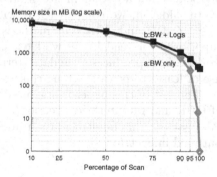

(b) Memory requirement.

Fig. 1. CPR with YCSB Workload E.

CPR is designed to satisfy the following requirements:

- **Strong consistency:** The caching layer must guarantee that data produced by a confirmed write is observed by all subsequent reads assuming the data store provides strong consistency [18].
- **Scale horizontally:** The throughput of the caching layer should increase linearly as a function of its servers.

- **General purpose for use with alternative data stores and caches.** The caching layer should use off-the-shelf hardware and software components. It must function with alternative data stores based on different data models, e.g., MySQL using the relational data model and MongoDB using the JSON data model.
- **Support alternative policies for processing writes.** These include write-around, write-through and write-back. While write-around deletes those cached entries impacted by an update to the data store, write-through updates them. Write-back updates the cached entries and buffers the write in the caching layer. It may store multiple replicas of a buffered write to enhance its availability. The degree of replication should be a configurable parameter. Different applications may require different write policies and the caching layer must provide all three policies.

CPR realizes the above requirements using off-the-shelf hardware and software components. It uses leases [11] to provide strong consistency and prevent undesirable race conditions that insert stale data in the cache. It implements all three write policies. It uses configurable log records to tolerate failures that may destroy contents of its volatile in-memory data structures.

We evaluate CPR using the YCSB [7] benchmark. Obtained results show performance of CPR is maximized with the write-back policy and selective range predicates that are small in size. Moreover, it scales horizontally with write-back.

In addition, we compare CPR with an implementation of range predicate using ZADD and ZRANGE methods of Redis. Obtained results show CPR's superiority for read heavy workloads. While Redis is superior for write-heavy workloads, it produces stale data (termed *anomalies* [4]). This highlights CPR's use of leases to provide strong consistency.

The rest of this paper is organized as follows. Section 2 provides an overview of CPR and its interfaces. Section 3 details a specific implementation of CPR. We evaluate this implementation in Sect. 4. Our future research directions are outlined in Sect. 5.

2   CPR

CPR is a scalable solution consisting of one or more Dendrites. A *Dendrite* is an extensible component that facilitates communication with (1) a Cache Manager Instance (CMI) such as memcached and (2) a data store such as MySQL or MongoDB. It implements the following interfaces:

CPR Dendrite instance DI = Initialize (Collection-name, Domain-name, Domain-type, Min, Max, Coordinator address, Write-Policy, β)
An application must invoke Initialize to obtain an instance of Dendrite for get, insert, delete, and update commands. This method assumes a coordinator that provides it with the necessary configuration parameters, including the identity of other Dendrites and their assigned ranges. With implementation of Sect. 3, it

also obtains IP:Port address of the individual CMIs from the Coordinator. The arguments of Initialize include:

- Collection-name identifies the table (SQL) or collection (MongoDB) that is referenced by the range predicate.
- Domain-name specifies an attribute that is queried using range predicate. It pertains to a column of a table (SQL) or a property of a collection (MongoDB).
- Domain-type may be an integer, text, real, float, date.
- Minimum value of the specified domain-name (optional).
- Maximum value of the specified domain-name (optional).
- Coordinator address specifies the network address (e.g., a URL, IP:Port) of the coordinator for obtaining leases on ranges.
- Write-Policy is either write-back, write-through, or write-around.
- β is the maximum tolerated percentage of duplicated data between two cached result sets. See below for additional details.

Value = DI.Get (Lower-bound, Upper-bound, Query execute function)

Get is invoked on an instance of Dendrite obtained using the Initialize method. Lower and upper bound values define the interval referenced by the range predicate of the query. Their values are inclusive and must match the domain-type inputted to Initialize. Query execute function is invoked with a cache miss to compute a cached entry. In our implementation of Sect. 3, a cached entry is identified as a (key, value) pair where "value" is the cached result set while the "key" uniquely identifies this value.

Success = DI.Insert (Lower-bound, Upper-bound, DML command, DML execute function, Cache update function)

Insert is invoked on a Dendrite instance of CPR obtained using Initialize method. Lower and upper bound specify the interval impacted by the insert. Their values are inclusive and must match the domain-type inputted to Initialize. DML command is issued at run time and inserts a new row (document) in the table (collection). DML execute function is a function used to apply the DML command to a table (collection). Cache update function is specified with a write-through and write-back policy. It describes how to update the cached entry impacted by this insert.

Success = DI.Delete (Lower-bound, Upper-bound, DML command, DML execute function, Cache update function) with a description similar to Insert.

Success = DI.Update (Lower-bound, Upper-bound, DML command, DML execute function, Cache update function) with a description similar to Insert.

The value of β limits the percentage of duplicated data across the cached result sets of two predicates relative to the predicate with the fewest number of records. Its value ranges from 0% to 100%. While $\beta > 0$ allows two cached result sets with duplicated data, $\beta = 0\%$ de-duplicates them to (a) maximize utilization of cache space by increasing its cache hit rate, and (b) minimize the number of cached entries impacted by insert, delete, and update commands.

A Dendrite is extensible and allows a software developer to implement the interfaces for insert, delete, modify that impact the cached result sets of a range predicate. These interfaces are the building blocks for implementing query processing. A Dendrite employs an order-preserving in-memory data structure to maintain three different variables named Predicate Interval Tree (PrInT), Lease Manager Interval Tree (LeMInT), and Buffered Write Interval Tree (BuWrInT).

PrInT indexes the cached predicates and their result sets. The lower and upper bounds of a predicate identify an *interval*. It is associated with the key of the cached result-set. PrInT stores this pairing by indexing the interval, facilitating fast lookups when the predicate is issued again. Given a predicate, PrInT may identify other cached entries that either overlap or contain this predicate. These can be used to compute the results of a predicate, see [9] for additional details. To simplify discussion and without loss of generality, the following describes processing predicates issued repeatedly with $\beta = 100\%$.

With writes (insert, delete, update), the Dendrite interface requires the application to specify the interval [lower-bound, upper-bound] impacted by the write's range predicate. If the predicate is exact-match (i.e., an equality predicate such as id = C where C is a constant) then its specified interval is a point ([C, C]). CPR uses this interval to index into PrInT and identify the impacted cached entries. With the write-around policy, the Dendrite deletes the impacted cached entries. With the write-through and write-back policies, the Dendrite invokes the input "Cache update function" to update each impacted cached entry. Both write-around and write-through update the data store by invoking the provided DML execute function with the input DML command.

With the write-back policy, a Dendrite maintains a Buffered Write Interval Tree (BuWrInT). This tree associates the interval impacted by the write with the key of its buffered write stored in the cache. The buffered write maintains changes by the write and is applied to the data store asynchronously[1].

CPR uses BuWrInT to process a predicate that observes a cache miss as follows. First, it uses the interval referenced by the predicate to identify the buffered writes that overlap it. Next, it applies these writes (if any) to the persistent store and removes them from BuWrInT. Finally, it issues the predicate to the persistent store for processing, caches the result set, and associates it with the interval corresponding to the predicate in the PrInT.

With concurrent threads, a Dendrite preserves consistency of the cached entries using a Lease Manager Interval Tree, LeMInT. This tree maintains Shared (read) and eXclusive (write) leases on intervals that are read and written, respectively. A get obtains a Shared lease on its referenced interval while an insert/delete/update obtains an eXclusive lease on its referenced interval. The maximum number of entries in LeMInT is dictated by the number of concurrent threads processing predicates.

---

[1] Order of applying writes may be important, see Sect. 3.2.

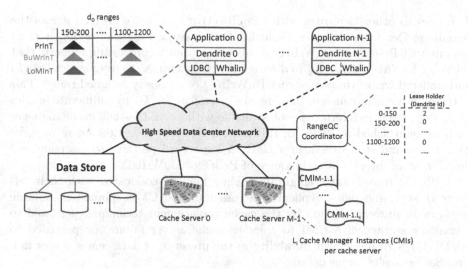

Fig. 2. A scalable multi-node CPR.

There are a variety of ways to implement Dendrites: In a client library, a data store, a cache manager instance (CMI), a middleware that uses a data store, in a trusted mobile[2] client with intermittent network connectivity, among others. Next section describes one implementation as a client library. In [9], we compare this implementation with an alternative that implements a Dendrite in a CMI.

3   A Scalable Implementation of CPR

This section describes an implementation of CPR using IQ-Twemcached [11] as the CMI and either MySQL or MongoDB as candidate data stores, see Fig. 2. It consists of D Dendrites and one Coordinator. The Dendrite may be a standalone process or a library component. Figure 2 shows the latter where a Dendrite is a library integrated in a Client. This figure shows the Coordinator as a stand-alone process. There may be shadow Coordinators that resume the responsibility of the Coordinator once it fails, similar to RamCloud's [17] Coordinator.

The domain of the attribute (property) referenced by the predicate is range partitioned across D Dendrites. Dendrite D_i is assigned d_i ranges. A Dendrite obtains its ranges from the Coordinator. The Coordinator assigns a range to at most one Dendrite by granting it a lease with a fixed life time. A Dendrite may renew its lease to continue serving requests for the range [3, 23].

Given D Dendrites and d_i ranges assigned to each Dendrite D_i, there are $\sum_{i=0}^{D-1} d_i$ instances of PrInT, LeMInT, and BuWrInT. Each implemented using an interval tree [13, 22]. When Dendrite D_i fails, the coordinator assigns its

---

[2] An untrusted mobile client may open possibilities for a Denial of Service (DoS) attack or data corruption.

d_i ranges to other Dendrites with the objective to balance its load across the remaining Dendrites. When a Dendrite D_r is assigned a range of D_i, it must re-construct PrInT and BuWrInT of this range prior to processing requests that reference it. This requires D_r to discover the cache entries (to reconstruct PrInT) and buffered writes (to reconstruct BuWrInT) of its newly assigned range. This is trivial if a cache manager implements interfaces for D_r to enumerate entries of a range. Such an interface is not available with an off-the-shelf cache manager such as memcached or Redis. In this case, a Dendrite generates *log* records for each range and stores them in a CMI. A log record pertains to insertion and deletion of an interval in an instance of PrInT or BuWrInT.

CPR log records are configurable. They may be co-located with their referenced key-value pairs, replicated across multiple CMIs, pinned in volatile memory to prevent eviction by the cache replacement technique, persisted to secondary storage of a CMI to tolerate cache server failure, or persisted to NVDIMM-N to implement durability in the presence of data center power failure. See next section for details.

In our implementation, the key that identifies a cached entry is a function of the collection-name, domain-name, and the specified lower and upper bound for a range predicate, see Fig. 3a. When a Get for a predicate is issued to Dendrite D_i, D_i constructs its key and looks it up in the cache server S_j, $j = h(key)$. If it finds the results then it produces it as output for consumption by the application. With a cache miss (or a write such as insert, delete, or update), Dendrites cooperate with one another by processing these requests on behalf of one another. Only the Dendrite(s) with the assigned range overlapping the predicate may process either a cache miss or a write action.

When a Client invokes a Dendrite D_i to process a cache miss, D_i looks up the range partitioning information to determine which Dendrite should service this request. If no range contains or overlaps this predicate, D_i contacts the Coordinator for a lease on this predicate. The Coordinator either (a) provides D_i with updated range partitioning information that identifies another Dendrite responsible for the range or (b) grants D_i a lease on a range that contains the referenced predicate. With the former, D_i forwards the predicate to the Dendrite responsible for this range. With the latter, D_i assumes responsibility for the range by constructing its PrInT, LeMInT and BuWrInT. While LeMInT starts as an empty tree always, D_i retrieves log records for PrInT and BuWrInT from the IQ-Twemcached servers to reconstruct the content of these trees.

Once these trees are constructed, D_i processes a cache miss by obtaining a Shared lease on the interval referenced by the predicate in LeMInT. D_i executes the function that queries the database to compute the key-value pair (k_j, v_j) representing the cache entry. D_i pairs k_j with the interval corresponding to its referenced range. It generates a log record for this insertion and stores it in server S_c, $i = h(k_j)$. Next, it stores this (k_j, v_j) in the IQ-Twemcached server S_c. It inserts pairing of interval with k_i in PrInT. Finally, D_i releases its Shared lease on the referenced interval in LeMInT.

```
Get(lb, ub, QFunc)
 1: key= computeKey(lb, ub).
 2: value= cache.get(key).
 3: if (cache hit) then
 4:     return value.
 5: cache.acquireILease(key).
 6: LeMInT.acquireSharedLease(lb, ub).
 7: if (policy== write-back) then
 8:     buffKeys = BuWrInT.getKeys(lb, ub).
 9:     buffWrites                           =
    cache.readAndAcquireQLeases(buffKeys).
10:     db.apply(buffWrites).
11:     cache.deleteAndReleaseQLeases(buffKeys).
12:     BuWrInT.delete(lb, ub).  // generates a log
    record.
13: value= db.get(rangeQuery).
14: cache.setAndReleaseILease(key, value).
15: PrInT.insert(lb, ub, key).  // generates a log record.
16: LeMInT.releaseSharedLease(lb, ub).
17: return value.
```

(a) Get operation.

```
Update(lb, ub, DML cmd, DML Func, Cache Up-
    date Func)
 1: LeMInT.acquireExclusiveLease(lb, ub).
 2: overlappers= PrInT.overlappers(lb, ub).
 3: for each interval in overlappers do
 4:     key= interval.getKey() from PrInT.
 5:     cache.readAndAcquireQLease(key).
 6:     if (policy== write-back or write-through)
    then
 7:         Execute Cache Update Func using key as its input.
 8:     if (policy== write-around) then
 9:         cache.delete(key).
10:         PrInT.delete(lb, ub).  // generates a log
    record.
11:     cache.releaseQLease(key).
12: if (policy== write-around or write-through)
    then
13:     db.apply( DML cmd, DML Func).
14: if (policy= write-back) then
15:     buffKeys, buffWrites = generte(DML Func,
    DML cmd).
16:     cache.set(buffKeys, buffWrites).
17:     BuWrInT.insert(lb, ub, buffKeys).  // gener-
    ates a log record.
18: LeMInT.releaseExclusiveLease(lb, ub).
```

(b) Update operation.

Fig. 3. Pseudo-code for Get and Update. Insert and Delete pseudo-code is similar to Update. Inhibit and Quarantine leases [11] are provided by IQ-Twemcached.

The above applies to write-around and write-through. Write-back is similar with one difference. Prior to querying the data store, it uses BuWrInT to identify buffered writes that overlap the interval referenced by the predicate. It applies these buffered writes to the data store and then executes the function that queries the database for the (k_j, v_j) pair to store in the cache. This provides strong consistency with write-back.

Dendrite D_i processes a write, such as insert, delete, or update by requiring it to specify its referenced interval [lb, ub], see Fig. 3b. The write specifies the same value for the lower and upper bounds when specifying a point, i.e., an equality predicate such as id = 5 is represented as [5, 5]. D_i obtains an eXclusive lease on the interval in LeMInT. Next, D_i looks up the overlapping and contained intervals in PrInT to identify the impacted cached entries. With write-around, D_i deletes the impacted key-value pairs from the cache along with their intervals in PrInT. In contrast, with write-through and write-back policies, D_i executes its input *Cache update function*, see Sect. 2 and Fig. 3b. In our implementation, this function updates the cached entry using a read-modify-write operation.

Next, with write-around and write-through, D_i applies the write to the data store. With write-back, D_i generates the buffered write and its log record. It appends the log record first and then inserts the buffered write in the caching layer, replicating these records at least 3 times and pinning them in the cache. It inserts the (interval, key) pairing in BuWrInT. Finally, D_i releases its exclusive lease of its interval in LeMInT.

3.1   Log Records

CPR employs configurable log records to recover from a Dendrite failure. Consider a range of a failed Dendrite D_i assigned to D_r. D_r must re-construct D_i's PrInT and BuWrInT for this range prior to its failure in order to process requests. PrInT is required to decide whether a write impacts a cached entry. BuWrInT is required with the write-back policy only. It identifies buffered writes and their intervals.

A Dendrite generates log records for each interval it either inserts or deletes from PrInT or BuWrInT. The configuration of a log record dictates whether it is co-located with its referenced cache entry, replicated for high availability, pinned in memory, persisted for durability, or a hybrid of these.

PrInT log records are configured to be co-located with their referenced cache entry in a CMI, pinned in its memory, and have one replica. A CMI failure destroys both the cache entry and its log record because CMI memory (DRAM) is volatile.

BuWrInT log records are also configured to be co-located with their referenced buffered writes and pinned in memory of a CMI. However, they have 3 or more replicas across CMIs assigned to different cache servers, see Fig. 2. This enhances availability in the presence of cache server failures. (Buffered writes are also replicated 3 or more times on the same CMIs as the log records.) Finally, the log records (along with their referenced buffered writes) are configured to persist to NVDIMM-N to implement durability in the presence of data center power failure, see Sect. 3.4. Both buffered writes and their log records cannot be lost because they pertain to acknowledged writes.

A log record contains the following information:

- insert:LSN:lowerbound:upperbound:key
- delete:LSN:lowerbound:upperbound

The first entry of the log record is the action, either insert or delete. It is followed with the Log Sequence Number (LSN), a monotonically increasing number for the log records corresponding to a range. The lower and upper bounds identify the interval impacted by the action. While insert maintains the identity of the impacted key, this information is not required for the delete log record.

An application write may impact multiple intervals of PrInT. With write-around, D_i deletes cache entries corresponding to each interval. It also deletes each interval from PrInT and generates its "delete" log record. These log records are hash partitioned across IQ-Twemcached servers using their referenced key.

With insert into either PrInT or BuWrInT, its log entry is generated and appended first. This results in two KVS operations: Append to the log record, insert the key-value pair in the cache. When deleting an interval from either PrInT or BuWrInT, D_i deletes the cache entry from IQ-Twemcached server CMI_j synchronously and generates its log records to be appended asynchronously. This does not compromise either strong consistency or correctness because the existence of an interval in the interval-tree does not mean the corresponding key must exist in the cache (e.g., it may have been evicted by IQ-Twemcached's LRU policy). This does enhance performance by minimizing the number of round-trip messages issued by D_i to a cache server for deletes from PrInT and BuWrInT.

Our implementation of asynchronous generation of delete log records maintains M buffers, one for each cache server. When a delete for an interval is issued, we hash partition on the key to append its delete log record to buffer j = h(key). Once the buffer reaches a threshold, say α, one append[3] is issued for the α log records, as long as the maximum value size is not violated.

Batching of delete log entries may cause them to be out of order with the inserts. When applying the log records to reconstruct an interval tree, a Dendrite sorts the entries using their LSN prior to applying them to construct the interval tree.

Multiple Dendrites may generate log records for the same CMI concurrently. To minimize contention for a single cache entry (key-value pair), a Dendrite partitions the log records across multiple cache entries on a CMI.

Many inserts and deletes may reference the same lower and upper bounds. We compact the log records by eliminating the inserts and deletes that nullify one another, i.e., reference the same lower and upper bounds.

3.2 Write-Back and Dependent Buffered Writes

With the write-back policy, multiple writes may impact either the same interval or overlapping intervals. CPR's synchronization primitives (LeMInT and IQ leases) dictate their serial execution to the cache entries. The background threads must apply the buffered writes to the data store in the same serial order.

CPR maintains the serial order of writes by extending a buffered write to maintain the identity of one or more buffered writes that it depends on. This results in an acyclic graph. Prior to applying a buffered write to the data store, all buffered writes it depends on must be applied first. This may navigate multiple buffered writes recursively. The termination condition is when a buffered write depends on no other buffered write or all buffered writes it depends on do not exist (because they have been applied to the data store and deleted). At that point, the buffered write is applied and processing of buffered writes falls out of recursion.

The dependency graph between buffered writes is constructed incrementally as CPR executes writes that reference overlapping intervals one by one. Processing of a write inserts its referenced interval associated with its buffered write in BuWrInT. If this insert results in one or more overlapping intervals then there are buffered writes it depends on.

3.3 Strong Consistency

CPR uses leases instead of locks for strong consistency. Leases granted on a data item have a fixed lifetime. If the lease expires (due to the grantee failing), its data item is released making it available for processing once again.

---

[3] We extended IQ-Twemcached with a command that appends multiple values to a key.

CPR uses two types of leases: LeMInT leases granted by a Dendrite on an interval, and Inhibit (I) and Quarantine (Q) leases granted by an IQ-Twemcached CMI on a key-value pair. These leases serve different purposes. LeMInT leases prevent read-write and write-write race conditions on cached intervals. Since LeMInT is an order preserving interval tree, it detects conflicts between a reader (writer) and a writer acquiring Shared/eXclusive leases referencing intervals that overlap, causing one to wait for the other to either commit or abort. The IQ leases implement the concept of a *session* [11]. An application implements its read and write actions using a session that acquires either an Inhibit or a Quarantine lease on a key-value pair. Once a write is granted a Q lease on a key k_i, IQ-Twemcached constructs a copy of v_i and applies all updates of this session to this copy. Once the application commits a session, it releases its Q lease and switches copy of v_i with v_i atomically. Should the application fail prior to committing, its Q lease times out and its copy of v_i (that may have been updated) is discarded.

We provide a formal proof of strong consistency of CPR for different write policies in [9].

3.4 Durability of Writes

With the write-back policy, durability of writes is compromised when a CMI failures results in loss of either buffered writes or log records of BuWrInT. Without BuWrInT, an application is not able to discover buffered writes to apply them to the data store. Hence, we replicate both buffered writes and log records of BuWrInT to enhance availability in the presence of CMI failures. Each buffered write or log record has three replicas on three CMIs assigned to different cache servers. With a write, all replicas of its buffered write and the log record for BuWrInT must be stored successfully before it is acknowledged as success. Failure to store a replica results in executing the write using the write-through policy (after applying all relevant buffered writes). Key-value pairs for buffered writes and log records are pinned in memory, preventing their eviction, see Sects. 3 for details.

Replication by itself is not enough to survive data center power failure that causes all the pending buffered writes and log records of BuWrInT to be lost. These key-value pairs should be stored on non-volatile memory such as NVDIMM-N [21].

4   Evaluation

In [9], we quantify tradeoffs associated with CPR using two different data stores based on different data models, MySQL and MongoDB, highlighting CPR's benefits and limitations. The key lessons learned from this evaluation are as follows:

1. CPR with the write-back policy provides the highest performance benefit.
2. CPR scales horizontally (with write-back) to support a higher throughput as a function of its cache servers.

3. The percentage improvement observed with CPR depends on the size of cached entries. This size depends on the selectivity factor of the range predicate and its number of projected attributes. When cached entries are large, CPR may provide a performance inferior to a data store by itself.

Moreover, [9] presents a comparison of CPR with how Redis implements processing of range predicates. With a read heavy workload, CPR is superior to Redis by utilizing clients to maintain PrInT. With a write heavy workload, while our implementation with Redis is significantly faster, it produces anomalies. This highlights the need for LeMInT to prevent undesirable race conditions that produce stale data.

Finally, in [9], We compare extreme settings of β, 0% and 100%, showing $\beta = 0\%$ enhances performance of write-heavy workloads. $\beta = 100\%$ enhances performance of read-heavy workloads.

We use Emulab [25] d430 nodes with 10 Gbps network connectivity for all experiments. Each node is a Dell poweredge R430 server configured with two 2.4 GHz 64 bit 8-Core Haswell processors, 64 GB of DRAM, 200 GB of Intel SATA SSD, and two 1 TB SATA hard disk drive. We vary the number of nodes used for the caching layer from 1 to 8. Each node hosts 16 IQ-Twemcached instances each configured with 3 GB of memory. There are 16 YCSB clients issuing requests. Each is configured with a Dendrite instance of CPR. A single node is dedicated to a data store, either MySQL or MongoDB configured to use 48 GB of DRAM. To maximize the performance of each data store, we used the SATA SSD in all our experiments. We have conducted experiments using the hard disk drive and observe CPR to provide a significantly higher performance benefit compared with a data store by itself.

Presented results are obtained using YCSB databases consisting of one and ten million records. The size of each record is 1000 bytes. Unless stated otherwise, the ten million record database is used for evaluation purposes.

We consider a variant of YCSB Workload E with uniform access pattern. Both generate a fixed percentage of scans and updates. The scan fetches α records ($\alpha = 5$ unless specified otherwise). The update modifies columns of a record using its primary key value. The difference between the two workloads is the number of columns fetched by the scan and modified by the update. While scan/update fetches/updates all ten 100 byte columns of the qualifying records with $YCSB^*$, it fetches/updates only one 100 byte column of the qualifying record with $YCSB^1$. We refer to a workload using its percentage of scan, e.g., $f = 10\%$ scan. The remainder are updates, e.g., $1 - f = 90\%$.

Due to lack of space, this section presents only one result, namely, the trade-offs associated with CPR using the alternative write-policies. Figure 4 shows the percentage improvement with these alternative configurations when compared with a data store by itself. The x-axis of this figure shows different mixes of update and scan commands. The y-axis reports the percentage improvement in throughput obtained by measuring the throughput of the data store by itself (T_{DS}) and once extended with CPR using one IQ-Twemcached server (T_{CPR}),

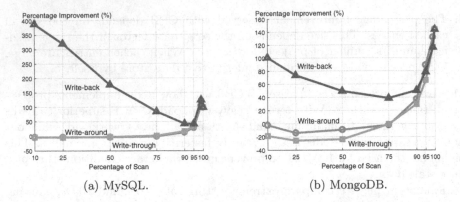

(a) MySQL.   (b) MongoDB.

Fig. 4. Percentage improvement observed with alternative write policies using $YCSB^*$ and scan cardinality 5.

$\%Improvement = \frac{T_{CPR}-T_{DS}}{T_{DS}}$. A y-axis value below 0 means CPR degraded the performance of a data store instead of enhancing it.

Figure 4 shows the write-back policy outperforms the other two policies by a wide margin with a write-heavy workload, 10% scan. It is able to do so by buffering writes in the cache, eliminating the data store from the critical path of the write operations. Both write-around and write-through perform the update to the data store synchronously. They incur the delay attributed to a sustained queue of requests on the SSD of the data store due to the high frequency of updates. Moreover, their cache misses incur the same delay. With the write-back policy, a scan that observes a cache miss applies the pending buffered writes for its referenced interval (if any) prior to querying the data store. Ten background threads apply the buffered writes to the data store. This enables the write-back policy to provide a superior performance with write-heavy workloads.

The write-around and write-through policies enhance performance when scan constitutes more than 90% of the workload, i.e., a read-heavy workload. These workloads eliminate the sustained queue of requests on SSD of the data store, causing the network bandwidth of the cache server to dictate the overall system performance. Hence, all write policies provide comparable performance benefits.

5   Future Work

Our future research directions are two folds. First, we are investigating techniques that decide the optimal value of β dynamically. A low β value reduces duplicated data in cache (maximize utilization of cache space), while a high β value creates coarser cache entries with duplicated data between two or more entries. A future work is to develop an algorithm to decide the optimal value of β between 0% and 100%. This algorithm may consider available cache space and network latency and bandwidth. The algorithm would dynamically adjust β to enhance metrics such as service time or throughput.

Second, we are evaluating alternative Dendrite implementations. For example, a Dendrite might be implemented in a CMI or a middleware. We speculate different implementations will provide different benefits for a given workload and application use case scenario. An understanding of the tradeoffs enables a system designer to select the most appropriate implementation for a given workload and application use case scenario.

Acknowledgments. We gratefully acknowledge use of Utah Emulab network testbed [25] ("Emulab") for all experimental results presented in this paper.

References

1. InnoDB memcached Plugin. https://dev.mysql.com/doc/refman/8.0/en/innodb-memcached.html. Accessed 02 June 2018
2. ZRANGE. https://redis.io/commands/zrange. Accessed 02 June 2018
3. Adya, A., et al.: Slicer: auto-sharding for datacenter applications. In: OSDI (2016)
4. Alabdulkarim, Y., Almaymoni, M., Ghandeharizadeh, S.: Polygraph: a plug-n-play framework to quantify anomalies. In: ICDE (2018)
5. Arulraj, J., Levandoski, J.J., Minhas, U.F., Larson, P.: BzTree: a high-performance latch-free range index for non-volatile memory. In: VLDB (2017)
6. Comer, D.: Ubiquitous B-tree. ACM Comput. Surv. **11**(2), 121–137 (1979)
7. Cooper, B.F., Silberstein, A., Tam, E., Ramakrishnan, R., Sears, R.: Benchmarking cloud serving systems with YCSB. In: Cloud Computing (2010)
8. Du, J., Miller, R.J., Glavic, B., Tan, W.: DeepSea: progressive workload-aware partitioning of materialized views in scalable data analytics. In: EDBT (2017)
9. Ghandeharizadeh, S., Alabdulkarim, Y., Nguyen, H.: CPR: client-side processing of range predicates. Technical report 2018–03, USC Database Laboratory (2018)
10. Ghandeharizadeh, S., Nguyen, H.: Design, implementation, and evaluation of write-back policy with cache augmented data stores. PVLDB **12**(8), 836–849 (2019)
11. Ghandeharizadeh, S., Yap, J., Nguyen, H.: Strong consistency in cache augmented SQL systems. In: Middleware (2014)
12. Ghemawat, S., Dean, J.: LevelDB (2011). http://code.google.com/p/leveldb
13. Jagadish, H.V.: On indexing line segments. In: VLDB, pp. 614–625 (1990)
14. Lamoureux, M.G., Nickerson, B.G.: Deterministic skip list data structures: efficient alternatives to balanced search trees. In: APICS (1995)
15. Lu, L., Pillai, T.S., Gopalakrishnan, H., Arpaci-Dusseau, A.C., Arpaci-Dusseau, R.H.: WiscKey: separating keys from values in SSD-conscious storage. Trans. Storage **13**(1), 5:1–5:28 (2017)
16. O'Neil, P., Cheng, E., Gawlick, D., O'Neil, E.: The Log-structured merge-tree (LSM-tree). Acta Inf. **33**(4), 351–385 (1996)
17. Ousterhout, J.K., et al.: The case for RAMClouds: scalable high-performance storage entirely in DRAM. Oper. Syst. Rev. **43**(4), 92–105 (2009)
18. Papadimitriou, C.H.: The serializability of concurrent database updates. J. ACM (JACM) **26**(4), 631–653 (1979)
19. Ports, D.R.K., Clements, A.T., Zhang, I., Madden, S., Liskov, B.: Transactional consistency and automatic management in an application data cache. In: OSDI, pp. 279–292 (2010)
20. Raddick, J., Thakar, A.R., Szalay, A.S., Santos, R.D.C.: Ten years of SkyServer I: tracking web and SQL e-science usage. Comput. Sci. Eng. **16**(4), 22–31 (2014)

21. Sainio, A.: NVDIMM: changes are here so what's next. In-Memory Computing Summit, 2016 (2016)
22. Sedgewick, R., Wayne, K.: Algorithms (Fourth edition deluxe). Addison-Wesley, Boston (2016)
23. Taft, R., et al.: E-store: fine-grained elastic partitioning for distributed transaction processing. PVLDB **8**(3), 245–256 (2014)
24. TPC Corp. TPC-C Benchmark. http://www.tpc.org/tpcc/
25. White, B., et al.: An integrated experimental environment for distributed systems and networks, New York, vol. 36, pp. 255–270. ACM, December 2002

Correction to: Cloud Computing – CLOUD 2019

Dilma Da Silva, Qingyang Wang, and Liang-Jie Zhang

Correction to:
D. Da Silva et al. (Eds.): *Cloud Computing – CLOUD 2019,*
LNCS 11513, https://doi.org/10.1007/978-3-030-23502-4

The original version of the book was revised; the following corrections have been incorporated:

In Chapter "An Approach to Failure Prediction in Cluster by Self-Updating Cause-and-Effect Graph":

- Typographical errors throughout the chapter were corrected
- Figure 10 was replaced because it was a duplicate

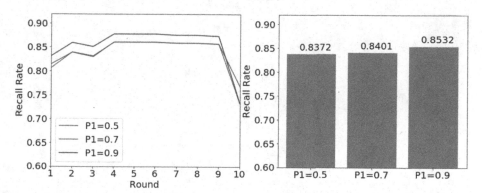

- Unused references were removed
- A missing reference was added

In Chapter "Towards Decentralized Deep Learning with Differential Privacy", typographical errors were corrected to help the reader to better understand the content.

The updated version of these chapters can be found at
https://doi.org/10.1007/978-3-030-23502-4_9
https://doi.org/10.1007/978-3-030-23502-4_10
https://doi.org/10.1007/978-3-030-23502-4

Author Index

Printed in the United States
By Bookmasters

Printed in the United States
By Bookmasters